WORKLOAD TRANSITION

Implications for Individual and Team Performance

Beverly Messick Huey and Christopher D. Wickens, *editors*

Panel on Workload Transition

Committee on Human Factors

Commission on Behavioral and Social Sciences and Education

National Research Council

NATIONAL ACADEMY PRESS
Washington, DC   1993

This work relates to Department of the Army grant MDA 903-89-K-0074 issued by the Defense Supply Service Washington. However, the content does not necessarily reflect the position or the policy of the government, and no official endorsement should be inferred.

The United States government has at least a royalty-free, nonexclusive and irrevocable license throughout the world for government purposes to publish, translate, reproduce, deliver, perform, dispose of, and to authorize others so as to do, all or any portion of this work.

Library of Congress Cataloging-in-Publication Data

Workload transition : implications for individual and team performance
  / Beverly Messick Huey and Christopher D. Wickens, eds. ; Panel on
  Workload Transition, Committee on Human Factors, Commission on
  Behavioral and Social Sciences and Education, National Research
  Council.
       p. cm.
     Includes bibliographical references and index.
     ISBN 0-309-04796-X
     1. Job stress. 2. Tank crews—Job stress. 3. Emergency medical
  personnel—Job stress. 4. Nuclear power plant operators—Job
  stress. 5. Fatigue. I. Huey, Beverly Messick. II. Wickens,
  Christopher D. III. National Research Council (U.S.). Panel on
  Workload Transition.
  RC963.48.W67   1993
  155.9'042—dc20   93-363
                                                           CIP

Additional copies are available from:
National Academy Press
2101 Constitution Avenue N.W.
Washington, DC 20418

B045

The National Academy of Sciences is a private, nonprofit, self-perpetuating society of distinguished scholars engaged in scientific and engineering research, dedicated to the furtherance of science and technology and to their use for the general welfare. Upon the authority of the charter granted to it by the Congress in 1863, the Academy has a mandate that requires it to advise the federal government on scientific and technical matters. Dr. Frank Press is president of the National Academy of Sciences.

The National Academy of Engineering was established in 1964, under the charter of the National Academy of Sciences, as a parallel organization of outstanding engineers. It is autonomous in its administration and in the selection of its members, sharing with the National Academy of Sciences the responsibility for advising the federal government. The National Academy of Engineering also sponsors engineering programs aimed at meeting national needs, encourages education and research, and recognizes the superior achievements of engineers. Dr. Robert M. White is president of the National Academy of Engineering.

The Institute of Medicine was established in 1970 by the National Academy of Sciences to secure the services of eminent members of appropriate professions in the examination of policy matters pertaining to the health of the public. The Institute acts under the responsibility given to the National Academy of Sciences by its congressional charter to be an adviser to the federal government and, upon its own initiative, to identify issues of medical care, research, and education. Dr. Kenneth I. Shine is president of the Institute of Medicine.

The National Research Council was established by the National Academy of Sciences in 1916 to associate the broad community of science and technology with the Academy's purposes of furthering knowledge and advising the federal government. Functioning in accordance with general policies determined by the Academy, the Council has become the principal operating agency of both the National Academy of Sciences and the National Academy of Engineering in providing services to the government, the public, and the scientific and engineering communities. The Council is administered jointly by both Academies and the Institute of Medicine. Dr. Frank Press and Dr. Robert White are chairman and vice chairman, respectively, of the National Research Council.

Foreword

The Committee on Human Factors was established in October 1980 by the Commission on Behavioral and Social Sciences and Education of the National Research Council. The committee is sponsored by the Air Force Office of Scientific Research, the Army Research Institute for the Behavioral and Social Sciences, the National Aeronautics and Space Administration, the Air Force Armstrong Aerospace Medical Research Laboratory, the Army Advanced Systems Research Office, the Army Human Engineering Laboratory, the Army Natick RD&E Center, the Federal Aviation Administration, the Nuclear Regulatory Commission, the Naval Training Systems Center, and the U.S. Coast Guard. The principal objectives of the committee are to provide new perspectives on theoretical and methodological issues, to identify basic research needed to expand and strengthen the scientific basis of human factors, and to attract scientists both inside and outside the field for interactive communication and performance of needed research.

Human factors issues arise in every domain in which humans interact with the products of a technological society. To perform its role effectively, the committee draws on experts from a wide range of scientific and engineering disciplines. Members of the committee include specialists in such fields as psychology, engineering, biomechanics, physiology, medicine, cognitive sciences, machine intelligence, computer science, sociology, education, and human factors engineering. Other disciplines are represented in the working groups, workshops, and symposia organized by the committee. Each of these disciplines contributes to the basic data, theory, and methods required to improve the scientific basis of human factors.

Acknowledgments

In 1988, the U.S. Army Human Engineering Laboratory approached the Committee on Human Factors to undertake a study of the effects of prolonged periods of underload on the performance of tank crews. As the committee evaluated the request, it realized that the key problems were less related to performance during underload itself, about which a fair amount is known and published, than to the consequences of prolonged underload (and concomitant sleep loss) on subsequent performance when workload is suddenly increased by the need to enter combat. Further study revealed this situation to be common across a number of team-oriented systems, such as emergency medical services personnel and nuclear power plant personnel responding to emergencies. Because of the perceived importance of this team transition situation, its commonality across systems, and the absence of a coherent research base, the committee chose to undertake the study.

Our approach was intentionally broad, focusing on multiple systems and not just tank crews. This choice of breadth was intentional as, aware of the scarce research base on tanks, we realized that generalizable research conclusions could be obtained only by casting our net broadly. We also felt that a broad net might assemble a set of coherent research conclusions with relevance to other systems as well as tanks. With these goals in mind, the committee assembled a panel of experts, spanning a wide range of fields relevant to the team transition situation.

The work of this study was performed by a small group of experts from key areas in workload, training, vigilance, circadian rhythms and performance effects of sleep loss and fatigue, cognitive switching, situation awareness, and crew communication and coordination. As chair, I want to thank the panel members for their extensive contributions, their many thoughtful position papers, and their gracious collaboration throughout this study. I want to personally acknowledge the work of Vern Battiste for his review of geographic orientation; Karen Cook for her contributions in the area of stress and social psychology; Charles Czeisler in the area of circadian rhythms, sleep loss, and fatigue; Sandy Hart in the area of workload; Bob Helmreich in the area of crew coordination and leadership; Gordon Logan in the area of cognitive switching; Mike Maddox in the area of workspace design and stress; Joyce Shields in the area of training; Joel Warm for his contributions in the area of vigilance and target detection; and Beverly Huey for her contributions in the area of stress and the review of analogous systems. Beverly Huey, Committee on Human Factors staff officer, not only organized and participated in the meetings of the panel, but also willingly and effectively worked with the chair to organize and assemble this report and contributed to its editing. Charles Dixon, Betty Ehrman Messick, and Evelyn Simeon provided secretarial assistance in preparing this document for review.

Beverly Huey and I would like to extend our sincere appreciation for the assistance and information provided by numerous representatives of analogous systems of interest: Todd Brown of the Safety Research Division of the Association of American Railroads; James Danaher, of the National Transportation Safety Board; Russell Dynes, head of the Disaster Research Center; Mark Mandler of the U.S. Coast Guard R&D Center; Merrill Messick, Jr., of the Maryland State Police and the Bel Air Volunteer Fire Company, Inc.; Richard Pain of the National Research Council's Transportation Research Board; James Reason of the University of Manchester; Ronald Schaefer of Shocktrauma; Steve Sheek of the Office of Marine Safety, Security, and Environmental Protection, U.S. Coast Guard; Barry Sweedler of the National Transportation Safety Board; Marc Wilson, doctoral candidate at George Washington University; Gene Worthington of the Maryland State Firemen's Association and the Level Volunteer Fire Company, Inc.; and Wayne Young of the National Research Council's Marine Board.

The panel received invaluable contributions from many people. Major Brad Scott gave a briefing on the psychological aspects of tank crew operations. Bernard Corona and Ron Whitaker set up presentations that were given by personnel of the U.S. Army Human Engineering Laboratory, Behavioral Research Division. Frederick Baldwin and Captain Ravell of the U.S. Combat Systems Test Activity gave panel members the opportunity to ride in a tank. Jack Thorpe of the Defense Advanced Research Projects Agency gave a demonstration of SIMNET, the U.S. Army's computer-based battlefield simulator.

The panel appreciates the cooperation, support, and advice it received from many individuals, especially that of John Lockett and Kenneth Caldwell. John Lockett arranged a site visit to Aberdeen Proving Ground, where the panel had the invaluable opportunity to experience a tank ride, and provided access to pertinent background materials; Kenneth Caldwell acted as technical consultant to the panel, contributing his years of experience as a tank commander to better our understanding of the nature of armored operations.

Christopher D. Wickens, *Chair*
Panel on Workload Transition

Contents

WORKLOAD TRANSITION

Implications for Individual and Team Performance

Summary

Systems in a variety of settings can be characterized by having a team of operators, functioning for some period of time under relatively routine conditions, then being abruptly confronted with abnormal and sometimes emergency circumstances to which they must rapidly respond in an appropriate manner. We term these features the *team transition* situation. We begin with some examples of these types of teams:

(1) The crew of a nuclear power control room becomes aware of a transient event in the reactor and must attempt to establish the appropriate procedures to maintain or restore plant safety.

(2) The crew of a commercial airline suddenly becomes aware of a life-threatening malfunction. Again, the team (i.e., flight deck personnel, maintenance personnel, and air traffic controllers) must rapidly perceive, problem solve, and respond to ensure the safety of the aircraft.

(3) Personnel in a hospital emergency room, on a quiet night, are suddenly confronted with victims of a serious automobile accident. Rapid problem solving and perhaps prioritization of causalities must be coupled with the precise exercise of procedural skills and coordination with the emergency room staff.

(4) An emergency medical service (EMS) team is suddenly called on in the middle of the night to make a helicopter flight to pick up a critically ill patient. The weather is bad, and the destination is unfamiliar.

(5) An M1A1 army tank crew stands ready and waiting at the edge of a battlefield, its crew of four having waited in a state of combat readiness for

1

36 hours. Suddenly hostile shots land close by, and the crew must immediately become an effective fighting unit.

For many of these kinds of teams, there is evidence, both formal and anecdotal, of failures of the team to effectively manage crisis situations. Three Mile Island, the crash of Eastern Airlines L1011 into the Everglades in 1972, and the Exxon Valdez incident are graphic examples. Against these failures, however, may be balanced the many instances in which a team has successfully managed the crisis. The ability of the pilots of the United Airlines flight, which suffered a total hydraulics failure near Sioux City, Iowa, is a salient example.

BACKGROUND

In 1988, in response to a request from the U.S. Army Human Engineering Laboratory, the Committee on Human Factors of the National Research Council undertook a project to provide advice and guidance on the effects of prolonged work underload on the subsequent performance of critical tasks and on approaches that could be employed to offset or compensate for decrements in performance that otherwise might occur. This information was requested in anticipation of Army plans to develop tanks with smaller crews than those currently found in M1A1 tanks. Crew downsizing would result in some tasks being automated or redistributed among remaining crew positions. During active deployment, the reduction in crew size is likely to increase workload, thus increasing the potential for performance failures and errors unless compensatory measures are devised. A concern of the Army was whether the response to high workload would be further exacerbated when it follows long periods of waiting.

Although the concept of workload transition has been given little, if any, attention and even less research emphasis, it is nevertheless an important problem encountered in many work settings such as those identified above. This generic aspect of suddenly having to perform important activities after a period of relative or complete inactivity lends special interest to the problem posed by the Human Engineering Laboratory. While some underload situations may lend themselves to administrative solutions, the uncertain environment of tank combat requires research solutions that identify those technologies that may be used to offset the possibility of negative effects on performance.

The objectives of this study were to: (1) review the concept of work underload and assess the state of research knowledge and its effects on subsequent high-workload task performance; (2) evaluate the components of the critical high-workload onset tasks to assess which components are most likely to be vulnerable to decrements from prior underload or the sudden onset of workload; and (3) identify and evaluate techniques that might be used by designers to compensate for, or offset, likely performance decrements.

A cursory analysis of the work underload problem reveals that several partially related domains of research are relevant to the problem: workload, stress, sleep loss and circadian rhythms, vigilance, geographic orientation, cognitive task management, decision making, crew communications, leadership and team coordination, and training.

ANALOGOUS SYSTEMS

When empirical data are scarce, insight and advances in knowledge may be achieved by sharing knowledge from similar systems or paradigms. However, the application of conclusions drawn from one domain to another must proceed cautiously and identify the ways in which the two domains are similar or different. There are five general features of similarity in the team transition process: time, structure of the event, environment, personal risk, and organizational structure. Time refers to the abruptness with which a crisis transition unfolds, the expectancy or perceived probability that a transition will occur, and the length of time that a crew must remain on watch before an event may occur. The structure of the event refers to the extent to which its nature is predictable and whether the desired response can be effectively preprogrammed. The environment describes the physical conditions. Personal risk is the extent to which the team is exposed to risk of personal injury or death, both to themselves and to others. Finally, organizational structure has three subcomponents: team structure or command authority, team integrity or continuity of team membership over time, and autonomy or extent to which the team functions alone rather than in close coordination with a higher organizational structure.

Characteristics of commercial airline crews, nuclear power plant control room crews, railroad freight train crews, merchant and military ship crews, natural disaster relief teams, emergency medical services crews, and trauma center and emergency room crews are briefly presented, followed by a few cautious generalizations which can be extended to the tank environment. First, in each system, appropriate duty schedules are very important. At present, these appear to be lacking in ship, railroad, and trauma center systems, to name but a few. In most of these systems this factor has been identified as contributing to numerous accidents.

Second, lack of a communication protocol appears to have serious consequences on crew performance. Many crews operate in more isolation than is advisable. When the triggering event is complex or unstructured, continuous situation awareness in the pretransition period is likely to increase the probability of more efficient and adaptive problem solving during the transition. This situation awareness is also likely to reduce the crew's stress and perceived workload.

WORKLOAD

A characteristic of most post-transition periods is a large number of task demands, often imposed with very severe time constraints. These tasks are often characterized by the description of high workload. Although workload and performance are clearly related, their relationship is much more complex than originally thought.

From mission requirements and models of human behavior, nominal workload profiles can be developed for different equipment and missions. However, unexpected events, environmental stressors, and other factors may alter significantly the workload a particular crew experiences. Considerable research has been performed to understand, manipulate, and measure workload of specific tasks or intervals of time. However, relatively little is known about the effects of moving from one level of workload to another. Different crews cope with such changes in different ways, but neither optimal strategies nor the performance consequences of suboptimal strategies have been identified. Regardless of the specific sources of workload, adequate training and preparation, adopting strategies and tactics most appropriate for the situation, effective leadership and effective crew coordination can counteract some of the detrimental effects of imposed task demands, moving from one mode of behavior to another, environmental stressors, and fatigue.

STRESS

The post-transition phase will impose a substantial degree of stress, incorporating time pressure at a minimum, but also danger and various other environmental stressors. Stressors may include features of the work environment such as noise, vibration, heat, poor lighting, toxic substances, and acceleration, as well as psychological factors such as anxiety, fatigue, and danger. These stressors may have different manifestations: subjective experience, physiological change, and performance decrements. The differential effects of many environmental factors have been demonstrated on the performance and physical workload of various types of tasks. Psychological stressors related to danger and anxiety have also been associated with specific changes in cognitive processes. Stress, similar to workload, has been found to interact with a host of factors and affect performance in complex ways; however, there are a variety of techniques that may be adopted to minimize the degrading effects of stress on human performance: design solutions, the use of strategies, and training.

SLEEP DISRUPTION AND FATIGUE

Performance following workload transitions is affected by three factors related to the daily cycle of sleep and wakefulness: a 24-hour circadian rhythmicity (indexed by body temperature), sleep deprivation, and sleep inertia. Psychomotor and cognitive performance on a variety of tasks in round-the-clock operations is at its worst during nighttime hours, generally reaching a nadir just before dawn. Circadian variations in alertness, cognitive performance, short-term memory, sleep tendency, spontaneous sleep duration, awakening, and rapid eye movement sleep propensity all remain closely coupled to the body temperature cycle.

Many studies have documented the deleterious effects of both sleep loss and misalignment of circadian phase on performance and safety. Tasks that require consistent, sustained alertness or perceptual-motor activities were found to be most sensitive to sleep loss in a 48-hour field test; and self-initiated activities, such as planning and maintaining situational awareness, degraded most quickly.

There is no known technique available to sustain human performance at an acceptable level for 72 continuous hours; however careful planning can result in the development of countermeasures, such as caffeine and other stimulants, increased physical activity, naps, monetary incentives, diet, and intensive social contact that can reduce the impact of sleep disruption on the performance of crew members. While these techniques can mitigate the deterioration of performance on the first night of sleep loss, none is effective in overcoming the impairments of performance that occur on the second or third nights of continuous operations.

VIGILANCE

A large portion of the responsibility of armored vehicle teams, and indeed the teams of many analogous systems, prior to transition is simply to monitor the environment for events that might signal the need for the team to mobilize into action. This is particularly true for gunners who bear the primary responsibility for target acquisition. Several factors are identified that might affect the vigilant behavior of armor crews: psychophysical variables (the modality, conspicuity and probability of signals, nonsignal event rate, task complexity), environmental variables (noise, vibration), and operator state (sleep loss, task-induced stress).

Although there is considerable literature on vigilance, very little information is available on the effects of transitions on vigilance performance. Studies to examine this varied event rate or dual task load to produce transitions in workload. Evidence suggests that performance suffers following transitions, relative to steady-state workload conditions. A number of general approaches for enhancing the quality of sustained attention in operational settings have been suggested, including reductions in signal uncertainty, the moderation of environmental sources of stress, and training.

GEOGRAPHIC ORIENTATION

There is a strong similarity in factors related to geographic orientation between tank crews and helicopter pilots, both of whom often operate in environments in which there are no explicit visible or electronic routes to follow. Local terrain features may obscure their view of significant landmarks, making it difficult to relate local terrain features to a more global context. Because electronic aids must have a line of site with the target and tanks have few navigation instruments, helicopter and tank crews must correlate features viewed in the external scene or described by other crew members with those depicted on paper maps. This may require mental transformations and rotations and accurate estimates of speed and distance traveled to determined when a landmark should be visible and when choice points have been reached or missed. The difficulty of maintaining geographic orientation depends on the availability and visibility of distinctive landmarks, familiarity with the area, and the adequacy of maps, premission planning, and crew coordination.

DECISION MAKING

Team decision making depends jointly on the decision-making capabilities of the team leader and on information flow. Analysis of decision-making studies reveals that shortcomings in decision making may result from limitations in a number of the processes necessary to execute a decision, from initial information gathering to final choice. In order to be able to make a good decision, one must have good situational awareness. Decision makers bring with them a number of biases and heuristics, including: (1) salience bias—the tendency to focus on the most salient cue, rather than that which may be most informative and diagnostic; (2) availability heuristic—the tendency to base one's actions on the hypothesis that is most available in memory; (3) anchoring heuristic—the tendency to stay with a current hypothesis and inadequately consider new information that might shift one's beliefs in favor of a different hypothesis; and (4) confirmation bias—the tendency to seek new information that supports one's currently held hypothesis and to ignore or inadequately weigh information that may support an alternative hypothesis.

To counteract the limitations of human decision making, four general remediation solutions have been proposed: computer-based decision aiding, debias training, domain training, and development of team cohesion.

STRATEGIC TASK MANAGEMENT

Strategic task management involves several components. One component is the switching between tasks or between different strategies in performing a task. Research in basic laboratory environments suggests that this switching can be done rapidly and efficiently, and that differences between people in switching speed can predict differences in performance in complex tasks such as driving or flying. The speed with which activities can be initiated depends on expectancy and the degree of uncertainty of possible alternative activities. Action can also be stopped rapidly, although under high stress there may be a tendency to inhibit action stopping or switching. That is, activities may persist longer than they should.

Another aspect of strategic task management is the management of task priorities: addressing high-priority tasks before those of lower priority. Effective management depends, in part, on good situation awareness: knowing what tasks are currently in the queue that need to be done. Studies of task priority management indicate that people are good but not perfect in managing tasks. Some aircraft accidents result from neglect of high-priority monitoring tasks, such as monitoring altitude. When task demands change, people are not always very good at rescheduling their activities, and there is a tendency to procrastinate in performing some tasks. Preview of upcoming task demands appears to improve task management skills.

TEAM LEADERSHIP AND CREW COORDINATION

Optimal team performance during a workload transition depends heavily on effective crew resource management—personnel within the team sharing information effectively and coordinating their monitoring and task performance responsibilities. A breakdown in leadership and coordination among crew members may result in flawed decision making and improper actions. The impact of automation on reduced crew complement and the role of personality factors as determinants of crew performance are issues that need to be further addressed.

Communications is another variable that impacts crew performance. Standardizing and restricting vocabulary, presenting redundant information (e.g., presenting the same information both visually and auditorially), and sending many short messages rather than fewer long ones all foster good communications by reducing the possibility of confusion or misinterpretation. Research indicates that effective crews exchange information and use available resources better than noneffective ones.

Given that the crew leader bears ultimate responsibility for the crew's performance and safety, he or she is the most important single component of the crew. Two leader behavior patterns have been found to be the source of poor crew performance: (1) autocratic behaviors that inhibit communication from subordinates and (2) failure to coordinate and guide actions of crew members.

TRAINING FOR EMERGENCY RESPONSES

Given that the final design of the tank or any other system takes into consideration all of the above factors, adequate training is essential to ensure effective performance, with acceptable levels of crew workload. Initial training introduces crew members to the tasks they will perform and provides instruction and/or practice in conducting specific elements. Unit training provides additional experience, places task components in context, and promotes team skills. Extended practice enables parallel processing and the development of alternative strategies and reduces the need for much conscious decision making evident early in practice. For example, psychomotor skills progress from continuous, conscious error correction and compensation to the execution of well-learned, automatic motor programs.

Training and experience facilitate the development of mental models that enable the prediction of future states from present evidence and frees operators from the need to monitor status displays continuously. Experts are more likely to perceive task goals and performance criteria correctly, thinking in terms of larger units of activity than novices. They complete subtasks without conscious attention, recognize patterns of information, and initiate action sequences with single decisions. They can use established patterns of motor responses, efficient strategies, and exert timely and appropriate effort. Finally, experts are likely to notice and recover from their own errors and system failures earlier and more easily than novices. All of these differences between novice, or less capable, operators and expert, or more capable, operators determine the workload cost of achieving the same level of performance and may establish the maximum levels of performance that can be achieved, regardless of the effort exerted. For example, if routine tasks are performed automatically and correctly, additional resources will be available to perform nonroutine tasks.

Training and specific skill acquisition extend an individual's capability to handle workload; however, certain contributors to high workload, such as the necessity to perceive faster, are not amenable to training. Many of these factors are related to and limited by cognitive abilities of the individual.

The specific performance requirements for tank crews span the continuum from performance of complex, problem-solving tasks to routine, procedural tasks. For example, the tank crew should be capable of performing certain tasks automatically, while the commander must possess the flexible adaptability to apply multidimensional thinking and decision making when appropriate. The training demands for these two are very different.

To perform in an expert fashion under stress, commanders and crews must have a thorough understanding of the system, should have automated the lower-level procedural skills required to respond appropriately, and must be able to respond to unique circumstances. The primary decision maker or commander must have the opportunity to practice emergency problem solving and decision making, as well as routine proceduralized tasks. Practice under realistic, challenging conditions will allow better use of mental resources for the nonroutine elements of the emergency situation.

Three training approaches have particular relevance for the training of crew members who may be required to respond to emergency situations: simulation networking (SIMNET), embedded training, and crew resource management (CRM) training. SIMNET allows individual crew members through battalion commanders to practice tasks and roles in a realistic, complex simulation environment necessary to develop the appropriate skills. The technology of embedded training allows individuals to practice procedural tasks in the operational environment. CRM training focuses on the crew's management of resources and communications.

RECOMMENDATIONS FOR RESEARCH

In carrying out its charge, the panel identified existing research results that could be applied and research that needs to be conducted to answer important questions and inform operational policy. A large number of recommendations appear throughout the report, but those considered most important are identified below. Recommendations for research appear first, followed by recommendations for the implementation of research results.

Research Recommendations

• The effects of such factors as speed-accuracy tradeoffs, task scheduling, and task duration on operator performance under different levels of workload are not well defined and need additional research.
• More research is needed on team workload management strategies and their effectiveness, such as the effect of teammate cooperation on performance.
• More research is needed to identify the joint effects of stress, fatigue, training, crew coordination, and environmental stressors on operator workload in transition situations.
• Quantitative scales to rate the attributes that can be placed on the different workload drivers for the development of predictive workload models need to be developed.
• Continued research and development to validate global operator models of human performance in complex systems are needed.

• The tradeoff between costs and benefits of automation needs to be examined in this environment.

• Research should be conducted on the effects of stress on communication.

• Research is needed on the minimum nap time necessary to prevent or mitigate performance degradations.

• Research is needed on the effects of team monitoring.

• More research regarding the effectiveness of debiasing needs to be conducted.

• Additional research is needed to identify the speed, strengths, and limitations of activity switching in high workload/high stress environments, especially the extent and prevalence of cognitive tunnel vision.

• Research is needed to examine the impact of partially reliable preview.

• Research on task rescheduling according to an optimal prioritization scheme needs to be conducted.

• Research is needed to examine the factors that enhance crew compatibility and productivity as well as the individual characteristics that predict how an individual and team will function productively.

• Additional areas for consideration include assessment of the social-psychological impact of automation and reduced crew complement and an investigation of the role of personality factors as determinants of crew performance.

• Research is needed on the impact of stress on task performance under varying degrees and types of training.

• Research is needed for the validation of training approaches against performance in a combat-like environment.

Application of Research Results

• Adequate training and preparation, adapting strategies and tactics most appropriate for the situation, effective leadership, and smooth crew coordination could counteract some of the detrimental effects of imposed task demands.

• In order to better adapt to the transition situation, design solutions and personal solutions need to be identified and employed. For example, design solutions would include the following:

— using familiar elements and eliminating nonessential ones,
— displaying information that is directly necessary,
— highlighting information,
— integrating displays,
— making on-line emergency procedures brief and succinct, and
— providing procedural instructions that are phrased as actions to be taken, not as prohibited actions or system state descriptions.

Personal solutions include the following:
- — preplanning, anticipating, and rehearsing actions to be taken under stress,
- — employing cognitive approaches to stress might be taken, i.e., providing information, and
- — using team-building and environmental buffers to minimize communication problems.
- To minimize some of the physical stress and discomfort:
  - — tighter, more comfortable headgear should be developed,
  - — the displays and controls should be analyzed and rearranged,
  - — the placement and design of the radio equipment should be examined,
  - — shock isolation, such as seat shock absorbers, and personal restraints should be used, and
  - — temperature extremes should be eliminated.
- A duty schedule, with special attention to the cycle time, is essential to good crew performance.
- Sleep periods should be mandated and enforced, especially for operators who perform low-level vigilance monitoring tasks or complex cognitive tasks.
- Preemptive naps should be scheduled in a staggered manner across time and crew members.
- Countermeasures for sleep loss (e.g., stimulants, increased physical activity, naps, monetary incentives, diet, and increased social activity), which are not effective after the second or third nights of continuous operations, should not be used.
- A minimum level of comfort and darkness for sleep should be provided.
- Computer assistance would assist target detection, because human monitors need adequate sleep.
- Designers should try to provide simultaneous-type displays for target acquisition functions.
- Crews should be instructed on the biases and nonoptimal strategies of their vigilance functions to optimize their response strategies.
- Crews should be trained with target cueing or with knowledge of results in tasks requiring sustained attention.
- Crews should be provided with accurate, possibly electronic, navigational information.
- Navigational systems should support north-up (to facilitate mission planning and communication between individuals who do not share the same perspective) and track-up (to facilitate wayfinding, locating targets, and communication between individuals who share same perspective) map formats.

- Both planned route and current position should be displayed on the maps.
- Design efforts must address the potential confusion of the source of communications under high workload.
- Teams should maintain their integrity over some period of time.
- Crew composition, which has been found to affect performance, has three possible solutions:
  - crew resource management training,
  - select out operators who have been found to inhibit the development of effective communication, and
  - crew composition/creation.
- In training, repetition is needed, and a greater variety of tasks need to be practiced.
- Training to the point of automatic processing for proceduralized tasks is required.
- There should be maximum utilization of SIMNET.
- Emergency problem solving and decision-making management needs to be practiced.
- Emergency problem solving must be trained first in a nonstressed environment.
- Fault diagnosis must be taught in complex systems.

1

Team Transitions

Across a wide number of different systems in our society a common situation may be found: a team of operators, functioning for some period of time under relatively routine conditions, is abruptly confronted with abnormal and sometimes emergency circumstances, to which they must rapidly respond in an appropriate fashion. We call this the team transition situation. Let us consider a number of diverse examples, to realize the importance and ubiquity of this situation.

(1) The crew of a nuclear power control room becomes aware of a transient event somewhere in the reactor and within minutes (or even seconds) must try to establish the appropriate procedures to restore or maintain plant safety. This process may sometimes require a high level of cognitive activity as the nature of a fault is diagnosed (Rubinstein and Mason, 1979).

(2) Closely parallel to the nuclear power plant incident is the response of the crew of a commercial airline, which suddenly becomes aware of a life-threatening malfunction—the loss of an engine or, in the case of United Airlines flight 232, complete loss of hydraulic power near Sioux City, Iowa (Predmore, 1991). Here again the team (flight deck personnel working with air traffic controllers and maintenance personnel) must rapidly perceive the problem and engage in problem-solving behavior to ensure the safety of the aircraft.

(3) On a quiet night, personnel in a hospital emergency room are suddenly confronted with the victims of a serious automobile accident. Rapid problem solving and perhaps prioritization of possible causes must be coupled

with the precise exercise of procedural skills and coordination with the emergency room staff.

(4) A firefighting unit is suddenly called to a multialarm blaze in the middle of the night. Multiple units arrive on the scene within minutes and find themselves confronted with a burning chemical plant with potential toxic and explosive material (Klein, 1989).

(5) Shipboard personnel respond to an explosion that not only results in a fire that they must combat, but also destroys the integrity of the hull and therefore the seaworthiness of the vessel (Wagenaar and Groeneweg, 1988).

(6) A tornado, hurricane, or earthquake severely damages a community. Within minutes or hours a major disaster relief effort must be mobilized to care for wounded and homeless residents and attempt to restore necessary services.

(7) An emergency medical service (EMS) team is suddenly called on to make a helicopter flight to pick up a critically ill patient. The flight will take place at night, in bad weather, to an unfamiliar destination.

(8) Finally, an army tank crew stands ready and waiting at the edge of a battlefield, its crew of four having waited in a state of combat readiness for 36 hours. Hostile shots suddenly land close by, and the crew must immediately become an effective fighting unit. The situation confronted by this crew will provide the focus for much of the material in this report.

BACKGROUND

The Army plans to develop tanks with reduced crew sizes. To do this, tasks now performed by at least one crew member will be automated or redistributed among the remaining crew positions. During active deployment, the reduction in crew size is likely to increase workload, thus increasing the potential for performance failures and errors unless compensatory measures are devised.

Aside from a potentially high combat workload, the tank crew of the future may be faced with the additional problem of a long period of work underload and inactivity prior to active engagement in combat. Military doctrine calls for crews to remain with their tanks for periods as long as 72 hours before being called into combat or withdrawn. During such a period of passive waiting, the tasks of the crew will consist mainly of monitoring communication channels and visual displays, sleeping, and so forth. This period of low-level alertness may suddenly be followed by a high level of activity, when the order to engage the enemy is received. At this juncture, when stress and workload are high, decrements in the ability to focus attention, to implement and prioritize activities, and to retain information in short-term memory may be differentially impaired.

The U.S. Army Human Engineering Laboratory requested that the Committee on Human Factors conduct a study to provide advice and guidance on the effects of prolonged work underload on the subsequent performance of critical tasks and on approaches that could be employed to offset or compensate for decrements in performance that otherwise might occur. Given descriptions of the critical tasks required of each crew member at the onset of combat, the study had three objectives:

(1) To review the concept of workload and the state of research knowledge of its effects on subsequent high workload task performance;

(2) To evaluate the components of the critical tasks at combat onset to assess which components are most likely to be vulnerable to decrements from prior underload or the sudden onset of high workload; and

(3) To identify and evaluate techniques that might be used by future tank planners and designers to compensate for, or offset, likely performance decrements.

To obtain further information about the issues involved, staff received an orientation on current tank design and discussed the potential problem of underload followed by overload. Individuals with expertise in workload were then contacted to obtain their views about the effects of underload on sudden performance of important tasks. It was the consensus of those contacted that, while the concept of work underload-overload transition has been given little, if any, attention and even less research emphasis, it is nevertheless an important problem encountered in many work settings ranging from naval patrols in enemy waters (e.g., the Persian Gulf) to rescue squads and other public emergency service workplaces. However, for the purposes of this study the tank crew is the predominant focus.

TEAM PERFORMANCE DURING TRANSITIONS

Although there are many case studies of situations in which teams failed to perform effectively when faced with an abrupt transition from one level of workload to another, little research has been performed to examine team performance under such circumstances. The Three Mile Island incident (Rubinstein and Mason, 1979) and the grounding of the ship Exxon Valdez (National Transportation Safety Board, 1990) are examples of situations in which a team failed to respond appropriately. At other times, crews have performed these functions routinely and professionally, reflecting the fact that most such transitions go unnoticed. At still other times, the heroic and effective efforts of teams in times of crisis are worthy of note. Here the recent performance of the crew of United Flight 232 can be singled out in bringing the severely crippled airliner, without its steering control, to the ground (Predmore, 1991).

The point here is not to argue that performance in team transition situations is either exceptionally good or exceptionally poor. Rather, it is to suggest that there is a confluence of elements defining a large class of events, which potentially impact the health and safety of a large number of people, about which little is known. Transition situations are characterized by: (1) a team of people who must coordinate and communicate; (2) an event that occurs at an unexpected time following a long duration of waiting; and (3) the impact of the event that may produce (a) substantial risk to the health and safety of the team and possibly others; (b) an increase, or qualitative change in workload; and (c) a concomitant increase in stress.

This chapter briefly describes the duties of the tank crew and the characteristics of the tank environment. It provides an operational context for the in-depth analysis of human performance problems with teams in transition that are treated in subsequent chapters. The chapter ends with an overview of some of the main features of the transition process.

CREW PERFORMANCE REQUIREMENTS

The duties of the four members of a tank crew (commander, gunner, driver, and loader), as well as the operators of many complex systems, may be grouped into seven categories: (1) planning, preparation, and organization; (2) monitoring; (3) information seeking; (4) decision making; (5) maintenance; (6) control and operation; and (7) communications. The requirement to perform each of these functions varies between mission segments and between crew members. Principles drawn from previous research can be used to develop an expected workload profile for each crew member and mission phase. However, unexpected events, emergencies, or the incapacitation of one crew member can alter the workload that the crew actually experiences.

Planning and Preparation

Before a mission or engagement, planning and preparation are the primary sources of workload for a tank crew, particularly for the tank commander. The lead time for formulating plans may be hours or even days. Plans are developed at every level of command and transmitted down the chain of command through briefings, written orders, or radio transmissions. Planning is based on intelligence reports, which may or may not be current, and is driven by military doctrine and strategic goals. This type of planning is generally more self-motivated than event-driven, and it may or may not occur under external time pressure. If planning and preparation are sufficient, then performance during the subsequent engagement or mission is more likely to be acceptable. If events occur as expected and if few changes in the plans are required, then the workload of individual tank crews will be much lower than if planning is insufficient or inappropriate.

During an engagement or once a mission has begun, planning and preparation occupy less of the crew's time. Previously developed plans have established the goals and tactics that are followed, at least until events occur that make these plans inoperative. At this point, individual tank crews may have to act independently, and control begins to shift down the chain of command. The need to change the plan or develop a new plan is driven by rapidly evolving events external to the tank (see Chapter 9). However, an individual tank commander's knowledge of the global situation may be extremely limited at this point; and less information is available up the chain of command about the position, status, and intentions of individual tanks or units. When planning and decision making must be performed on-line, time pressure may be acute, and the plans that are developed tend to focus on immediate events, rather than long-term strategies. The workload of planning in real time is high.

Routine Monitoring

Before a mission or while preparing for an engagement, tank crews are responsible for some types of monitoring (see Chapter 6). The crew of each tank must stand watch, and members of a unit share the responsibility for mutual security. If the proposed reduction in tank crew complement occurs, standing watch will require more time for the remaining crew members, further contributing to fatigue problems already encountered in the field with crews of four (see Chapter 5). Most of the monitoring activities associated with the tank and its weapons systems are preventive. In general, premission monitoring is of relatively long duration, self-motivated (rather than driven by changes in the situation), and precautionary.

During a mission, continual monitoring is required to maintain situational awareness (see Chapters 7 and 8). The situation may change very rapidly and tank crews must rely on their own assessment of the local situation rather than on formal briefings. Thus, monitoring activities impose significantly higher workload during a mission than before. When the tank is moving, the driver is responsible for monitoring the state of the vehicle, the gunner is responsible for monitoring the weapons systems; the loader is responsible for monitoring ammunition supplies; and the tank commander must monitor the global situation inside and outside the tank. Each member of the tank crew must ensure that the others are aware of relevant information. The tank commander must transfer such information to other members of the unit and up the chain of command.

Maintenance

Before a mission, tank crews devote considerable time to maintaining their equipment (e.g., the tank, weapons systems, personal equipment), themselves (e.g., resting, eating), and resupply. These activities are generally routine, established by procedures and schedules. Depending on the time pressure under which these tasks are performed, workload may be very low or moderately high. Each crew member has specific duties that must be performed at regular intervals. The tank commander is responsible for ensuring that each crew member has completed his duties, as well as performing his own duties. He is also responsible for ensuring that each crew member has sufficient rest and food. If a defensive position is being established, the driver and loader may experience relatively high physical workload while positioning and concealing the tank.

The primary difference between maintenance activities performed before and during a mission is that the former are routine and proceduralized, whereas the latter are performed in response to problems or driven by events. During an engagement, only the most critical maintenance or repairs are performed in response to an urgent need. Rest and meals no longer occur at regular intervals or according to a schedule, but rather when the situation allows. Resupply becomes far less predictable as well; tank crews may have to make do with what they can carry with them for extended periods of time. Because maintenance performed during a mission is generally not routine, it is likely to impose higher workload. Furthermore, the support system available to facilitate maintenance before a mission may not be available once an engagement begins.

Information Seeking

Before a mission, intelligence briefings provide the primary source of information. The plans and strategies that are evolved are relatively static (although they may change as new information is received). If adequate briefings are given, crews within a tank, unit, or company share common information about the situation and each other's intentions. During this phase, situational assessment is primarily predictive in nature.

During a mission, the situation is no longer static, and gathering information about friendly as well as enemy forces is more difficult. Information transmitted by radio between tanks and intercom systems within a tank may be piecemeal and confusing. Each tank commander must update his mental model of the situation by piecing together incomplete information from a variety of sources and transmit relevant information to members of his crew, the unit, and up the chain of command. Obtaining information directly from the surrounding environment becomes an important element of the crew's duties during a mission.

When the tank is moving, remaining geographically oriented is critically important, imposes higher workload, and is more compensatory than predictive (see Chapter 7). The tank commander and driver must work together to correlate the visual scene with information on maps to determine their current and projected position. The tank commander must work with the gunner to identify and classify targets as they are observed and transmit information about their location. All of these information-seeking, interpreting, integrating, and sharing tasks are performed under time pressure and stress with only minimally sophisticated instruments. Thus, workload is much higher and performance may suffer. Uncertainty and complexity are greater, information quality is reduced, interruptions and interference are common, and the crew has little control over the rate or sequence of events.

Decision Making

At each level of command, the leader must select an appropriate strategy, given the mission goals and current situation, and adopt tactics that support the selected strategy. He must determine and convey the tank's position, situation, intentions, and ability to execute the original plan up the chain of command. If a tank's current position puts the crew in jeopardy or the crew will not be able to achieve its assignment, the tank commander must select a new position and the safest route to get there.

If failures occur or if the tank is hit by enemy fire, the commander must determine the extent of damage and choose the most appropriate action, based on status reports from the crew. Furthermore, the act of classifying and prioritizing targets and selecting the most appropriate weapons is an important decision that can affect the degree to which a tank succeeds or fails in accomplishing its goal and maintaining its security.

Control and Operation

Before a mission, tank control and operation of weapons systems plays a very small role in a tank crew's workload. Depending on whether a defensive or offensive position is being established, the crew may or may not have to move to a new position. However, this activity generally follows a well-specified plan and may impose relatively low workload.

During a mission, however, the tank may move rapidly over unfamiliar terrain. Vehicle control demands most of the driver's attention and considerable attention from the tank commander. The task is dynamic and unpredictable and can impose relatively continuous workload. Workload is increased further if visibility is limited by terrain, weather, smoke, or restrictions in forward visibility and field of view when the crew is closed up in the tank. The gunner is responsible for locating and aiming at targets with the primary weapons systems, although the tank commander shares this responsibility. The primary source of workload for the gunner in this phase is determining the range of a target and aiming accurately, while verbally coordinating his actions with the loader, the tank commander, and the driver.

Communications

Both before and during a mission, radio communications among tanks and intercom communications within a tank may impose significant workload. Before a mission, however, considerably more information is transmitted face to face through formal and informal briefings. This type of interaction is not possible during a mission, when the radio is the only link between tanks and when noise and physical separation between crew members makes direct verbal interactions difficult (see Chapter 8). Particularly in the midst of a battle, communications between and within channels may overlap and transmission clarity is reduced. Although the format of transmissions is highly stylized, the content and organization of messages transmitted under stress is less than optimal, therefore increasing the workload of the recipient. During a mission, communications are likely to focus on the immediate situation only. Particularly for the tank commander, monitoring the radio and transmitting information impose a significant amount of workload during a mission. Within a tank, the shared intercom frequency not only facilitates coordination, but also creates a significant monitoring demand for all crew members. Both before and after transition, the efficiency of communications and the coordination of cooperative actions may be governed very much by the leadership offered by the tank commander (see Chapter 10).

WORKSTATION CHARACTERISTICS

The physical environment of the tank crew establishes the context within which the above-mentioned aspects of performance are carried out. Crew workstation design has the potential for either enhancing or degrading crew performance. The M1A1 Main Battle Tank is a 60-plus ton mobile workplace for its crew members (Figure 1.1). Accurate weapons delivery is its primary purpose. Most of the design emphasis has thus been placed on propulsion, armor, and fire control systems. In an effort to produce a safe, or at least survivable, battlefield environment for crew members, the tank has been designed to be extremely mobile, present a small target to enemies,

FIGURE 1.1   Photo of an M1A1 Main Battle Tank.   Courtesy of the U.S. Army
Human Engineering Laboratory.

provide a structurally sound shield against enemy ordnance, and provide a
capsule that can be sealed against chemical/biological weapons (referred to
as "buttoned up").   The crew workstations inside a tank (see, for example,
Figure 1.2) are well defined, as are the normal work tasks of each crew
member.   There is one workstation for each of the four crew members.
Each workstation consists of a seat and the displays, controls, and weapons
that are required for the crew member to perform his job function.

The driver is stationed in the front of the tank, beneath the main gun
and turret.   His seat is recumbent with a movable headrest.   The steering
yoke, throttle, transmission, and brake controls are positioned at the front of
the driver's workstation.   The driver is responsible for monitoring all engine
parameters as well as the status of the hydraulic systems in the tank.   He
can look outside the vehicle by placing his head through a hatch in the tank
deck.   When the tank is buttoned up, the driver sees the outside world
through three fixed vision blocks (narrow windows with ballistic glass) that
are 7 1/4 inches long and 1 3/4 inches high built into the hatch cover.

The other three crew members are stationed inside the turret of the
tank.   The loader's workstation is just to the left of the main gun breech.

FIGURE 1.2   Top-down view of the tank commander's workstation in an M1A1 Main Battle Tank. Courtesy of the U.S. Army Human Engineering Laboratory.

His seat is oriented slightly sideways to allow him to take ammunition from the storage locker on his right (at the rear of the turret) and transfer it to the main gun breech on his left. When the main gun is fired, the recoil causes the breech to move backward in the turret. The loader must move his legs and other appendages out of the way of this recoil. A hatch is located directly above his head. When the tank is open he can see the outside world through the hatch by standing on his seat. When the tank is buttoned up, the loader views the outside world through vision blocks.

The gunner has the most complex workstation in the tank because he has been provided with the most advanced technology. He is positioned to the right of the main gun and slightly below the loader's level. His workstation consists of a seat and all the aiming and other fire control systems in the tank. In addition to the main sighting system, the gunner's workstation includes an auxiliary sighting system, a laser rangefinder, a thermal imaging system, and a ballistic fire control computer. The gunner has the main responsibility for acquiring targets visually, tracking them with the aiming system, adjusting any fire control solutions in the computer, and firing the main gun. The gunner is second-in-command of the tank crew; he takes over in the event that the tank commander is unable to function.

The tank commander's workstation is located directly behind and above the gunner. It consists of a seat, all communication controls, the controls for actuating certain auxiliary armaments on the tank (e.g., grenade launchers, smoke generators, and chaff canisters), and a main gun firing mechanism to be used if the gunner's main firing switch is inoperative or the gunner is disabled. The tank commander is responsible for the overall operation of the tank and its crew. He is directly responsible for the tactical movement and placement of the tank, selection of targets, decisions about the type of ammunition to be used, the final decision to fire the main gun, and all communication with both his counterparts in other tanks in his platoon and the higher command structure.

Several aspects of tank crew workstations fall short of acceptable human factors design criteria. One characteristic common to all four workstations is the lack of seatbelts or any other mechanism (such as pneumatic chair suspension) that might counteract the sudden and strong accelerations associated with vehicle movement. The driver's seat is the only one in the tank that is recumbent, allowing the driver to recline. The driver's seat provides much more body support than the other seats in the tank. This support, together with the availability of structures that allow the driver to brace himself for sideways accelerations, allows the driver to function under much higher accelerations than the other crew members. It is a commonly accepted fact among tank crews that a driver can operate the tank in such a manner as to cause injury to the other crew members while causing none to himself.

At least two of the tank crew workstations have obvious problems with the placement of controls and displays. In the driver's workstation, the steering and propulsion controls are well placed, allowing the driver to look outside the vehicle and steer the tank much like an automobile when the tank is not buttoned up. In many cases, he must rely on the commander's verbal steering commands and drive blind or drive with offset eyepoint (i.e., similar to using a periscope to see the outside world). However, many of the displays that the driver is supposed to monitor are placed orthogonal to his line of vision, so that he must lean forward and look sideways to see them. In the gunner's workstation, the main gunsight is centrally located in the gunner's field of vision and well within his reach. However, other components, most notably the fire control computer console, are placed in extremely awkward locations.

Another common workstation design problem concerns ingress and egress. It is quite difficult to get into and out of certain crew member workstations. The gunner's station is probably the most difficult to get into and out of, since it has no direct hatch access. The gunner must come through the tank commander's or the loader's hatch and then thread his way down into his workstation. Such access problems are a direct result of competing design goals. As mentioned earlier, tank designers endeavor to make the tank as small as possible, as fast as possible, and as powerful in firepower, as possible. Crew member workstations are probably relegated to a fairly low priority in the overall design scheme.

FRAMEWORK OF THE REPORT

Given this description of the tank environment, features of which are elaborated in the report, we now turn to Figure 1.3, which provides a framework for the report. It describes the variables that characterize the transition to action, the performance variables that are most affected by the transition, and the variables that moderate the effect of the transition on performance and cognition. As mentioned before, this report focuses its attention most heavily on a single system—the tank and its crew—that we see as prototypical of many of the other systems in transition to be described in Chapter 2. It is our hope in doing so that we shall: (a) provide specific guidelines for human performance modeling and human factors engineering in the tank environment, (b) provide conclusions and offer a data base that will generalize to other teams in transition, and (c) stimulate research that may generalize to all such teams.

Four key changes characterize the transition (Part A of Figure 1.3): (1) psychological stress level, a qualitative change from the anxiety and fear of waiting to the high workload, time pressure, and mortal danger of the battle; (2) environmental change from quiet to noisy and possibly clear to smoky; (3) cognitive mode changes from a good deal of proactive planning and routine following of procedures (pre) to a reactive mode involving rapid decision making and problem solving (post); and (4) target search and acquisition transitions from a low to a high probability of finding a target. Part B shows processes that are affected by the transition and will be the focus of subsequent chapters in this report: (1) target search, detection, and recognition; (2) spatial orientation, navigation, and situation awareness; (3) decision making; (4) strategic planning; (5) communications and team coordination; (6) following of procedures; and (7) perceptual-motor interaction. It should be noted that all of these activities characterize sustained battlefield activity, as well as the immediate post-transition period. However, it is likely that spatial orientation, navigation and situation awareness, and strategic planning will undergo a particularly intense increase during the immediate post-transition period.

Finally, Part C is a partial list of variables that can affect or moderate the response to the transition: sleep loss, stress, human factors design, and training. Stress represents both a cause (Part A) and a moderating variable that can attenuate or enhance the effects of the transition on performance (Part C). Human factors design of the displays, controls, and working

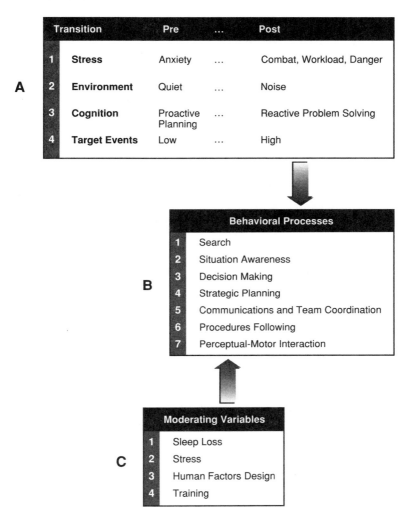

FIGURE 1.3 Variables that (A) characterize the transition, (B) are most affected by the transition, and (C) moderate the effect of the transition on performance and cognition.

environment may be assumed to influence transition performance in two respects: (a) good human factors design will improve the quality of performance as demands increase during the post-transition period and (b) good human factors principles may be applied specifically to address the problems of updating situation awareness in the crisis period immediately following the transition. This second application is quite analogous to the concerns expressed in the nuclear industry for displays that will support the rapid diagnosis of complex faults (Woods, 1988). Finally, training may be the single most important variable to influence performance during transition. Training may focus on the skills that are disrupted during transition or on mitigating the detrimental effects of stress.

This framework sets a context for the chapters that follow. The first part of the report contains information from analogous systems that may provide insight on the variables that may affect performance during the transition and examines the workload domain--which is the overriding context that interacts with moderating variables to affect performance. Chapter 2 presents an analysis of the features of similarity and contrast between the tank environment and other analogous systems and references relevant case studies and accident reports in other domains. Chapter 3 reviews workload: its sources, measurement, consequences, relationship to performance, and so forth.

The report then focuses on key variables that influence crews' abilities to adapt to a transition: stress (Chapter 4) and sleep disruption and fatigue (Chapter 5). The report turns then to the specific domains of tank crew performance that may be influenced by the transition process: vigilance and target detection (Chapter 6), situation and geographic awareness (Chapter 7), decision making (Chapter 8), strategic task management (Chapter 9), and team structure, communications, and leadership (Chapter 10). Finally, it discusses possible remediations of some of the moderating variables such as training (Chapter 11) and integrates and synthesizes the panel's most important recommendations (Chapter 12).

Two final points should be noted. First, our listing of specific tank crew behaviors is not exhaustive (i.e., Part B of Figure 1.3). The panel selected a subset of tasks specific to particular members of the tank crew, primarily the commander and the gunner, as the focus of analysis. This selection was not random but was based on information obtained from a series of briefings provided by professional armor personnel at Aberdeen Proving Ground and in Washington, DC. These briefings revealed certain critical areas of vulnerability to transition-related effects, on which we have focused our analysis. Second, the chapters that follow, while maintaining a consistent structural format, vary to some degree in the extent to which they emphasize the broader issue of transitions across various systems or the specific tank system, emphasizing, but not exclusively, the transition aspects of the tank.

REFERENCES

Klein, G.A.
   1989   Recognition-primed decisions. Pp. 47-92 in W. Rouse, ed., *Advances in Man-Machine Systems Research, Volume 5*. Greenwich, Connecticut: JAI Press.

National Transportation Safety Board
1990   *Marine Accident Report—Grounding of the U.S. Tankship EXXON VALDEZ on Bligh Reef, Prince William Sound, near Valdez, Alaska, March 24, 1989.* Report No. NTSB/Mar-90/04. Washington, DC: National Transportation Safety Board.

Predmore, S.C.
1991   Micro-coding of cockpit communications in accident analyses: Crew coordination in the United Airlines flight 232 accident. In R.S. Jensen, ed., *Proceedings of the 6th International Symposium on Aviation Psychology.* Columbus, Ohio: Ohio State University, Department of Aviation.

Rubinstein, T., and A.F. Mason
1979   The accident that shouldn't have happened: An analysis of Three Mile Island. *IEEE Spectrum* 16:33-57.

Wagenaar, W.A., and J. Groeneweg
1988   Accidents at sea: Multiple causes and impossible consequences. Pp. 133-144 in E. Hollnagel, G. Mancini, and D.D. Woods, eds., *Cognitive Engineering in Complex Dynamic Worlds.* London: Academic Press.

Woods, D.D.
1988   Commentary: Cognitive engineering in complex and dynamic worlds. Pp. 115-129 in E. Hollnagel, G. Mancini, and D.D. Woods, eds., *Cognitive Engineering in Complex Dynamic Worlds.* London: Academic Press.

2

Analogous Systems

Human factors analysis gains value from its ability to generalize across domains. This is particularly true when empirical data are scarce and advances in understanding may be achieved by sharing knowledge from similar systems or paradigms. Yet the application of conclusions drawn in one domain to another must proceed cautiously and identify the ways in which the two domains are similar or different. It is with this caution in mind that we proceed with these comparisons, which may be based on a number of criteria, such as unique characteristics of the transition within each system (e.g., expectancy of an emergency occurring, level of risk, physical environment) and factors of the system contributing to the emergency (e.g., faulty decision making, duty schedule, crew structure, communications, human factors design).

The first part of the chapter enumerates the features of similarity in the team transition process in terms of five general categories: time, structure of the event, environment, risk, and organizational structure. These features are then described for each of the analogous systems of interest. Within the discussion of each system, relevant case studies are referenced illustrating how causes and contributing factors of an emergency or accident may be generalized, with caution, to the tank environment.

FEATURES OF SIMILARITY

Time

The time element contains three areas of concern: the time constant of transition, expectancy, and the pretransition period.

The time constant of the transition refers to the abruptness with which a crisis transition unfolds and how it affects the manner in which the team is able to respond. For example, the transitions and responses to those transitions in a nuclear reactor typically unfold in a matter of seconds and minutes; those at a fire scene or on the battlefield may involve minutes and possibly hours; the response to natural disasters may unfold over hours and days.

Situations differ widely in the extent to which operators can expect that a transition will occur. Expectancy is a variable often driven by the frequency with which transitions have occurred in the past. For example, nuclear power operators rarely encounter serious failures. In spite of their recurrent simulator training to deal with emergencies, they operate under the assumption that the plant will continue to function normally. A similar situation probably exists for air crews of commercial airliners.

In contrast, shock trauma and hospital emergency room crews maintain a fairly continuous level of preparation for medical emergencies and accident victims, as they can be expected at any time. Tank crews fall somewhere between these levels of expectancy. They are mobilized for an engagement, know that such an engagement will probably occur some time in the future, but they do not know precisely when. The difference in expectancy is potentially important, as it influences the speed with which people can respond to discrete events (Wickens, 1992), as well as to system failures (Wickens and Kessel, 1981).

The pretransition period is related to, but distinct from, expectancy and describes the length of time that a given crew must remain on watch before an event may occur. For example, flight crews or nuclear power operators may be on duty for eight to ten hours before an event occurs (if at all), whereas hospital personnel may be on call for days, and battlefield necessities may call on the tank crew to maintain themselves on station for as long as 72 to 96 hours. This time period clearly has the potential to influence the quantity and quality of rest in a way that can influence the post-transition performance.

Structure of the Event

The structure of the event refers to the extent to which its nature is predictable and whether the desired response can be effectively preprogrammed. Cognitively, this process may be described as updating a mental picture of the evolving situation. Because of the high complexity of nuclear power plants and the resulting complexity and multiplicity of their features when emergencies occur, reactor designers encounter major challenges in training operators for specific sequences of procedures or actions to be followed, given the variability of possible failures (Woods, 1988). In contrast, the pilot of an emergency medical services (EMS) team will have a fairly proceduralized set of actions to be carried out in the process of getting the helicopter aloft and then to its destination, although the destination and the route flown to and from that destination may be wholly unpredictable. The degree of predictability of response in tank crew operations falls somewhere in between.

Environment

Physical conditions of the environment play a potentially important role in the response to the transition. The conditions of the flight deck or nuclear power plant control room are relatively friendly—temperature controlled, low to modest noise level, comfortable, and relatively free of vibration. This is in marked contrast to the tank environment, in which four operators work within cramped, noisy, and vibrating conditions, often under excessive temperatures.

Personal Risk

Transition teams differ in terms of the extent to which they are exposed to risk of personal injury or death, both to themselves and to others. Risk may be realized at three different levels (i.e., before or after the transition period or not at all). For the tank crew, there is a feeling of risk the moment they enter the combat arena, whether in the pre- or post-transition period. The aircraft pilot or nuclear power plant operator experiences little risk until after a transition event occurs; the emergency room personnel or disaster relief organization may never feel the risk at all. Both risk and environmental factors influence the stress that is experienced in a way that can have serious effects on the abilities of crews to function effectively.

Organizational Structure

Organizational structure has three subcomponents: team structure (command authority), team integrity, and organizational autonomy.

The dimension of team structure or command authority defines the extent to which the unit does (e.g., the tank crew or flight deck) or does not (e.g., the nuclear power control room team) have a clearly defined chain of command or authority gradient. The authority gradient and its relation to the definition of job responsibilities can have a complex effect on performance efficiency (Foushee and Helmreich, 1988; Wickens et al., 1989; see also Chapter 10).

Team integrity refers to the extent to which crew members are maintained as an integral crew over time or continue to belong to the same unit.

Tank crews generally possess such integrity. In contrast, U.S. airline crews are typically formed uniquely for each sequence of flights. It is generally assumed that team integrity is beneficial for team emergency response, although airlines believe that common training and proceduralized activities can compensate. This issue has been identified as important by other researchers as well (see, for example, Druckman and Bjork, 1991).

Organizational autonomy defines the extent to which a unit functions alone or in close coordination with a higher organizational structure. Nuclear power plant operators respond to emergencies as a fairly self-contained unit, as do emergency room staffs. Firefighting units may have to coordinate with other units when the situation is serious. Tank crews nearly always need to do so. The need for extra-group communications and coordination typically places an added burden on the ability to cope with the transition.

Summary

The features of similarity described above are summarized in Figure 2.1, which identifies the set of features, and offers a line connecting the feature levels of the designated transition teams. Comparisons of two prototypical teams are shown: the tank (x) and the aircrew (o) (discussed below).

COMMERCIAL AIRLINES

Commercial airline crews typically consist of two or three members: the captain (or pilot), the first officer (or copilot), and possibly a second officer (or flight engineer), in addition to a support team of maintenance workers, air traffic controllers, cabin crew, and so forth. These crews may be on flights that take as little as half an hour or as long as 15 hours or more. The crews do not remain intact from flight to flight, so little crew planning can occur prior to the predeparture briefing.

The reader is referred to Chapter 10 for a detailed discussion of the important aspects of leadership and coordination in the cockpit that affect team performance under stress caused by transitions in workload. A number of airline accidents have been attributed to inadequate cockpit coordination and management (National Transportation Safety Board, 1985a). In one case the National Transportation Safety Board reported that in many of these accidents there appeared to be little captain leadership and planning guidance for the flight (National Transportation Safety Board, 1985a) which led to the conclusion that all crew members should be required to be trained in crew coordination and decision-making skills that are essential to the safe operation of aircraft.

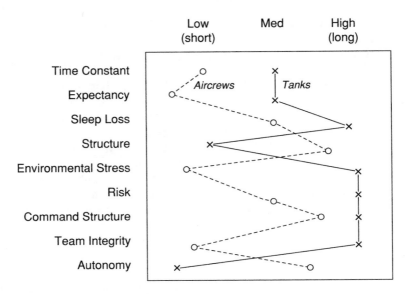

FIGURE 2.1   Similarity of team transitions.

As Figure 2.1 shows, air crews often have little advance warning that a crisis is about to occur, and when it does the crew must respond within seconds or, at most, a few minutes, depending on the event. However, as in the nuclear power environment, the probability that a transition or serious event will occur is quite low. When a transition does occur, though, one factor that is likely to affect the capability of the crew to respond appropriately and rapidly is the current flight and duty schedule of the crew members, which may be a period of 8 to 10 hours.

As in a number of other systems, such as emergency medical services, the pilot will have a fairly proceduralized set of actions to be carried out in the process of taking off, flying, and landing. The environment is temperature controlled but noisy, which makes intracockpit communications difficult without the use of headsets and interphone (National Transportation Safety Board, 1980). In addition, the cockpit is cramped, especially considering the number of displays and controls that are present. If a transition occurs, the extent to which the crew is exposed to risk of personal injury is moderate. However, the crew will usually experience little risk until after the transition event occurs.

In commercial airlines, the cockpit crew has a clearly defined chain of authority; however, U.S. crew members are never given the opportunity to adjust to how a particular pilot manages the crew because the crew composition is reconstituted for each flight. Finally, the crew does not operate in isolation but must coordinate and communicate with air traffic control, cabin crew, and maintenance. As identified in aircraft accident reports, several airline accidents have been attributed to a breakdown in air traffic control coordination (National Transportation Safety Board, 1985a, 1987). At the same time, the availability of air traffic control can often serve as a valuable asset to flight crews in time of crisis.

Upon examination of Figure 2.1, it appears that tank crews and airline crews do not have a great deal in common. Their time constants during transitions, expectancies of transitions occurring, environmental stress, team integrity or continuity, and group autonomy are very different. However, they are very much alike when one examines their duty schedules and command structure. These latter two factors affect vigilance and monitoring behavior (Chapter 6) and communication flow (Chapter 10), which have been found to degrade team performance in both environments, as well as in numerous other systems. This seems to suggest that the communication flow and the type of information that is shared should be fairly well structured and should be heard and understood by the receiver(s). Crew members need to receive pertinent information that is likely to affect team and system performance in a timely and easily interpretable format. These shared aspects between the two environments are highlighted in Chapter 10.

A number of major transportation accidents raise serious concerns about the far-reaching effects of physiological conditioning (including fatigue and sleep patterns) and circadian rhythm factors in transportation system safety, in addition to the effects of the physical environment or workspace, training, communication structure, and crew structure on system safety. Accident investigations reveal that poor work-rest scheduling can jeopardize safety in most transportation modes (Graeber, 1988). It appears that employees and first-line supervisors in the transportation industry do not receive training on the effects of work-rest schedules on safety and performance. Yet commercial airline crews frequently encounter irregular and often unpredictable work-rest patterns. It appears that, with minor exceptions, neither management nor the labor segment of the transportation industry properly considers the adverse effects of irregular and unpredictable cycles of work and rest on its vehicle-operating personnel.

RAILROADS

Railroad freight train crews until recent years were composed of 5-person crews; however, the current typical crew consists of 3- and, increasingly, 2-person crews. Amtrak and many other commuter trains are known to run with a crew of 1 in some areas. The typical 5-person crew is composed of an engineer, a conductor, 2 brakemen, and a fireman. The 3-person crew includes an engineer, a conductor, and a brakeman in the cab;

the 2-person crew does not have a brakeman. The engineer is responsible for controlling the train. He has the written dispatch orders, receives information from the dispatcher, and is the sole decision maker. Both the engineer and conductor know the makeup of the train, but the trainmaster, the manager of the yard with respect to the movement of freight, determines the makeup, and the conductor keeps a manifest. This information will influence the decisions made concerning stopping distances and train speed, especially when approaching curves and up/down grades. The brakeman couples and uncouples train cars, releases the hand brakes, and so forth. On all freight trains, there is a clear division of labor that has evolved since the 1800s. For example, eliminating the brakeman's position would have no effect on that of the engineer (T. Brown, personal communication, 1992).

When a transition event unfolds in the railway industry, it does so in a matter of seconds. As in the commercial airline industry, the expectation that a transition will occur is quite low. The railway crew is "on watch" or "on call" at all times while on duty. This may affect the quantity and quality of the rest they get. At times, crew members have gotten only a few hours of sleep at a time, which leads to chronic sleep deprivation and has been cited as a contributing factor in at least one railway accident (National Transportation Safety Board, 1989); however, a recent study (General Accounting Office, 1992) analyzed accident data of 30 engineers from each of 4 railroads and found no relationship between hours on duty and human-factors-related accidents. At least 80 percent of the engineers surveyed work, on average, 10 or fewer consecutive hours, but the time at which they were called to duty varied greatly and may have been a contributing factor.

Railroad cab crews have highly irregular work-rest cycles; work and rest hours begin and end at any hour of the day or night. If a crew works up to 8 hours, the law requires that they have 8 hours off immediately after. Crew members are called at least one hour in advance of reporting time, but normally two hours ahead. These calls can come at any time. The maximum number of consecutive hours an employee in the U.S. railroad train service may actually be on duty in a 24-hour period is 12 hours, and the minimum time off duty between work assignments is 8 hours, but there are no required rest days. If the crew works 8 to 12 hours, they are required to then have 10 hours off duty. This results in some crew members not being permitted to report for duty when a run is scheduled. Thus, there are "extra-boards," normally engineers with less seniority, on call to take trips. Crews with required rest and sufficient seniority can bid on any job.

Local runs and passenger trains have more predictable schedules, and these trains, like the tank crews, have an average degree of team integrity. For example, passenger train crews typically work approximately 2 1/2 consecutive hours; freight train crews may work on trips that last anywhere from 4 to 20 hours or more with a 2- to 3-hour rest in the middle of the trip (Michaut and McGaughey, 1972). These short-run crews are trained for a specific territory, and they can probably be trained for certain response procedures. The National Transportation Safety Board has made the recommendation that the railway industry needs to (1) regulate the hours of work and compulsory rest; (2) standardize work schedules; (3) improve control over noise, temperature, vibration, etc.; and (4) evaluate, monitor, and maintain employee health (Belanger, 1989).

Although there are strict requirements concerning duty schedules, codified in the Hours of Service Act, at present it is not possible to mandate sleep periods; nor would such a mandate necessarily be effective. When employees are off duty, the railway industry cannot regulate what they do, and some workers may have very few hours of sleep before going on duty. As discussed in previous sections and in Chapter 5, these irregular schedules can have serious effects on circadian rhythms and job performance (Smiley, 1990). In the railway industry, irregular schedules have been cited in numerous investigations as a contributing factor to railway accidents (National Transportation Safety Board, 1985b, 1989; Smiley, 1990). One report notes (National Transportation Safety Board, 1989b:2):

> The changing nature of railroad operations and competitive factors have materially increased the relative number of train crew members who must work irregular and unpredictable shifts on a long-term basis. Lacking proper training and education in the physiology of fatigue, many may allow themselves to become chronically deprived of sleep, and develop physiological problems that could adversely affect their performance and the safety of train operations. Other transportation industry operators are exposed to shift work, but the work and rest cycles of railroad extra-board and pool train crews are often more irregular and unpredictable.

When a transition occurs (in this case, the train crew determines that an accident is going to occur or can occur unless some immediate action is taken), the structure of the event is moderately predictable and, to a small extent, so is the nature of the required action. If a collision is about to occur, the emergency brakes are probably applied; however the degree of application, etc., will be affected by the makeup of the train, the environment (e.g., whether there is a grade), etc. It appears that the coordination factors or individual cognitive factors are of a different criticality than is the case with other teams, such as the tank crew. There is little risk to the train crew in the pretransition period and during the transition. However, there is moderate to high personal risk in the post-transition period.

The train crew is highly autonomous. It receives dispatch orders, observes signals and responds accordingly, regulates the speed of the locomotive, and so forth. There is communication via portable radios between the cab crew and any train personnel who may be in trailing units of the train (i.e., the rear brakeman if there is a 4- or 5-person crew, or the conductor). There is communication between the train dispatcher and the engineer; however, according to Smiley (1990), the dispatchers are not required to notify the engineer verbally by radio of expected meets or other conditions that may exist. This raises a number of safety issues that are similar in the tank environment. One cannot be sure of the level of situation awareness on the part of the engineer, and the dispatchers may not realize the criticality of this potential lack of awareness. Note, however, that in T. Brown's experience (personal communication, 1992), there was constant communication between engineer and dispatcher, particularly with regard to meets and passes; to operate otherwise would have disastrous consequences.

The environment is another feature that the locomotive cab and the tank have in common. Both are noisy, dirty, and uncomfortable (particularly the seating), vibrate, and have poor temperature control. Current design of new locomotives is focusing on ergonomically designing the seats in the cab (e.g., to provide lower-back support), insulation to reduce noise, addition of air conditioning, vibration damping, and numerous changes in information presentation. The analog dial and pointer are being replaced by more sophisticated digital displays, and some prototypes are scheduled to be evaluated in 1992 (T. Brown, personal communication, 1992).

A third attribute that the rail crews have in common with the tank crews concerns the assumption that the crews are underloaded much of the time. Vigilance tasks have been viewed as minimally demanding, tedious situations (Dember and Warm, 1979; Parasuraman, 1984); however, current research is beginning to suggest that vigilance tasks can be quite demanding and induce much stress (see Chapter 6). Consequently, because locomotive crews, similar to armor crew members, perform tasks requiring vigilance functions, they may be stressed by the tasks that need to be completed, as well as by the environmental factors.

As noted by Devoe and Abernethy (1977), the engineer is very busy, but for stretches of time, there is little stimulation. The engineer must continually monitor and anticipate changes on the trip (e.g., grades, curves, obstructions on the track) and respond when required. However, there may be long periods of inactivity ranging from 5 to 20 minutes (Michaut and McGaughey, 1972). Unlike the tank environment, however, when a change is input to the locomotive, the response of the system is slow and complex. Thus, the two systems are, dynamically, different and therefore may require different cognitive processes of the decision makers.

In summary, the locomotive and tank environments share their greatest degree of similarity in the pretransition period, and here the common themes focus more on the efficiency of the individual operator, as influenced by vigilance, stress, and sleep disruption, than on the coordination of the team.

NUCLEAR POWER PLANTS

Nuclear power plant operators work in a control room that is very spacious, well-lit, and air-conditioned. Control rooms are supplied with potable water coolers, cooking facilities, and adjacent toilets. Operators sit in comfortable office-type chairs and are free to move around the control room. In fact, they *must* move about the control room to acquire the information they need to determine whether the plant is operating correctly. Information, which is acquired mostly visually, comes from hundreds of instruments arranged on rather large control panels. Nuclear power plant control rooms normally operate in a semibuttoned-up mode, in that access to control rooms is controlled by locked doors and security badge readers. Control rooms are furnished with their own atmospheric control systems, including filters for smoke, particulates, and radioactive gases.

Operators of nuclear power plants, once selected, are put through an extensive training program. These operators have the equivalent of a 2-year associate degree when they complete their formal training. They are tested after completing a prescribed training program that is administered by the utility owning the particular plant for which the operator will be licensed. Individual operators are licensed at one of two levels by the Nuclear Regulatory Commission: reactor operator or senior reactor operator. Both require plant experience, but a senior reactor operator must have significantly more. All candidates for reactor operator work for some period of time in the plant operating areas as equipment operators. This allows them to become familiar with the layout of the plant and the location and operation of all equipment and systems within the it. Many nuclear power plant operators come to the industry after having served in the U.S. Navy as nuclear submarine crew members. Like crews in tanks, but unlike those in commercial aviation, teams in a given control room are typically constituted for a fairly long period of time.

Prior to the Three Mile Island accident, there were no formal requirements regarding specific nuclear power plant crew structure (other than the requirement for a specific number of crew members and their licensing level), technical support personnel and systems, or the maximum number of hours worked by crew members in any given work period. There was also no enforceable standard for individual crew members' duties during either normal or emergency operation. Many of these details have been specified since that accident. There is still, however, no federal standard for individual crew duties. Some emergency procedures are sufficiently formalized to specify each crew member's assigned duties at any point in time, but individual operators are free to deviate from procedures if they deem the procedure to be ineffective.

Unlike military crews, nuclear power plant crews do not use a standardized communication protocol.   There is no equivalent in nuclear power plants to the short, understandable, and practiced protocol used by tank crews to identify targets and their location, specify armament and ammunition to be used against targets, and to inform other crew members of the status of tank systems (see Chapter 10).   There is also no requirement in nuclear power plants to coordinate activities with external groups, except in certain classes of declared emergency situations.   Even in these emergency conditions, a nuclear power plant control room is very much an autonomous entity.

The one operational area in which nuclear power plant operating crews and tank crews differ greatly is in terms of the expectation of events that must be dealt with in a timely manner.   Things do not often go wrong in nuclear power plants—at least they don't go wrong to the extent that an emergency situation is encountered.   Statistically speaking, nuclear power plants are very safe, at least as far as the nuclear portion is concerned. Workers in nuclear power plants are subject to the same dangers as anyone working in an industrial plant in which heavy, rotating equipment and vast quantities of high pressure steam are employed.   However, no death has been directly caused by an accident in the nuclear portion of a U.S. nuclear power plant.   The result of this safety factor is that nuclear power plant operating crews don't expect anything to go wrong, and usually it doesn't.

The operation of a nuclear power plant, as in many process-oriented plants, is essentially a crew effort rather than an individual job, oriented toward procedural operation.   As in the rail industry and the tank environment, the essential nature of the job is predominantly vigilance-oriented. There are extended periods of low activity with the possibility of sudden emergency or urgent operation.   Thus, the nuclear power plant industry has the same potential problems with vigilance as the rail industry.   Nuclear power plant operators encounter periods of extreme cognitive underload, especially during evening and late night work shifts, followed potentially by extreme sensory and cognitive overload.   If a nuclear plant is operating properly, then virtually no operator intervention is required and the crew's job becomes one of a classic continuous vigilance task complicated by the fact that the operators know the automatic monitoring systems will probably alert them if something goes wrong.   One can imagine the extreme boredom and fatigue that can occur at three o'clock in the morning with everything operating smoothly, no maintenance procedures in effect, and the steady hum of the plant surrounding the control room.

An operating crew working in this situation at one moment can find the whole plant going haywire the next.   It has been said that things happen relatively slowly in nuclear plants and, in general, that is true.   However, in the event of a major accident or equipment failure, the control room is almost instantaneously transformed into a buzzing, ringing, flashing arcade.

Most control rooms contain between 2,000 and 4,000 lighted-tile annunciators to warn operators of specific malfunctions. These annunciators seem to work well for isolated failures in specific equipment. In any major event, however, a large proportion of these annunciators begin to flash and the alerting horns, bells, and buzzers begin to sound. The operating crew is then faced with the task of making sure the plant is being safely shut down, diagnosing the problem(s), and activating their emergency procedures—all the while trying to acknowledge and silence the visual and auditory alarms. If a major accident does occur, it is potentially serious in terms of injury, loss of life, and property damage.

It is in this transition period that another feature common to the tank and the power plant is encountered, in terms of the structure of the event. In both cases (and in contrast to railway incidents), the nature of the workload triggering event may be quite complex, imposing heavily on the operator's cognitive skills. For this reason, a heavy premium may be placed on the continuous maintenance of pretransition situation awareness: which systems are working, which systems are receiving maintenance, and what is the current state of the plant. It was, in fact, failure in this regard that was partially responsible fo the Three Mile Island disaster (Rubinstein and Mason, 1979).

MERCHANT AND MILITARY SHIPS

Historically, U.S. merchant ships consisted of three departments: engine, steward, and deck; however, in recent years, crew members' responsibilities have been reallocated and crew size has been reduced due to the implementation of automation and mechanization. Shipboard automation has had the greatest impact on the engineering department, in which a majority of monitoring tasks (e.g., watch-standing) have been automated, resulting in a periodically unattended engine room on new vessels, while labor-intensive intermittent deck tasks have remained numerous (National Research Council, 1990). The maintenance department, whose members can perform both engine and deck jobs as well as routine maintenance, has evolved in order to facilitate a more even distribution of this labor between deck and engineering personnel.

Recently built U.S. flag vessels have a typical crew size of 20 to 24, in contrast with the 40 to 45 found aboard smaller ships of 30 years ago. Similarly designed foreign flag vessels currently have crew sizes ranging from 12 to 16, and in highly automated foreign flag ships, there may be as few as 8 to 12 crew members on board. This reduction in crew size has raised the question of system safety. But in the last 20 years, as ship size has increased and crew size has diminished, there has been a concomitant worldwide reduction in vessel casualties and personnel injuries (National

Research Council, 1990). Nevertheless, there are indications that this general downward trend in marine casualties may be bottoming out. There are various factors, including a worldwide aging of the merchant fleets, that could potentially lead to a reversal of this trend (W. Young, personal communication, 1992).

Merchant shipping operations over the past decade have been characterized by great change in terms of technology, economics, and operating practices. Applied human performance research is quite limited; much of the more complete work is dated; and the safety data that are available are incomplete, especially with regard to human performance issues (National Research Council, 1990). Since the data and studies related to human systems have not been updated and since the commercial maritime sector is undergoing great change, broad generalizations need to be approached very carefully. Nevertheless, some insights might be available that could provide general implications to high-stress human performance in other systems, such as the tank environment.

The vessel command structure is clearly specified: the master, or captain, is in command and is responsible for the vessel at all times. When a ship approaches port, it usually is required to use an independent marine pilot who is federally or state-licensed. Typically, the pilot is placed in charge of navigation, makes maneuvering decisions, and gives maneuvering orders subject to overriding command authority of the master, who remains responsible for the safety of his vessel and crew.

The master attempts to hold to a schedule and to have the ship port arrival time coincide with normal work hours of longshore labor to minimize overtime costs, and he tries to have short turnarounds in port to minimize port costs and to maximize cargo service (and payback). As in many of the other systems described in this report, including tank crews, this setup, in conjunction with watch organization, results in sleep disruption and deprivation, which often leads to fatigue and performance decrements.

Coming into port, the master, third mate, and independent marine pilot (if there is one) are on the bridge, and the chief mate and second mate are involved in preparing for cargo operations. The second mate usually keeps watch during the graveyard shift (midnight to 4 am), and the chief mate has the 4 to 8 am watch; therefore, for the master and mates, there is limited rest time prior to entering port. Note that the chief and second and third mates supervise cargo operations, which are intense and also expose them to hazards during transhipment.

Crew integrity also varies among the different types of ships. Non-union U.S. tankers have the greatest continuity and, among U.S. union tankers, the master and chief engineer usually remain with the ship for repeated trips; however, the chief mates and first assistant engineers may be reconstituted for each trip (Pollard et al., 1990). A National Research Council (1990:34) report found that "all operators [surveyed] agreed that continuity of service by crew members is an important safety factor, particularly with sophisticated shipboard systems requiring intimate knowledge. Repeated service aboard the same vessel ensures familiarity with the equipment and promotes teamwork. Continuity is most desirable among key personnel (master, chief engineer, chief mate, and first assistant engineer), and is helpful with junior officers and unlicensed personnel as well." Tank crews, thus, appear to have greater team integrity than current U.S. ships, but it is highly desirable in both environments.

The military and merchant bridges are characterized by a fairly well-established structure for decision making and information flow. In the Navy, Coast Guard, and on other military vessels, communications is highly structured. The roles in merchant marine are reasonably well established for masters, mates, and pilots, but there is a considerable range of interpretation for their interaction; it is more a judgment call for the master and pilot. Teamwork is an essential part of professional development in the military; in the merchant marine setting, teamwork is taught in maritime schools and is expected aboard the ship within the general structure and role models exist, but the actual level of bridge team interaction is variable and generally consistent across the wide category of vessels. The situation is different for tugs because there is usually only one person in the pilot house.

Shipping, similar to other freight transportation modes, is often characterized by longer-than-average work weeks, nonstandard work days, intermittent extensive night operations, and periods of intense effort preceded by periods of inactivity (Pollard et al., 1990). Scheduling factors—frequency of port calls, operation in congested waters, arrival and departure times, long duty tours (especially those that exceed 75 days), and less time available to go ashore—all affect the fatigue (due to interference with crew members' sleep and circadian rhythms) and stress felt by crew members. Fatigue and excessive workload were determined to have been contributing factors in a number of marine accidents (e.g., National Transportation Safety Board, 1988a, 1990).

Work-rest schedules are affected by the type of work being performed, and workload and shipboard operations vary drastically, depending on the stage of the voyage. Workload is extremely high during mooring, cargo operations, and unmooring and is quite reduced in transit, during which time many maintenance tasks are performed. The negative effects of these schedules on performance following the transition are similar to those documented in other environments and suggest that crew work-rest schedules must be carefully planned. In addition, "Aboard merchant ships, current manning statutes as interpreted by federal courts set no upper limit on the hours a crew member may work" (National Research Council, 1990:75). This adds to the potential for safety-related incidents.

As in the rail industry and the tank environment, communications is a critical issue whose importance cannot be overemphasized. Merchant vessel operations are not conducted in a highly structured decision-making environment. Interactions lack the precision and protocols associated with military operations, tending instead to be more informal and ad hoc. Although there are self-enforcing international rules to prevent collisions at sea, they are designed to guide the interactions of two vessels. The rules become ambiguous when more than two vessels are involved, as frequently occurs in ports and waterways. Meeting and overtaking situations are characterized by informal coordination using voice radio rather than guidance by strict maneuvering protocols. Traffic regulation comparable to that in the aviation sector is not practiced, although interactive information sharing is available for some ports and waterways in the form of Vessel Traffic Services (VTS) (Ives et al., 1992).

Although human error is often cited as a factor in marine casualties, marine accident investigations primarily focus on proximate human causes of accidents rather than more subtle factors that underlie human performance. However, beginning in May 1992, the U.S. Coast Guard implemented the Marine Investigation Module (MINMOD), a greatly expanded data base, that focuses on human factors and human performance issues in marine casualties (S. Sheek, personal communication, 1992).

Successful military operations rely heavily on effective human performance of crews and task groups or forces operating cohesively as a single entity, even with modern warfighting technology. Individuals, individual ships, and combinations of units are expected to function effectively and efficiently, with precision and without hesitation. At the same time, reasonable flexibility for innovative and creative decision making is retained to accommodate the variabilities in the combat scenarios, with flexibility varying by the role and responsibility of each individual. The teamwork that is required itself requires that good order and discipline be established in the individuals throughout the organization. It also requires highly stylized operating standards and protocols. Well-defined authority is embedded in a hierarchical command structure to establish both a decision making and performance structure that can function effectively under the stress of time-critical situations. Effective teamwork is achieved through technical training of individuals through resident schools, short courses, and correspondence courses and by extensive, frequent, on-site training and drills. This approach concurrently accommodates the transfers that occur, prepares individuals to work effectively singly and as a unit team member, and establishes in each team member the time phasing required to respond instinctively under the pressure of high-stress operating conditions. The roles and responsibilities of individuals are continuously reinforced throughout the military organizations as a routine practice for professional and interpersonal relationships, thereby maintaining well-defined command relationships.

The operation of military ships while in company is characterized by high levels of precision. There are well-defined maneuvering schemes and execution protocols. Fleet maneuvering protocols are established in operational instructions and routinely practiced. The naval approach works well aboard individual units and for convoy operations. However, there are exceptional differences between what is found in a naval task force or group and what is found in the interaction of ships in the nonmilitary setting, particularly in ports and waterways. When military ships interact with merchant shipping, especially in confined harbors and waterways, associated human interactions devolve to a much less precise and largely informal decision-making structure.

Some port-state nations have established VTS to improve order and predictability in waterway interactions. These capabilities are essentially interactive information sharing communications networks with, in some cases, very limited positive control. A VTS, in effect, places a decision-making structure within the existing informal decision-making network that characterizes the marine operating environment. There are about 200 VTS facilities worldwide of varying capabilities; approximately 20 are located in the United States, some of which are operated by the U.S. Coast Guard and others are operated by the U.S. Army Corps of Engineers, other governmental organizations, and marine pilots (Ives et al., 1992).

It is believed that the use of a VTS will improve the accuracy and completeness of information and that, given this information, operator decision making will be improved. However, this depends on the relevance and accuracy of the communications on a single vessel, between vessels, or between a vessel and a VTS. There are substantial differences in communications between the military and maritime settings. In the Navy, internal as well as external communications are critical to successful warfighting. There are very precise standards and protocols for internal communications; external communications have been greatly improved by the composite warfare commander (CWC) concept by means of satellite down links, electronic means, etc. There are precise communications protocols for vessel interactions, but the protocols on the bridge are less precise.

In the merchant marine setting, although the roles of each individual on the ship bridge are well understood, how the members communicate varies greatly. Bridge crew communications tends to be much more informal, lacking the well-defined protocols and stylized language found in the Navy. Where there is a VTS, circuit discipline is enforced, especially when operated under military protocol. Military protocols are routinely employed in

VTS to ensure the clarity, brevity, and accuracy of the information exchange. Bridge commands are relatively well defined, standardized, and universal. Communications in maritime are voice VHF radio. This involves bridge communications (i.e., intrabridge communications) but not bridge-to-bridge communications (i.e., interbridge or intervessel communications), which has been identified as a contributing factor in at least one marine accident (National Transportation Safety Board, 1984).

Automatic radar plotting aids (ARPA) used by ships are capable of tracking and displaying the courses of a large number of targets automatically and of generating warnings regarding possible collisions in open water transits. These collision avoidance features are of marginal use in confined waterways and in situations where frequent maneuvering is required. However, in some situations this aid is one means of minimizing the possibility of collisions and groundings.

A somewhat dated review report has identified a set of prevailing conditions typically found at the time of many marine accidents (National Transportation Safety Board, 1981:18): the ships were outside an active vessel traffic service (communication control center) area, radar was not in operational use, there was no equipment failure, and the occurrence was during the 4 am to 8 am watch in clear visibility on a U.S. waterway on which the inland navigation rules were in effect. "The Safety Board found that ineffective communication was either a causal or a contributing factor in 7 out of 33 collisions. VHF communication problems ranged from the failure to keep a listing watch to the failure to transmit timely navigational intentions to the lack of a VHF communication requirement."

Watchkeepers at the vessel traffic center acquire, interpret, and distribute system-wide navigational information. VHF radio is the standard for marine communications. A single frequency is used for communications in each VTS sector, and a designated frequency is available for direct bridge-to-bridge communications between vessels (National Research Council, 1990); however, contact is not always established to confirm maneuvering intentions.

Characteristics of the physical environment, including noise levels and vibration, also vary from ship to ship. But in general it appears that, similar to the tank environment, these factors are present and may, unbeknownst to the crew, add to the stress already felt, although their magnitude tends to be somewhat less than in the tank. As noted by Pollard et al. (1990), ship crew members believe they adapt to these noise levels and, therefore, they believe their performance is not affected by this environmental stressor. However, as in the tank environment, sound (or changes in sound) can also be an important task relevant cue; in this case, it may be important for maneuvering purposes.

The ship is a complex system with many components related to compartments, hatches, fuel, and cargo locations, as well as weather, sea, and land characteristics that influence its ability to withstand damage. Hence, the structure of the event may be ill-defined, and the time constant may vary. If situation awareness of this state is absent in a pretransition period, disaster may result. For example, if a grounding or collision occurs in a confined waterway, the time constant may be short, and unpredictable response types may be required. However, for an accident in open water during transit, the time constant is longer and the response types may be more predictable.

NATURAL DISASTERS

Emergency workers who are responding to a natural disaster constitute a normal population working under abnormal conditions. Floods and hurricanes usually are preceded by a buildup that allows time for warning and subsequent preparation for impact. Major aircraft disasters, explosions, earthquakes, or tornadoes typically allow far less preparation for the specific event. For the first 2 weeks following the occurrence of a major disaster, Red Cross staff members work 12 to 14 hour days. After the second week, they get half a day off. Individuals who are on a disaster assignment for 2 or 3 months may get 1 day off after the third week (Eby, 1985).

The core resources of the team already exists, and volunteers are incorporated into the system. Although central planning should focus on ways to effectively allocate human and material resources, the allocation decisions, themselves, are made without much preplanning (Dynes, 1989). Training of as much of the team as possible in simulated disasters appears to be a necessary precondition for effective disaster management (Rolfe, 1989).

The probability of a natural disaster occurring varies, depending on location; however, even in an area in which it is most expected (e.g., earthquakes in California), the probability of occurrence is still quite low. The response to the event is predictable; however, the decisions that need to be made will be unique. The decision making is decentralized and pluralistic, and the team, similar to the tank crew, must coordinate and cooperate with many other groups and teams to be most effective.

The physical conditions of the environment are typically poor, due to the nature of the event, but the extent to which the team is exposed to risk of personal injury is minimal following the disaster. The environment during a natural disaster is similar to that of the tank crew engaging in battle, in that people attempt to protect themselves inside buildings, etc., during the natural disaster just as tank crew members in battle remain buttoned up in the tank. Immediately following the natural disaster, however, when the relief teams are working, many team members are out in the open with little protection from the elements. The environment, although different, leaves much to be desired.

As can be ascertained, teams in this environment are similar to tank crews in that their sleep schedules are similarly disrupted, the stress is somewhat comparable (although the response period following the transition is much longer for teams responding to the natural disaster), and the team must coordinate with others to accomplish its goals. While the nature of the response to disasters is, in many respects, quite different from the tank environment, it is noteworthy that this is one of the few transition team situations that has received systematic study (Dynes, 1989). The author's conclusion in the study indicated that the teams involved were in fact quite effective in their response.

EMERGENCY MEDICAL SERVICES

Emergency medical service (EMS) helicopter crews (also called medevac—medical evacuation) consist of a pilot and a critical care medic; EMS ambulances operate with a 2-person or sometimes a 3-person crew—a driver and 1 or 2 medics. These medics are recertified every year on practical and written cardiopulmonary resuscitation techniques. Upon arrival at the scene of the event, the medic(s) performs an assessment of the level of injury, following a set protocol that dictates beginning with an assessment of the head and neck, then of the chest, the groin, the legs, and finally the feet. The medic checks the vital signs and the eyes, then decides where the patient will go and consults with the doctor at the chosen location. The consulting doctor is the one who will care for the patient when he or she arrives at the hospital; however, this doctor may later turn the care of the patient over to another doctor. The medics communicate using written and oral protocols. During the assessment, medics go through a process of pattern matching. In addition, medics, like tank crew personnel, must be concerned about self-preservation, their personal safety, and what to do if there is a hostile environment.

In the 1960s and early 1970s, emergency medical services were used almost solely to transport injured patients as quickly as possible to the nearest hospital. The first commercial EMS helicopter program in the United States started in 1972, and commercial EMS helicopter activity has increased sharply since 1980 because some "surgeons began to suggest that accident victims would fare better if they were taken to larger hospitals that had all the necessary manpower, equipment, and supplies close at hand. The surgeons produced statistics to prove that accident victims survived more often at large hospitals than at small ones" (Doelp, 1989:59). As a result, many patients were being transported to hospitals that were not near the accident scene. This generated a need for patient transporters to be specially trained to begin treating the injured before reaching the hospital, because what happens during the first hour after the onset of the injury (coined the Golden Hour) is critical to the probability of the patient's survival (Franklin and Doelp, 1980).

The EMS crew is usually on the way to the scene of the event in a matter of minutes, and once on the scene the injury assessment occurs as soon as possible depending upon the location of the patient (e.g., if there has been an automobile accident, when the medics can physically get to the patient to perform the assessment), but usually within a few minutes.

The average number of calls the EMS crews respond to each year is dependent on the environment. It is not uncommon for an ambulance crew in a suburban area to average 2,300 calls in a year (which is an average of almost 200 calls per month or approximately 6.5 calls per 24-hour period) (Maryland State Firemen's Association, 1991), although the number of calls may vary from 500 to 4,000 or more calls per year depending on the suburban location. At this level, the crews should always be prepared for incoming calls. However, in a rural area, they may average one-fifth to one-tenth this number of calls, which would result in one call every 20 to 25 hours, on average (Maryland State Firemen's Association, 1991). Although not as great a probability of occurring, rural EMS crews still have a high expectancy of a call coming in each day. None of the crews can anticipate when these will occur; however, when storms are in the area or a fire has been called in, the likelihood of a medical emergency is greater.

The length of duty for EMS crews varies depending on the type of organization they work for. For example, volunteer ambulance crews sometimes schedule duty, but unlike paid ambulance crews, this staffing may not be active 24 hours each day. These paid ambulance crews work normal 8-hour shifts, which may be extended depending on the requirements of the situation. EMS helicopter crews work on shift schedules, and the greatest number of calls are received at night, many times in bad weather (which may be one of the contributing factors of the accident that generated the need for medical services in the first place), and their mission requires landing and takeoff from unimproved landing areas. The pilot must receive 10 consecutive hours of rest in any 24-hour period if the combined duty and rest periods total 24 hours. Each flight crew member must have 13 rest periods of at least 24 consecutive hours every 90 days. The EMS helicopter pilot must have 8 hours of consecutive rest every 24 hours and 10 hours of consecutive rest before reporting to the hospital for availability for flight time. An EMS pilot may not be on duty longer than 72 hours (Doelp, 1989). It is interesting to note that, according to Doelp (1989:36), "The majority of EMS pilots responded that next to combat flying, the EMS flight environment is the most stressful and challenging." This may be attributable to the fact that, in addition to poor environmental conditions, the EMS helicopter pilot and crew must respond quickly, often do not have the time to plan the flight, and must make decisions knowing that human life is at stake.

The probability of the EMS helicopter crashing is nearly twice that of other noncombat helicopter operations (National Transportation Safety Board, 1988b). Of the 59 EMS helicopter accidents in the National Transportation Safety Board's data base between May 1978 and December 1986, 18 were weather-related. Of the 18, 15 involved reduced visibility and spatial disorientation and occurred below 1,200 feet in uncontrolled airspace; the remaining 3 accidents resulted in hard landings due to heavy winds. Thus, the risk of personal injury or death to the EMS helicopter crew is greater than for either other helicopter crews or for EMS ambulance crews.

The continuity of the crew in the EMS ambulance crew, again, is dependent on the organization. In paid companies, the crew remains the same approximately 75 percent of the time; in volunteer companies, the crew could change with every call, but the individuals usually know each other. There is a thin level of hierarchy in commercial EMS. The crew may be responsible only to themselves and the protocol, but EMS ambulance crews that belong to a firefighting company may have a thicker level of hierarchy, which may extend from the battalion chief down. The medics for the first few minutes may function alone, but as soon as the assessment has been made and a hospital chosen, the medics will be in almost constant communication with a doctor at that hospital or center. All services performed from then on will be done in coordination with the waiting doctor.

Crews in this system are similar to tank crews in a few major respects. First, duty schedules have been identified as having an influence on the probability of success; and the sharing of information is essential. If the EMS helicopter is flying at night and in bad weather, the risk of personal injury is realized, but not as greatly as a tank crew entering battle. Finally, as discussed in Chapter 7, the issue of navigation and geographic orientation is critical in both environments.

TRAUMA CENTERS AND EMERGENCY ROOMS

Trauma center and emergency room teams consist of doctors, nurses, and an anesthesiologist, prepared to care for injured patients who are brought to the center or hospital for treatment. The exact composition of the medical team is determined by the operating procedures of the trauma center or hospital, and their requirements vary depending on the community in which they operate. For example, at Children's Hospital National Medical Center in Washington, DC, the nucleus of the trauma team consists of the trauma coordinator, the surgical resident, the resident in the intensive care unit, the nurse in charge, and at least one other nurse. This team is assisted by a support group that includes an X-ray technician, lab technicians, blood bank technicians, and a social worker (Doelp, 1989).

Time is probably the most critical element in medical services. In recent years, surgeons have come to realize that the first hour of treatment is critical to the patient's recovery (Franklin and Doelp, 1980). The crisis transition or event (i.e., treatment of an arriving injured patient) unfolds in a matter of seconds and minutes. There is a great probability that one or more patients will arrive during the team members duty period, and the team members will work long hours.

Like EMS teams, adult trauma centers (such as the Maryland Institute for Emergency Medical Services—known as Shocktrauma), pediatric trauma centers (such as the Children's Hospital National Medical Center), and emergency rooms in hospitals around the country maintain a fairly continuous level of preparation for patients or accident victims that can be expected at any time. Often the trauma centers receive only a few minutes advance notice that a patient is on the way. During this time the hospital or trauma center and its team members must be notified by a communications center (such as SYSCOM for Shocktrauma and ECIC—the Emergency Communications and Information Center—for Children's Hospital). The team members then converge on the arrival, code, or emergency room to prepare for the arriving patient.

The hospital teams, especially in the trauma centers, are on duty much longer than teams in many other environments. The medical teams in the Children's Hospital National Medical Center are on call one day out of three; and according to Doelp (1989), for the day the resident is on call, he or she must stay at the hospital all night to be available to the nursing staff. If there are no problems, the resident may sleep, but this is a rare occasion. The off-call day is a normal workday, which includes two sets of rounds (one morning and one evening) and a full day in the operating room. Workdays usually last longer than 12 hours. The surgical residents get one day off every other weekend. Each trauma center and hospital have different schedules, but they are similar in nature. Hence, it is undoubtedly the case that sleep disruption is often present in emergency room personnel, although the extent to which this has had deleterious effects on performance has not been well documented.

The event is relatively predictable. According to Doelp (1989:78-9), "Trauma medicine is, first and foremost, checklist medicine [a treatment protocol]." This means that there is a written set of procedures that are to be followed for each patient. The checklist is the same as that described above for emergency medical services. A series of tests are conducted to determine the type and extent of injury to each area instead of treating injuries in a nonrational order in which certain symptoms could easily be missed or overlooked.

The environment in treatment or emergency rooms, unlike that of the tank, is cool (often between 65° and 69° F), there is much lighting, and much of the noise comes from the medical team and the patient, if he or she is conscious and feeling pain; however, the room is not inherently noisy. At times, there may be some problem with cramped working space, but this cannot be avoided, in that all members of the team may be working on the patient. The treatment or emergency room itself may be quite spacious.

Until recent years, the team probably would not have been considered to be at risk of personal injury. But with the outbreak of AIDS and the amount of blood that may be found, especially in the treatment room of the trauma center, the team is at a much greater risk of exposure to personal injury. The team may therefore feel the stress of risk.

Trauma center and emergency room teams have a low chain of command. In emergency rooms around the country, nurses follow the directives given by the doctors, and technicians and others in the support group follow the directives of the nurses. At Shocktrauma and Children's Hospital, unlike most hospitals around the country, nurses have almost as much authority as the doctors. At Children's Hospital, the trauma coordinator is in charge of what is happening in the treatment room, and the nurse in charge supervises the emergency room nursing staff. The members of the team in the emergency room interact with their support group outside the room to have X-rays taken, receive additional units of blood, have tests conducted on blood samples taken, etc. The core team cannot work in isolation; it must coordinate with other teams and individuals to be successful in its mission.

The residents who work on these teams go on rounds with the chief resident, who reviews each patient's status, progress, and treatment. In addition, the work in the emergency rooms is reviewed by the trauma center director or an assistant, and problems that have been identified are discussed with the appropriate team member(s).

While working in the emergency rooms, the medical teams have a high level of integrity—they work closely together and on similar duty schedules. There appears, however, to be a large rate of turnover of personnel in emergency rooms, especially in the trauma centers, possibly due to the high level of stress inherent in the job. This reduces the amount of team continuity that would otherwise be achieved and increases the on-the-job training that is necessary.

CAUTIOUS GENERALIZATIONS

From this discussion of the analogous systems of interest, a few conclusions can be extended to the tank environment. First, in each system, appropriate duty schedules are of utmost importance. At present, these appear to be lacking in maritime, railroad, and trauma center systems, to name but a few. In most of these systems this factor has been identified as contributing to numerous accidents. As discussed in Chapter 5, if work-rest schedules were employed that are synchronous with the circadian rhythm, fatigue and possibly stress levels would be reduced, resulting in better responses to transitions and, in some cases, fewer system transitions.

Second, lack of a communication protocol appears to have serious consequences on crew performance. Many crews operate in more isolation than would appear prudent. Railway crews as well as a number of ship crews, if they had been given more verbal information from the dispatcher or communications center, may have prevented the accidents that occurred. Tank crews must communicate with other crews to increase the probability of successful mission completion; however, as discussed in upcoming chapters, other factors interfere and cause confusion and miscommunication. This miscommunication has also occurred in a number of maritime accidents. If some of these analogous systems, like the tank crews, had a standardized terminology and protocol, miscommunication could be reduced and the likelihood of accidents would also diminish. When the triggering event is complex or unstructured, then strong support for continuous situation awareness—the state of the system and environment—in the pretransition period will be likely to support more efficient and adaptive problem solving during the transition.

Although this section has focused on what these analogous systems have to offer to the tank environment, one could also ask what conclusions drawn in the tank environment can be generalized to these other systems. Such conclusions emerge from our discussions in the following chapters and are integrated in Chapter 13. Next we examine workload factors and stressors that affect performance during the transition as well as processes that are inherent in transition.

REFERENCES

Belanger, J.D.
    1989   Railway safety. *Current Issue Review.* Canada: Library of Parliament.
Dember, W.N., and J.S. Warm
    1979   *Psychology of Perception, Second Edition.* New York: Holt, Rinehart and Winston.
Devoe, D.B., and C.N. Abernethy
    1977   *Maintaining Alertness in Railroad Locomotive Crews.* Transportation Systems Center, U.S. Department of Transportation. Report No. FRA/ORD-77/22. Washington, DC: Federal Railroad Administration.
Doelp, A.
    1989   *In the Blink of an Eye: Inside a Children's Trauma Center.* New York: Ballantine Books.
Druckman, D., and R.A. Bjork, eds.
    1991   *In the Mind's Eye: Enhancing Human Performance.* Committee on Techniques

for the Enhancement of Human Performance. Washington, DC: National Academy Press.

Dynes, R.
1989   *Community Emergency Planning: False Assumptions and Inappropriate Analogies.* Paper presented at the Workshop on Safety Control and Risk Management. Karlstad, Sweden: Swedish Rescue Services and World Bank.

Eby, D.L.
1989   A disaster worker's response. Pp. 119-125 in *Role Stressors and Supports for Emergency Workers.* Rockville, Maryland: U.S. Department of Health and Human Services.

Foushee, H.C., and R.L. Helmreich
1988   Group interaction and flightcrew performance. In E. Wiener and D. Nagel, eds., *Human Factors in Aviation.* San Diego, California: Academic Press.

Franklin, J., and A. Doelp
1980   *Shock-Trauma.* New York: St. Martin's Press.

General Accounting Office
1992   *Engineer Workshift Links and Schedule Variability.* Report No. GAO/RCED-92-133. Washington, DC: U.S. General Accounting Office.

Graeber, R.C.
1988   Aircrew fatigue and circadian rhythmicity. Pp. 305-344 in E. Wiener and D. Nagel, eds., *Human Factors in Aviation.* San Diego, California: Academic Press.

Ives, P.L., Jr., W. Parker, F. Seitz, and W. Young
1992   Assessment of Vessel Traffic Services. Unpublished background paper prepared for the Marine Board, Committee on Advances in Navigation and Piloting. Marine Board, National Research Council.

Maryland Sate Firemen's Association
1991   Maryland State Firemen's Association 1991 Statistical Report.

Michaut, G.M.E., and T.P. McGaughey
1972   *Work Conditions and Equipment Design in Diesel Locomotives: Feasibility Study and Recommendations.* Canadian Institute of Guided Ground Transport. Canada: Queen's University.

National Research Council
1990   *Crew Size and Maritime Safety.* Committee on the Effect of Smaller Crews on Maritime Safety, Marine Board, Commission on Engineering and Technical Systems. Washington, DC: National Academy Press.

National Transportation Safety Board
1980   *Aircraft Accident Report—Air New England, Inc., deHavilland DHC-6-300, N383EX, Hyannis, Massachusetts, June 17, 1979.* Report No. NTSB/AAR-80/1. Washington, DC: Bureau of Accident Investigation.
1981   *Special Study—Major Marine Collisions and Effects of Preventive Recommendations.* Report No. NTSB/MSS-81/1. Washington, DC: Bureau of Technology.
1984   *Sinking of the U.S. Tug #2 While Assisting in the Docking of the USS William V. Pragg, Pensacola, Florida, October 12, 1983.* Washington, DC: National Transportation Safety Board.
1985a   *Aircraft Accident Report—US Air, Incorporated Flight 183 McDonnell Douglas DC9-31, N964VJ, Detroit Metropolitan Airport, Detroit, Michigan, June 13, 1984.* Report No. NTSB/AAR-85/01. Washington, DC: Bureau of Accident Investigation.
1985b   *Railroad Accident Report—Head-On Collision of Burlington Northern Railroad Freight Trains Extra 6714 West and Extra 7820 East at Wiggins, Colorado, April 13, 1984 and Rear-End Collision of Burlington North Railroad Freight Trains*

7843 *East and Extra ATSF 8112 East Near Newcastle, Wyoming April 22, 1985.* Report No. NTSB/RAR-85/04. Washington, DC: National Transportation Safety Board.

1987   *Aircraft Accident Report—Midair Collision of Nabisco Brands, Inc., Dassault Falcon, DA50, N784B and Air Pegasus Corporation, Piper Archer, PA28-181, N1977H, Fairview, New Jersey, November 10, 1985.* Report No. NTSB/AAR-87/05. Washington, DC: Bureau of Accident Investigation.

1988a   *Collision between the USS RICHARD L. PAGE (FFG-5) and the U.S. Fishing Vessel CHICKADEE, the Atlantic Ocean, April 21, 1987.* Washington, DC: Bureau of Accident Investigation.

1988b   *Safety Study—Commercial Emergency Medical Service Helicopter Operations.* Report No. NTSB/SS-88/01. Washington, DC: National Transportation Safety Board.

1989a   *Railroad Accident Report—Head-End Collision of Consolidated Rail Corporation Freight Trains UBT-506 and TV-61 near Thompsontown, Pennsylvania, January 14, 1988.* Washington, DC: National Transportation Safety Board.

1989b   Safety Recommendation. Letter Report Dated May 12, 1989. Washington, DC: National Transportation Safety Board.

1990   *Marine Accident Report—Grounding of the U.S. Tankship EXXON VALDEZ on Bligh Reef, Prince William Sound, near Valdez, Alaska, March 24, 1989.* Report No. NTSB/MAR-90/04. Washington, DC: Office of Surface Transportation Safety.

Parasuraman, R.
1984   The psychobiology of sustained attention. Pp. 61-101 in J.S. Warm, ed., *Sustained Attention in Human Performance.* Chichester, UK: Wiley.

Pollard, J.K., E.D. Sussman, and M. Stearns
1990   *Shipboard Crew Fatigue, Safety, and Reduced Manning.* U.S. Department of Transportation, Research and Special Programs Administration. Report No. DOT-MA-RD-840-90014. Washington, DC: Office of Technology Assessment.

Rolfe, J.M.
1989   The end-of-flight simulation. In D. Mangelsdorff, ed., *Proceedings of the 7th User Stress Workshop.* Consultation Report No. 91-0001. Washington, DC: U.S. Army Health Services Command.

Rubinstein, T., and A.F. Mason
1979   The accident that shouldn't have happened: An analysis of Three Mile Island. *IEEE Spectrum* 16:33-57.

Smiley, A.M.
1990   The Hinton train disaster. *Accident Analysis and Prevention* 22(5):443-455.

Wickens, C.D.
1992   *Engineering Psychology and Human Performance.* New York: Harper Collins.

Wickens, C.D., and C. Kessel
1981   Failure detection in dynamic systems. In J. Rasmussen and W. Rouse, eds., *Human Detection and Diagnosis of System Failures.* New York: Plenum Press.

Wickens, C.D., R. Marsh, M. Raby, S. Straus, R. Cooper, C.L. Hulin, and F. Switzer
1989   Aircrew performance as a function of automation and crew composition: A simulator study. *Proceedings of the Human Factors Society 33rd Annual Meeting.* Santa Monica, California: Human Factors Society.

Woods, D.D.
1988   Commentary: Cognitive engineering in complex and dynamic worlds. Pp. 115-129 in E. Hollnagel, G. Mancini, and D.D. Woods, eds., *Cognitive Engineering in Complex Dynamic Worlds.* London: Academic Press.

3

Workload Factors

A characteristic of most post-transition periods is a large number of task demands, often imposed with very severe time constraints. These tasks are often characterized by the description of high workload. The term *workload* has intuitive meaning for most people; everyone has experienced periods of high or low workload in their daily life in response to different situations. Psychologists have invoked the concept in theories of attention and performance. Aircraft designers, manufacturers, operators, and regulatory agencies have identified operator workload as a critical factor in system effectiveness. However, the word *workload* did not appear in many dictionaries until the 1970s; and operational definitions proposed by psychologists and engineers continue to disagree about its source(s), mechanism(s), consequence(s), and measurement. Furthermore, although workload and performance are clearly related, it has proven to be a much more complex relationship than originally thought.

WORKLOAD CHARACTERISTICS

Sources

Over the past 20 years, workload has been equated with: (1) imposed task demands—if the difficulty, number, rate, or complexity of the demands imposed on an operator are increased, workload is assumed to increase; (2) the level of performance an operator is able to achieve—if errors increase or control precision degrades, workload is assumed to increase; (3) the mental and physical effort an operator exerts—workload reflects an operator's response to a task, rather than task demands directly; and (4) an operator's perceptions—if an operator feels effortful and loaded, then workload has, in fact, increased even though task demands or performance have not changed. Most contemporary definitions assume that workload emerges from the interaction between a specific operator and the assigned task (Gopher and Donchin, 1986; Hart, 1986; Hart and Wickens, 1990).

Consequences

The consequences of optimal or suboptimal levels of workload depend on the structure of a specific task, the environment in which it is performed, and operator characteristics. As task difficulty increases, performance often, but not always, degrades; response times and errors increase for discrete tasks, control variability and error increase for tracking tasks, and fewer tasks are completed within an interval of time. The workload imposed by one task may interfere with the performance of other concurrent activities. The subjective experience of excessively low or high workload may prompt operators to adopt different task-performance strategies. Prolonged periods of high workload may result in operator fatigue. An increase in psychological stress that often accompanies high workload may result in elevated heart rate.

Measures

To some extent, these apparent complexities have been caused by (1) the practice of using the same term (workload) to refer to the demands imposed on an operator; the effort exerted to accomplish those demands; and the physiological, subjective, or performance consequences of an operator's actions and (2) the naive assumption that different measures of workload index the same entity. In fact, different measures are sensitive to different aspects of workload and are appropriate for answering different questions. Thus, the results of most workload studies are interpreted far too broadly, given the complexity of the phenomena and the limited range of factors to which each type of measure is sensitive. The problem is compounded by the absence of a generally accepted definition, standardized procedures and units of measurement, or an absolute standard against which to compare a particular task or candidate measure.

Relationship Between Workload and Performance

Designers, manufacturers, and operators of complex systems have been more interested in the association between workload and performance than in theoretical issues. They assume that human performance is most reliable under moderate workload that does not change suddenly or unpredictably (Kantowitz and Casper, 1988). When workload is too high, errors arise from an operator's inability to cope with critical task demands. When workload is too low, errors may arise from loss of vigilance and boredom (see Chapter 6). However, the actual relationship between the effort an operator invests in a task and the performance he or she is able to achieve is much more complex.

O'Donnell and Eggemeier (1986) suggested that the relationship between workload and performance changes as overall task difficulty is increased. For relatively easy tasks, operators can maintain consistent performance by exerting additional effort if task demands are increased. For moderately difficult tasks, they cannot maintain consistent performance even if they exert additional effort. For extremely difficult tasks, operators do not have the capacity to exert additional effort in response to further increases in task demands, so performance decrements no longer reflect a change in workload.

Navon and Gopher (1979) suggested that this relationship depends on the structure of the task, differentiating between situations in which additional resource investment would (resource-limited) or would not (data-limited) result in improved performance. For data-limited tasks, additional effort cannot improve performance. If sufficient information is available, the task can be performed. If it is not, the task cannot be performed adequately. For resource-limited tasks, however, additional effort can result in improved performance.

Hart (1989) and Hart and Wickens (1990) discussed the importance of operator strategies in determining the relationship between workload and performance. People may not try to achieve perfect performance or accomplish tasks immediately. Rather, they manage their attention and effort, rescheduling, deferring, or shedding less important tasks to achieve acceptable performance and maintain a reasonable level of workload for the duration of the task (see Chapter 9 for some discussion of how effectively this scheduling is accomplished). In a recent interview, Broadbent (1990:7) stated that humans are "dynamic, self-regulating systems, with each function monitored and modified by others." Thus, to optimize their interaction with a complex system, operator beliefs, values, and intentions must be considered. Because it is clear that humans have interests beyond optimizing traditional indices of system performance (Rouse, 1979), simple linear models cannot provide an accurate description of their behavior.

Despite the apparent confusion about what workload is (one might fairly say that anything can cause workload) and what its effects might be, there are some factors that stand out as being particularly salient. The duties assigned to the crews of tanks, helicopters, jets, nuclear power plants, and so on impose a set of requirements that vary in magnitude and composition from one moment to the next, from one type of activity or mission phase to another, and from one crew position to another. The operational requirements of the tank crew are composed of a variety of behaviors that have been studied in isolation (in laboratory research) or in different combinations (in simulation and field studies) to determine the specific task-related, equipment-related, environmental, and operator-related factors that influence workload and performance. From this research, general principles may be drawn to estimate the effects of performing specific activities on the operators of a particular system performing a mission. The following pages contain a review of data regarding the primary factors that drive workload, showing how these drivers are relevant to a variety of transition teams.

WORKLOAD DRIVERS: REVIEW OF RESEARCH

The intrinsic difficulty of the activities that an operator must perform establishes the target or nominal level of workload. The difficulty of a particular task may be influenced by any one or several of the following factors: (1) the goals and performance criteria set for a particular task; (2) the structure of the task; (3) the quality, format, and modality in which information is presented; (4) the cognitive processing required; and (5) the characteristics of the response devices. Although the fundamental source of workload is literally the "work" that is "loaded" on an operator, the behavior and workload experiences of a particular operator may be influenced by other factors as well. For example, fatigue, stress, training, crew coordination, and environmental stressors (e.g., heat, cold, vibration, noise, and danger) may have a significant impact on operator workload. Although the influence of these factors is obvious in operational situations, little research has been performed to establish their relationship with operator workload, and they are ignored in most workload theories. The relationship between these factors and team performance are reviewed in other chapters.

Given the limitations of human memory, vision, physical strength, and so forth, some tasks may stretch or even exceed an operator's capacities; other tasks impose so few demands that they may be performed concurrently with other tasks. Thousands of experiments have been conducted in which a variety of task-difficulty manipulations were imposed to examine different aspects of the human information processing system and to define and quantify the limits of human capabilities. The following section summarizes the results of a representative sampling of this work.

Task Structure

The way in which a task or combination of tasks is organized, the rate at which information is presented or error signals change, the length of time the task must be performed, and the levels of speed and accuracy that the operator must try to achieve have a significant impact on the workload imposed during its performance. A significant number of the experiments conducted to analyze human operators' responses to different levels of workload have included some variation in the rate of presentation for discrete tasks or disturbance bandwidth for control tasks. Thus, a considerable amount is known about these factors. Relatively less information is available about the effects of speed-accuracy tradeoffs, task schedules, and task duration.

Performance Criteria and Strategies

The difficulty of almost any task can be altered by a requirement for additional speed or accuracy. As criteria for acceptable performance become more stringent, the workload associated with attaining adequate performance increases (Yeh and Wickens, 1988). People may adopt either externally imposed performance criteria or personal criteria (which may or may not be more stringent). Workload and performance are influenced by the objective consequences of failing to meet task requirements as well. People are more likely to try to meet performance standards if their job or personal safety are on the line, than if the consequence of poor performance is simply a "bad score." In addition, operators may act less conservatively, take more risks, and try new techniques when there are no dire consequences of failure.

In general, manual controllers of dynamic systems such as the tank driver try to follow a particular course or path, while minimizing the effects of external disturbances. Error will increase if control inputs are too little, too late, or in the wrong direction. If operators overcontrol (i.e., make control inputs that are faster or larger than necessary), they create additional workload for themselves (i.e., they must compensate for the errors that they generate) and run the risk of destabilizing the system. Thus, although minimizing error is the goal of most control activities, smoothness and stability may be equally important.

Similarly, in discrete control tasks like target acquisition, performance strategies can be described by a tradeoff between the speed and accuracy of the movements. Faster movements are made with less accuracy, and more precise movements are made more slowly. This tradeoff is described by a mathematical model known as Fitts's Law. This relationship has proven to be extremely robust (Keele, 1986) for a wide range of target types, widths, and distances, limbs (e.g., fingers, arms), system dynamics (e.g., displacement of the joystick controls cursor position or velocity), control devices (e.g., computer mouse, joystick, rotary knob), and displays (e.g., computer screen, direct view of nearby or distant target). More recent research has demonstrated that Fitts's Law also holds for targets that vary dynamically in size (Johnson and Hart, 1987) or position (Jagacinski et al., 1980). A similar relationship has been found between the movement difficulty and subjective workload (Hart et al., 1984b; Johnson and Hart, 1987; Mosier and Hart, 1986).

Instructions to maximize either speed or accuracy influence the workload and performance associated with discrete responses, target acquisition, and continuous control. If operators are instructed or choose to maximize precision, the cost may be an increase in time for task completion. Conversely, if they maximize speed, then accuracy may be reduced. Depending on the situation, either speed or accuracy may be more important. Thus, the overall quality of performance depends on the operators' correct assessment of which factor is most critical. For example, correctly identifying a target (as friend or foe) is more important than firing quickly (and running the risk of hitting a friend), even though verifying the identity of a target may take longer than making a snap judgment. If the position of a helicopter or tank is not yet known to an enemy, making the first shot count (e.g., accuracy) is extremely important, as firing a weapon will reveal its position. Alternatively, if a tank is being fired on or the engine of a helicopter fails, a rapid response is essential. Smooth control and on-time arrival may be more important to an airline pilot than keeping the needles precisely centered on the intended flight path, while extreme precision is required to accomplish inflight refueling.

Different components of a complex task may have different functional priority with respect to the overall goals of the task or temporal priority (if they are not completed by a deadline, they can no longer be performed at all). Operators may adopt different resource allocation and scheduling strategies to satisfy external instructions or personal goals. Within limits, people are able to maintain a particular level of performance on one task (at the expense of another) or to share attention equally or in graded amounts between two tasks (Gopher et al., 1982). They may adopt a fixed policy for resource allocation or dynamically modulate it in response to changes in task demands or priority over time. People are better able to dynamically allocate the same resource across tasks in response to priority instructions (e.g., devote more processing resources to a tracking task than to a concurrent running memory task) than to dynamically allocate graded amounts of different resources (e.g., devote more visual resources to one task than auditory resources to another). Shifting task priorities and resource allocation policies in response to transient changes in task demands is particularly difficult (Tsang and Wickens, 1988) and may inhibit an effective response to workload transitions. In practice, humans tend to maintain a particular strategy of resource allocation, even though the situation has changed.

To achieve required levels of performance on competing tasks, subjects try to perform tasks simultaneously, or allow high-priority tasks to preempt their attention whenever their performance begins to degrade. In operational situations, task prioritization may be formalized, based on safety or mission-related concerns. For example, all pilots are taught to aviate, navigate, and communicate, in that order of importance. However, even low-priority tasks can assume temporal priority (i.e., verbal communications do not wait for an operator to get around to them) because they grab attention (they are loud, bright, unexpected, etc.) or because they can be completed quickly (thereby getting them out of the way).

An operator's ability to respond to changing priorities is influenced by the total demands of concurrent tasks, their resource requirements, instructions, feedback, and training (Tsang and Wickens, 1988). Although little research has been performed to relate priority manipulations and dynamic resource allocation to workload, it is reasonable to assume that workload is likely to increase when performance strategies must be changed in response to a shift in task priority. Furthermore, if operators select an inappropriate strategy (e.g., focusing more resources than required on one task and too little on another), resources are wasted with a resulting cost in performance, workload, or both.

It appears that people can learn more efficient methods of responding to task-specific, priority manipulations through training (Gopher et al., 1989). Furthermore, more generic skills developed in one task (i.e., a video game) can transfer to another (i.e., flight), thereby facilitating performance (Gopher et al., 1988).

Task Schedule

The way operators organize their time and resources to perform complex tasks has a significant impact on the workload experienced and performance achieved. To some extent, task scheduling depends on external factors (e.g., instructions, procedures, information availability, deadlines, the length of time a task can be safely ignored, etc). In laboratory research, tasks that are to be performed sequentially are generally presented sequentially and those that are to be performed concurrently are presented concurrently, to elicit a particular response strategy. In realistically complex situations, however, operators may have greater flexibility in how they perform multiple tasks. They may choose to perform different task combinations either simultaneously, alternatively, or sequentially, with different workload and performance costs.

Sequential performance may decrease workload and result in a better quality of performance. However, this strategy may delay the completion of some task components. Concurrent performance may increase workload and result in a poorer quality of performance, although the time to complete all of the tasks may be less. When tasks are performed simultaneously, workload and performance depend on the cognitive and physical resources required. If two tasks require the same resources, and if their demands exceed available capacity, performance on one or both of them will suffer. When operators alternate between several tasks (or perform them sequentially), resource competition is no longer an issue, although switching attention may require additional time and effort (see Chapter 9). In addition, switching from one stimulus-response modality to another takes more time and effort than switching between tasks that require the same stimulus-response modalities. For example, visual-spatial target acquisitions take longer and impose higher workload when the correct target is identified auditorially, rather than visually, or represented verbally rather than spatially (Hart et al., 1986).

If operators are allowed some scheduling flexibility, they may adopt different strategies depending on the characteristics of a particular task combination. For example, King et al. (1989) found that subjects faced with performing a three-axis tracking task while also completing a series of discrete tasks adopted both time-sharing and switching strategies. Discrete tasks that could be completed quickly preempted the tracking task. Subjects were able to maintain single-task performance levels on the discrete tasks without seriously disrupting control performance because they required little time away from tracking. Subjects also alternated between the control task and discrete tasks that took several seconds to complete. Response times increased significantly over single-task levels, and subjective workload was high, possibly reflecting the added cost of switching back and forth. Moray and Liao (1988) found that when the presentation rate of four concurrent tasks was increased until there was insufficient time to service all of the tasks, subjects simply stopped performing some of the tasks to protect performance on the others.

When performing familiar tasks, in which variations in task demands are relatively predictable, completing some tasks ahead of schedule and developing contingency plans during periods of low workload can reduce workload and improve performance during later periods of high workload. For example, Pepitone et al. (1988) found that contingency planning significantly improved the quality of later decisions made under time stress and resulted in safer flights. Furthermore, if the time required to complete specific tasks and the time remaining in which to complete them are known, then operators can develop more efficient task-performance schedules.

When events unfold as planned and well-rehearsed sequences of actions can be relied on, cognitive demands are lower, performance better, and workload less than when unexpected events occur. Thus, developing a range of contingency plans for potential events is a valuable workload management tool. Planning ahead requires time and effort, however. For example, Vienneau and Gozzo (1987) found that helicopter pilot workload was higher during the planning stage immediately preceding the execution of a maneuver than during the maneuver itself. Thus, predicted load levels (based on physical activities) lagged the actual load levels by one event. Hart and Hauser (1987) obtained similar results with fixed-wing pilots. Premission workload levels were higher than those of all but the most demanding flight segments.

In laboratory research, random intertrial intervals and lack of preview about upcoming events generally preclude anything but a reactive strategy. However, the little research that has been performed on this topic suggests that people are able to develop more efficient strategies if given the opportunity. For example, Tulga and Sheridan (1980) examined decision makers' performance in a dynamic, multitask simulation. The number, durations, deadlines, and payoff of tasks and intertask arrival times were manipulated. With moderately complex schedules, operators adopted relatively optimal scheduling strategies. However, they reverted to a reactive strategy when the situation became too complex. Using a similar paradigm, Hart et al. (1984a) found that proficient subjects adopted a time-sharing strategy, rather than a sequential strategy, and actively controlled the flow of task elements (e.g., requesting tasks ahead of schedule during periods of low workload, deferring some tasks during periods of high workload, and shedding tasks they could not complete), thus completing twice as many tasks in the same interval of time as low-scoring subjects, who were more reactive and performed task elements sequentially, even though there was sufficient time to alternate between tasks.

In operational situations, team members may request assistance from each other as a strategy for coping with excessive task demands. Although the effects of team workload management strategies are not well known, it seems reasonable to assume that the appropriate management of human and system resources can result in adequate performance and acceptable workload, even in the face of relatively high task demands. A team commander must monitor the workload of team members and shift responsibilities to avoid an uneven distribution of workload across people and time. However, when a crew adopts a reactive strategy or is forced into one by externally paced and unpredictable task demands, performance is more likely to suffer and workload will be higher.

Rate of Presentation

Almost any task within an operator's capabilities can be performed correctly and with acceptable workload if sufficient time is available. Conversely, if sufficient time is not provided to perform a single task, or if the interval between task elements is reduced below some critical value, then task completion is not possible, no matter how much effort is invested. In between, where internal or external constraints impose some time pressure but task performance is still feasible, the usual finding is that subjective workload increases as time pressure increases. However, people may adopt different coping strategies to deal with an increase in time pressure (e.g., trade accuracy for speed, shed or defer some tasks, reduce their performance criteria), thereby reducing the effects of time pressure on their workload.

There are structural limitations in the speed with which humans can perceive, process, and respond to successive inputs. For example, perceptual events that occur within roughly 100 milliseconds of each other are combined into a single perceived event (Card et al., 1986). If one stimulus is presented before a previous one has been fully processed, responses to the second will be delayed, presumably because the central processor can operate on only one task at a time (Welford, 1967). Card et al. (1986) estimated the duration of the entire perception-processing-action feedback loop to take between 200 and 500 milliseconds. Thus, since the discrete micromovements that combine to create continuous control activities require only about 70 milliseconds (Keele, 1986), a series of motor movements can be executed open-loop between corrections guided by visual feedback. For discrete responses, the lower limit of reaction time is in the range of 70-100 milliseconds. However, the minimum time required to complete any particular keystroke or button press is determined by the duration of the perceptual and cognitive processes required to select the correct response. For example, Card et al. (1986), in their summary of research, identified the minimum processing times associated with: (1) number of potential responses (response times increase by 90-150 milliseconds for each additional alternative), (2) comparisons with remembered items in short-term memory (30-70 milliseconds for each additional item, depending on their complexity), (3) meaningfulness (a range of 158 to 500 milliseconds per typing keystroke for text, random words, and random letters, with text being the fastest and random letters the slowest), (4) matching stimulus input to an internal representation (310, 380, and 450 milliseconds, respectively, for physical, name, and class matches), and so on.

Obviously, the minimum time required to perform the complex activities typical of the real world is longer and more difficult to predict. However, the same principles hold. If operators are not allowed sufficient time to encode and process information, select a response, and execute the response, then performance quality will suffer and higher workload will be experienced.

In continuous control tasks, such as that performed by the tank driver, the operator's goal is to minimize the time-averaged difference between a target (e.g., a nominal flight path, a driving lane, a point or line on a screen) and the output of a dynamic system. This goal is accomplished by manipulating available control mechanisms (e.g., aircraft control inputs, steering commands, or joystick inputs). The difficulty of this task is directly influenced by the predictability, frequency, and amplitude of the disturbances (e.g., winds) for which the operator is trying to compensate. People may be able to compensate perfectly for highly predictable, low-frequency disturbances; error and workload generally increase at higher frequencies (see, for example, Moray and Liao, 1988). Random or quasi-random signals composed of many frequencies are less predictable and therefore impose even higher workload. As more frequencies are combined to create a complex signal, it becomes more difficult for an operator to track. An increase in bandwidth (the upper limit of the frequencies represented in a complex signal), such as that caused by driving an unpredictable course at faster speeds is usually associated with an increase in workload as well (see, for example, Hauser et al., 1983; King et al., 1989); operators must enter corrections and monitor the visual display more often with high-bandwidth disturbances. However, people may be less sensitive to the effects of bandwidth on workload than they are to other manipulations of tracking task difficulty (Vidulich and Wickens, 1984, 1986). There is evidence from scores of dual-task experiments that low-bandwidth tracking tasks (e.g., less that 0.5 Hz) allow the operator sufficient time to simultaneously perform many types of concurrent tasks. However, it is difficult for them to maintain the same level of performance on high-bandwidth tasks (e.g., greater than 1.0 Hz) while also performing other activities. Maintaining acceptable performance when a signal is very unpredictable simply demands too much time and attention.

The relationship between rate of presentation (or response) and workload or performance may be U-shaped. For extremely slow or infrequent tasks, loss of vigilance has been associated with slower response time and higher subjective workload; boredom is unpleasant for many people (Hancock and Warm, 1989). A moderate increase in presentation rate may increase arousal and result in faster response times, but at the cost of an increase in workload (see, for example, Moray and Liao, 1988). Beyond some point, further increases in presentation rate generally result in an increase in subjective workload, errors, or delayed responses as operators attempt to share their attention between temporally overlapping activities. For example, Pepitone et al. (1987) found that pilot workload was significantly positively correlated with the rate at which flight-related tasks were imposed while pilots flew a simulator. As presentation rate was increased from once every 2.4 minutes to once every 0.8 minutes, subjective workload increased significantly.

For complex tasks, the pattern of performance decrements that occurs when there is insufficient time to monitor, process, and respond to all task components depends on the strategy an operator adopts. For example, Moray and Liao (1988) found that increased task frequency had different effects on the performance of each of four concurrent tasks. For choice reaction time and arithmetic tasks, response time became faster but accuracy suffered as task pacing increased. In addition, tracking error increased and target identification responses were delayed. In this experiment, there was no catastrophic collapse in performance, but rather a graceful degradation controlled by the operator's tactical allocation of attention; the operator appeared to give high priority to the choice response task and low priority to the relatively infrequent monitoring task in order to manage workload.

Complexity of Task Demands

As the number of alternative choices among which an operator must select increases, the time required to respond correctly generally increases. Hick (1952) and Hyman (1953) postulated the Hick-Hyman Law, which asserts that response latency increases linearly as the logarithm of the number of alternatives is increased. Later research demonstrated a reliable relationship between the number of alternatives and workload. For example, Kantowitz et al. (1984) found that performance was worse and workload was higher for a four-choice task than for a two-choice task in the context of simulated flight. Furthermore, performance on tasks with many alternatives is more likely to be disrupted by concurrent activities than is performance on a single-alternative response task.

As the complexity of a task or combination of tasks performed concurrently increases, workload often increases as well. For example, Bittner et al. (1988) found that the workload of mobile air defense system crews was significantly higher when attacked by two helicopters than by one in a field test. Hurst and Rose (1978) found that air traffic controllers reported higher workload as the number of aircraft under their control increased. However, it is the cognitive complexity of a task that influences workload, more than the absolute number of task elements (Kantowitz and Casper, 1988). Although Hart and Hauser (1987) found that communications frequency was significantly correlated with the workload of test pilots, more detailed analyses of pilot communications suggested that other factors have an even more significant impact on workload: delayed, unexpected, or very complex messages or clearances that result in a change of plans impose higher workload than do routine messages conveying expected information (Acton et al., 1983; Hart and Bortolussi, 1984). Aretz (1990) found that map complexity had a more powerful effect on the cognitive operations required for navigation than any other variable; each additional landmark added to the map increased response time by 450 milliseconds.

Variability of Task Demands

People develop expectations about how much effort a specific task should require. If a particular instance is more difficult than expected, workload will seem even higher than it actually is. Furthermore, people may select a strategy that is inappropriate for the current situation, based on expectations from prior experiences.

Operator workload may vary dramatically over time within a task. As load levels increase or decrease, the rate or intensity of effort exerted during the immediately preceding interval may influence subsequent behavior. Thus the task performance strategies operators adopt, and the level of performance they achieve, cannot be predicted from the current load level alone (Matthews, 1986). Instead, when task demands change cyclicly or randomly, people may persist with a previously successful strategy (Poulton, 1982) or fail to anticipate or recognize a change in task demands (Cumming and Croft, 1973). Thus, they maintain an inappropriately high response rate (when task demands have shifted from high to low) or an inappropriately low response rate (when task demands have shifted from low to high). In the first case, persistence of the previous strategy may benefit performance but result in unnecessarily high workload; in the second case, performance will degrade.

Rapid changes in demand level may result in a sudden change in arousal level and require a number of resources to be recruited for task performance. This shift takes time and requires effort. For example, Thornton (1985) demonstrated that an unexpected peak of workload introduced in a relatively low workload task, elevated subjective workload for the whole segment, particularly if it occurred late in the interval. If task difficulty was changed more gradually, however, performance was not disrupted and rated workload more accurately reflected the average demands of each segment in a series of target acquisition tasks (Staveland et al., 1986).

Hart and Bortolussi (1984) examined pilots' opinions about the effects of sudden changes in task demands. They found that almost any additional task, deviation in flight plan, or system failure resulted in increased workload and degraded performance, particularly when changes occurred during phases of flight that already imposed high workload. On the average, routine events or activities increased workload by 6 percent, system failures increased workload by 30 percent, and pilot errors increased workload by 16 percent. The effect of pilot error on subsequent performance and workload was particularly interesting. Through experience, pilots had come to expect that additional errors would follow those already committed and that workload would be elevated when resolving an error (i.e., they must recognize the occurrence of an error and then develop and execute a plan for resolving it). Errors may force an operator out of routine, low workload, patterns of behavior and, in fact, completely change the character of the task until the error is resolved. Significant increases in stress were associated with operator errors and system failures, even when the effort required to deal with the problem was low. In contrast, other events (e.g., communications) increased workload but did not change stress.

Task Duration

The relationship between task demands, effort, and performance is moderated by task duration. People may be able and willing to exert considerable effort or accept inactivity and boredom for brief intervals, but not for very long. Particularly in familiar and predictable situations, experienced operators will pace themselves, working at a rate and effort level that they can sustain for the expected duration of the task. If they do not pace themselves appropriately (either because they are inexperienced or the situation is different than expected), then performance is likely to suffer as the mission progresses. Good leadership ensures that members of a team can maintain performance throughout an entire mission by setting an appropriate pace.

When performing prolonged tasks, particularly those that are repetitive and monotonous or present little task-relevant information, people become bored. When this occurs, performance becomes less efficient (e.g., operators make errors, miss relevant signals, respond less frequently or more slowly, or change their decision criteria) (Hockey, 1986). Fatigue may arise from excessive demands imposed on an operator for a prolonged period. Physical and mental fatigue may occur as a direct result of the effort exerted to perform a task, while emotional fatigue may reflect prolonged exposure to the stressful environment in which a task is performed (Rotondo, 1978). Thus, when difficult or stressful activities must be performed for a prolonged period, operators' capacities may be diminished and their performance will suffer unless they exert additional effort. These effects are discussed in more detail in Chapters 5 and 6. Although some of the subjective symptoms of boredom are similar to those of fatigue, the effects of boredom are more easily reversed by a change in the situation.

Within limits, however, task duration alone does not appear to have a consistent influence on workload or performance. Research has shown that difficulty, stimulus-response compatibility, resource competition, presentation rate, and so on have a more significant effect. For example, in most simulation and flight research, workload ratings are obtained for each segment of flight. Even though takeoff and landing segments last only a few minutes and cruise segments last considerably longer, pilot workload ratings reflect the difficulty rather than the duration of a segment (Bortolussi et al., 1987; Hart and Hauser, 1987). Pepitone et al. (1987) developed flight scenarios in which segment length and within-segment difficulty were not confounded. Here, too, workload covaried with the number and frequency of tasks performed within a segment, not with flight segment duration. In fact, workload was lower during longer segments than during shorter segments. Similarly, Hart and Hauser (1987) found that overall workload and subjective fatigue were unrelated to the duration of flights performed at night in the Kuiper Airborne Observatory of the National Aeronautics and Space Administration.

Task Requirements and Procedures

It should be clear from the preceding discussion that the introduction of automation must be preceded by a careful analysis of task requirements and human capabilities. Such analysis is also critical for the distribution of tasks across people within a team. The design questions here concern who should perform which tasks to maintain an adequate balance of information processing load across operators and machines, yet to operate within the constraints of the command hierarchy within the system. Should tasks be redistributed to other operators because of overload? Or should they be redistributed to computers, which are lighter in weight and, for many tasks, more reliable? How should the operator monitor the state of an automatically controlled system? If tasks are shifted or shared between operators, is the reduction in task load on the two operators greater than the increase in communications load necessary to coordinate between them?

The potential to address these sorts of complex multielement design issues is provided by interactive computer simulation design tools, which incorporate models of task scheduling, crew interaction, anthropometry, display layout, and operator time-sharing (Elkind et al., 1990). Two parallel approaches potentially have much to offer at this level: the CREWCUT project sponsored by the U.S. Army Human Engineering Laboratory (Hahler et al., 1991; Lockett et al., 1990; Prevost and Banda, 1991; Wickens, 1992a) focuses directly on developing a simulation model for tank crew operators; and the MIDAS (Man-Machine Integration, Design, and Analysis System) project developed at NASA Ames Research Center (Bamba et al., 1991), although it originally focused on rotorcraft, is designed for a broader range of multicrew systems. The research effort on modeling distributed decision making carried out by Kleinman and his colleagues, described in Chapter 10, would appear to have considerable potential to predict the implications of different organizational structures on team performance.

Finally, the issue of task requirements is closely related to the procedures that are either mandated or, in some cases, relieved by operating procedures. The Federal Aviation Administration, for example, has adopted a host of operating procedures intended to improve air safety, although adherence to some of these will not necessarily decrease workload and may increase it. Adopting policies mandating adherence to a sleep schedule (see Chapter 5) certainly falls in this category. New procedures and regulations, however, should be introduced with caution and careful analysis of their potentially less obvious side effects. Sometimes the costs (and burden on the operator) to implement may far outweigh the benefit, particularly if the regulation was introduced with the intention of "locking out" a very infrequent operator error, whose cause could not be established with certainty in the first place.

Input Variables

Operators require information to perform most tasks. They may obtain necessary information from memory; however, this section addresses information gained from external sources through an operator's eyes and ears while the task is being performed. The operators of complex systems are bombarded by visual and auditory inputs. Their perceptual systems translate the information detected by their eyes and ears into internal representations that may be subject to deeper analysis. Because so much information may be presented at the same time, operators must divide their attention among these different sources, seeking, interpreting, and integrating relevant information. There is no question that crew workload is influenced by the number and complexity of the information sources that must be monitored and the quality of the information they provide. However, the influence of purely perceptual factors on workload has been examined in less depth than have information processing, memory, and response mechanisms.

The workload associated with perceiving an auditory or visual signal depends on a number of factors, such as intensity (i.e., whether or not it is above threshold), signal/noise ratio (i.e., the similarity of the signal to the background in which it is presented), rate of change (i.e., whether a change is fast enough or large enough to be noticeable), distinctiveness, frequency, and familiarity, among other factors. If it is difficult to identify a signal, workload is likely to increase.

Information From Visual Displays

Analog and digital instruments provide information about the state of the system and, in many vehicles, additional information is provided about the current location, orientation, speed, altitude, depth, and heading of the vehicle and the environment through which it is moving. The display format may be analog or digital, abstract or representational, and one- or multidimensional. The reference coordinate systems (e.g., earth-centered, vehicle-centered) differ across displays. Because the quality, format, and content of displays vary, the perceptual demands their use imposes on an operator also vary. And, because there may be many information sources that an operator must monitor, formal procedures may be established to ensure that visual scan patterns sample different displays often enough and that competing auditory messages are prioritized.

Electronic displays are beginning to replace analog gauges in most aircraft, power plants, automobiles, and other complex systems. All too often, digital readouts have replaced analog. Whereas pilots of earlier aircraft simply had to check the general orientation of a number of needles to assure themselves that system state was normal, digital readouts must be read individually, present unnecessarily precise information for most uses, and do not provide readily interpreted trend information. Since analog displays can be checked more quickly and with less workload than digital readouts (Hanson et al., 1981), the influence of this design decision is obvious. Furthermore, an alphanumeric display (which is represented in memory verbally) must be transformed into a spatial representation to be integrated into the pilot's internal model of the environment, vehicle orientation, and state.

Display design should foster an appropriate distribution of attention, given the relative importance of different display elements. If a display is poorly designed, it may capture the operator's attention for an inordinate amount of time to extract relevant data. Thus, other important sources of information inside or outside the cockpit may be ignored. For example, Harris et al. (1982) found that different analog display formats and placements required significantly different amounts of visual attention and created different levels of workload. They found that a bar graph type of vertical speed indicator located in a more logical position on the panel could be interpreted more quickly, thus reducing pilots' mental workload. The more appropriate format and placement required shorter visual dwell times.

Interface design affects both workload and the cognitive strategies adopted (Woods, 1989). For example, the design of display elements and their organization can force even a highly skilled user from automatic perceptual processes to effortful cognitive processes, or vice versa. Particularly for displays with which complex, automated systems are monitored, the format should promote the development of an accurate understanding of the relation between components of the system and provide information of a nature that is necessary for solving different types of problems. This appears to be particularly critical in extremely complex systems, such as the nuclear reactor (Woods, 1989).

When information from several sources must be integrated to perform a single operation, there are workload and performance benefits if the information requires the same type of processing and is displayed in an integrated format. Carswell and Wickens (1987) demonstrated that independent tasks are performed best with separate displays; integrated tasks are performed best with similar, integrated displays. Display integration was created by depicting movement in different axes of control as variations in different dimensions of a single triangular object. Performance was also improved when displays with similar formats were grouped, by placing them in proximity to each other. In addition, when similar or related information is displayed on several instruments, performance can be improved by coding it in a similar manner (e.g., by color, shape, or numeric rather than pictorial format) (Boles and Wickens, 1987). Sequentially presented information can be integrated by its temporal organization.

Wickens et al. (1988) suggested that cockpit displays could be used more effectively if they were congruent with a pilot's mental model of the environment. Compatibility might be improved by the use of: (1) 3-dimensional perspective displays (rather than 2-dimensional planar displays); (2) color coding that corresponds with population stereotypes (e.g., red to indicate stop or slow down, green to go or speed up); and (3) consistent color coding of similar information across displays to aid integration. Workload will also increase if there is a lack of consistency across displays (Andre and Wickens, 1992). Inconsistent formats should be avoided whenever possible. There are times, however, when changes in format are necessary and inevitable. For example, when an operator must cross-check between a fixed north-up map and a forward field of view out the cockpit window (see Chapter 7), or between a small-scale and large-scale map. In these cases, there are principles of visual momentum that effectively link the different displays together, showing how information depicted in one relates to the other (Andre et al., 1991; Aretz, 1991; Wickens, 1992b; Woods, 1984).

Perceptual workload is related to the operator's goal. For example, looking at a specific display to read its value and glancing at the display during a routine scan to detect anomalies require different types of perceptual processes. Scanning known locations for information that is presented in a consistent format (e.g., checking an instrument) is less demanding than searching for any target that might appear at any location (e.g., scanning a radar display for potential threats) (Liu and Wickens, 1990). Thus, the source of perceptual difficulties may be different: determining the exact value of a particular instrument may depend on legibility or character size; detecting a change in the location of a pointer may depend on its rate or magnitude of change.

Information From the Visual Scene

In the real world, operators often rely on visual cues in the external scene (i.e., optical flow, structural transformations, terrain features) to estimate their orientation, speed, altitude, heading, and location. They may have to do so because their instruments are not sufficiently accurate to perform a particular task (e.g., helicopter instruments are unreliable at very low altitudes or slow speeds) or because the information is not available (e.g., there is no compass in a tank).

Perceiving spatial relationships and states is difficult if available visual cues are insufficient. For example, changes in optical flow may be too slow to provide useful guidance information at very slow speeds (Bennett et al., 1990). In addition, variations in optical variables may be misinterpreted, even though they are perceptible. For example, Perrone (1984) found that pilots do not extract the appropriate cues from an external scene when estimating approach angle. Instead, they rely on simpler but less reliable cues. Kaiser et al. (1990) found that accurate perception of surface slope depends on the orientation of the observer's flight path relative to the terrain. Estimates are more accurate when the observer moves parallel to the slope than toward it. Compensating for such perceptual errors may result in a significant increase in workload during a critical phase of flight.

At night, the crews of tanks and helicopters use visual aids (such as night vision goggles and thermal imaging systems) when monitoring the environment. Although these devices do provide information that would otherwise be unavailable, visual acuity, depth cues, and field of view are limited. Thus, perceiving objects and distances is more difficult, and peripheral motion cues are unavailable or difficult to obtain. In addition, object perception with thermal imaging systems is considerably more difficult than with direct vision. The visual display represents thermal differences rather than reflected light. Thus, objects may look very different than they do with the naked eye (Foyle et al., 1990); surface texture and shading are limited or inconsistent with the viewer's expectations; shadows, convex, and concave areas may be either bright or dark depending on the polarity selected; and objects may disappear if their temperature is similar to that of their surround. Again, the perceptual demands thus imposed add significantly to operator workload. A different but related visual factor that may affect performance and workload is the use of spectacles or contact lenses. The National Research Council's Committee on Vision (1990; Flattau, 1991) has documented the advantages and disadvantages of their use in military aviation. These concerns should also be taken into consideration in this environment.

In either monitoring or search tasks, attention is directed toward different positions in space, particular information sources, or both. In monitoring, the operator routinely scans one or more sources to detect the presence of a previously specified signal or a change in the value of a particular parameter. This task involves both temporal uncertainty (i.e., signals occur infrequently and at unpredictable times) and spatial uncertainty (i.e., a signal may occur in any one of many spatial locations or information sources). In addition, monitoring continuously varying signals is more difficult than detecting the occurrence of a discrete event. In the former, signals may not be uniquely specified and the operator must infer a change in system state by integrating information from multiple sources (Wiener, 1984). The time required to scan an array of instruments, and the demands thus imposed, are influenced by the number of different fixations required. Moving the eyes from one fixation to another takes from 70 to 700 milliseconds (Card et al., 1986). A detailed discussion of the workload and performance effects of monitoring is presented in Chapter 6.

Information From Auditory Displays

Auditory information may be presented as aural displays (warning tones, beeps, synthetic voice messages) or voice communications among the crew or with people located elsewhere. The increasing use of aural warnings (a proliferation of beeps, buzzes, tones, etc.) in aviation demands increasing perceptual accuracy to distinguish among the possibilities. Environmental noise may create significant perceptual problems, particularly in tanks or helicopters. Furthermore, transmission quality may make it difficult to perceive a radio or intercom. Finally, many communications channels are filled with messages directed toward others. Thus, crews must monitor messages intended for other crews (in order to maintain situational awareness) while identifying and paying particular attention to messages intended for them.

An aural message lasts for a finite amount of time, and elements of the message are presented sequentially. Thus, auditory messages have a certain attention grabbing quality because they must be perceived as they occur. If operators delay, they may miss important information. Furthermore, long messages may impose additional memory demands. Perceiving individual components is only the first step of perceiving the meaning of the whole message. (Speech communication is discussed further in Chapter 10.)

Regional accents or computer-generated speech may increase the workload of speech perception. For example, the use of synthesized, rather than natural, speech for warning messages is becoming more common. Although the artificial sound of the voice commands the operator's attention, specific perceptual problems are created by speech quality (e.g., the pilots of transport aircraft reported significant difficulties interpreting synthesized voice messages used to convey critical warnings).

Thus, auditory workload is increasing as quickly as visual workload in many complex systems. For example, civil and military pilots must monitor an increasing number of communication frequencies to maintain coordination, as well as a variety of aural warnings. Soon auditory workload is likely to become as significant a workload problem as visual workload.

Because the visual and auditory demands imposed on the operators of many complex systems are so high, and because incoming information may be degraded or difficult to interpret, problems associated with the initial perception of needed information impose additional demands on later cognitive processes required to identify, interpret, and integrate the information. Despite the likelihood that a relationship exists between perceptual difficulty and workload, relatively little workload research has focused on purely perceptual factors. Instead, the focus has been on the processes required to interpret, transform, and remember information and formulate a response.

Information Processing Variables

As the cognitive processing required to interpret incoming information and select a response increases from simple rules of thumb to complex algorithms, inference, or deduction, response time generally increases; errors are more frequent; and experienced workload is higher.

Level of Processing

Different factors affect the processing required at one or more stages of human information processing. For example, signal quality affects the initial processing stage, and uncertainty affects the response selection stage (Gopher and Donchin, 1986). Craik and Lockhart (1972) suggested that preliminary analyses focus on the physical features of a stimulus, while later stages are more concerned with matching the input against information stored in memory, extracting meaning, and enrichment or elaboration. Familiar, meaningful input, which is compatible with existing cognitive representations, is processed at a deeper level more quickly than is unfamiliar, or less meaningful, input. Within this framework, workload might be linked to the level and depth of analysis required to interpret and retain information.

Rasmussen (1982) identified three categories of tasks, differentiated by the level of processing required for their performance. Levels of processing were associated with degrees of uncertainty. The greater the uncertainty associated with selecting an appropriate response for a particular situation, the higher the cognitive demands placed on an operator. For *skill-based tasks*, which are exemplified by highly practiced perceptual-motor skills, there is a clear and unambiguous relationship between system states and required responses, and no uncertainty about the mapping from stimulus to action. *Rule-based tasks* are characterized by a set of appropriate actions governed by explicit procedures. Once an operator has correctly recognized the situation, the choice of actions is deterministic, following a set of if-then rules. *Knowledge-based tasks* are characterized by uncertainty, requirements to develop novel solutions, and delayed or limited feedback. These activities require operators to perform complex interpretation and decision making. Although tasks may be readily assigned to Rasmussen's three categories, recent evidence suggests that their ordering of skill-rule-knowledge does not necessarily correspond to their level of workload. For example, Moray et al. (1988) found that skill-based tasks did impose significant workload on people performing a complex video-game-like laboratory task. In fact, subjective workload estimates were often dominated by the difficulty of the skill-based component of the task.

Since there is less uncertainty associated with skill- and rule-based behaviors, these tasks are often candidates for automation. Knowledge-based tasks are left for the human operator, as they are difficult or impossible to automate. While it is in this domain that humans continue to outperform machines, these functions are more difficult to learn, easier to forget (as they are often quite abstract), and impose high workload (Hart and Sheridan, 1984). In support of this concept, Tanaka et al. (1983) demonstrated that automation did in fact reduce the workload of skill-based tasks, but not rule- and knowledge-based tasks, in a laboratory flight simulation. However, unexpected and abnormal events increased the workload of rule- and knowledge-based tasks.

Closely related to the skill-rule-knowledge continuum is the dichotomy between automatic and controlled processing. If there is a unique and consistent mapping between signals and actions, rapid and automatic processing develops with experience (Schneider and Shiffrin, 1977). Processing is fast, inflexible, difficult to suppress (once learned), and not limited by short-term memory capacity or attention. Workload is generally low. Similar improvements may be found even when stimulus-response relationships vary, provided the rules relating types of stimuli to appropriate responses are consistent (Kramer et al., 1988). When the relationship between signals and responses is not consistent, automatic behavior cannot develop. Processing remains serial and capacity-limited in the mode known as control processing. The higher-order mental processes required to select a response increase response time and impose higher workload. Thus, a consistent relationship between the location, appearance, and meaning of a particular display element, or class of features, will improve performance and reduce workload. As an example, automatic processing will be more likely to develop with a fixed display that has a fixed mode of information presentation than a variable mode or multifunction display.

Processing Resources

More recently, performance limitations have also been linked to the availability of resources (i.e., hypothetical entities that represent the capacity or mental energy available to perform a task). Early models (see, for example, Kahneman, 1973), assumed that resources were limited in quantity but relatively nonspecific. Performance suffers if any task or combination of tasks requires more capacity than is available. Evidence for an undifferentiated pool of resources came from the observation that apparently unrelated activities interfere with each other's performance. Kahneman further suggested that the arousal induced by some task requirements might in fact increase available capacity. Although common experience supports the notion that people can perform incredible feats when highly motivated, the concept of flexible capacity proved to be difficult to test.

The common observation that tasks interfere with each other to different degrees suggests the existence of independent resources for perceiving, encoding, processing, and responding to different types of information. The seminal papers written by Norman and Bobrow (1975) and Navon and Gopher (1979) resulted in hundreds of experiments designed to identify and describe such resources. Most of these studies used a dual-task paradigm in which pairs of tasks were presented that imposed various demands on different resources. Wickens's (1980) multiple resource model proposed the following dimensions: input modality (visual/auditory), processing stage (perceptual-central/response), processing code (spatial/verbal), and response modality (manual/verbal). The relationship between performance in single- and dual-task conditions was interpreted as evidence of competition for the same resource or independent use of different resources.

The general finding has been that when the resource requirements of two tasks are the same (e.g., visual perception, spatial processing, manual response) and exceed an operator's capacities, then response latency, accuracy, or both on one or both tasks will suffer. But if, for example, one task is presented auditorily (rather than visually) or requires verbal (rather than spatial) processing or a vocal (rather than manual) response, it is more likely that both tasks can be performed as well together as separately. For example, Vidulich and Tsang (1985) found that performance was better and workload lower when a visual-spatial-manual tracking task was paired with a spatial transformation task presented auditorily and performed verbally than with a visual-manual version. Similar results were found in a more complex environment. Vidulich and Bortolussi (1988) conducted two simulations of advanced Army scout/attack helicopter missions to evaluate alternative methods of entering discrete commands. Although commands took longer to enter using a voice recognition system than with manual switches (and subjective workload was higher), single- to dual-task performance decrements were less for voice commands than manual. Furthermore, simultaneous helicopter control performance was better with voice commands. Manual discrete tasks competed with manual flight control for limited resources, whereas vocal discrete tasks did not.

Wickens's (1980, 1991) multiple resource model, based on extensive experimental data, provides a useful tool for the designers of complex systems. This model predicts the time-sharing efficiency likely for different task combinations based on their resource-demand profile (see, for example, Wickens, 1989). It provides a framework for evaluating the effects of alternative design concepts on operator performance and improving the human-machine interface. If an operator's visual capabilities are exceeded by ongoing activities, then alternative display modes might be considered. If control activities exceed an operator's manual capabilities, vocal controls might be substituted for some tasks, and so on.

Although the research performed by Wickens and his colleagues clearly demonstrated the performance problems associated with specific combinations of task parameters, the relationship between resource concepts and workload, at least subjective estimates of workload, was less clear (see, for example, Vidulich and Wickens, 1986; Yeh and Wickens, 1988). Although humans appear to be aware of the total demands imposed on them (created by variations in task frequency, difficulty, and number), their estimates of workload are relatively insensitive to resource competition. If this is true, then it presents the operator of a complex system with a significant problem. If humans are not aware of the potentially detrimental effects of specific task combinations on performance, then they might not adopt the most efficient strategies for performing particular combinations of tasks that momentarily exceed their capacities.

Memory Requirements

Most models of the human mind distinguish among different types of memory: (1) modality-specific sensory registers (in which auditory and visual stimuli are represented literally for no more than a few seconds); (2) some type of resource-demanding short-term or working memory (in which a limited number of items are held for seconds or minutes); and (3) long-term memory (in which vast quantities of information are held for long periods of time). Although attention is not required for information to enter sensory registers, the information will be lost by the process of displacement unless it is transferred into working memory for further processing (Neisser, 1976). Short-term memory is used to temporarily hold and manipulate new information or that retrieved from long-term memory. Only some of the information once held in short-term memory is transferred to long-term memory for more permanent retention. It is unlikely that the products of preliminary or intermediate analyses are retained. Craik and Lockhart (1972) suggested that the persistence of information in memory, and the way it is encoded, depend on the level or depth of processing it received initially.

Because there are severe limitations in the number of separate items that can be retained in working memory at any point in time, errors are more likely for tasks that exceed this capacity (Card, 1989). Miller (1956) placed this limit at seven items, plus or minus two. However, he also suggested that chunking related information could increase this apparent limitation. Chunks were described as composite units created by grouping, organizing, or recoding a group of otherwise separate elements based on rules stored in long-term memory. Although a useful concept, the possibility of chunking eliminates the feasibility of assessing the processing demands of tasks based solely on their formal properties or surface structure.

Information decays rapidly from short-term memory, and not all information is retained equally well. For example, the last items in a list are generally recalled most accurately (i.e., recency effect), followed by the first items in a list (i.e., primacy effect) (Postman and Phillips, 1965). Although information can be retained in working memory almost indefinitely by active rehearsal (Baddeley, 1986), some or all of it may be lost if new information or higher-priority tasks intervene (i.e., it is difficult to remember a telephone number while also engaging in a conversation). However, there may be different types of working memory capable of retaining and processing different types of information. For example, Baddeley and Hitch (1974) proposed two relatively independent processors: one that stores and manipulates verbal information, and another that stores and manipulates visual-spatial images.

As the demands imposed on short-term memory are increased, tasks are perceived as being more difficult. Thus, tasks that require short-term memory often impose greater workload than do tasks that require retrieval of information from long-term memory. For example, Berg and Sheridan (1984) found that pilot workload was significantly higher and flying performance was significantly worse for flights that imposed short-term memory demands than for those that required long-term memory.

Since memory is fallible, particularly when interruptions occur, written procedures and checklists are used in many operational environments to reduce operator workload and decrease the probability of errors. However, since retrieving the appropriate page from a manual may take an unacceptable amount of time in an emergency situation, critical items (e.g., the first few steps in an emergency checklist) are committed to memory. This ensures a rapid and appropriate response when stress or time pressure interfere with operators' analytical and decision-making abilities. Alternatively, people may deliberately bring information that they anticipate needing into working memory, where it will be readily accessible. They recognize that it takes time to access information from long-term memory and that they may forget important information under time stress.

A series of actions that often occur together may become integrated into a high-level action sequence and represented in memory as a single event. However, if information is remembered as an element of an ordered list, or if a series of actions are represented as an integrated unit, it is more difficult to retrieve an individual element of this series from memory. Just because people possess relevant knowledge in long-term memory does not guarantee that this knowledge will be activated when needed (Woods, 1989).

Display-Control Compatibility

The way in which information displays are mapped onto the appropriate responses influences both workload and performance. In general, responses are faster and more accurate when there is a spatial correspondence between the position and direction of movement of stimuli and control responses, correspondence with population stereotypes, compatibility between stimulus and response modalities, and agreement of control dynamics with task requirements (Jagacinski, 1989). As one example, the traditional relationship between helicopter controls and displays places the instrument for altitude (which is controlled with the left hand) on the right and for speed (which is controlled with the right hand) on the left. Craig et al. (1983) found that a more compatible arrangement resulted in faster movement times than did the traditional arrangement (e.g., responses were 1 to 2 seconds faster with a compatible arrangement).

The compatibility between display modality, response modality, and type of processing required to perform a task also influences performance and workload (Vidulich and Wickens, 1986; Wickens et al., 1983). For both discrete and continuous control tasks, single-task performance and time-sharing efficiency are better when display modality is compatible with: (1) the way information is cognitively represented and processed (e.g., visual displays are more compatible with spatial processing; auditory displays are more compatible with verbal processing) and (2) response modality (e.g., auditory displays are more compatible with vocal responses; visual displays are more compatible with manual responses). Since incompatible arrangements impose additional information processing demands, it is reasonable to assume they should increase workload, as well as slow performance (Andre and Wickens, 1992).

If information must be transformed from one format or orientation to another to complete a task, workload and response time are increased. For example, King et al. (1989) found that response time and subjective workload increased when mental rotation was required to bring two items into alignment for comparison. Aretz (1990) found, as others have, that the time required to mentally rotate a map to bring it into alignment with the external scene increased from 3.7 to 4.2 seconds as the difference in orientation increased from 0 to 180 degrees.

If information must be transformed from one form to another to perform sequential tasks, response time is longer and subjective workload is higher than if the two tasks share common input modalities and processing codes. For example, Hart et al. (1986) found that visual-spatial target acquisitions took longer and imposed higher workload when the target to be acquired was identified by auditory rather than visual displays or by verbally coded rather than spatially coded commands.

These and other results suggest that unrelated but concurrent tasks benefit from displays that require different sensory modalities, processing codes, and response modalities. However, performance on functionally related, sequential tasks benefits from compatible display modalities, central processing codes, and response modalities. The former reduces competition for limited resources (thereby reducing workload and improving performance), whereas the latter promotes subjective integration and reduces the need for transformation (also reducing workload and improving performance).

Output Variables

Although the intrinsic difficulty of a task determines the demands imposed on an operator, the interface that is provided to accomplish the task has a significant influence on the workload actually experienced. Poorly designed controls, high-order system dynamics, inadequate displays, and incompatible controls and displays may make it difficult for an operator to accomplish even relatively easy tasks.

Control Design

Many real-world tasks require discrete, transient, periodic, or relatively continuous control inputs in response to direct or indirect feedback from the environment. Pilots move the control yoke to change heading or altitude, drivers steer their vehicles down a road, and gunners track and acquire a target. The workload of these activities depends on the independent and joint effects of: (1) the frequency, duration, and force of control inputs required to change (e.g., complete a turn, move the reticle over the target) or maintain the state of the system (e.g., minimizing the effects of disturbances created by uneven road surface, wind gusts), (2) the way control inputs map onto a change in system state, (3) the way changes in system state are displayed, (4) the physical characteristics and dynamics of the control device(s), (5) the number of axes controlled, (6) the availability of predictability and preview, and (7) the required precision. Although control tasks may impose relatively constant physical demands (i.e., operators' hands and feet are busy), cognitive demands may be low (i.e., perceptual-motor tasks may require little thought for an experienced operator, such as a backhoe operator).

Manual control workload is influenced by the physical and dynamic characteristics of the control device itself and of the system controlled. There may be one (or many) control devices used to operate a system. A single control input may impact several systems, or coordinated use of several controls may be required to make a single change in system state. Control devices may be single- or multiaxis. The more complex the control system, the greater the workload of the operator. For example, the more axes that must be controlled simultaneously, the higher the workload of pilots in simulated flight (Kantowitz et al., 1984; King et al., 1989). For most vehicle control tasks, workload and performance are influenced by interrelationships among axes of control. For example, if a helicopter pilot pulls back on the cyclic to gain altitude, he must simultaneously add power (with the collective) to maintain a constant speed. If he banks to the right to execute a turn, he must increase pressure on the pedals to counteract the additional torque. These complex interrelationships among control devices, control surfaces, and vehicle state impose additional cognitive load on operators.

Control Gain and Display Gain

Control gain refers to the displacement or force required to achieve a given change in system state. In high-gain systems, small control movements produce large outputs. In low-gain systems, large control movements are required to achieve the same effect. Display gain refers to the way in which changes in system state are presented to the operator. A high-gain display reflects even minor variations in system state; while, a low-gain display reflects only those changes that exceed some threshold. Although humans are able to compensate for variations in control and display gain over a wide range (Wickens, 1986), additional workload is imposed when control or display gain exceeds an optimal range, is poorly matched, or is inappropriate for a specific task. If gain is too high, the effects of even small corrections are magnified and the operator must make very fine adjustments to avoid introducing errors. Oscillations and overcorrections are often the result. If gain is too low, frequent or large-amplitude movements may be required, inducing physical fatigue. While high-gain systems reduce the workload of the initial phase of target acquisitions (the higher the gain, the smaller the control displacement required), they impose additional workload during the final phase (the higher the gain, the finer the corrections required to remain over the target area).

Control Lag and Display Lag

A lag in the system's response to a control input can increase operator workload, although a pure time delay is not particularly disruptive when inputs are predictable (Wickens, 1986). Generally, as the delay between a control input and a change in the display of system state increases, tracking error and workload increase. Levison et al. (1979) found that performance was disrupted by delays as small as 80 milliseconds between simulator motion and visual displays. Preview can improve performance and reduce workload; that is, when the operator can see ahead and anticipate future control requirements (e.g., view turns in the road ahead, predict periodicities in disturbances) operators can shift from a reactive to a proactive mode of behavior. Time lags coupled with high gains produce dynamics that are likely to be unstable and oscillatory.

Order of Control

Control dynamics generally fall into one of three categories (or are a combination of more than one): (1) Zero-order or position controls are the easiest to conceptualize and use. A deflection of the control stick causes the controlled element to move in the direction the stick was deflected. If the stick is held steady in one position, the controlled element remains stationary. (2) First-order or velocity controls command rate. If stick deflection is constant, velocity and direction are constant; the greater the stick deflection, the faster the controlled element moves in that direction. (3) Second-order or acceleration controls command rate of change; the greater the stick deflection, the faster the controlled element accelerates in that direction. If stick deflection is held constant, the controlled element will move in the commanded direction at an increasing velocity.

Although tracking performance and workload are not generally different between zero- and first-order controls, they differ significantly between first- and second-order controls (Vidulich and Wickens, 1984; Wickens, 1986). The difficulty of higher-order control is attributed to the amount of lead, or prediction, an operator must generate to achieve the same level of performance, the information processing required, and the complexity and number of inputs necessary to achieve the same result. For target acquisition, as with continuous tracking, the higher the order of control, the greater the demands placed on the operator. Put very simplistically, position, velocity, and acceleration controls require a minimum of one, two, or three control inputs to bring and hold a reticle over a target.

Computer Aiding and Automation

Computer aiding and automation are introduced to reduce operator workload, increase safety, improve performance, and extend mission capability. In automobiles, automatic transmission and cruise control reduce the need for gear changes and continuous operation of the gas pedal. In transport aircraft, autopilots achieve and maintain the flight path based on information entered by the pilot before takeoff or modified inflight by single, discrete commands. In military jets, terrain following/terrain avoidance algorithms process mission, terrain, and threat data to project and follow an optimal flight path. In many environments, even system monitoring is accomplished automatically, providing the operator with visual and/or auditory alarms when a failure occurs. Expert systems are being developed for use in high-performance aircraft that will infer the pilots' intentions and evaluate the degree to which his commands support, or conflict with, his current goals (Rouse et al., 1990).

Given the increasing complexity of many advanced systems, operators are no longer able to control the system without assistance. Thus, various methods of alleviating their workload have been introduced. For example, direct displays of system parameters (which may be noisy, high-order, and unintegrated) might be replaced by displays that filter noisy inputs, appear to be of a lower order, and integrate the outputs of related subsystems. Predictor displays can depict estimates of the future state or position of the system based on its current state and assumptions about the operator's future control activity (Wickens, 1986) and present this information to the operator in graphic form. Because predictor displays perform some integration and projection for operators, thus allowing them to be proactive rather than reactive, they often improve the accuracy and smoothness of control activities and reduce operator workload.

Stability augmentation systems reduce the frequency and order of control inputs required of an operator. For example, a number of the stability-control augmentation systems evaluated in a simulated advanced Army helicopter significantly reduced pilot workload (Haworth et al., 1987), but the benefits varied across mission segments. Fully automatic systems allow an operator to enter a desired outcome directly (e.g., a new heading) while underlying subsystems manipulate the control surfaces to achieve the desired state. In fact, as the level of control augmentation increases beyond some point, the role of the operator shifts from that of manual controller to system monitor.

Vienneau and Gozzo (1987) evaluated the effects of automating eight different subsystems in simulated military missions conducted in a single-pilot advanced scout/attack helicopter. They found, as did Haworth et al. (1987), that automation aided pilots in managing workload peaks and reduced overall workload. For example, computer-aided systems for communications (with voice-activated frequency selection) and navigation (with a digital map display) reduced flight path deviations by an average of 67 percent and time en route by 70 percent. Again, differential benefits were found across mission segments and greater improvements were found for high-workload activities. Vienneau and Gozzo suggested that workload reductions might be achieved by either the addition of automated subsystems or by increasing the efficiency of the human's interface with the system.

Automation does not always reduce operator workload. Often, it simply replaces one form of workload (the physical demands of manual control) with another (the perceptual-cognitive demands of monitoring the system) (Hart and Sheridan, 1984). Designers tend to automate tasks that are easy to automate. As discussed earlier, these are usually the skill-based tasks that are also easy for a human to perform. This often leaves the operator with a collection of unrelated activities to perform that are too ambiguous or unpredictable to automate and that impose equally high demands on the operator. Finally, automation reduces an operator's direct involvement with and knowledge of the system and may make it more difficult to detect errors or assume control if the automated system fails. For example, Wickens and Kessel (1979) found that people are better able to detect a sudden change in system state when manually controlling a system than when supervising the performance of an automated system. Thus, opportunities for system error may, in fact, increase. Long delays between an operator input and its ultimate effect decrease the probability of detecting and rectifying a human error (Kantowitz and Casper, 1988) or a system error. Although airline pilots have found automation to be useful, they do not necessarily agree that it has reduced their overall workload (Wiener, 1989; Wiener and Curry, 1980).

In many cases, automation is introduced to allow a reduction in crew size or an increase in mission capability. This creates the potential for increasing the workload of remaining crew members if the level of automation is not sufficient. Even with a fully functioning system, it is difficult to replace a human operator completely with an automatic system. For example, Haworth et al. (1987) found it was impossible to achieve the same level of workload typical of two-pilot crews for the single pilots of a highly automated simulation of an advanced Army helicopter. In addition, workload and performance predictions and system evaluations (on which crew complement decisions are based) assume the appropriate use of available automation. If the systems are too numerous or complex to be used effectively, or if they fail, the burden of accomplishing the mission rests on the operator(s), who may experience far higher workload than anticipated. Finally, the controversy continues about how to allocate tasks between humans and machines and whether the operator should retain control or allow an automated system to override human decisions.

SUMMARY

In some cases, it is apparent that human limitations reflect the consequences of poorly designed controls, displays, and automatic subsystems.

In others, task demands simply exceed the operator's capabilities either momentarily or for extended periods. Despite their limitations, humans are remarkably flexible, adaptable, and capable. They can improvise, compensate for inadequate information and system or human failures, adjust to novel situations, exhibit graceful (rather than catastrophic) degradation, plan ahead, predict the outcome of familiar and unfamiliar events, and learn from experience. However, the consequences of extreme demands and requirements to act creatively and adaptively impose significant workload on the human operators of complex systems.

Regardless of the specific source(s) of workload at any point in time, adequate training and preparation, adopting strategies and tactics most appropriate for the situation, effective leadership, and smooth crew coordination can counteract some of the detrimental effects of imposed task demands, transitioning from one mode of behavior to another, environmental stressors, and fatigue. The more actions that have become automatic through training and experience and the more predictable events seem through planning and rehearsal or availability of preview information, the more likely it will be that crews will respond appropriately and sustain adequate performance for as long as necessary.

There are several significant factors that characterize the transition from low to high workload mission phases. One, of course, is the absolute level of workload. There is no question that workload is higher during an engagement than before. However, the fact that the sources of workload are significantly different between the two phases may present a greater problem. The nature of the task demands shifts from preparation to action; from static to dynamic; from long lead times to short; from passive monitoring and maintenance to active information seeking, control, and operating; from direct interaction to radio communications; from predictive to compensatory behaviors; from planning to reaction; from organized procedures and schedules to spontaneous actions.

Crews may adopt different strategies for coping with a sudden increase in workload. They may choose to process fewer events (e.g., selectively attend to fewer tasks, defer activities, monitor fewer channels, ignore information about expected events, or consider fewer alternative hypotheses). Alternatively, they may choose to process events less completely (e.g., sample information sources less often, seek less corroborating evidence, be satisfied with partial feedback, narrow the field of attention, pursue fewer possible explanations, or limit their anticipation of what might happen next) (Woods, 1989). Although either of these strategies might be effective in reducing workload in the near term, they also might shift such workload to a later time. Furthermore, incomplete attention to the current situation and tasks is more likely to result in errors, which will impose additional workload to rectify.

A shift in the nature of task demands, accompanied by an increase in time pressure and uncertainty, requires a significant change in the team's behaviors and strategies, which in itself imposes additional workload. In addition, boredom, impatience, or apprehension (which may characterize the premission phase) are replaced by stress and fear following a transition. While the latter factors increase the level of arousal and focus the attention of the crew (a potential benefit for performance) they may impair the crew's ability to perform accurately and effectively, thereby increasing the effort it must exert to maintain acceptable performance. These stress effects are addressed in the next chapter.

REFERENCES

Acton, W.H., M.S. Crabtree, J.C. Simons, F.E. Gomer, and J.S. Eckel
1983   Quantification of crew workload imposed by communications-related tasks in commercial transport aircraft. Pp. 239-243 in *Proceedings of the Human Factors Society 27th Annual Meeting*. Santa Monica, California: Human Factors Society.

Andre, A.D., and C.D. Wickens
1992   Compatibility and consistency in display-control systems. *Human Factors* 34(6).

Andre, A.D., C.D. Wickens, L. Moorman, and M.M. Boeschelli
1991   Display formatting techniques for improving situation awareness in the aircraft cockpit. *International Journal of Aviation Psychology* 1(3):205-218.

Aretz, A.J.
1990   Map display design. Pp. 89-93 in *Proceedings of the Human Factors Society 34th Annual Meeting*. Santa Monica, California: Human Factors Society.

Baddeley, A.D.
1986   *Working Memory*. Oxford: Clarendon Press.

Baddeley, A.D., and G.J. Hitch
1974   Working memory. In G.H. Bower, ed., *The Psychology of Learning and Motivation: Advances in Research and Theory, Volume 8*. New York: Academic Press.

Bamba, Z., D. Bushnell, S. Chen, A. Chiu, C. Nuekom, S. Nishimura, M. Prevost, R. Shankar, L. Staveland, and G. Smith
1991   *Army-NASA Aircrew Aircraft Integration Program (A^3I): Man-Machine Integration, Design, and Analysis Systems (MIDAS)*. Report No. TN-91-8216-000. Palo Alto, California: Sterling Federal Systems, Inc.

Bennett, C.T., M. Schwirzke, and J.S. Tittle
1990   Perceptual and Performance Consequences of Flight in Virtual Worlds. Poster presented at the Workshop on Human-Machine Interfaces for Teleoperators and Virtual Environments. Santa Barbara, California.

Berg, S.L., and T.B. Sheridan
1984   Measuring workload differences between short-term memory and long-term memory scenarios in a simulation flight environment. Pp. 397-416 in *Proceedings of the 20th Annual Conference on Manual Control*. Report No. NASA CP-2341. Washington, DC: National Aeronautics and Space Administration.

Bittner, A., J.C. Byers, S.G. Hill, A.L. Zaklad, and R.E. Christ
1988   *Generic Workload Ratings of a Mobile Air Defense System (LOS-F-H)*. Willow Grove, Pennsylvania: Analytics, Inc.

Boles, D.B., and C.D. Wickens
1987   Display formatting in information integration and nonintegration tasks. *Human Factors* 29(4):395-406.

Bortolussi, M.R., S.G. Hart, and R.J. Shively
  1987   Measuring moment-to-moment pilot workload using synchronous presentations of secondary tasks in a motion-base simulator. Pp. 625-657 in *Proceedings of the Fourth Symposium on Aviation Psychology*. Columbus, Ohio: Ohio State University.

Broadbent, D.E.
  1990   Fellows profile: Donald Broadbent. Pp. 7 in *The Human Factors Society Bulletin*. Santa Monica, California: Human Factors Society.

Card, S.K.
  1989   Models of working memory. Pp. 203-214 in J. Elkind, S. Card, J. Hochberg, and B. Huey, eds., *Human Performance Models for Computer-Aided Engineering*. Washington, DC: National Academy Press.

Card, S.K., T.P. Moran, and A. Newell
  1986   The model human processor. Pp. 45.1-45.35 in K. Boff, L. Kauffman, and J.P. Thomas, eds., *Handbook of Perception and Human Performance*. New York: Wiley and Sons.

Carswell, M., and C.D. Wickens
  1987   Information integration and the object display: An interaction of task demands and display superiority. *Ergonomics* 30:511-528.

Craig, K.M., E.J. Hartzell, and S.L. Dunbar
  1983   Helicopter pilot responses as a function of compatibility of the control-display configuration. Pp. 100-115 in *Proceedings of the 19th Annual Conference on Manual Control*. Washington, DC: National Aeronautics and Space Administration.

Craik, F.I., and R.S. Lockhart
  1972   Levels of processing: A framework for memory research. *Journal of Verbal Learning and Verbal Behavior* 11:671-684.

Cumming, R.W., and P.G. Croft
  1973   Human information processing under varying task demand. *Ergonomics* 16:581-586.

Flattau, P.E., ed.
  1991   *Consideration in Contact Lens Use Under Adverse Conditions: Proceedings of a Symposium*. Committee on Vision, National Research Council. Washington, DC: National Academy Press.

Foyle, D.C., M.S. Brickner, L. Staveland, and B.D. Sanford
  1990   Human object recognition as a function of display parameters using TV and infrared imagery. *Proceedings of the Society for Information Displays 1990 International Symposium*.

Gopher, D., M. Brickner, and D. Navon
  1982   Different difficulty manipulations interact differently with task emphasis: Evidence for multiple resources. *Journal of Experimental Psychology: Human Perception and Performance* 8(1):146-157.

Gopher, D., and E. Donchin
  1986   Workload: An examination of the concept. Pp. 41.1-41.49 in K. Boff, L. Kauffman, and J.P. Thomas, eds., *Handbook of Perception and Human Performance*. New York: Wiley and Sons.

Gopher, D., M. Weil, T. Bareket, and S. Caspi
  1988   Fidelity of task structure as a guiding principle in the development of skill trainers based upon complex computer games. Pp. 1266-1275 in *Proceedings of the Human Factors Society 32nd Annual Meeting*. Santa Monica, California: Human Factors Society.

Gopher, D., M. Weil, and D. Siegel
    1989   Practice under changing priorities: An approach to training complex skill. *Acta Psychologica* 71(1-3):147-177.
Hahler, B., S. Dahl, K.R. Laughery, Jr., J. Lockett, III, and B. Thein
    1991   CREWCUT: A tool for modeling the effects of high workload on human performance. Pp. 1210-1214 in *Proceedings of the Human Factors Society 35th Annual Meeting*. Santa Monica, California: Human Factors Society.
Hancock, P.A., and J.S. Warm
    1989   A dynamic model of stress and sustained attention. *Human Factors* 31:519-537.
Hanson, R.H., D.G. Payne, R.J. Shively, and B.H. Kantowitz
    1981   Process control simulation research in monitoring analog and digital displays. Pp. 154-158 in *Proceedings of the Human Factors Society 25th Annual Meeting*. Santa Monica, California: Human Factors Society.
Harris, R.L., Sr., J.R. Tole, A.R. Ephrath, and A.T. Stephens
    1982   How a new instrument affects pilots' mental workload. Pp. 1010-1013 in *Proceedings of the Human Factors Society 26th Annual Meeting*. Santa Monica, California: Human Factors Society.
Hart, S.G.
    1986   Theory and measurement of human workload. Pp. 396-456 in J. Zeidner, ed., *Human Productivity Enhancement: Training and Human Factors in System Design, Volume 1*. New York: Praeger.
    1989   Crew workload management strategies: A critical factor in system performance. Pp. 22-27 in *Proceedings of the Fifth International Symposium on Aviation Psychology*. Columbus, Ohio: Ohio State University.
Hart, S.G., V. Battiste, and P.T. Lester
    1984a   POPCORN: A supervisory control simulation for workload and performance research. Pp. 431-454 in *Proceedings of the 20th Annual Conference on Manual Control, Volume 1*. Report No. NASA-C-2341. Washington, DC: National Aeronautics and Space Administration.
Hart, S.G., and M.R. Bortolussi
    1984   Pilot errors as a source of workload. *Human Factors* 26(5):545-556.
Hart, S.G., and J.R. Hauser
    1987   Inflight application of three pilot workload measurement techniques. *Aviation, Space, and Environmental Medicine* 58(5):402-410.
Hart, S.G., J.J. Sellers, and G. Guthart
    1984b   The impact of response selection and response execution difficulty on the subjective experience of workload. Pp. 732-736 in *Proceedings of the Human Factors Society 28th Annual Meeting*. Santa Monica, California: Human Factors Society.
Hart, S.G., and T.B. Sheridan
    1984   Pilot workload, performance, and aircraft control automation. Pp. 18.1-18.12 in *Proceedings of the AGARD Symposium on Human Factors Considerations in High Performance Aircraft Conference Proceedings No. 371*. Neuilly sur Seine, France: NATO Advisory Group for Aerospace Research and Development.
Hart, S.G., R.J. Shively, M.A. Vidulich, and R.C. Miller
    1986   The effects of stimulus modality and task integrality: Predicting dual-task performance and workload from single task levels. Pp. 5.1-5.18 in *Proceedings of the 21st Annual Conference on Manual Control*. Report No. NASA CP-2428. Washington, DC: National Aeronautics and Space Administration.
Hart, S.G., and C.D. Wickens
    1990   Workload assessment and prediction. In H.R. Booher, ed., *MANPRINT: An Emerging Technology. Advanced Concepts for Integrating People, Machines, and Organizations*. New York: Van Nostrand and Reinhold.

Hauser, J.R., M.E. Childress, and S.G. Hart
  1983   Rating consistency and component salience in subjective workload estimation. Pp. 127-149 in *Proceedings of the 18th Annual Conference on Manual Control.* Report No. AFWAL-TR-8-3021. Wright-Patterson Air Force Base, Ohio: Air Force Flight Dynamics Laboratory.

Haworth, L.A., A. Atencio, C.C. Bivens, R.J. Shively, and D. Delgado
  1987   *Advanced Helicopter Cockpit and Control Configurations for Helicopter Combat Missions.* Report No. NASA TM-100017. Washington, DC: National Aeronautics and Space Administration.

Hughes, D.
  1989   Glass cockpit study reveals human factors problems. *Aviation Week and Space Technology* August 7:32-35.

Hick, W.E.
  1952   On the rate of gain of information. *Quarterly Journal of Experimental Psychology* 4:11-26.

Hockey, G.R.J.
  1986   Changes in operator efficiency as a function of environmental stress, fatigue, and circadian rhythms. Pp. 44.1-44.49 in K. Boff, L. Kauffman, and J.P. Thomas, eds., *Handbook of Perception and Human Performance.* New York: Wiley and Sons.

Hurst, M.W., and R.M. Rose
  1978   Objective job difficulty, behavioral responses, and sector characteristics in air route traffic control centers. *Ergonomics* 21(9):697-708.

Hyman, R.
  1953   Stimulus information as a determinant of reaction time. *Journal of Experimental Psychology* 45:188-196.

Jagacinski, R.J.
  1989   Target acquisition: Performance measures, process models, and design implications. Pp. 135-150 in G. McMillan, ed., *Applications of Models to System Design.* New York: Plenum Press.

Jagacinski, R.J., D.W. Repperger, S.L. Ward, and M.S. Moran
  1980   A test of Fitts' Law with moving targets. *Human Factors* 22:225-233.

Johnson, W.W., and S.G. Hart
  1987   Step tracking shrinking targets. Pp. 248-252 in *Proceedings of the Human Factors Society 31st Annual Meeting.* Santa Monica, California: Human Factors Society.

Kahneman, D.
  1973   *Attention and Effort.* Englewood Cliffs, New Jersey: Prentice-Hall.

Kaiser, M.K., J.S. Perrone, G.J. Anderson, J.L. Lappin, and D.R. Proffitt
  1990   The Effect of Motion on Surface Slant Perception. Paper presented at the Annual Meeting of the Association for Research in Vision and Ophthalmology (ARVO). Sarasota, Florida.

Kantowitz, B.H., and P.A. Casper
  1988   Human workload in aviation. Pp. 157-187 in E. Wiener and D. Nagel, eds., *Human Factors in Aviation.* San Diego, California: Academic Press.

Kantowitz, B.H., S.G. Hart, and M. Bortolussi
  1983   Measuring pilot workload in a motion-based simulator: I. Asynchronous secondary choice-reaction task. Pp. 359-372 in *Proceedings of the Human Factors Society 27th Annual Meeting.* Santa Monica, California: Human Factors Society.

Kantowitz, B.H., S.G. Hart, M.R. Bortolussi, R.J. Shively, and S.C. Kantowitz
  1984   Measuring pilot workload in a moving-base simulator: II. Building levels of load. Pp. 359-372 in *Proceedings of the 20th Annual Conference on Manual Control.*

Report No. NASA CP-2341. Washington, DC: National Aeronautics and Space Administration.

Keele, S.W.
1986   Motor control. Pp. 30.1-30.60 in K. Boff, L. Kauffman, and J.P. Thomas, eds., *Handbook of Perception and Human Performance.* New York: Wiley and Sons.

King, T., J. Hamerman-Matsumoto, and S. Hart
1989   Dissociation revisited: Workload and performance in a simulated flight task. Pp. 796-801 in *Proceedings of the Fifth International Symposium on Aviation Psychology.* Columbus, Ohio: Ohio State University.

Kramer, A., D. Strayer, and Y. Liu
1988   The role of consistency in automatic processing. Pp. 266-270 in *The Proceedings of the Eleventh Biennial Psychology in the Department of Defense Symposium.* Colorado Springs, Colorado: U.S. Air Force Academy.

Levison, W.H., R.E. Lancroft, and A.M. Junker
1979   Effects of simulator delays on performance and learning in a roll-axis tracking task. *Proceedings of the Fifteenth Annual Conference on Manual Control.* Report No. AFFDL-TR-7-3134. Wright-Patterson Air Force Base, Ohio: Air Force Flight Dynamics Laboratory.

Liu, Y., and C.D. Wickens
1990   Visual scanning with or without spatial uncertainty and time-sharing performance. Unpublished paper, Aviation Research Laboratory, University of Illinois.

Lockett, J.F., T. Plocher, and S. Dahl
1990   Crew reduction in armored vehicles ergonomic study (CRAVES). In E.J. Lovesey, ed., *Contemporary Ergonomics.* London: Taylor and Francis.

Matthews, M.L.
1986   The influence of visual workload history on visual performance. *Human Factors* 28(6):623-632.

Miller, G.A.
1956   The magical number seven, plus or minus two: Some limits on our capacity for processing information. *Psychological Review* 63:81-97.

Moray, N., E. Kruschelnicky, P. Eisen, L. Money, and I.B. Turksen
1988   The mental workload of skill-based, rule-based, and knowledge-based tasks and their combination. Pp. 164-167 in *Proceedings of the Human Factors Society 32nd Annual Meeting.* Santa Monica, California: Human Factors Society.

Moray, N.P., and J. Liao
1988   *A Quantitative Model of Excess Workload, Subjective Workload Estimation, and Performance Degradation.* Report No. EPL-88-03. Urbana-Champaign: University of Illinois, Department of Mechanical and Industrial Engineering.

Mosier, K.L., and S.G. Hart
1986   Levels of information processing in a Fitts' Law task. Pp. 4.1-4.15 in *Proceedings of the 21st Annual Conference on Manual Control.* Report No. NASA CP-2428. Washington, DC: National Aeronautics and Space Administration.

National Research Council
1990   *Contact Lens Use Under Adverse Conditions: Applications in Military Aviation.* Committee on Vision. Washington, DC: National Academy Press.

Navon, D., and D. Gopher
1979   On the economy of the human-processing system. *Psychological Review* 86(3):214-255.

Neisser, U.
1976   *Cognition and Reality: Principles and Implications of Cognitive Psychology.* San Francisco, California: Freeman.

Norman, D.A., and D.G. Bobrow
   1975   On data-limited and resource-limited processes. *Journal of Cognitive Psychology* 7(1):44-64.
O'Donnell, R.D., and F.T. Eggemeier
   1986   Workload assessment methodology. Pp. 42.1-42.49 in K. Boff, L. Kauffman, and J.P. Thomas, eds., *Handbook of Perception and Human Performance*. New York: Wiley and Sons.
Pepitone, D.D., T. King, and M. Murphy
   1988   The role of flight planning in aircrew decision performance. *Proceedings of the SAE Aerospace Technology Conference and Exposition*. SAE Technical Paper Series #881517. Warrendale, Pennsylvania: The Society of Automotive Engineers.
Pepitone, D.D., R.J. Shively, and M.R. Bortolussi
   1987   Pilot workload prediction. *Proceedings of the SAE Aerospace Technology Conference and Exposition*. SAE Technical Paper Series #871771. Warrendale, Pennsylvania: The Society of Automotive Engineers.
Perrone, H.A.
   1984   Visual slant misperception and the "black hole" landing situation. *Aviation, Space, and Environmental Medicine* 1020-1025.
Postman, L., and L.W. Phillips
   1965   Short-term temporal changes in free recall. *Quarterly Journal of Experimental Psychology* 17:132-138.
Poulton, E.C.
   1982   Influential companions: Effects of one strategy on another in the within-subjects designs of cognitive psychology. *Psychological Bulletin* 91:673-690.
Prevost, M., and C.P. Banda
   1991   Visualizing tool for human machine interface designers. Pp. 58-66 in *Proceedings of the Society of Photo-optical Instrument Designers*. Bellingham, Washington: Society of Photo-optical Instrument Designers.
Rasmussen, J.
   1982   The role of cognitive models of operators in the design, operation, and licensing of nuclear power plants. Pp. 13-35 in *Proceedings of the Workshop on Cognitive Modeling of Nuclear Plant Control Room Operators*. Report Nos. NUREG/CR-3114; ONRL-TM-8614. Washington, DC: U.S. Nuclear Regulatory Commission.
Rotondo, G.
   1978   Workload and operational fatigue in helicopter pilots. *Aviation Space and Environmental Medicine* 430-436.
Rouse, W.B.
   1979   Approaches to mental workload. Pp. 255-262 in N. Moray, ed., *Mental Workload: Its Theory and Measurement*. New York: Plenum Press.
Rouse, W.B., N.D. Geddes, and J.M. Hammer
   1990   Computer-aided fighter pilots. *IEEE Spectrum* 27(3):38-40.
Schneider, W., and R.M. Shiffrin
   1977   Controlled and automatic human information processing: Decision research and attention. *Psychological Review* 84:1-66.
Staveland, L.E., S.G. Hart, and Y.Y. Yeh
   1986   Memory and subjective workload assessment. Pp. 7.1-7.13 in *Proceedings of the 21st Annual Conference on Manual Control*. Report No. NASA-CP-2428. Washington, DC: National Aeronautics and Space Administration.
Tanaka, K., A. Buharali, and T.B. Sheridan
   1983   Mental workload in supervisory control of automated aircraft. Pp. 40-58 in *Pro-

ceedings of the 19th Annual Conference on Manual Control. Cambridge, Massachusetts: Massachusetts Institute of Technology.

Thornton, D.C.
  1985   An investigation of the "von Restorff" phenomenon in post-test workload ratings. Pp. 760-763 in *Proceedings of the Human Factors Society 29th Annual Meeting.* Santa Monica, California: Human Factors Society.

Tsang, P.S., and C.D. Wickens
  1988   The structural constraints and strategic control of resource allocation. *Human Performance* 1:45-72.

Tulga, M.K., and T.B. Sheridan
  1980   Dynamic decisions and workload in multitask supervisory control. *IEEE Transactions on Systems, Man, and Cybernetics* SMC-10:217-232.

Vidulich, M., and M. Bortolussi
  1988   A dissociation of objective and subjective workload measures in assessing the impact of speech controls in advanced helicopters. Pp. 1471-1476 in *Proceedings of the Human Factors Society 32nd Annual Meeting.* Santa Monica, California: Human Factors Society.

Vidulich, M.A., and P.S. Tsang
  1985   Techniques of subjective workload assessment: A comparison of two methodologies. Pp. 239-246 in *Proceedings of the Third Symposium on Aviation Psychology.* Columbus, Ohio: Ohio State University.

Vidulich, M.A., and C.D. Wickens
  1984   Subjective workload assessment and voluntary control of effort in a tracking task. Pp. 57-72 in *Proceedings of the 20th Annual Conference on Manual Control.* Report No. NASA-CP-2341. Washington, DC: National Aeronautics and Space Administration.
  1986   Causes of dissociation between subjective workload measures and performance. *Applied Ergonomics* 17:291-296.

Vienneau, R., and F. Gozzo
  1987   Estimating pilots workload and its impact on system performance. Pp. 91-102 in *Proceedings of the American Helicopter Society 43rd Annual Forum and Technology Display.* New York: American Helicopter Society.

Welford, A.T.
  1967   A single channel operation in the brain. *Acta Psychologica* 27:5-22.

Wickens, C.D.
  1980   The structure of attentional resources. Pp. 239-257 in R. Nickerson, ed., *Attention and Performance, Volume VIII.* Englewood Cliffs, New Jersey: Erlbaum.
  1986   The effects of control dynamics on performance. Pp. 39.1-39.60 in K.Boff, L. Kauffman, and J.P. Thomas, eds., *Handbook of Perception and Human Performance.* New York: Wiley and Sons.
  1989   Models of multitask situations. Pp. 259-273 in G. McMillan, ed., *Applications of Models to System Design.* New York: Plenum Press.
  1991   *Internal Model of Complex Dynamic Systems.* Report No. ARI-RN-91-64. Urbana-Champaign, Illinois: Illinois University at Urbana-Champaign Department of Psychology.
  1992a   Computational models of human performance. Invited Address. *Sixth Annual Conference on Psychology in the Department of Defense.* U.S. Air Force Academy, Colorado.
  1992b   *Engineering Psychology and Human Performance, 2nd Edition.* New York: Harper Collins Publishers.

Wickens, C.D., I. Haskell, and K. Harte
  1988   Ergonomic design for perspective flight-path displays. *Proceedings of the 1988 International Conference on Systems, Man, and Cybernetics.* New York: Institute of Electrical and Electronics Engineers.

Wickens, C.D., and C. Kessel
  1979   The effects of participatory mode and task workload on the detection of dynamic system failures. *IEEE Transactions on Systems, Man, and Cybernetics* SMC-9(1):24-34.

Wickens, C.D., D.L. Sandry, and M.A. Vidulich
  1983   Compatibility and resource competition between modalities of input, central processing, and output. *Human Factors* 25(2):227-248.

Wiener, E.
  1984   Vigilance and inspection. In J.S. Warm, ed., *Sustained Attention in Human Performance.* London: Wiley.
  1989   Reflections on human error: Matters of life and death. Pp. 1-7 in *Proceedings of the Human Factors Society 33rd Annual Meeting.* Santa Monica, California: Human Factors Society.

Wiener, E.L., and R.E. Curry
  1980   Flight-deck automation: Promises and problems. *Ergonomics* 23:995-1011.

Woods, D.D.
  1984   Visual momentum: A concept to improve the cognitive coupling of person and computer. *International Journal of Man-Machine Studies* 21(3):229-244.
  1989   Modeling and predicting human error. Pp. 248-274 in J. Elkind, S. Card, J. Hochberg and B. Huey, eds., *Human Performance Models for Computer-Aided Engineering.* Washington, DC: National Academy Press.

Yeh, Y.Y., and C.D. Wickens
  1988   Dissociation of performance and subjective measures of workload. *Human Factors* 30(1):111-120.

4

Stress

The battlefield environment is a stressful place and, as graphically described by Keegan (1976), those stresses are amplified within the armored vehicle. Indeed, the post-transition phase of any team situation will impose a substantial degree of stress, incorporating time pressure at a minimum, often augmented by danger, noise, and a host of other environmental stressors. The concept of stress as it influences human performance may be understood in the context of Figure 4.1. At the top of the figure are identified a set of stressors; these are influences on information processing and cognition that are not inherent in the content of the information itself. Stressors may include features of the work environment like noise, vibration, heat, dim lighting, and high acceleration, as well as such psychological factors as anxiety, fatigue, and danger. Such stressors may have different manifestations: subjective experience, physiological changes, and performance decrements.

Stressors may affect a subjective experience. For example, individuals are usually (but not always) able to report a feeling of frustration, or arousal, as a consequence of a stressor. Closely linked, a change in physiology is often observable. This might be a short-term change—such as the influence on heart rate associated with the demands of flying as pilot-in-command (Hart and Hauser, 1987) or the stress of controlling air traffic in high-load situations (Romhert, 1979). Or it might be a more sustained effect, such as the change in the output of catecholamines, measured in the urine, after periods of simulated combat maneuvers flying in an F16 (Burton et al., 1977), inflight emergencies, or actual battlefield events (Bourne, 1971).

The subjective and physiological characteristics are often, but not invariantly, linked. The subjective experience of stress may also mediate performance. For example, one who does not realize the risk or danger of a particular situation will experience less stress than one who does a subjective appraisal of the situation, thereby mediating stress effects on performance (Coyne and Lazarus, 1980).

As Figure 4.1 shows, the effects may be either direct or indirect. Direct effects are stressors that influence the quality of information perceived by the human operator or the precision of the motor response. For example, vibration will reduce the quality of visual input (as well as the quality of motor output), and noise will do the same for auditory input. Time stress may simply curtail the amount of information that can be perceived, in a way that will quite naturally degrade performance. Direct effects also include the effects of noise on working memory (Poulton, 1976); rehearsal of a set of instructions or coordinates, for example, will be more difficult in noise. Direct effects can also include the distraction experienced by an operator who is concerned about personal problems or danger, who may therefore redirect attention to thinking about those problems, rather than to the job at hand.

Some direct-effect stressors (e.g., noise or vibration) as well as others for which no direct effect can be observed (e.g., anxiety or fear) also influence the efficiency of information processing. In this chapter we first consider stressors that are characteristic of the physical work environment in which the tank crew operates, described in Chapter 1. We then address what is known about the effects of psychological stress on performance

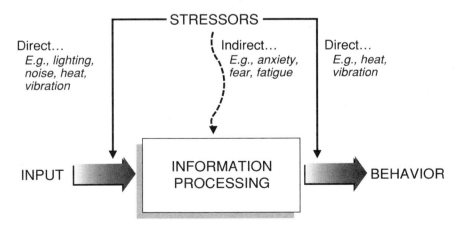

FIGURE 4.1   Influence of stress on human performance.

under conditions of high anxiety and arousal. Finally, we consider stress in the context of team performance, examining the characteristics of teams that make them more stress resistant. The discussion emphasizes to a greater extent the stress effects present in the post-transition period. In Chapter 5 we consider the most potent stressors of the pretransition period: sleep loss and fatigue and their influence on both pre- and post-transition performance.

STRESS IN THE WORK ENVIRONMENT

The term *work environment* encompasses all the variables that determine the physical comfort level of users. These include ambient temperature, relative humidity, atmospheric pressure, airflow, the presence or absence of noxious fumes or toxic substances, motion, acceleration (normally expressed as G-loading), and ambient sound and light levels. For most of these parameters there exist absolute limits within which humans can function and beyond which they cannot function or, for some variables, even survive. There are, in general, much narrower limits within which humans feel comfortable. An example of such a comfort zone is contained in the American Society of Heating, Refrigerating, and Air-Conditioning Engineers (ASHRAE) comfort standard (American Society of Heating, Refrigerating, and Air-Conditioning Engineers, 1985). The definitive military human factors standard, MIL-STD-1472C (U.S. Department of Defense, 1981), specifies such zones for several environmental variables.

The degree to which comfort enhances performance is a function of the nature of the tasks that must be completed. The differential effects of many environmental factors have been demonstrated on the performance and physical workload of various types of tasks. There are well-known relationships between certain environmental variables, such as ambient temperature and relative humidity and the ability to do physical work (Occupational Safety and Health Administration, 1974). Among the factors known to increase workload or, more accurately, to decrease performance are high levels of ambient noise (Davies and Jones, 1982), high temperature and humidity (Hancock, 1981), low temperature (Enander, 1984), and motion and vibration (International Organization for Standardization, 1978). Obviously, high levels of toxic materials in the environment can have a substantial impact on the user's ability to perform tasks.

The tank environment combines some of the most potent factors that have been shown to adversely affect performance. Even in a nonchemical/biological-warfare (non-CBW) battlefield scenario, tank crew members are subjected to elevated temperature and humidity due to the fact that tanks are not air conditioned. Heat casualties are quite common during training in field exercises. It is also common for the interior of the tank to be filled with noxious fumes from leaking hydraulic fluid and spent propellant from ordnance. When buttoned up, the interior of the tank is pressurized by an air movement system that brings outside air in through filters that remove particulate and some chemical components. This air is not conditioned for temperature or humidity. In the CBW battlefield environment, these conditions are exacerbated by the requirements of wearing environmentally protective clothing or "MOPP gear" and remaining buttoned up inside the tank for long periods of time.

Even in non-CBW environments, all crew members must wear helmets with integral earphones and a movable microphone. The purpose of these helmets is not so much to protect crew members from external ordnance as it is to protect them from head injuries caused by hitting the interior surface of the tank while it is moving over terrain. The large, fully enclosing earphones insulate the crew members from noise generated by the tank running gear. The helmet allows crew members to communicate with each other and with other tanks in their platoon. Unfortunately, the helmets are heavy and tend to trap heat. The earpieces press against the sides of the head causing discomfort after even short periods of time.

It is reasonable to infer that environmentally extreme conditions will affect some tasks more than others. Some tank crew positions are primarily physically oriented, i.e., those of loader and driver, whereas others are concerned mainly with cognitive tasks, i.e., those of gunner and tank commander. However, even those crew positions that are physically oriented have task responsibilities that require mental sharpness. Specifically, all crew members are expected to search for threats and targets. During operations of long duration, the crew is put on a sleep-wake cycle that requires all crew members to assume the responsibility of searching for enemy threats. The result of this division of responsibilities is that adverse environmental factors are likely to increase the workload of all tank crew members and, consequently, decrease the performance of the tank crew as a whole.

Long-duration operations also bring into play another environmental factor that should be noted. Tanks contain no toilet facilities. When buttoned-up, crew members are not allowed to leave the confines of the tank. The unpleasant, but inevitable result of these restrictions is that all bodily functions must be accommodated within the tank. It is probably an understatement to observe that such a situation can lead to an environment that is not conducive to superior task performance.

STRESS AND HUMAN PERFORMANCE

Many aspects of the relation between stress and performance are related to the construct of arousal. The relation between stress-induced arousal and performance has sometimes been described in terms of an inverted U-shaped function, as shown in Figure 4.2. With increasing arousal, performance

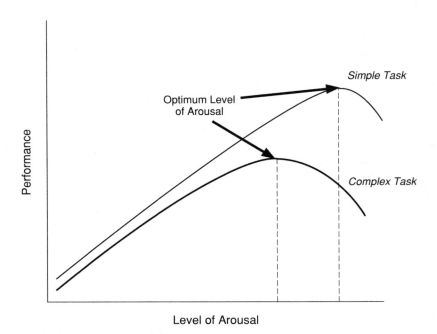

FIGURE 4.2 The Yerkes-Dodson law. The solid portion of the curve represents the arousal effects. The dashed portion represents the effects caused by attentional narrowing.

first improves, up to an optimal level, and then deteriorates when arousal is too high. Based on data originally collected in 1908, the relation is sometimes called the Yerkes-Dodson law (Yerkes and Dodson, 1908) and has served as a framework for understanding human performance under stress by more recent investigators (Broadbent, 1971; Easterbrook, 1959; Kahneman, 1973). An example of the role of stress in the inverted-U relation is provided by an experiment carried out by Simonov et al. (1977). Simonov et al. measured performance of parachute jumpers on a visual detection task, as the time of their first jump approached. As time passed and their level of stress (assessed by physiological measures) continuously increased, performance first improved and then degraded until just prior to the jump.

Elaborating on the Yerkes-Dodson law, analysis and synthesis of experimental data carried out by Easterbrook (1959) and Kahneman (1973) suggested that the upward and downward "limbs" of the inverted-U shown in the figure are the results of different factors. The upward limb appears to result from an energizing process, which simply expands the amount of cognitive effort or resources mobilized for task performance. In contrast, the downward limb is the consequence of a more specific effect of high arousal on the selectivity of attention, which causes the operator to focus on a more restricted set of environmental or internal sources of information. An appropriate metaphor is to say that high levels of stress narrow the spotlight of attention.

Extending this argument logically leads to the conclusion that high arousal should be more detrimental to tasks that require the processing of several information sources (i.e., complex tasks) than to tasks which depend on only a few cues (i.e., executing a well-practiced skill). This difference in arousal effects resulting from task complexity is depicted by the differences between the two curves in Figure 4.2. The optimum level of arousal for the simple (or the more highly practiced) task is higher than for the complex task.

A relevant example of the different effects of stress on performance as a function of complexity is an experiment carried out by Berkun (1964). Using Army soldiers engaged in simulated (but highly realistic) tasks, Berkun employed three different experimental manipulations to induce a very realistic experience of stress. In one manipulation, subjects were led to believe that the aircraft in which they were flying was in danger of crashing—as they attempted to fill out an insurance form. In a second manipulation imposed during combat exercises, subjects were led to believe that artillery shells were exploding around them as a result of a confusion about their location, as they tried to follow procedures to initiate a radio call to redirect the fire. In the third manipulation, subjects believed that a demolition that they had initiated had accidentally caused a serious injury to one of their fellow soldiers, and they were now required to call for medical assistance. Thus, in all cases, subjects were deceived to believe that they, or someone for whom they felt responsible, were at serious mortal risk. Berkun found that in all three cases, the high level of stress and arousal induced by the anxiety or perceived danger led to degraded performance on following the necessary procedures. However, this degradation was less for soldiers with greater experience. This last finding may be placed nicely into the context of Figure 4.2, if it is assumed that the more skilled soldier faces a less complex task in problem solving. Much of the perceptual and short-term memory requirements of task solution are replaced by direct recall from long-term memory. The increased arousal caused by stress then exerts a less degrading effect.

While Berkun's study clearly illustrates the loss of performance under stress, it is less illuminating regarding the qualitative manner in which performance is affected. This issue of qualitative stress effects will now be addressed in more detail.

QUALITATIVE PATTERN OF STRESS EFFECTS

Hockey (1984, 1986) expanded on the two factors (arousal and tunneling) that underlie the Yerkes-Dodson law and has attempted to identify more subtle patterns of stress effects on performance. Reviewing a large number of studies that examined the effects of stress on human performance, Hockey distilled the pattern of stress effects into the form shown in Table 4.1. Each stressor appears to be identified by a profile or signature of effects across a set of five critical information processing components: general arousal, selectivity of attention, speed and accuracy of performance, and capacity of short-term memory (working memory).

The focus in this section is on a stressor that is an important characteristic of many operational environments in the team transition situation: the anxiety, fear, or arousal associated with failures of task performance or dangerous, threatening environments (Idzikowski and Baddeley, 1983a, 1983b). This fear is often coupled with a shortage of time to deal with the crisis. (The direct effects of time pressure on performance were discussed in some detail in Chapter 3.) This stressor may characterize the experiences of the flight crew, following an engine stall in midair in which both danger and time stress are imposed; the nuclear control room personnel, following initial alerting of a failure; or the tank crew moving into combat. Idzikowski and Baddeley (1983a, 1983b) present a review of research and case study findings related to this form of stress; the reader can refer to treatments by Hamilton and Warburton (1984), Broadbent (1971), and Hockey (1986) for broader discussions of stress. In the following review of research, we also capitalize on the psychological equivalence of signature patterns between noise and anxiety as shown in the table, allowing us to extrapolate from the effects of noise to those of danger-producing anxiety. It is reasonable, also, to assume that in the noisy and dangerous environment of the tank, these two effects would be additive. In the following discussion, we use the term *stress* to refer to the combined effects of danger, anxiety, and noise. Within the framework of teams in transition addressed in this report, the transition effects involve a rapid jump from the left to the right side of the Yerkes-Dodson curve. Our focus in Chapter 5 is on the left side of the curve. Here we address performance effects on the right or high end.

Attentional Tunneling

Weltman et al. (1971) compared the performance of two groups of divers on a central and peripheral signal detection task. One group was led to believe it was under conditions of a 60 foot dive in a pressure chamber; the other was not. In fact, there was no change in pressure for either group. Both groups showed similar performance on the central task, but perfor-

TABLE 4.1 The Patterning of Stress Effects Across Different
Performance Indicators.

	Performance Indicators Speeded Responding					
	GA	SEL	S	A	STM	Sources/Reviews
Noise	+	+	0	−	−	2,3,4,5,7,8
Anxiety	+	+	0	−	−	4,12
Incentive	+	+	+	+	+	2,4,5
Stimulant drugs	+	+	+	0	−	2,4,13
Later time of day	+	?	+	−	−	1,2,4,5,6,8
Heat	+	+	0	−	0	2,4,11
Alcohol	−	+	−	−	−	2,4,7,8,13
Depressant drugs	−	−	−	−	−	2,4,10,13
Fatigue	−	+	−	−	0	2,4,9
Sleep loss	−	−	−	−	0	2,4,5,7,8
Earlier time of day	−	?	−	+	+	1,2,4,5,6,8

The table summarizes the typical outcome in various studies using these stress variables in terms of their effect on the five behavioral indicators show: GA — general alertness/activation (subjective or physiological arousal); SEL — selectivity of attention; S and A refer to overall speed and accuracy measures in speeded responding tasks; STM — short-term memory. A plus (+) indicates a general increase in this measure, a zero either no change or no consistent trend across studies, and a minus (−) a general tendency for a reduction in the level of the indicator. A question mark is used to indicate cells where there is insufficient data. Sources of data: (1) Blake (1967a, 1971); (2) Broadbent (1971); (3) Broadbent (1978); (4) Davies & Parasuraman (1982); (5) M.W. Eysenck (1982); (6) Folkard (1983); (7) Hamilton, Hockey, & Rejman (1977); (8) Hockey (1979); (9) Holding (1983); (10) Johnson and Chernik (1982); (11) Ramsey (1983); (12) Wachtel (1967, 1968); (13) Wesnes and Warburton (1983).

SOURCE: G.R.J. Hockey, "Changes in Operator Efficiency as a Function of Stress, Fatigue, and Circadian Rhythms." P. 44-39 in K.R. Boff, L. Kaufman, and J.P. Thomas (eds.), *Handbook of Perception and Human Performance*. Chichester, England: John Wiley and Sons, 1986. Reprinted by permission.

mance on the peripheral task was significantly degraded for the pressure group. This group also showed greater anxiety-related increases in heart rate, substantiating the increased level of stress. Stress may also cause a focusing of attention on one particular task or cognitive activity, as well as on a particular perceptual channel. In the analysis of cockpit voice recordings at times of high stress prior to accidents, Helmreich has found evidence of severe breakdowns in the pilots' ability to handle multiple tasks or multiple concerns.

Although perceptual or cognitive tunneling produced by stress usually degrades performance, it is also possible to envision circumstances in which this tunneling may actually facilitate performance, in which focused attention on critical task aspects is desired. Indeed, this positive effect was observed in a study by Houston (1969), who found that noise stress improved the focus of attention on the relevant aspect of a stimulus and reduced the distracting effect of irrelevant aspects.

Data provided by Houston's experiment and others suggest that the attentional or cognitive tunneling resulting from stress is defined in terms of subjective importance or priority. That is, performance of those tasks or processing of that information thought to be most important remains unaffected or perhaps is enhanced (through arousal), while processing information with lower perceived priority is filtered (Bacon, 1974; Broadbent, 1971). In one sense, this kind of tunneling is optimal, but it will produce undesirable effects if the subjective importance that defines the attended channel proves to be unwarranted. Such was the case, for example, in the incident of the Three Mile Island nuclear power plant (Rubinstein and Mason, 1979). Immediately after the crisis in the plant developed and under the high stress caused by the initial failure, the operators appeared to be fixated on a single faulty indicator, supporting an incorrect belief that the water level in the reactor was too high, thereby preventing their attention from focusing on more reliable indicators that supported the opposite (and correct) hypothesis. As suggested by this example and elaborated below, this narrowing effect can be directly related to biases in decision making. But for the operator who has a well-structured and accurate model of task demands and a well-developed skill in discriminating sources of useful (versus trivial) information, it can be expected that stress should lead to little degradation of performance, as reflected by the behavior of the United Airlines flight 232 crew (Predmore, 1991).

Working Memory Loss

Mandler (1979) has discussed the degrading effects of anxiety on working memory. Correspondingly, many of the difficulties in following procedures that Berkun (1964) observed when his Army subjects were placed under the stress of perceived danger can also be attributed to reduced working memory capacity. Logie and Baddeley (1983) and Lewis and Baddeley (1981) have noted similar working memory decrements of divers performing at depth. Idzikowski and Baddeley (1983a, 1983b) observed an anxiety-related working memory loss of speakers waiting in the wings to give their first public speech. Noise, as well as danger and anxiety, has also produced consistent effects on working memory (Hockey, 1986). While it is intuitively evident that the presence of noise would disrupt the ability to rehearse verbal information in working memory (Poulton, 1976), it appears also that the combined stress effects of noise and anxiety may disrupt spatial working memory systems as well (Stokes et al., 1990; Stokes and Raby,

1989). Indeed, in a simulation study of pilot decision making, Wickens et al. (1988) observed that the effects of noise stress were greatest on decision problems that relied on spatial visualization for their successful resolution.

Communications

Successful communications depend heavily on working memory, to remember what has just been said. Hence, it is not surprising that communications have sometimes broken down under conditions of stress. Analyses of crew communications in accidents in which a prolonged inflight emergency preceded ultimate disaster provide compelling evidence of the communication breakdowns that occur under conditions of extreme threat. These include fragmented communications, failures to process the information communicated, and inability to deal with multiple tasks or concerns (Predmore, 1991).

Long-Term Memory

While stress appears to disrupt working memory, it appears to have less of an effect on the retrieval of information from long-term memory, to the extent that information is well rehearsed and memorized. For example, in their study of pilot judgment, Wickens et al. (1988) found that those judgments requiring direct retrieval of facts from long-term memory were relatively unimpaired by stress.

The differences in Berkun's findings between more and less skilled soldiers is also consistent with this view. Stokes et al. (1990) found that the decision-making performance of novice pilots deteriorated under stress, whereas performance of a group of highly trained pilots in the same circumstances was not affected. Presumably the latter group was more able to rely on direct retrieval of information from long-term memory in making their decisions.

Similar to the narrowing effect that stress exerts on perception and selective attention, however, stress appears to restrict the information retrieved from long-term memory more specifically to those habits that are well learned or overlearned (Eysenck, 1976). Although there do not appear to be much experimental data supporting this claim, at least one study shows that increased stress actually eliminates some of the benefits of expertise and training in decision making (Ben Zur and Breznitz, 1981). Studies by Fitts and Seeger (1953) and Fuchs (1962) and analyses of aircraft accidents carried out by Allnutt (1987) have all suggested that stress will lead to a regression to earlier learned and more compatible response patterns, when these patterns may conflict with incompatible (but appropriate) ones. Collectively, these findings suggest the importance of extensive training in procedures and actions that may need to be taken in emergency. They further emphasize that such procedures should require only actions of high compatibility. The findings, however, emphasize the extent to which creative innovative problem solving may be degraded under stress since, by definition, such problem solving will not have been accomplished in the same way in the past and hence repetitive practice of the same steps cannot be achieved.

Strategic Shifts

There is some evidence from behavioral studies that stress leads to consistent shifts in processing strategy. In the study of the anxiety brought on by the first parachute jump, for example, Simonov et al. (1977) observed a shift in detection performance that can be characterized by a riskier criterion setting. The paratroopers were simply more likely to respond "yes" and hence made more hits and more false alarms. Hockey (1986) concludes that there is a general effect of noise and/or anxiety stress on the speed-accuracy tradeoff, shifting performance to a less accurate but not slower level. In their study of pilot judgment, Wickens et al. (1988) found that judgments were less accurate but not necessarily slower under the combined stress effects of noise, time pressure, and threat of loss of income.

The tendency of those under the stress of an emergency to shift performance from accurate to fast (but error prone) responding has been cited as a concern in operator response to complex failures in nuclear power control rooms. The operator often has a desire to do something rapidly, when in fact this impatience is often counterproductive until the nature of the failure is well understood. In the Three Mile Island incident the hasty action of the control room operators was to shut down an automated device that had in fact been properly doing its job.

Decision Making

Understanding the effects of stress on decision making has always been of great interest to the human factors profession. The importance of this knowledge has been enhanced by the analysis of the faulty decisions made in the Three Mile Island incident and, more recently, by concerns over the decisions made in the U.S.S. Vincennes incident (U.S. Navy, 1988; see also Chapter 8). Both of these incidents are particularly relevant to the focus of this report because of the involvement of teams of operators in making decisions following a fairly abrupt transition of system state, under a high level of stress. The concern that decisions degrade under stress is reinforced by anecdotes and case studies of poor pilot judgments that have occurred under stressful conditions of bad weather, spatial disorientation, or aircraft failure (Jensen, 1982; Nagel, 1988; Simmel et al., 1987). However, caution must be exercised in forming firm conclusions on the basis of post hoc accident analysis for, without tight experimental control, it is often difficult to know if a real-world decision that failed was in fact a poor one in foresight as well as in hindsight. Furthermore, it is often difficult to tell whether stress was itself a causal factor in the poor decision or whether the conditions that produced the stress were also those that, for example, degraded the information available in such a way that the poorer decision became more likely.

To predict the effects of stress on decision making, one approach is to adopt a componential approach (Wickens and Flach, 1988). Since different decisions may involve varying dependence on such components as working memory, attention, and long-term memory retrieval, each decision may be affected differently by stress as a function of the components on which it depends and of the differential effects of stress on those components as described in the previous pages (Wickens et al., 1988).

An alternative approach is to examine the results of experiments that impose stress on decision making, diagnosis, and problem-solving tasks. While few such studies exist, their results are consistent with the picture of a stress-sensitive decision-making process. Such studies have not only shown that decisions of various sorts degrade under stress but have also concluded that this degradation takes specific forms. Thus, for example, Cowen (1952) found that subjects perseverated longer with inappropriate or rigid problem solutions under the stress produced by threat of shock, a sort of action tunneling that is consistent with the idea of attentional tunneling. Keinan et al. (1987) found that the allocation of attention to a word problem became increasingly nonoptimal and unsystematic as stress was imposed by the threat of an electrical shock. The investigators also observed that this stressor produced a premature closure: subjects terminated their decision before all alternatives had been considered. Ben Zur and Breznitz (1981) found that stress, while leading to some filtering of information, also led subjects to give more weight to negative task dimensions and, as a consequence, make less risky decisions.

Driskell and Salas (1991) observed that stress actually increased the receptivity of members of a dyad to judgments provided by the other member in reaching a problem solution. They imposed stress on U.S. Navy personnel who believed they were one component of a cooperative decision-making dyad. In fact, unknown to the subjects, the other component of the dyad was always the same source of computer-generated information for all subjects. The investigators were interested in the extent to which perceived stress influenced the receptivity to information received from a team member when that member was perceived to be either above or below them in the military chain of command. Not surprisingly, greater receptivity to information was shown when the member was perceived of higher rank. But whether the rank was higher or lower, both groups were more willing to accept the information under the conditions of perceived stress.

As we have discussed above, Wickens et al. (1988) observed that the combined stress of noise, time pressure, risk, and task loading produced a general degradation of pilot judgments on a computer-based flight simulation. The stress effect, however, was selectively observed only on decision problems that were difficult in terms of their spatial memory demand. As noted before, their data indicated that decisions did not degrade under stress when long-term memory retrieval was the primary mechanism. These conclusions are related to those drawn by Klein (1989), who argues that expert firefighters use direct long-term memory retrieval to make their decisions. Given this characteristic, experts making decisions about familiar courses of action should be less likely to suffer degrading effects of stress.

The conclusion drawn by Klein, however, is partially contradicted by a study carried out by Koehler and McKinney (1991), who evaluated the decision-making performance of Air Force pilots in 195 aircraft malfunction mishaps. Their analysis of decision quality revealed that experts (long-time pilots) did not necessarily perform better than relatively new pilots under the high-stress conditions of an inflight malfunction. Although this conclusion must be tempered by the fact that experts were more often flying a lead aircraft in formation, thereby adding to their attention demands, a second finding is consistent with the picture presented here. That is, expert performance was particularly disrupted when the malfunctions were novel and unique, more so than the performance of the novices. This is consistent with the view that experts had available well-learned solutions in long-term memory for the routine problems that were not available for the unique ones. The novices had fewer such solutions available for either problem type, and the loss in their performance from routine to unique would therefore be less.

Attention and Arousal

As indicated by the Yerkes-Dodson law depicted in Figure 4.2, a stressor can sometimes have a facilitating effect on performance if that stressor moves the operator closer to the optimal level of arousal. There are, indeed, studies that have shown improved performance at higher stress levels. For example, Kennedy and Coulter (1975) found that performance on a vigilance monitoring task was improved by the threat of a shock. Hockey (1970) found that noise stress improved performance on a tracking task presented centrally although, consistent with perceptual tunneling effects, the same stressor disrupted peripheral monitoring performance. Lazarus and Ericksen (1952) observed that the threat of failure improved performance on a cognitive test for those subjects of higher ability, although it degraded performance for those of lower ability. This interaction is interpretable in the framework of the Yerkes-Dodson law, if it is assumed that the task was of greater complexity for the low-ability subjects, and they were therefore presumably already operating above their optimal level of arousal in the absence of the threat, while the higher-ability subjects, for whom the task was less complex, were below their optimal level.

Conclusion

What emerges from this literature are a series of somewhat tentative conclusions that must be offered without an extensive empirical data base. In particular, most of the experimental studies have used fairly generic laboratory tasks, therefore avoiding the examination of skilled operators, experiencing stress in a domain in which they are experts. Hence the extent to which stress may produce failures of processes in memory and attention in such skilled operators cannot be asserted with confidence. Furthermore, given the qualitative differences in expert versus novice performance on routine tasks, it may well be that the documented stress effects on attention and working memory would not influence expert performance to the extent that those processes are not involved in the expert's performance of routine tasks (Stokes et al., 1990). The negative effects of stress on experts performing nonroutine tasks within their domain still awaits empirical validation, because it is clear that case studies provide contradictory information (Koehler and McKinney, 1991).

MEDIATING EFFECTS

The effects of a given stressor on performance may be mediated by at least two other factors: additional stressors that may be present and individual differences in personality. With regard to the first of these mediating influences, the effects of combinations of stressors is often complex (Broadbent, 1971). Thus, it is not possible to say that the effect of two stressors in combination is the sum of their individual effects nor even necessarily that it is greater than that sum (a positive interaction). Sometimes the effects of one stressor may compensate for another's degrading effects. Fortunately, however, these interactive effects may sometimes be understood in the context of the inverted-U function (Broadbent, 1971). For example, although both sleep loss and noise will typically degrade performance, their effect in combination is generally less than either effect alone (Wilkinson, 1963). This effect makes sense when it is realized that each is pulling arousal in a different direction on the function depicted in Figure 4.2, and the net effect is to maintain arousal nearer the peak.

Individual differences between operator personality types describe a second mediating effect. These are complex, not well understood, and their full treatment is beyond the scope of this chapter. Locus of control describes the extent to which individuals believe that they, rather than other forces, have control over the things that influence their lives. These two beliefs describe an internal versus external locus of control, respectively. There is some evidence that those with an internal locus of control are less stressed by anxiety-provoking situations, because of their belief that they can exert some control over the situation. The distinction between introverted and extroverted personality types has also been found to mediate the effects of stressors. In general, extroverts are more affected by all stressors, although more specific patterns of difference between the two personality types, the time of day (am versus pm), and stimulants that increase or decrease the level of arousal have also been reported (Hockey, 1986). A description of these effects is beyond the scope of this chapter.

Closely related is the idea of cognitive appraisal (Coyne and Lazarus, 1980). Two individuals could be placed in identical situations of danger. The one who correctly appraises the personal danger of the situation will be more likely to realize stress effects on performance. Stress effects here will also be mediated by differences in the extent to which individuals believe they can cope with the stress-inducing events.

COPING WITH STRESS

There are a variety of different techniques that may be adopted in the effort to minimize the degrading effects of stress on human performance. Roughly these may be categorized into design solutions that address the task and personal solutions that address the operator (either through strategies or training) or the characteristics of the whole team.

Design Solutions

Design solutions may focus on good human factors of displays. If perceptual narrowing among information sources or unsystematic scanning does take place, then reducing the amount of unnecessary information (visual clutter) and increasing its organization will surely buffer the degrading effects of stress. For example, Zhang and Wickens (1990) found that integrating the separate displays of information into a single object display reduced the degrading effects of noise on performance in a multitask environment. Schwartz and Howell (1985) observed that graphical rather than numerical data display could reduce the derogating effects of time pressure on a command-and-control task.

Whitaker and Klein (1990) have identified five principles for designing stress-resistant displays: metaphors (use of the familiar), streamlining (eliminating nonessential elements), functional prototypes (display information directly necessary for action), foregrounding or highlighting, and fusion or display integration. Similarly, it is clear that any design efforts that minimize the need for operators to maintain or transform information in working memory should be effective. Emergency procedures, which must be referred to on-line, must be clear and simply phrased as they will undoubtedly need to be followed under the very circumstances that make working memory for their contents extremely fragile.

It is desirable also that procedural instructions of what to do are redundantly coded with speech as well as print, should avoid arbitrary symbolic coding (abbreviations or tones other than general alerting alarms), and should be phrased in direct statements of what action to take, not as statements of what *not* to do (avoid negatives) or statements that only describe the current state of the system. This is the policy inherent in voice alerts for aircraft in times of emergencies, in which commands are directed to the pilot of what to do to avoid collision (e.g., "pull up") (Chappel, 1989). Also, whenever possible, the number of steps that need to be taken in following emergency procedures should be minimized. Adhering to fundamental principles of design compatibility in all of its forms (Wickens, 1992) is certainly one of the best techniques for minimizing the damaging effects of stress on performance.

Strategies

There are strategies that can be adopted by the operator to minimize the degrading effects of stress. Certainly one of the most effective of these is planning, anticipating, and rehearsing actions to be taken under stress— either expected actions or those required by emergencies. While advance planning requires working memory capacity at the time it is being done, such planning can compensate for the fact that fewer resources will be available under stressful conditions. Furthermore, research has shown that, if individuals can predict, understand, and have knowledge of and a sense of control over the stressor, then they are more likely to develop successful coping strategies (Bourne, 1971).

Training

A number of investigators have reported that well-learned responses appear less subject to interference from extraneous environmental conditions (Krueger, 1989; Kubala and Warnick, 1979; Webb and Levy, 1984; Williams and Williams, 1966). Zajonc (1965) suggested that increased stress leads to the increased probability of selecting the dominant response with a consequent decrease in the probability of selecting other responses. Thus, under conditions in which the best learned (dominant) response is the most appropriate, stress may lead to enhanced performance.

In addition to training for automaticity, there is also a family of training approaches aimed at reducing stress reactions. Relaxation training (Wolpe, 1958) and biofeedback techniques (DeWitt, 1980; Lawrence and Johnson, 1977) are both designed to reduce stress levels. Another important approach is cognitive training. Cognitive training or cognitive restructuring refers to a wide variety of techniques that help individuals modify their thoughts and perceptions of stress (DeWitt, 1980; Ellis, 1974; Lazarus, 1968). For example, in one study DeWitt (1980) combined cognitive and biofeedback training for football and basketball players. Subjects improved significantly in pre- and post-treatment performance ratings and reported greater comfort and confidence.

In a review of relaxation training, biofeedback techniques, and cognitive restructuring, Druckman and Swets (1988:123) concluded that "there is no evidence to indicate that biofeedback training has any effect on stress or on performance under conditions of stress." They found cognitive restructuring and the simple provision of realistic information to be most useful in reducing stress. These stress management procedures focus on the reduction of uncertainty and the increase in control that follows from this reduction. At the same time, others warn that stress reduction is not necessarily beneficial to performance. A soldier's stress may be seen as legitimate and valuable; reducing it to very low levels may reduce combat performance.

Earlier in this chapter the beneficial effects of training were discussed—in particular, extensive training of key emergency procedures so that these will become the dominant and easily retrieved habits from long-term memory, when stress imposes that bias. In fact, a case can possibly be made that training for emergency procedures should be given greater priority than training for routine operations. This emphasis should be particularly realized whenever emergency procedures (or those to be followed in high-stress situations) are in some way inconsistent with those followed in normal operations. For example, under normal operations, Step A precedes Step B, but under an emergency the two steps are to be reversed in sequence. Clearly, as a design solution, systems should be designed so that procedures followed under an emergency are as consistent as possible with those followed under normal operations, and the perceptual cues for any changes are prominent and easily visible.

It is also true that successful experience in a stressful situation can greatly reduce the anticipated anxiety of repeated performance. For example, Ursin et al. (1978) assessed physiological measures of stress prior to the first and second parachute jump made by a group of paratroop trainees. The investigators observed a large drop in those measures between the two jumps, signaling the relief, as it were, that successful performance was possible. In this regard, it is not surprising that, in a wide variety of contexts, research findings demonstrate the efficacy of prestress training, geared at providing preparatory information in order to reduce the novelty of the stressful situation. Novelty, as Rose (1987) and others have indicated, is a primary component of the intensity of the stress response: the greater the novelty, the greater the intensity of the stress experienced in many settings. Thus, training should be a crucial component of any program to enable tank crews to manage stressful environments.

Finally, there appears to be considerable merit in training that makes crews aware of the potentially degrading effects of stress. Survey data collected from civilian and military flight crews using the Cockpit Management Attitudes Questionnaire (CMAQ) contain items aimed at determining attitudes regarding personal awareness of the effects of external stressors on human performance. In particular, a Recognition of Stressor Effects subscale of the CMAQ measures perceptions of personal capabilities when faced with stressful conditions and the ability to put aside stresses caused by personal problems when faced with the need to perform at high efficiency. One of the striking findings from the survey data is how little awareness flight crews have of the deleterious effects of stress on individual and group performance (Helmreich, 1984). The model pilot tends to endorse a position reflecting an ability to leave behind personal problems and a perception that personal performance is unaffected by life-threatening, emergency conditions. Such attitudes represent the classic model of the "white scarf" aviator.

TEAM MODELS: IMPLICATIONS FOR STRESS MANAGEMENT

The bulk of the research on stress addresses individual-level responses (physiological, psychological, and behavioral) often in laboratory settings removed from the more complex contexts in which multiple stressors usually occur. Prevention and intervention programs are also often addressed as individual-level strategies for reducing negative stress-related consequences (e.g., therapy, exercise, training programs). Fewer studies examine the group and organizational level structures and processes that might be modified in order to diminish the problems created for individuals enduring a high level of stress in the workplace. A simple example is the case with air traffic controllers. Studies typically focus on the effects of the stress of their jobs on their own responses, physiological and psychological (as well as on their families). As Matteson (1987) suggests, stress may often be relieved, not by training particular individuals in how to cope with stress, but by altering the conditions that create the negative stress responses. Human and organizational resources can be used, for example, to hire more controllers to handle peak times and high volumes of traffic. Kahn (1987) concludes a recent review of stress research indicating optimism about the potential for organizational-level interventions.

While research findings concerning the responses of individuals in various occupations to stressful situations or encounters are important, perhaps even more useful for the investigation of teams in transitions, such as tank crew operations in stressful environments, are the studies of teams and team-building strategies. Numerof (1987) and Salas and coworkers (Baker and Salas, 1992; Driskell and Salas, 1992; Tannenbaum et al., 1992) provide models of team characteristics that may be relevant to teams in a workload transition. Teams are defined by Numerof as groups that have a high level of energy directed toward accomplishing a goal, usually in settings in which the tasks to be performed require multiple inputs and cannot be handled by any individual alone, which is generally true of tank crews during periods of engagement. Effective teams are referred to as groups that have a combination of high loyalty, morale, commitment, adaptability, and exchange and coordinate information. These good team qualities, which may provide a buffer against organizational stress, include: effective leadership, appropriate selection of members, commitment and cohesion, open climate, achievement motivation, effective work methods, clarity of procedures, giving and acceptance of constructive criticism, individual initiative, high creativity, positive intergroup relations, and role clarity.

These characteristics are briefly described below, based on Numerof's (1987) review. Various studies support the significance of the individual components of the model, but what remains to be specified is the relative impact of each component on team performance and the optimal mix. Effective leadership is viewed as one of the most important components, given the wealth of research on this factor (see Chapter 10). What appears to be critical is the ability of the leader to change leadership style based on the requirements of the situation and to integrate the needs and individual abilities of the team members to meet the demands of the task situation. We will expand on our discussion of this factor subsequently, given its significance for team performance.

Appropriate selection of members refers to the extent to which the individuals are well matched as a team to the task requirements. This includes the match between each individual and the job requirements, or what is referred to above as the job-person fit. This issue is discussed in greater detail in Chapter 10 in the context of airline crews, on which there has been a great deal of research involving the task and social skills required to maximize crew performance in the cockpit—in particular, to optimize crew performance and decision-making skills under the high stress produced by emergency situations.

Commitment and group cohesion are referred to frequently in the literature on group productivity and effective teams. The usual assumption is that high levels of cohesion and commitment enhance group productivity. While this is generally true (see review by Ridgeway, 1983), high cohesion may also result in lower group productivity if the performance norms of the group run counter to those of the overall organization (e.g., the normative pressures in some work groups that limit work output or the rate of production). Furthermore, highly cohesive groups may also be subject to the problem identified by Janis (1972) as groupthink, situations in which group members who offer information or criticisms that deviate from the more popular decision in the group are ignored. According to Ridgeway (1983), this high level of cohesiveness may cause groups to make poorer decisions than they otherwise might. And yet highly cohesive groups often have more trust in each other and coordinate their behavior more. It has been found (Kelley et al., 1965) that outside stress makes it harder for members to trust one another and coordinate their behavior together, which greatly increases the social difficulty of the group's task, although some evidence provided by Driskell and Salas (1991) suggests that this may not invariably be true. Therefore, more cohesive groups whose members have good interpersonal relationships should perform better under high stress conditions (Shils and Janowitz, 1948).

Many of the remaining team components are self-evident; thus, only those that are less so are discussed. An open climate is critical because it represents a team that has open direct communication and trust. In such groups members often feel at ease in taking what they consider appropriate risks, which in turn enhances opportunities for innovation and creativity.

Achievement motivation refers to the extent to which team members are motivated toward performance goals and are willing to use feedback mechanisms to improve performance over time. Individual initiative is also an important component in effective teams since members are encouraged to emphasize their own unique contributions and to raise constructive questions concerning procedures or suggestions and actions of other group members. Risk-taking is also encouraged, as is creativity. These factors may be less important during routine activity for tank crews, but they may be crucial during the transition phase and periods of high stress.

The significance of cohesion, described above, arises in the context of team-building activities since teams may become isolated and more oriented to the enhancement of group performance, at the expense of other teams or units. For tank crew teams this is essential because of the interunit communication and coordination required for successful maneuvers. Positive intergroup relations and corporate role clarity are critical for this reason. The former refers to the nature of the working relations with other teams or units, the latter to a clear picture of the way in which each team fits into a larger whole. Training could enhance both of these factors through simulation exercises and team-building strategies that increase cohesion without increasing intergroup competition. Often intergroup competition is used to enhance group cohesion, which would be counterproductive for the situation in which intergroup cooperation is required, as in the transition phase and during subsequent maneuvers.

However, to the extent that team building is useful to improve performance, raise levels of trust and commitment, and reduce stress that results from external factors as well as internal factors such as poor integration, lack of goal clarity, low levels of participation, and commitment, then strong leadership is required to counteract the stress created by a more open climate involving more feedback and open management of conflict. Thus, we return to the importance of leadership.

Good team qualities provide a buffer against stress, organizational as well as environmental. Trust, participation in decision making relevant to the work being performed, excellent communications, and a commitment to collaboration have all been identified as conducive to effective team-building processes (Numerof, 1987; Tannenbaum et al., 1992). Organizational resistance to effective team building comes from two sources, perceived threat and resistance to change. While some of these characteristics are not particularly relevant to the tank crew environment, other features are of central importance given that tank crews fit the above definition of a team (i.e., a group that requires coordination and cooperation to produce an outcome that no individual alone can produce).

Various organizational effects resulting from the failure to implement good team-building strategies for both group and organizational-level outcomes have also been identified (Numerof, 1987). For example, suboptimization occurs when organizational objectives are not clearly communicated. Individuals may perform their own functions appropriately, but coordination is lacking. Organizational objectives may not be clearly defined or may change often and thus result in greater stress and uncertainty. If there is low commitment to the group and/or the organization and low cohesion, stress in the group will be high and team performance will be impaired. In organizations in which work is characterized by high levels of interdependence, frequent problem-solving efforts, and high demands for accuracy and/or timeliness, team building is very important (Numerof, 1987). For tank crews and, similarly, air crews, this model has implications for selection, recruitment, training, and the organization of roles and work assignments. In addition to environmental buffers (e.g., alterations in the actual tank environment), team-building efforts can be employed to minimize communication problems and the stress-related inefficiencies in decision-making and problem-solving tasks, described in later chapters.

SUMMARY

It is clear that considerably less is known about stress effects, and the appropriate techniques for their remediation, than about many other aspects of performance. This shortcoming results in part because of the great difficulty in conducting research in the area—i.e., imposing realistic, credible stressors in a controlled setting in a way that is also consistent with the ethics of research. Still, enough data are available from incident reports, from the research described above, and from the extensive reviews provided by Broadbent (1971) and Hockey (1986) to construct a reasonably coherent picture of those effects and suggest some possible remediations, as we have done.

REFERENCES

Allnutt, M.F.
  1987   Human factors in accidents. *British Journal of Anaesthesia* 59:856-864.
American Society of Heating, Refrigerating, and Air-Conditioning Engineers
  1985   *American Society of Heating, Refrigerating, and Air-Conditioning Engineers Handbook: Fundamentals.* New York: ASHRAE.
Bacon, S.J.
  1974   Arousal and the range of cue utilization. *Journal of Experimental Psychology* 102:81-87.
Baker, D.P., and E. Salas
  1992   Principles for measuring teamwork skills. *Human Factors* 34(4):469-475.
Ben Zur, H., and S.J. Breznitz
  1981   The effect of time pressure on risky choice behavior. *Acta Psychologica* 47:89-104.
Berkun, M.M.
  1964   Performance decrement under psychological stress. *Human Factors* 6:21.
Blake, M.J.F.
  1967   Time of day effects in performance on a range of tasks. *Psychonomic Science* 9:349-350.
  1971   Temperament and time of day. In W.P. Colquhoun, ed., *Biological Rhythms and Human Behavior.* London: Academic Press.
Bourne, P.G.
  1971   Altered adrenal function in two combat situations in Vietnam. In B.E. Elefherion and J.P. Scott, eds., *The Physiology of Aggression and Defeat.* New York: Plenum.
Broadbent, D.E.
  1971   *Decision and Stress.* New York: Academic Press.
  1978   The current state of noise research: Reply to Poulton. *Psychological Bulletin* 85:1052-1067.
Burton, R.R., W.F. Storm, L.W. Johnson, and S.D. Leverett, Jr.
  1977   Stress responses of pilots flying high-performance aircraft during aerial combat maneuvers. *Aviation Space and Environmental Medicine* 48(4):301-307.
Chappel, S.
  1989   Avoiding a maneuvering aircraft with TCAS. In R. Jensen, ed., *Proceedings of*

the Fifth International Symposium on Aviation Psychology. Columbus, Ohio: Ohio State University.

Cowen, E.L.
1952   The influence of varying degrees of psychosocial stress on problem-solving rigidity. Journal of Abnormal and Social Psychology 47:512-519.

Coyne, J.C., and R.S. Lazarus
1980   Cognitive style, stress perception, and coping. Pp. 144-158 in I.L. Kutash, L.B. Schlesinger, and associates, eds., Handbook on Stress and Anxiety. San Francisco, California: Josey-Bass.

Davies, D., and D. Jones
1982   Hearing and noise. In W. Singleton, ed., The Body at Work. New York: Cambridge University Press.

Davies, D.R., and R. Parasuraman
1982   The Psychology of Vigilance. London: Academic Press.

DeWitt, D.J.
1980   Cognitive and biofeedback training for stress reduction with university athletes. Journal of Sport Psychology 2:288-294.

Driskell, J.E., and E. Salas
1991   Group decision making under stress. Journal of Applied Psychology 76(3):473-478.
1992   Collective behavior and team performance. Human Factors 34(3):277-288.

Druckman, D., and J.A. Swets, eds.
1988   Enhancing Human Performance. Washington, DC: National Academy Press.

Easterbrook, J.A.
1959   The effect of emotion on cue utilization and the organization of behavior. Psychological Review 66:183-201.

Ellis, A.
1974   Humanistic Psychotherapy: The Rational Emotive Approach. New York: McGraw-Hill.

Enander, A.
1984   Performance and sensory aspects of work in cold conditions: A review. Ergonomics 27(4):365-378.

Eysenck, M.W.
1976   Arousal, learning, and memory. Psychological Bulletin 83:389-404.
1982   Attention and Arousal: Cognition and Performance. Berlin: Springer-Verlag.

Fitts, P.M., and C.M. Seeger
1953   S-R compatibility: Spatial characteristics of stimulus and response codes. Journal of Experimental Psychology 46:199-210.

Folkard, S.
1983   Diurnal variation. In G.R.J. Hockey, ed., Stress and Fatigue in Human Performance. Chichester, England: Wiley.

Fuchs, A.
1962   The progressive-regressive hypothesis in perceptual-motor skill learning. Journal of Experimental Psychology 63:177-181.

Hamilton, P., G.R.J. Hockey, and M. Rejman
1977   The place of the concept of activation in human information processing theory: An integrative approach. In S. Dornic, ed., Attention and Performance, Volume 6. New York: Academic Press.

Hamilton, V., and D.M. Warburton, eds.
1984   Human Stress and Cognition: An Information Processing Approach. Chichester: Wiley.

Hancock, P.A.
    1981   The limitation of human performance in extreme heat conditions. Pp. 74 in *Proceedings of the Human Factors Society 25th Annual Meeting*. Santa Monica, California: The Human Factors Society.

Hart, S.G., and J.R. Hauser
    1987   Inflight application of three pilot workload measurement techniques. *Aviation Space, and Environmental Medicine* 58(5):402-410.

Helmreich, R.
    1984   Cockpit management attitudes. *Human Factors* 26:583-589.

Hockey, G.R.J.
    1970   Effect of loud noise on attentional selectivity. *Quarterly Journal of Experimental Psychology* 22:28-36.
    1979   Stress and the cognitive components of skilled performance. In V. Hamilton and D.M. Warburton, eds., *Human Stress and Cognition: An Information Processing Approach*. Chichester, England: Wiley.
    1984   Varieties of attentional state: The effect of the environment. In R.S. Parasuraman and D.R. Davies, eds., *Varieties of Attention*. Orlando, Florida: Academic Press.
    1986   Changes in operator efficiency as a function of environmental stress, fatigue, and circadian rhythms. Pp. 41.1-41.49 in K. Boff, L. Kaufman, and J.P. Thomas, eds., *Handbook of Perception and Human Performance*. New York: Wiley and Sons.

Holding, D.H.
    1983   Fatigue. In G.R.J. Hockey, ed., *Stress and Fatigue in Human Performance*. Chichester, England: Wiley.

Houston, B.K.
    1969   Noise, task difficulty, and Stroop color-word performance. *Journal of Experimental Psychology* 82:403-404.

Idzikowski, C., and A.D. Baddeley
    1983a   Fear and dangerous environments. In G.R.J. Hockey, ed., *Stress and Fatigue in Human Performance*. London: Wiley.
    1983b   Waiting in the wings: Apprehension, public speaking, and performance. *Ergonomics* 26:575-583.

International Organization for Standardization
    1978   *Guide for the Evaluation of Human Exposure to Whole-Body Vibration*. ISO-2631.

Janis, I.L.
    1972   *Victims of Groupthink*. New York: Harcourt, Brace.

Jensen, R.S.
    1982   Pilot judgment: Training and evaluation. *Human Factors* 24:61-74.

Johnson, L.C., and D.A. Chernik
    1982   Sedative-hypnotics and human performance. *Psychopharmacology* 76:101-113.

Kahn, R.L.
    1987   Work stress in the 1980s: Research and practice. Pp. 311-320 in J.C. Quick, R.S. Bhagat, J.E. Dalton, and J.D. Quick, eds., *Work Stress: Health Care Systems in the Workplace*. New York: Praeger.

Kahneman, D.
    1973   *Attention and Effort*. Englewood Cliffs, New Jersey: Prentice-Hall.

Keegan, J.
    1976   *In the Face of Battle*. New York: Penguin Books.

Keinan, G., N. Friedlan, and Y. Benporat
    1987   Decision making under stress: Scanning of alternatives under physical threat. *Acta Psychologica* 64:219-228.

Kelley, H.H., J.C. Condry, Jr., A.E. Dalke, and A.H. Hill
    1965   Collective behavior in a simulated panic situation. *Journal of Experimental Social Psychology* 1:20-54.
Kennedy, R.S., and X.B. Coulter
    1975   Research note: The interactions among stress, vigilance, and task complexity. *Human Factors* 17:106-109.
Klein, G.A.
    1989   Recognition-primed decisions. Pp. 47-92 in W. Rouse, ed., *Advances in Man-Machine Systems Research, Volume 5.* Greenwich, Connecticut: JAI Press.
Koehler, J.J., and E.H. McKinney
    1991   *Uniqueness of Task, Experience, and Decision Making Performance: A Study of 176 U.S. Air Force Mishaps.*
Krueger, G.P.
    1989   Sustained work, fatigue, sleep loss, and performance: A review of the issues. *Work and Stress* 3:129-141.
Kubala, A.L., and W.L. Warnick
    1979   *A Review of Selected Literature on Stresses Affecting Soldiers in Combat.* Alexandria, Virginia: Human Resources Research Organization.
Lawrence, G.H.
    1984   *Biofeedback and Performance: An Update.* Technical Report No. 658. Alexandria, Virginia: U.S. Army Research Institute for the Behavioral and Social Sciences.
Lawrence, G.H., and L.C. Johnson
    1977   Biofeedback and performance. Pp. 163-179 in G. Schwartz and J. Beatty, eds., *Biofeedback Theory and Research.* New York: Academic Press.
Lazarus, R.S.
    1968   Emotions and adaptation: Conceptual and empirical relations. Pp. 175-270 in W.J. Arnold, ed., *Nebraska Symposium on Motivation, Volume 16.* Lincoln, Nebraska: University of Nebraska Press.
Lazarus, R.S., and C.W. Ericksen
    1952   Effects of failure stress on skilled performance. *Journal of Experimental Psychology* 43:100-105.
Lewis, V.J., and A.D. Baddeley
    1981   Cognitive performance, sleep quality, and mood during deep oxyhelium diving. *Ergonomics* 24:773-793.
Logie, R.H., and A.D. Baddeley
    1983   A trimex saturation dive to 660 m: Studies of cognitive performance, mood, and sleep quality. *Ergonomics* 26:359-374.
Mandler, G.
    1979   Thought processes, consciousness, and stress. In V. Hamilton and D.M. Warburton, eds., *Human Stress and Cognition: An Information Processing Approach.* Chichester, England: Wiley and Sons.
Matteson, M.T.
    1987   Individual-organizational relationships: Implications for preventing job stress and burnout. Pp. 156-170 in J.C. Quick, R.S. Bhagat, J.E. Dalton, and J.D. Quick, eds., *Work Stress: Health Care Systems in the Workplace.* New York: Praeger.
Nagel, D.C.
    1988   Human error in aviation operations. Pp. 263-303 in E. Wiener and D. Nagel, eds., *Human Factors in Aviation.* New York: Academic Press.
National Research Council
    1983   *Video Displays, Work, and Vision.* Panel on Impact of Video Viewing on Vision of Workers, Committee on Vision. Washington, DC: National Academy Press.

Numerof, R.E.
    1987   Team-building interventions: An organizational stress moderator. Pp. 171-194 in
            J.C. Quick, R.S. Bhagat, J.E. Dalton, and J.D. Quick, eds., *Work Stress: Health
            Care Systems in the Workplace.* New York: Praeger.
Occupational Safety and Health Administration (OSHA)
    1974   Recommendation for a Standard for Work in Hot Environments (Draft #5). Avail-
            able from the U.S. Government Printing Office, Washington, DC.
Poulton, E.C.
    1976   *Tracking Skill and Manual Control.* New York: Academic Press.
Predmore, S.C.
    1991   Micro-coding of cockpit communications in accident analyses: Crew coordination
            in the United Airlines flight 232 accident. In R.S. Jensen, ed., *Proceedings of the
            Sixth International Symposium on Aviation Psychology.* Columbus, Ohio: Ohio
            State University, Department of Aviation.
Ramsey, J.D.
    1983   Heat and cold. In G.R.J. Hockey, ed., *Stress and Fatigue in Human Performance.*
            Chichester, England: Wiley.
Ridgeway, C.L.
    1983   *The Dynamics of Small Groups.* New York: St. Martin's Press.
Romhert, W.
    1979   Determination of stress and strain at real work places: Methods and results of
            field studies with air traffic control offices. In N. Moray, ed., *Mental Workload.*
            New York: Plenum Press.
Rose, R.M.
    1987   Neuroendocrine effects of work stress. Pp. 130-147 in J.C. Quick, R.S. Bhagat,
            J.E. Dalton, and J.D. Quick, eds., *Work Stress: Health Care Systems in the Work-
            place.* New York: Praeger.
Rubinstein, T., and A.F. Mason
    1979   The accident that shouldn't have happened: An analysis of Three Mile Island.
            IEEE Spectrum 16:33-57.
Schwartz, D.R., and W.C. Howell
    1985   Optional stopping performance under graphic and numeric CRT formatting. *Hu-
            man Factors* 27:433-444.
Shils, E., and M. Janowitz
    1948   Cohesion and disintegration in the Wehrmacht in World War II. Public Opinion
            Quarterly 12:280-315, and Related Concepts: A Bibliography. Project No. 172-
            288, Contr. Nonr 996(02). New London, Connecticut.
Simmel, E.C., M. Cerkovnik, and J.E. McCarthy
    1987   Sources of stress affecting pilot judgment. Pp. 190-194 in *Proceedings of the
            Fourth International Symposium on Aviation Psychology.* Columbus, Ohio: Ohio
            State University, Department of Aviation.
Simonov, P.V., M.V. Frolov, V.F. Evtushenko, and E.P. Suiridov
    1977   *Aviation, Space, and Environmental Medicine* 48:856-858.
Stokes, A.F., and M. Raby
    1989   Stress and cognitive performance in trainee pilots. *Proceedings of the Human
            Factors Society 33rd Annual Meeting.* Santa Monica, California: Human Factors
            Society.
Stokes, A.F., A. Belger, and K. Zhang
    1990   *Investigation of Factors Comprising a Model of Pilot Decision Making, Part 2:
            Anxiety and Cognitive Strategies in Expert and Novice Aviators.* Report No. ARL-
            90-9/SCEEE-90-2. Savoy, Illinois: University of Illinois, Aviation Research Laboratory.

Tannenbaum, S.I., R.L. Beard, and E. Salas
    1992   Team building and its influence on team effectiveness: An examination of conceptual and empirical developments. Pp. 117-134 in K. Kelley, ed., *Issues, Theory, and Research in Industrial/Organizational Psychology.* Amsterdam: Elsevier Science Publishers.

U.S. Navy
    1988   *Investigation Report: Formal Investigation into the Circumstances Surrounding the Downing of Iran Air Flight 655 on 3 July 1988.* Washington, DC: Department of Defense Investigation Report.

Ursin, H., E. Badde, and S. Levine, eds.
    1978   *Psychobiology of Stress: A Study of Coping Men.* New York: Academic Press.

U.S. Department of Defense
    1981   *Human Engineering Design Criteria for Military Systems, Equipment, and Facilities.* MIL-STD-1472C. Washington, DC: U.S. Government Printing Office.

Wachtel, P.L.
    1967   Conceptions of broad and narrow attention. *Psychological Bulletin* 68:417-429.
    1968   Anxiety, attention, and coping with threat. *Journal of Abnormal Psychology* 73:137-143.

Webb, W.B., and C.M. Levy
    1984   Effects of spaced and repeated total sleep deprivation. *Ergonomics* 27:45-48.

Weltman, G., J.E. Smith, and G.H. Egstrom
    1971   Perceptual narrowing during simulated pressure-chamber exposure. *Human Factors* 13(2):99-107.

Wesnes, K., and D.M. Warburton
    1983   Stress and drugs. In G.R.J. Hockey, ed., *Stress and Fatigue in Human Performance.* Chichester, England: Wiley.

Whitaker, L.A., and G.A. Klein
    1990   Stress resistant displays. Pp. 335-339 in *Proceedings of the Eleventh Symposium: Psychology in the Department of Defense.* Colorado Springs, Colorado: U.S. Air Force Academy.

Wickens, C.D.
    1991   Processing resources and attention. In D. Damos, ed., *Multiple Task Performance.* London, England: Taylor and Francis.
    1992   *Engineering Psychology and Human Performance.* New York: Harper Collins.

Wickens, C.D., and J. Flach
    1988   Human information processing. Pp. 111-155 in E. Wiener and D. Nagel, eds., *Human Factors in Aviation.* New York: Academic Press.

Wickens, C.D., A.F. Stokes, B. Barnett, and F. Hyman
    1988   Stress and pilot judgment: An empirical study using MIDIS, a microcomputer-based simulation. *Proceedings of the Human Factors Society 32nd Annual Meeting.* Santa Monica, California: Human Factors Society.

Wilkinson, R.T.
    1963   Interaction of noise with knowledge of results and sleep deprivation. *Journal of Experimental Psychology* 66:332-337.

Williams, H.L., and C.L. Williams
    1966   Nocturnal EEG profiles and performance. *Psychophysiology* 3:164-175.

Wolpe, J.
    1958   *Reciprocal Inhibition Therapy.* Stanford, California: Stanford University Press.

Yerkes, R.M., and J.D. Dodson
    1908   The relation of strength of stimulus to rapidity of habit formation. *Journal of Comparative Neurological Psychology* 18:459-482.

Zajonc, R.B.
  1965   Social facilitation. *Science* 149:269-274.
Zhang, K., and C.D. Wickens
  1990   Effects of noise and workload on performance with two object displays vs. a separated display. *Proceedings of the Human Factors Society 34th Annual Meeting*. Santa Monica, California: Human Factors Society.

5

Sleep Disruption and Fatigue

Performance following abrupt workload transitions during duty cycles of extended duration is markedly affected by three factors related to the daily cycle of sleep and wakefulness. When called on to work and sleep at irregular intervals for prolonged periods of time, these three factors can interact in an additive manner to create major impairments in performance. The first factor is circadian rhythmicity, which produces a near-24-hour internally driven cycle in alertness and performance. The second is sleep deprivation, the effects of which are evident after only a few hours of lost sleep. The third is sleep inertia, which results in impaired performance immediately on awakening from sleep. These three factors combine to make it exceedingly difficult to work effectively or safely for prolonged periods of time without a carefully planned strategy of countermeasures designed to address each factor. The purpose of this chapter is to review current understanding of each of these factors and their potential relevance to performance during workload transitions.

CIRCADIAN EFFECTS ON PROLONGED PERFORMANCE

It has long been recognized that psychomotor and cognitive performance on a variety of tasks in round-the-clock operations is at its worst during nighttime hours, generally reaching a nadir just before dawn (Bjerner et al., 1955). In fact, the intrinsic nature of such daily rhythms was first demonstrated 260 years ago, when a French astronomer proved that the daily rhythm in leaf movement persisted even if a plant were kept in total darkness throughout night and day (deMairan, 1729). More than a century and a half ago, Duhamel discovered that these self-sustained oscillations persisted with a period that was close to (i.e., circa) but generally not exactly one day (hence our word *circadian*) when an organism was isolated from the periodic environmental light-dark cycle (DeCandolle, 1832). However, the manner by which the light-dark cycle synchronized an endogenous circadian rhythm with a non-24-hour period to the 24-hour day was not discovered until 30 years ago (DeCoursey, 1960; Hastings and Sweeney, 1958). At that time, it was found that brief exposures to light could induce phase shifts in endogenous circadian rhythms, and that the amount and direction of such shifts was dependent on the timing of the initial light exposure. The universality of this property of the circadian timing system was extended to humans only within the past three years (Czeisler et al., 1989).

Furthermore, the neurophysiologic basis for the generation of circadian rhythms in mammals was first uncovered less than 20 years ago. Ablation studies performed independently in two different laboratories indicated that bilateral destruction of a pair of hypothalamic neuronal clusters located on either side of the anterior tip of the third ventricle resulted in a loss of both endocrine and behavioral circadian rhythms (Moore and Eichler, 1972; Stephan and Zucker, 1972). It was further demonstrated that these central nervous system structures, the suprachiasmatic nuclei (SCN) of the hypothalamus, received a direct, monosynaptic input from the retina via the retinohypothalamic tract (RHT) (Moore and Lenn, 1972). These initial studies, which suggested that the SCN might serve as a light-sensitive pacemaker of the mammalian circadian timing system, have subsequently been supported by a variety of experimental manipulations. Multiunit recordings demonstrated a prominent circadian rhythm in the firing rate of SCN neurons, along with those in a number of other brain structures (Inouye and Kawamura, 1982). However, when the SCN were isolated from the rest of the brain via knife cuts, a circadian rhythm in firing rate was found only within the SCN (Inouye and Kawamura, 1979). It would thus appear that a periodic signal emanating from the SCN drives a prominent circadian variation in central nervous system activation, as reflected by neuronal firing rate. Yet, surprisingly, neurophysiologic studies involving microinjection of tetrodotoxin have demonstrated that the firing of SCN neurons is not required for maintenance of the SCN's timekeeping function (Schwartz et al., 1987).

Two different experimental paradigms have unambiguously established the link between this paired central nervous system structure and behavior. First, direct electrical stimulation of the mammalian SCN induces phase shifts in the behavioral rest-activity cycle comparable to those induced by brief exposures to light (Rusak and Groos, 1982). Second, transplantation of fetal SCN tissue rapidly restores rhythmicity of the behavioral rest-activity cycle in SCN-lesioned animals (Drucker-Colin et al., 1984; Lehman et al., 1987; Sawaki et al., 1984). In fact, SCN transplantation from a mutant animal with an abnormally short intrinsic circadian period into a wild type animal whose own SCN had previously been destroyed results in an animal with a behavioral rest-activity cycle period comparable to that of the mutant (Ralph et al., 1990). It has thus been demonstrated that the genotype of the SCN determines the expression of this behavioral phenotype.

The links between the SCN and human behavior are, of course, less definitively established. However, both the SCN and the RHT have been identified in the human brain (Hofman et al., 1988; Lydic et al., 1980; Sadun et al., 1984). More than 60 years ago it was recognized that damage to the anterior tip of the hypothalamus resulted in abnormalities of the circadian sleep-wake cycle, leading to the suggestion that the neural center responsible for the timing of sleep might be located in that region (Fulton and Bailey, 1929). Yet the first demonstration that human circadian rhythms persist in the absence of environmental time cues occurred only 30 years ago (Aschoff and Wever, 1962; Siffre, 1964). At that time, it was discovered that the intrinsic period of the human circadian pacemaker was typically longer than 24 hours, implying that our internal clock required resetting to an earlier hour each day. Those studies further demonstrated that a number of behavioral rhythms, including the rest-activity cycle and circadian variations in cognitive and psychomotor performance, persisted in the absence of environmental time cues (Aschoff et al., 1971, 1972; Wever, 1979).

However, subjects in isolation from environmental time cues do not always choose to sleep and wake in synchrony with circadian variations in physiological variables, such as body temperature and cortisol secretion (Aschoff, 1965). Whenever human subjects have been studied in environments free of environmental time cues for more than two months, the timing of the self-selected rest-activity cycle loses synchrony with the stable, near-24-hour oscillations that can be detected in physiological variables such as the body temperature cycle (Czeisler, 1978; Czeisler and Jewett, 1990). Yet even under such conditions of internal desynchrony, prominent circadian variations in alertness, cognitive performance, short-term memory, sleep tendency, spontaneous sleep duration, awakening and rapid eye movement (REM) sleep propensity all remain closely coupled to the body temperature cycle (Czeisler, 1978; Czeisler et al., 1980a, 1980b; Johnson et al., 1992; Zulley et al., 1981). Thus, no matter what sleep-wake schedule subjects choose to adopt in temporal isolation, they are, on average, most alert and perform best during their biologic day, as marked by the crest of the body temperature cycle; as might be expected, they are least likely to choose to sleep during those hours. Correspondingly, subjects are least alert, perform most poorly, and most often choose to be asleep during their biologic night, as marked by the temperature nadir. Moreover, these daily variations persist even when subjects are unaware of the time of day and are choosing to sleep and wake out of synchrony with these physiologic and behavioral rhythms.

It is thus not surprising that field studies of human performance among shift workers demonstrate strikingly similar results. During the latter half of the night, responses to calls for service take the longest; performance on an F-104 flight simulator is worst; shooting range performance among military personnel is least efficient; mental arithmetic is slowest; alertness is lowest; short-term memory is markedly impaired; and the rate of single-vehicle truck accidents due to sleepiness is by far the greatest (Czeisler et al., 1986; Folkard et al., 1978; Froberg et al., 1975; Harris, 1977; Klein et al., 1977). These circadian rhythms in performance variables parallel the wide variety of circadian rhythms in physiologic variables—including daily variations in thermoregulation; hormone release; kidney, cardiac and respiratory function—which are controlled by the human circadian pacemaker (Babkoff et al., 1988; Czeisler, 1978, 1983; Froberg et al., 1975; Klein et al., 1977; Mills, 1974; Moore and Eichler, 1983; Wever, 1977).

Just as in all other eukaryotes, synchronization of the oscillations to the 24-hour day in humans is accomplished by means of exposure to the environmental light-dark cycle (Czeisler et al., 1989). Thus, during the latter half of the night, humans are at their mental and physiological trough; maintaining high levels of alertness and performance at this time is exceedingly difficult. In fact, more than half of night shift workers report that they nod off or fall asleep at least once per week when working the night shift. Ironically, night shift workers who must stay awake during these unproductive hours then experience difficulty sleeping during their biological day. Sleep during daylight hours is disturbed, being shorter in duration and more frequently interrupted (Foret and Lantin, 1972). These results from field studies are consistent with experimental data from subjects scheduled to attempt sleep at all times of day and night; sleep efficiency is at its lowest near the crest of the temperature cycle (Carskadon and Dement, 1975; Czeisler, 1978; Weitzman et al., 1974). Thus, night shift workers typically suffer from misalignment of circadian phase. That is, they are attempting to stay awake and perform complex tasks at a time of day that the human circadian clock has scheduled the central nervous system to be asleep and then attempting to sleep at the scheduled time of peak arousal. In and of itself, this misalignment of circadian phase results in deterioration of alertness and performance. In addition, because of the effect of circadian phase misalignment on sleep, night shift work inevitably results in acute and chronic sleep deprivation, which can independently impair performance.

SLEEP DEPRIVATION

Laboratory Studies

The first demonstration of the deleterious effects of total extended sleep deprivation on human performance was reported nearly a century ago. At that time, 88-90-hour sleep deprivation experiments were carried out at the Iowa Psychological Laboratory by Patrick and Gilbert. They reported that grip strength, reaction time, memory, acuteness of vision, and calculation performance were adversely affected in some, but not all, subjects. Since that time, there have been a variety of studies investigating the deleterious effects of partial and prolonged sleep deprivation on the ability to perform sensory, physical, and cognitive tasks. As will be discussed in more detail in the following chapter, vigilance on both visual and auditory performance tasks has been found to be impaired after sleep deprivation (Hamilton et al., 1972; Horne et al., 1983; Sanders and Reitsma, 1982; Taub and Berger, 1973; Webb and Levy, 1984; Wilkinson et al., 1966). Recall of verbal information is substantially reduced after even one night of sleep loss (Webb and Levy, 1984). During the second night of sleep loss, subjects were able to complete only half their baseline average of problems solved on the Wilkinson Addition Test (Carskadon and Dement, 1979). Loss of as little as 5 hours of nocturnal sleep results in a doubling of the number of errors in reading an electrocardiographic strip by resident physicians (Friedman et al., 1971). This decrease in performance appears to be due to impairments in perceptual encoding and storage, lapses of attention, and a decline in the ability to discriminate signals, rather than from a decline in willingness to respond (Horne et al., 1983; Morris et al., 1960; Sanders and Reitsma, 1982; Torsvall and Akerstedt, 1987; Williams et al., 1959). Sleep tendency increases markedly with both partial and total sleep deprivation (Carskadon and Dement, 1979, 1981), such that ultimately sleep and/or attention lapses intrude involuntarily onto the waking brain (Williams et al., 1959). Motor initiation and execution in response to visual stimuli are also impaired following sleep deprivation, resulting in a failure to perceive information present in the functional visual field (Sanders and Reitsma, 1982). Although additional incentives (e.g., monetary rewards) can raise signal detection to normal baseline levels for one night and the following day of sleep deprivation, by the second night detection rate falls regardless of the incentive offered (Horne, 1988). This may be why very long hours of work fail to increase total production in industrial settings (Chambers, 1961).

In addition to reduced ability to respond to sensory stimuli, both primary mental performance and high-order cognitive functioning also show significant deficits following sleep deprivation (Hawkins et al., 1985). In tests of mental arithmetic after sleep deprivation, speed of calculation is slower, calculation errors increase, and fewer calculations are attempted (Hamilton et al., 1972; Taub and Berger, 1973; Webb and Levy, 1984; Wilkinson et al., 1966). Furthermore, in memory tests subsequent recall of material learned under sleep deprivation is significantly less efficient than that of material learned under normal conditions (Folkard et al., 1977; Wilkinson, 1972). Moderate sleep loss seems to cause deficits in memory trace formation that are independent of the physiological lapses, or microsleeps, that will of course disrupt the initial perception of the material (Williams et al., 1966), and that occur with increasing frequency with each hour of additional sleep deprivation. Finally, sleep deprivation impairs information processing, resulting in increased time requirements for making decisions (Asken and Raham, 1983).

Several studies have employed protocols of extended wakefulness to investigate the interaction of the effects of sleep deprivation and circadian rhythmicity on reaction time, cognitive function, and shooting range performance (Babkoff et al., 1988; Carskadon and Dement, 1979; Dinges et al., 1987; Froberg et al., 1975). These studies have found that performance in all variables declines during the first night of sleep deprivation, reaching a nadir just before dawn. During the second day of sleep deprivation, performance remains near this low level and may even improve somewhat, although it remains below normal baseline levels. However, during the second night of sleep deprivation, performance drops sharply, reaching levels much lower than those observed previously. Both sleep deprivation and adverse circadian phase contribute to substantial impairment of perceptual, motor, and cognitive functioning under such conditions.

Operational Settings

Many studies have documented the deleterious effects of both sleep loss and misalignment of circadian phase on performance and safety. During the latter half of the night, there is an increased rate of errors in reading meters (Bjerner et al., 1955), longer delays in responding to calls by switchboard operators (Browne, 1949), and an increased rate of operational errors associated with falling asleep at the wheel by locomotive engineers (Kazutaka and Ohta, 1975). These findings may help to explain the manyfold increase in the rate of single-vehicle truck accidents due to sleepiness that occur in the early morning hours between 4 and 6 am (Harris, 1977). Yet in many operational settings, crews are willing to attempt to maintain sustained performance for even longer periods. These include hospital interns and residents, whose performance is greatly impaired by such extended work hours (Asken and Raham, 1983; Friedman et al., 1971; Hawkins et al., 1985; Poulton et al., 1978), along with pilots, paramedics, and firefighters. They generally become impaired during the first night of sleep loss and are very

ineffective after 40 to 72 hours without sleep. This is particularly true for
people with command responsibilities (Belenky et al., 1987). For example,
Haslam (1985) found steady deterioration in the performance of soldiers
who were allowed no sleep, 1.5 hours, or 3 hours of sleep each night for 9
consecutive days during a field exercise. Although physical fitness was not
affected, vigilance and performance on detailed cognitive tasks deteriorated
to 50 percent of premission levels. Although the group that did not sleep at
all was unable to function after 3 days, the groups allowed 1.5 hours of
sleep per night lasted for 6 days, and the group allowed 3 hours of sleep per
night completed the 9-day study. Studies of military paratroopers' shooting
performance over a 72-hour period showed a marked circadian variation in
performance with a superimposed deterioration as sleep loss accumulated,
consistent with the results of Babkoff et al. (1988) and Froberg et al. (1975).
Ainsworth and Bishop (1971) found that specific tank crew duties (e.g.,
those that required consistent, sustained alertness or perceptual-motor activities) were most sensitive to sleep loss in a 48-hour field test. Banderet
et al. (1981) found performance decrements within the first 24-48 hours in a
simulation of sustained operations in an artillery fire direction center. Significantly, they found that performance on self-initiated activities, such as
planning and maintaining situational awareness, degraded most quickly.

Even when operators are adequately rested, some types of missions are
more fatiguing than others (e.g., day attack missions are more fatiguing for
Army aviators than day medical evacuation (medevac) missions, while night
scout-reconnaissance are the most fatiguing (Duncan et al., 1980). In addition, different factors contribute to the fatigue created by different missions.
Exposure to hostile action was universally rated as the most important con-
tributor. Additional factors were related to: (1) the mission (e.g., command
pressure to complete the mission, duration of flying duty day, number of
takeoffs and landings); (2) vehicle design (e.g., vibration, seating discomfort); (3) scheduling (e.g., long or frequent standby periods, disrupted sleep
schedules); (4) specific duties (e.g., tasks that are monotonous, impose high
mental workload, or require monitoring heavy radio traffic); or (5) the environment (night versus day flights, weather problems). The Army has recognized these differences by specifying different recommended flight-time
limitations depending on the type of mission flown (U.S. Department of the
Army, 1985). In computing flight time, one hour of daytime nap-of-the-
earth flight was considered to be equal to 1.6 hours of daytime standard
flight, and one hour of nighttime flight performed with night vision goggles
was equivalent to 2.3 hours. These multipliers are used to determine the
maximum recommended flight time and duty period in a 24-hour period (8
and 18 hours of day standard flight, respectively).

The critical role of sleep deprivation in train crews was discussed in
Chapter 2. Although data regarding impairment in performance from sleep

deprivation in other team environments are less available, it is easy to generalize from the above results and envision that the sleep-deprived schedule that is characteristic of many medical personnel (particularly residents and interns [Doelp, 1989]) may leave them especially vulnerable to medical errors (Gopher et al., 1989).

SLEEP INERTIA

Sleep inertia occurs immediately on awakening and results in less effective functioning than before sleep onset. This postsleep decrement in performance is seen in a variety of tasks, including simple and complex reaction time, grip strength, steadiness and coordination, visual-perceptual tasks, memory, time estimates, complex behavior simulation tasks, and cognitive tasks (Asken and Raham, 1983; Dinges et al., 1985; Downey and Bonnet, 1987; Feltin and Broughton, 1968; Seminara and Shavelson, 1969; Wilkinson and Stretton, 1971). Sleep inertia is characterized by confusion and disorientation and usually results in high response latencies (Downey and Bonnet, 1987). The effects of sleep inertia may take many minutes to dissipate and tend to be more intense after sleep deprivation and when wakenings occur at an adverse circadian phase (Dinges et al., 1985; Downey and Bonnet, 1987).

IMPACT ON PERFORMANCE IN
EXTENDED-DUTY OPERATIONS

Army tank crews may be required to be in a state of readiness for up to 72 continuous hours prior to the onset of battle. Then, following an extended period of inactivity, they may be required to abruptly begin a combat engagement. In such circumstances, the effects of circadian rhythmicity, sleep deprivation, and sleep inertia may conspire to markedly weaken the performance of the tank crew at this very critical time, threatening both their effectiveness and their safety. Performance reaches its daily nadir in the last hours of the night, just prior to dawn. Since physiologic sleep tendency is low during the evening, crew members may not attempt to sleep until they have already suffered from considerable sleep loss. The imposition of strict work-rest schedules by the military will ensure that crew members' circadian pacemakers are mutually synchronized, resulting in all of them reaching their performance nadir simultaneously. Then, in the latter half of the night during extended periods of inactivity, crew members may find sleep irresistible. Struggling to stay awake, crew members may find themselves nodding off in much the same way as a very sleepy driver attempting to keep all four wheels on the road. Each time they do nod off, they will be further reducing their ability to respond to an immediate call to service, due to the lasting effects of sleep inertia. Added together, these factors can converge to create a critical zone of vulnerability from 3:00 am to 6:00 am, at just the times when night vision equipment would otherwise allow U.S. forces to enjoy a technical advantage over forces less well equipped.

POTENTIAL COUNTERMEASURES

There is no known technique available to sustain human performance at an acceptable level for 72 continuous hours. The effects of pharmaceutical agents meant to facilitate sleep often linger on after scheduled wake time, impairing performance, memory, or both. Similarly, pharmaceutical agents taken to promote wakefulness (e.g., caffeine, amphetamine) often interfere with the ability to catch some sleep when time permits and also directly impair psychomotor performance (Lipschutz et al., 1988).

As noted by Weiner (1985) and Pollard et al. (1990), amphetamines can aid individuals who are fatigued, but, after heavy use, sleep patterns may not return to normal for almost two months. According to Pollard et al., some laboratory studies have demonstrated a potential short-term effect; however, in the real world, use of amphetamines is likely to have serious negative effects. "As the effects of fatigue and lack of sleep increase, the operator may increase the dosage resulting in the build-up and finally predominance of the negative side effects of the drug. These include blurred vision, dizziness, loss of coordination, paranoia, and irregular heartbeat followed ultimately by physical collapse" (Pollard et al., 1990:A-2). Refer to Pollard et al. (1990) for a brief review of the effects of other central nervous system stimulants, central nervous system depressants, opiates, antidepressants, and hallucinogens on performance.

If such extended-duty performance is demanded, there will inevitably be a critical zone of vulnerability each day during which microsleep episodes involuntarily intrude on the waking brain, leading to dangerous lapses of attention (Torsvall and Akerstedt, 1987). In addition, if performance is abruptly required after a period of low workload, during which crew members are likely to have fallen asleep, then, because of sleep inertia, they may subsequently be disoriented, confused, and unable to consolidate memories or perform efficiently for at least 30 minutes after awakening. Such problems may be exacerbated by the fact that the individual crew members often have little subjective awareness of the extent of their impairment under such circumstances.

However, careful planning can result in the development of countermeasures that can reduce the impact of sleep disruption on the performance of tank crew members. Countermeasures that have been attempted in the face of such circumstances include caffeine (Lipschutz et al., 1988) and other stimulants, increased physical activity, naps, monetary incentives, diet, and intensive social contact. The duration of commercial airline flights has led the National Aeronautics and Space Administration to recommend scheduled cockpit naps as a potential countermeasure. Rosekind et al. (1991) examined the effects of naps on long-duration transoceanic flights with three-person crews and found (1) most of the pilots were able to sleep during flight and had an average nap time of 26 minutes; (2) compared with a control group that was not given the opportunity to nap, the pilots who napped responded more rapidly to vigilance signals in the cockpit; and (3) the pilots who napped were not disrupted in their ability to sleep after the flight terminated by having gotten the extra nap sleep during flight. This measure has been found to be so effective that the Federal Aviation Administration has recently modified regulations to allow scheduled napping in the cockpit.

While these techniques can mitigate the deterioration of performance on the first night, none is effective in overcoming the impairments of performance that occur on the second or third nights of continuous operation. Recent research demonstrates that properly timed exposure to bright light and darkness can induce complete physiologic adaptation to night work and day sleep within 2-3 days (Czeisler et al., 1990); however, even this new technology can only reschedule, but not eliminate, the daily trough in cognitive and psychomotor performance. Nonetheless, the use of properly timed exposure to bright light (both natural and artificial) and strict scheduling of exposure to darkness could enable commanders to disperse periods of vulnerability either within individual tank crews or across tank divisions. In that way, there would be no one time at which an entire division would be most vulnerable to the effects of sleep loss and fatigue.

Dinges and colleagues have demonstrated that the strategic placement of a single 2-hour nap can significantly reduce (but not eliminate) the periodic decrements of alertness and performance that occur during 54 hours of sleep deprivation (Dinges et al., 1987). In order to reduce the consequences of all crew members suffering from the effects of sleep inertia simultaneously, such preemptive naps should be scheduled in a staggered manner. Furthermore, naps must be a minimum of 10 minutes in duration in order to begin to restore the decrements due to sleep loss (Naitoh, 1980).

In terms of minimum sleep requirements, as noted above, Haslam (1985) found that soldiers allowed as little as 3 hours of sleep per night were able to continue functioning (although not at optimal levels) during a 9-day field study, whereas soldiers who did not sleep at all were judged to be militarily ineffective after three days. Krueger et al. (1985) found that Army aviators were able to maintain adequate flight control and navigation, but they began to make occasional judgment errors during 14 hours of precision instrument flight in a simulator on each of 5 successive days with only 4 hours of sleep each night.

Leadership also plays a critical role in moderating the potential effects of sleep disruption. For example, Haslam (1985) found that the leadership of an experienced noncommissioned officer allowed his platoon to sustain their performance for a longer time than could other, equally sleep-deprived platoons. It is the responsibility of the team leader to establish a work-rest schedule that ensures that each team member gets adequate rest, if the situation allows. DeSwart (1989) describes sleep management as a critical element of stress management techniques adopted by the Royal Netherlands Army. In addition, the team leader must get adequate rest to be able to perform his own duties. During a mission, the team leader must monitor the status of each team member, relieving or reducing the responsibilities of team members who are too tired to perform their duties.

Finally, it has been reported that individuals who sleep 9-10 hours per night for a week prior to sleep deprivation score consistently higher on performance tasks than those who have only slept 7-8 hours per night (Taub and Berger, 1973, 1976). Therefore, strict enforcement of a 10-hour sleep regimen in total darkness during the weeks of rising tensions that often precede the deployment of armored personnel carriers could result in substantial improvements in crew performance. Certainly, cumulative sleep deprivation should be avoided at all costs during such periods, since many studies have documented the impairments of performance associated with the habitual restriction of nocturnal sleep (Hamilton et al., 1972). While none of these countermeasures can eliminate the effects of this powerful homeostatic regulatory mechanism on human performance, they can dissipate the impact of sleep loss and misalignment of circadian phase and minimize their deleterious consequences during the critical transition period from inactivity to combat.

REFERENCES

Ainsworth, L.L., and H.P. Bishop
   1971   *The Effects of a 48-hour Period of Sustained Field Activity on Tank Crew Performance.* Alexandria, Virginia: Human Resources Research Organization.
Aschoff, J.
   1965   Circadian rhythms in man: A self-sustained oscillator with an inherent frequency underlies human 24-hour periodicity. *Science* 148:1427-1432.
Aschoff, J., M. Fatranska, H. Giedke, P. Doerr, D. Stamm, and H. Wisser
   1971   Human circadian rhythms in continuous darkness: Entrainment by social cues. *Science* 171:213-215.
Aschoff, J., H. Giedke, E. Poppel, and R. Wever
   1972   The influence of sleep interruption and of sleep deprivation on circadian rhythms in human performance. In W.E. Colquhoun, ed., *Aspects of Human Efficiency: Diurnal Rhythm and Loss of Sleep.* London: English University Press.
Aschoff, J., and R. Wever
   1962   Spontanperiodik des menschen bie ausschuluss aller zeitgeber. *Die Naturwissenschaften* 49:337-342.

Asken, M.J., and D.C. Raham
  1983   Resident performance and sleep deprivation: A review. *Journal of Medical Education* 58:382-388.
Babkoff, H., M. Mikelinder, T. Karlsson, and P. Kuklinski
  1988   The topology of performance curves during 72 hours of sleep loss: A memory and search task. *Journal of Experimental Biology* 40:737-756.
Banderet, L.E., J.W. Stokes, R. Farncesconi, D.M. Kowal, and P. Naitoh
  1981   *The Twenty-Four Hour Workday: Proceedings of a Symposium on Variations in Work-Sleep Schedules.* Cincinnati, Ohio: U.S. Department of Health and Human Services.
Belenky, G.L., G.P. Krueger, T.J. Balkin, D.B. Headley, and R.E. Solick
  1987   *Effects of Continuous Operations (CONOPS) on Soldier and Unit Performance: Review of the Literature and Strategies for Sustaining the Soldier in CONOPS.* Washington, DC: Walter Reed Army Institute of Research.
Bjerner, B., A. Holm, and A. Swensson
  1955   Diurnal variation in mental performance a study of three-shift workers. *British Journal of Industrial Medicine* 12:103-110.
Browne, R.C.
  1949   The day and night performance of teleprinter switchboard operators. *Journal of Occupational Psychology* 23:121-126.
Carskadon, M.A., and W.C. Dement
  1975   Sleep studies on a 90-minute day. *Electroencephalogram Clinical Neurophysiology* 39:145-155.
  1979   Effects of total sleep loss on sleep tendency. *Perceptual Motor Skills* 48:495-506.
  1981   Cumulative effects of sleep restriction on daytime sleepiness. *Psychophysiology* 18:107-113.
Chambers, E.G.
  1961   Industrial fatigue. *Occupational Psychology* 35:44-57.
Czeisler, C.A.
  1978   Internal Organization of Temperature, Sleep-Wake, and Neuroendocrine Rhythms Monitored in an Environment Free of Time Cues. Ph.D. Thesis. Stanford University, Stanford.
  1983   Testimony at hearing before the subcommittee on investigations and oversight of the Committee on Science and Technology, House of Representatives. Pp. 171-232 in *Biological Clocks and Shift Work Scheduling.* Washington, DC: U.S. Government Printing Office.
Czeisler, C.A., and M.E. Jewett
  1990   Human circadian physiology: Interaction of the behavioral rest-activity cycle with the output of the endogenous circadian pacemaker. Pp. 117-137 in M.J. Thorpy, ed., *Handbook of Sleep Disorders.* New York: Marcel Dekker, Inc.
Czeisler, C.A., M.P. Johnson, J.F. Duffy, E.N. Brown, J.M. Ronda, and R.E. Kronauer
  1990   Exposure to bright light and darkness to treat physiologic maladaptation to night work. *New England Journal of Medicine* 322:1253-1259.
Czeisler, C.A., W.A. Kennedy, and J.S. Allan
  1986   Circadian rhythms and performance decrements in the transportation industry. Pp. 146-171 in A.M. Coblentz, ed., *Proceedings of a Workshop on the Effects of Automation on Operator Performance.* Paris: Universite Rene Descartes.
Czeisler, C.A., R.E. Kronauer, J.S. Allan, J.F. Duffy, M.E. Jewett, E.N. Brown, and J.M. Ronda
  1989   Bright light induction of strong (Type 0) resetting of the human circadian pacemaker. *Science* 244:1328-1333.

Czeisler, C.A., E.D. Weitzman, M.C. Moore-Ede, J.C. Zimmerman, and R.S. Knauer
  1980a   Human sleep: Its duration and organization depend on its circadian phase. *Science* 210:1264-1267.
Czeisler, C.A., J.C. Zimmerman, J.M. Ronda, M.C. Moore-Ede, and E.D. Weitzman
  1980b   Timing of REM sleep is coupled to the circadian rhythm of body temperature in man. *Sleep* 2:329-346.
DeCandolle, A.P.
  1832   Du sommeil des feuilles. Pp. 854-862 in *Physiologie Vegetale, Exposition des Forces et des Fonctions Vitales des Vegetaux*. Paris, Bechet Jeune: Libraire de la Faculte de Medecine.
DeCoursey, P.J.
  1960   Daily light sensitivity rhythm in a rodent. *Science* 131:33-35.
deMairan, J.J.
  1729   Observation botanique. *Historie de l'Academie Royale des Sciences, Paris* 35:35.
deSwart, J.
  1989   Stress and stress management in the Royal Netherlands Army. In *Proceedings of the User's Stress Workshop*. Washington, DC: U.S. Army Health Services Command.
Dinges, D.F., K.T. Orne, and E.C. Orne
  1985   Assessing performance upon abrupt awakening from naps during quasi-continuous operations. *Behavioral Research Methods, Instruments, and Computers* 17:37-45.
Dinges, D.F., K.T. Orne, W.G. Whitehouse, and E.C. Orne
  1987   Temporal placement of a nap for alertness: Contributions of circadian phase and prior wakefulness. *Sleep* 10:313-329.
Doelp, A.
  1989   *In the Blink of an Eye: Inside a Children's Trauma Center*. New York: Ballantine Books.
Downey, R., and M.H. Bonnet
  1987   Performance during frequent sleep disruption. *Sleep* 10:354-363.
Drucker-Colin, R., R. Aguilar-Roblero, F. Garcia-Hernandez, F. Fernandez-Cancino, and F.B. Rattoni
  1984   Fetal suprachiasmatic nucleus transplants: Diurnal rhythm recovery of lesioned rats. *Brain Research* 311:353-357.
Duncan, C.E., M.G. Sanders, and K.A. Kimball
  1980   *Evaluation of Army Aviator Human Factors, Fatigue in a High Threat Environment*. Fort Rucker, Alabama: Army Aeromedical Research Laboratory.
Feltin, M., and R. Broughton
  1968   Differential effects of arousal from slow wave versus REM sleep. *Psychophysiology* 5:231.
Folkard, S., T.H. Monk, R. Bradbury, and J. Rosenthall
  1977   Time of day effects in school children's immediate and delayed recall of meaningful material. *British Journal of Psychology* 68:45-50.
Folkard, S., T.H. Monk, and M.C. Lobban
  1978   Short and long-term adjustment of circadian rhythms in "permanent" night nurses. *Ergonomics* 21:785-799.
Foret, J., and G. Lantin
  1972   The sleep of train drivers: An example of the effects of irregular work schedules on sleep. Pp. 273-282 in W.P. Colquhoun, ed., *Aspects of Human Efficiency Diurnal Rhythm and Loss of Sleep*. Cambridge, UK: English Universities Press Ltd.
Friedman, R.C., J.T. Bigger, and D.S. Kornfield
  1971   The intern and sleep loss. *New England Journal of Medicine* 285:201-203.

Froberg, J.E., C.G. Karlsson, L. Levi, and L. Lidberg
  1975   Circadian rhythms of catecholamine excretion, shooting range performance and
          self-ratings of fatigue during sleep deprivation. *Biological Psychology* 2:175-188.
Fulton, J.F., and P. Bailey
  1929   Tumors in the region of the third ventricle: Their diagnosis and relation to patho-
          logical sleep. *Journal of Nervous and Mental Diseases* 69:1-25, 145-164, 261-
          277.
Gopher, D., M. Weil, and D. Siegel
  1989   Practice under changing priorities: An approach to training complex skills. *Acta
          Psychologica* 71(1-3):147-177.
Hamilton, P., R.T. Wilkinson, and R.S. Edwards
  1972   A study of four days partial sleep deprivation. Pp. 101-113 in W.P. Colquhoun,
          ed., *Aspects of Human Efficiency*. London: English Universities Press, Ltd.
Harris, W.
  1977   Fatigue, circadian rhythm, and truck accidents. Pp. 133-146 in R. Mackie, ed.,
          Vigilance Theory, Operational Performance, and Physiological Correlates. New
          York: Plenum.
Haslam, D.R.
  1985   Sustained operations and military performance. *Behavior Research Methods, In-
          struments, and Computers* 17:9-95.
Hastings, J.W., and B.M. Sweeney
  1958   A persistent diurnal rhythm of luminescence in Gonyaulax polyedra. *Biological
          Bulletin* 115:440-458.
Hawkins, M.R., D.A. Vichick, H.D. Silsby, D.J. Kruzich, and R. Butler
  1985   Sleep and nutritional deprivation and performance of house officers. *Journal of
          Medical Education* 60:530-535.
Hofman, M.A., E. Fliers, E. Goudsmit, and D.F. Swaab
  1988   Morphometric analysis of the suprachiasmatic and paraventricular nuclei in the
          human brain: Sex differences and age-dependent changes. *Journal of Anatomy*
          160:127-143.
Horne, J.A.
  1988   *Why We Sleep*. Oxford: Oxford University Press.
Horne, J.A., N.R. Anderson, and R.T. Wilkinson
  1983   Effects of sleep deprivation on signal detection measures of vigilance: Implica-
          tions for sleep function. *Sleep* 6:347-358.
Inouye, S.T., and H. Kawamura
  1979   Persistence of circadian rhythmicity in a mammalian hypothalamic "island" con-
          taining the suprachiasmatic nucleus. *Proceedings of the National Academy of
          Sciences* 76:5962-5966.
  1982   Characteristics of a circadian pacemaker in the suprachiasmatic nucleus. *Journal
          of Comparative Physiology* 146:153-160.
Johnson, M.T., J.F. Duffy, D.J. Dijk, J.M. Ronda, C.M. Dyal, and C.A. Czeisler
  1992   Short-term memory, alertness, and performance: A reappraisal of their relation-
          ship to body temperature. *Journal of Sleep Research* 1:24-29.
Kazutaka, K., and T. Ohta
  1975   Incidence of near accidental drowsing in locomotive driving during a period of
          rotation. *Journal of Human Ergology* 4:65-76.
Klein, K.E., R. Herrmann, P. Kuklinski, and H.M. Wegmann
  1977   Circadian performance rhythms: Experimental studies in air operations. Pp. 111-
          132 in R.R. Mackie, ed., *Vigilance: Theory, Operational Performance, and Physi-
          ological Correlates*. New York: Plenum Press.

Krueger, G.P., R.N. Armstrong, and R.R. Cisco
  1985 *Aviator Performance in Week Long Extended Flight Operations in a Helicopter Simulator*. Fort Rucker, Alabama: U.S. Army Aeromedical Research Laboratory.

Lehman, M.N., R. Silver, W.R. Gladstone, R.M. Kahn, M. Gibson, and E.L. Bittman
  1987 Circadian rhythmicity restored by neural transplant: Immunocytochemical characterization of the graft and its integration with the host brain. *Journal of Neuroscience* 7:1626-1638.

Lipschutz, L., T. Roehrs, A. Spielman, H. Zwyghuizen, J. Lamphere, and T. Roth
  1988 Caffeine's alerting effects in sleepy normals. *Journal of Sleep Research* 17:49.

Lydic, R., W.C. Schoene, C.A. Czeisler, and M.C. Moore-Ede
  1980 Suprachiasmatic region of the human hypothalamus: Homolog to the primate circadian pacemaker? *Sleep* 2:355-361.

Mills, J.N.
  1974 Phase relations between components of human circadian rhythms. Pp. 560-563 in L.E. Scheving, F. Halberg, and J.E. Pauly, eds., *Chronobiology*. Tokyo, Igaku-Shoin Limited.

Moore, R.Y., and V.B. Eichler
  1972 Loss of a circadian adrenal corticosterone rhythm following suprachiasmatic lesions in the rat. *Brain Research* 42:201-206.
  1983 Organization and function of a central nervous system circadian oscillator: The suprachiasmatic hypothalamic nucleus. *Federation Proceedings* 42:2783-2789.

Moore, R.Y., and N.J. Lenn
  1972 A retinohypothalamic projection in the rat. *Journal of Comparative Neurology* 146:1-9.

Morris, G.O., R.L. Williams, and A. Lubin
  1960 Misperception and disorientation during sleep deprivation. *Archives of General Psychiatry* 2:247-254.

Naitoh, P.
  1980 *Chronopsychological Approach for Optimizing Human Performance*. San Diego, California: Naval Health Research Center.

Pollard, J.K., E.D. Sussman, and M. Stearns
  1990 *Shipboard Crew Fatigue, Safety, and Reduced Manning*. Report No. DOT-MA-RD-840-90014. U.S. Department of Transportation, Research, and Special Programs Administration. Washington, DC: Office of Technology Assessment.

Poulton, E.C., G.M. Hunt, A. Carpenter, and R.S. Edwards
  1978 The performance of junior hospital doctors following reduced sleep and long hours of work. *Ergonomics* 21:279-295.

Ralph, M.R., R.G. Foster, F.C. Davis, and M. Menaker
  1990 Transplanted suprachiasmatic nucleus determines circadian period. *Science* 247:975-978.

Rosekind, M.R., P.H. Gander, and D.F. Dinges
  1991 Alertness management in flight operations: Strategic napping. Pp. 1-12 in *Aerospace Technology Conference and Exposition*. Long Beach, California.

Rusak, B., and G. Groos
  1982 Suprachiasmatic stimulation phase shifts rodent circadian rhythms. *Science* 215:1407-1409.

Sadun, A.A., J.D. Schaechter, and L.E.H. Smith
  1984 A retinohypothalamic pathway in man: Light mediation of circadian rhythms. *Brain Research* 302:371-377.

Sanders, A.F., and W.D. Reitsma
  1982 The effect of sleep-loss on processing information in the functional visual field. *Acta Psychologica* 51:149-162.

Sawaki, Y., I. Nihonmatsu, and H. Kawamura
    1984   Transplantation of the neonatal suprachiasmatic nuclei into rats with complete bilateral suprachiasmatic lesions. *Neuroscience Research* 1:67-72.
Schwartz, W.J., R.A. Gross, and M.T. Morton
    1987   The suprachiasmatic nuclei contain a tetrodotoxin-resistant circadian pacemaker. *Proceedings of the National Academy of Sciences* 84:1694-1698.
Seminara, J.L., and R.J. Shavelson
    1969   Effectiveness of space crew performance subsequent to sudden sleep arousal. *Aerospace Medicine* 40:723-727.
Siffre, M.
    1964   *Beyond Time.* (Translated and edited by H. Briffault) New York: McGraw Hill.
Stephan, F.K., and I. Zucker
    1972   Circadian rhythms in drinking behavior and locomotor activity of rats are eliminated by hypothalmic legions. *Proceedings of the National Academy of Sciences* 69:1583-1586.
Taub, J.M., and R.J. Berger
    1973   Performance and mood following variations in the length and timing of sleep. *Psychophysiology* 10:559-570.
    1976   The effects of changing the phase and duration of sleep. *Journal of Experimental Psychology* 2:30-41.
Torsvall, L., and T. Akerstedt
    1987   Sleepiness on the job: Continuously measured EEG changes in train drivers. *Electroencephalogram Clinical Neurophysiology* 66:502-511.
U.S. Department of the Army
    1985   *Aviation: General Provisions, Training, Standardization, and Resource Management.* Army Regulation 95-3. Washington, DC: U.S. Army Headquarters.
Webb, W.B., and C.M. Levy
    1984   Effects of spaced and repeated total sleep deprivation. *Ergonomics* 27:45-58.
Weiner, N.
    1985   Norepinephrine, epinephrine, and the sympathomimetic amines. In A.G. Gilman, L.S. Goodman, T.W. Rall, and R. Murad, eds., *The Pharmacological Basis of Therapeutics.* New York: MacMillan.
Weitzman, E.D., C. Nogeire, M. Perlow, D. Fukushima, J. Sassin, P. McGregor, T.F. Gallagher, and L. Hellman
    1974   Effects of a prolonged 3-hour sleep-wake cycle on sleep stages, plasma cortisol, growth hormone, and body temperature in man. *Journal of Clinical Endocrinological Metabolism* 38:1018-1030.
Wever, R.A.
    1977   Quantitative studies of the interaction between different circadian oscillators within the human multi-oscillator system. *Proceedings of the International Society of Chronobiology* 12:525-535.
    1979   *The Circadian System of Man: Results of Experiments Under Temporal Isolation.* New York: Springer-Verlag.
Wilkinson, R.T.
    1972   Sleep deprivation - eight questions. Pp. 25-30 in W.P. Colquhoun, ed., *Aspects of Human Efficiency.* London: English Universities Press.
Wilkinson, R.T., R.S. Edwards, and E. Haines
    1966   Performance following a night of reduced sleep. *Psychonomic Science* 5:471-472.
Wilkinson, R.T., and M. Stretton
    1971   Performance after awakening at different times of night. *Psychonomic Science* 23:283-285.

Williams, H.L., C.F. Gieseking, and A. Lubin
  1966   Some effects of sleep loss on memory. *Perceptual Motor Skills* 23:1287-1293.
Williams, H.L., A. Lubin, and J.J. Goodnow
  1959   Impaired performance with acute sleep loss. *Psychology Monogram* 73:1-26.
Zulley, J., R. Wever, and J. Aschoff
  1981   The dependence of onset and duration of sleep on the circadian rhythm of rectal
            temperature. *Pfluegers Archiv* 391:314-318.

6

Vigilance and Target Detection

As noted in Chapter 1, a large portion of the responsibility of armored vehicle teams, and indeed the teams of many analogous systems, prior to transition is simply to monitor the environment for events that might signal the need for the team to mobilize into action. This task of monitoring for infrequent signals is one for which humans are not well suited, particularly after periods of sleep disruption. In this chapter we examine in detail the research on human performance in monitoring, vigilance, and target detection.

HISTORICAL BACKGROUND

World War II

Vigilance or sustained attention refers to the ability of observers to maintain their focus of attention and to remain alert to stimuli for prolonged periods of time (Davies and Parasuraman, 1982; Warm, 1984a). Systematic study of sustained attention began during World War II. It was stimulated by surprising fallibility in the performance of British airborne radar observers while on patrol for enemy submarines. These individuals were often required to maintain continuous observation of their radar scopes during long flights over the Bay of Biscay watching for telltale "blips" that signaled the presence of German U-boats in the sea below. Despite their extensive training and obvious motivation to perform well, the observers failed with increasing frequency to notice the critical signals displayed by their equipment as time on watch progressed. As a result, the submarines passed undetected and were free to prey on Allied shipping.

In response to a request from the Royal Air Force to study the problem, Mackworth (1948, 1961) initiated a series of ingenious experiments that formed the first systematic effort to bring the study of vigilance into the laboratory. Using a simulated radar display known as the "Clock Test," Mackworth was able to chart the course of performance over time and to confirm the suspicions generated in the field that the quality of sustained attention is fragile: it wanes over time. He found that his subjects became progressively more inefficient at detecting signals as the watch continued, and that this inefficiency did not take long to develop. In general, the accuracy of signal detections declined about 10 percent after only 30 minutes of watch, and then showed a more gradual decline during the remainder of the 2-hour session.

The progressive decline in performance over time noted in Mackworth's pioneering experiments has been confirmed in a large number of subsequent investigations. It has been labeled the "decrement function" or the "vigilance decrement" and is the most ubiquitous finding in vigilance studies. Many investigations using a broad assortment of vigilance tasks indicate that the decline in performance is complete from 20 to 35 minutes after the initiation of the vigil and at least half of the final loss is completed within the first 15 minutes (Teichner, 1974). Under especially demanding circumstances, the decrement can even appear within the very first few minutes of watch (Jerison, 1963; Nuechterlein et al., 1983). As Dember and Warm (1979) have noted, the most striking aspect of this finding is that it seems to result merely from the necessity of looking or listening for a relatively infrequent signal over a continuous period of time.

Implications of Automation for Vigilance

The study of vigilance has generated considerable interest among human factors and ergonomics specialists, who are concerned not only with the decrement function, but also with the factors that affect the overall level of performance. Comprehensive reviews of the extensive experimental literature on vigilant behavior can be found in Craig (1985a, 1985b, 1991), Davies (1985), Davies and Parasuraman (1982), Dember and Warm (1979), Parasuraman (1986), Warm (1977, 1984b), Warm and Berch (1985) and Warm and Parasuraman (1987).

The importance of vigilance research for human factors concerns is based in part on the fact that the surveillance problems encountered during World War II are still with us in one form or another. The generation of automatic control and computing systems for the acquisition, storage, and processing of information has altered the role of the human operator from that of active controller to a more executive function, a development that Sheridan (1970) has characterized as a shift from active to supervisory control. Vigilance is a crucial aspect of the reliability of human performance in a wide variety of activities including industrial quality control, robotic manufacturing, air traffic control, nuclear power plant operations, long distance driving, and the monitoring of life signs in medical settings (Warm, 1984a). As Parasuraman (1986) has noted, target detection in today's highly automated systems may be executed by instruments and controls, but the same problems of vigilance occur when the systems malfunction or unusual events appear. In some cases, the vigilance functions demanded of the operator can be overwhelming (Parasuraman, 1987; Wiener, 1984, 1985, 1987).

Implications for Armor Personnel

Modern tank warfare is still another situation in which vigilant behavior is critical. Indeed, the maintenance of a proper level of alertness is the price of survival in combat. As described in Armor Field Manual 17-12-1, *Tank Combat Table* (U.S. Department of the Army, undated), future battlefields are expected to require tank crews to move and engage rapidly under conditions in which our forces are intermingled with those of the enemy. Survival will depend on the crew's ability to detect and locate opposing forces rapidly in order to maintain the advantage of a first strike. Target acquisition, however, can be a difficult task for all crew members, especially the gunner. Toward that end, they must search both ground and sky, looking and listening for target signatures (critical signals) involving acoustic and visual patterns (engine noise, aircraft noise, broken vegetation, weapon smoke, glare from airplane canopies or wings), using just their eyes and ears or with the assistance of field glasses, telescopes, and thermal imagery. All of this must be accomplished under extreme conditions of heat, noise, vibration, and danger. In order to provide some insight into factors that might affect the vigilant behavior of armor crews and ways to counter threats to their ability to remain alert, this chapter describes a variety of task and environmental factors that have been discovered to play an important role in the quality of vigilance performance.

PSYCHOPHYSICAL DETERMINANTS

A Functional Equation

The Components of Vigilance

Performance efficiency in vigilance tasks is closely tied to the nature of the stimuli that demand attention. Consequently, the study of vigilance, like that of other perceptual phenomena, has profited from the precise determination of the stimulus conditions that influence performance. In summarizing these conditions, it is helpful to follow the framework of an empirically determined functional equation developed by Jerison (1959b) and modified by Warm and Berch (1985), which takes the following form:

$$P = f(M, S, U, B, C)$$

According to this relation, performance (*P*) is a function of the sensory modality of signals (*M*), the salience of signals (*S*), stimulus uncertainty (*U*), the characteristics of the background of nonsignal events in which critical signals for detection are embedded (*B*), and task complexity (*C*).

Signal Modality

Vigilance experiments have used auditory, visual, and cutaneous stimulation. However, the sensory modality of signals is not a matter of indifference when the quality of sustained attention is concerned. Auditory tasks tend to be associated with a higher level of overall efficiency and with greater stability over time than their cutaneous and visual analogs (Davies and Parasuraman, 1982; Warm and Jerison, 1984). In addition, intersensory correlations are often low or nonsignificant (Hatfield and Loeb, 1968).

Fortunately, techniques are available that can enhance visual performance and improve intersensory correlations in vigilance. The level of visual vigilance can be elevated to that characteristic of audition by closely coupling subjects to the display so that they cannot avoid stimulation by looking away (Hatfield and Loeb, 1968), and audiovisual correlations can be increased by equating the types of discriminations required in the two modalities (Galinsky et al., 1990; Hatfield and Loeb, 1968; Parasuraman and Davies, 1977). Performance with redundant displays in which analogous signals are presented simultaneously to the auditory and visual channels exceeds that with single-mode displays. The dual-mode superiority effect has been shown to stem from the integrative action of the sensory systems and not from a fortuitous combination of their independent activities (Craig et al., 1976; Doll and Hanna, 1989). It represents a potentially important technique for the general enhancement of monitoring efficiency.

Signal Salience

A common finding in studies of target detection under alerted conditions is that the frequency of detection is positively related to stimulus amplitude and duration. These factors are also important under conditions of sustained attention. Investigations by Adams (1956), Guralnick (1972), and Loeb and Binford (1963) have demonstrated that the overall quality of sustained attention can be enhanced and performance rendered more stable over time by increasing the amplitude of the signal-to-noise ratio of critical signals. In addition, Corcoran and his coworkers (Corcoran et al., 1977) have shown that it is also possible to reverse the typical time course of performance by "turning up the gain" on the sensory channel being monitored. Using acoustic pulses, they found that an abrupt increment in the amplitude of the stimuli midway through the vigil bolstered the frequency of signal detections for the remainder of the session. In addition to amplitude increments, signals can also be rendered more salient by increasing their duration. Signals of brief duration are more likely to be missed than those that remain visible for longer periods of time. Indeed, the rate of gain in detection efficiency is a negatively accelerated increasing function of duration up to a limit of about four seconds (Warm et al., 1970).

Stimulus Uncertainty

Alluisi (1966) has pointed out that, like lookouts in old-time sailing ships, subjects in vigilance experiments can be faced with considerable uncertainty regarding the signals they are to detect—they may not know when such signals will appear (temporal uncertainty) or where they will appear (spatial uncertainty). The same can be said for armor personnel in combat. Both types of uncertainty degrade performance efficiency.

One means of manipulating the subject's temporal uncertainty is through variations in the density or the number of critical signals presented during a vigilance session. The more frequently such signals occur within a fixed time period, the greater the a priori signal probability and the lower will be the subject's average uncertainty as to when critical signals will occur. The accuracy of signal detections varies directly as a function of signal density (Warm and Jerison, 1984). Increases in signal density also increase the speed of detection in a regular manner. Using an information theory analysis to measure the density-determined temporal uncertainty in the appearance of critical signals, Alluisi and his coworkers (Smith et al., 1966; Warm and Alluisi, 1971) found that response times to detections increased as a linear function of uncertainty.

An important aspect of the effects of signal probability in vigilance performance is that these effects perseverate. Several studies have demonstrated that subjects trained initially under conditions of high signal probability do better during subsequent testing than do those initially exposed to a low probability, regardless of the probability condition in effect (high or low) during the testing phase of the experiment (Colquhoun and Baddeley, 1964, 1967; Griffin et al., 1986; Krulewitz and Warm, 1977; McFarland and Halcomb, 1970).

Temporal uncertainty in vigilance experiments has also been manipulated through variations in the intervals of time between signals or the intersignal intervals. These intervals can be made quite regular and easily predictable or irregular and unpredictable. The speed and accuracy with which signal detections occur is greater in the context of regular compared with irregular signal conditions (Adams and Boulter, 1964; Warm et al., 1974).

Spatial uncertainty has been introduced into vigilance experiments by varying the probability that signals will appear in different locations of a monitored display or by using an unpredictable sequence of display locations. Under such conditions, performance efficiency is lowered and subjects tend to bias their attention toward those portions of the display in which the likelihood of signal appearance is highest (Adams and Boulter, 1964; Joshi et al., 1985; Milosevic, 1974; Nicely and Miller, 1957).

The Background Event Context

Vigilance experiments frequently employ dynamic displays in which critical signals for detection are embedded within a matrix of recurrent background events. For example, subjects may be asked to detect occasional brighter flashes of light in a background of dimmer flashes or the presence of a stronger pulse of acoustic stimulation in a background of less intense pulses. Although the background events may be neutral in the sense that they require no overt response, they are far from neutral in their influence on the quality of sustained attention. The frequency of background events, or the background event rate, is a very important determinant of performance efficiency. Both the speed and the accuracy of signal detections vary inversely with event rate, and the vigilance decrement tends to be more pronounced in the context of a fast compared with a slow event rate (Jerison and Pickett, 1964; Lanzetta et al., 1987; Parasuraman, 1979; Parasuraman and Davies, 1976).

From the earlier discussion of signal density, one might be tempted to conclude that the effects of event rate are artifactual. If critical signal density is held constant, as is usually the case when event rate is varied, increases in event rate reduce the conditional probability that a stimulus event is a critical signal. Thus, event rate may simply be another example of signal uncertainty. This is not the case, however. The quality of sustained attention decreases with increased event rate even when signal density is adjusted so that the conditional probability is equated within event rates (Loeb and Binford, 1968; Parasuraman, 1979; Taub and Osborne, 1968).

In addition to its own influence on performance, the background event rate also modifies that of other stimulus parameters. The effects associated with signal amplitude and signal regularity as well as the perseverative effects of signal density are dependent on the event rate context in which critical signals must be detected (Krulewitz and Warm, 1977; Metzger et al.,

1974; Moore and Gross, 1973). Moreover, the speed of probe detections for a secondary task also depends on the event rate in force in a primary vigilance task (Bowers, 1983; Parasuraman, 1985). Taken together, findings such as these have led several investigators to conclude that background event rate is probably the prepotent psychophysical factor in vigilance performance (Parasuraman et al., 1987).

For the most part, neutral events in vigilance experiments have been presented in temporally regular intervals, such as 1 event every 12 seconds at an event rate of 5 per minute or 1 event every 2 seconds at a faster rate of 30 per minute. Under such conditions, subjects can predict when an event that needs to be inspected for the possibility that it is a critical signal will appear. Accordingly, they can take task-contingent timeouts and rest between the appearance of events. Recent studies by Scerbo and his colleagues have denied subjects such rest intervals by using temporally irregular or asynchronous event schedules so that subjects could not be certain when an event that could be a signal would appear and had to observe the vigilance display continuously. As might be anticipated, event asynchrony degrades performance efficiency compared with a synchronous schedule of background events (Scerbo et al., 1987a, 1987b). The effects of both event rate and event asynchrony are striking; they demonstrate that signal detection in vigilance experiments is determined as much by what transpires in the interim between signals as by the characteristics of the signals themselves.

Stimulus Complexity

Vigilance studies typically make use of relatively simple perceptual discriminations involving the detection of discrete changes in the intensity, extensity, duration, or movement of stimuli on a single display (see Hancock, 1984, for a description of the kinds of displays used). In operational settings, however, more complex discriminations are often involved and observers may be required to cope with multiple signal sources. A number of attempts have been made to explore the consequences of increased task complexity for the quality of vigilant behavior, but the results are not clear cut.

In a well known study, Jerison (1963) asked observers to monitor three displays simultaneously and found that the vigilance decrement was greatly enhanced under such conditions. Rather than appearing after the first 5 or 10 minutes of watch, he found that the decrement could be observed from the very first signal onward. In contrast, however, are several experiments by Adams and his associates (Adams and Humes, 1963; Adams et al., 1963; Montague et al., 1965) that employed very complex vigilance tasks with multiple stimulus sources (from 6 to 36) under conditions in which any one source could present a signal at any moment in time. The vigilance decrement was either absent or minimal in these experiments even though the vigil lasted for several hours. However, the absolute level of vigilant performance (the number of signals missed) was far from perfect. Adams's findings have been confirmed recently by Warm and his collaborators who varied complexity by increasing the cognitive demand placed on observers in a vigilance task (Dember et al., 1984; Lysaght et al., 1984; Warm et al., 1984). But Loeb and his coworkers have reported that the beneficial effects of increased cognitive demand are limited—increasing demand beyond a rather low optimal level degrades performance and restores the decrement function (Loeb et al., 1987).

The problem of stimulus complexity is perplexing. Depending on the approach employed, it is possible to amplify or eliminate the vigilance decrement through modifications of complexity. Clearly, a resolution of these disparities will be necessary in order to develop a complete functional equation for the psychophysics of vigilance. Some insight into ways in which this conundrum might be unraveled comes from a study by Fisk and Schneider (1981), who approached the issue of complexity in terms of automatic and controlled processing theory (see Schneider and Shiffrin, 1977). According to this view, automatic processes are fast, fairly effortless, skilled behaviors while controlled processes refer to relatively slow, effortful, capacity-limited processes. In a carefully conducted experiment in which automatic processing was developed over several hundred trials, Fisk and Schneider found that the vigilance decrement was restricted to controlled processing tasks; automatic tasks were performed in a stable manner throughout the vigilance session. Evidently, proper training might be a key in aiding subjects to cope with demanding vigilance tasks.

Sensing and Decision Making

The Theory of Signal Detection

At first glance, a subject's success in correctly detecting a signal (a predesignated stimulus event) in vigilance or other detection situations may seem to be a rather direct measure of the individual's perceptual ability in that situation. However, if one examines the process of signal detection more carefully, it becomes evident that perceptual reports are not that simple (see Natsoulas, 1967); the affirmation of signal presence or absence does not depend solely on perceptual sensitivity. Such a report is also contingent on nonperceptual factors that include the subject's detection goals, expectations about the nature of the stimuli, and the anticipated consequences of correct and incorrect responses. Taken together, these factors compose the subject's response criterion or willingness to emit a detection response.

Failure to detect a signal can result from a lack of perceptual sensitivity for the signal or from a conservative criterion that leads the subject to withhold the detection response.

The theory of signal detection is concerned with these aspects of performance. It is a major theory for the general study of perception and has been used widely in investigations of sustained attention. A detailed tutorial on the nature of this approach is beyond the scope of this chapter. Appropriate descriptions can be found in Dember and Warm (1979), Green and Swets (1974), and McNicol (1972). For special sections on the application of signal detection theory to vigilance, see Davies and Parasuraman (1982) and Warm and Jerison (1984).

Applications to Vigilance

In essence, signal detection theory makes use of the frequency of correct detections (hits) and the frequency of false detections (false alarms), which also decline over time in vigilance studies, to derive two independent measures of performance: an index of perceptual sensitivity (d'), and an index of criterion in responding (β). The former describes the keenness of the observer's senses: the ability to discriminate signals from nonsignals. The latter describes the observer's tendency to say "yes, I see a signal," thus possibly detecting more signals but also generating more false alarms.

These measures have provided an important insight into the nature of the vigilance decrement. A substantial number of investigations have indicated that the decrement often does not involve a decline in alertness during a vigil (drop in d'). Instead, it reflects a shift to a more conservative response criterion (rise in β), perhaps because subjects develop more rational expectations of the actual signal probability in force with experience in the experiment (Davies and Parasuraman, 1982; Swets, 1977; Warm and Jerison, 1984; Williges, 1969). True perceptual decrements seem to be restricted to extremely demanding situations with low levels of signal discriminability, which may be brought about by low signal-to-noise ratios, fast event rates, and memory demanding tasks (Parasuraman et al., 1987).

Task Taxonomy

A major feature of vigilance tasks is their diversity. As noted earlier, such tasks can be presented in different sensory modalities and utilize a variety of psychophysical dimensions to define critical signals for detection. Davies and Parasuraman (1982) have argued, however, that there is an essential order to this diversity that can be made clear by appealing to a general view of attention known as resource theory. According to this position, the quality of performance in many situations is directly related to the amount of mental resources or capacity invested in the task at hand (Gopher and Kimchi, 1989; Kantowitz, 1985; see also Chapters 3 and 4). With that notion in mind, Davies and Parasuraman have suggested a classification system (taxonomy) in which vigilance tasks can be characterized as successive or simultaneous. The former are absolute judgment tasks in which subjects need to compare current input with a standard retained in working memory in order to separate signals and noise. Simultaneous tasks are comparative judgment tasks in which all of the information needed to distinguish signals from nonsignals is present in the stimuli themselves, and there is little involvement of recent memory for the signal feature. Davies and Parasuraman maintain that because of the memory imperative, successive tasks are more resource demanding than their simultaneous cohorts. A number of studies have supported this point of view. In so doing, they have adopted the strategy of comparing the effects of factors known to degrade the quality of sustained attention by increasing the subject's information processing load on the performance of successive and simultaneous tasks. If the former are more resource demanding than the latter, then any factor that places an additional drain on the subject's information processing resources should have a more pronounced effect on vigilance efficiency when presented within the context of a successive compared with a simultaneous task. Along these lines, the degrading effects of increments in event rate, event asynchrony, and the spatial uncertainty of signals have all been found to be more notable with successive than with simultaneous tasks (Joshi et al., 1985; Lanzetta et al., 1987; Scerbo et al., 1987a).

ENVIRONMENTAL STRESS

Environment and Task

In addition to psychophysical factors, vigilance performance is influenced considerably by conditions in the ambient environment. These conditions are often termed environmental stressors. The concept of stress, which is discussed more fully in Chapter 4, is difficult to define, but for the purpose of this chapter, stress is considered to be any threat to the physical or psychological well-being of the organism (Wingate, 1972). The discussion centers on the effects on vigilance of four basic stressors that are particularly likely to be a part of the combat environment of tanks: temperature, noise, vibration, and sleep loss.

Temperature

As in the case of the psychophysics of vigilance, Mackworth's seminal studies (1948, 1961) also provided the earliest data regarding the effects of heat on performance efficiency. Using a range of effective temperatures from 21 to 36 degrees centigrade, he found an inverted U-shaped function between performance efficiency and the temperature of the testing chamber. Performance was maximal at about 26 degrees centigrade and was poorer at temperatures on either side of that point. Later studies have demonstrated that while performance may improve when subjects are first exposed to moderate levels of heat (Kerslake and Poulton, 1965), the quality of vigilant behavior is impaired with continued exposure to temperatures above 32 degrees centigrade. In these conditions the probability of signal detection declines, as does d´, the sensitivity (Benor and Shvartz, 1971; Mackie and O'Hanlon, 1977; Pepler, 1953; Poulton and Edwards, 1974; Poulton et al., 1974).

The effects of heat stress on vigilance performance have also been studied more directly in terms of body temperature itself. Bell and his colleagues have found that performance suffers with rising body temperature (Bell et al., 1964), while other studies have reported that performance efficiency improves with elevations in body temperature (Colquhoun and Goldman, 1972; Wilkinson et al., 1964). In an effort to account for this disparity, Hancock (1984) has noted that the subjects' body temperatures were rising during the vigilance session in the Bell et al. (1964) experiment, while in the other studies, subjects were established in a static hyperthermic state during the session. Hancock (1984, 1986) has suggested that the key to understanding the effects of thermal stress lies in the action of the stressor on deep body temperature. Vigilance performance breaks down with perturbations in core temperature, remains unaffected when there is no variation in that temperature, and can be facilitated when subjects are established in a static hyperthermic state. Only a few studies have examined the effects of cold on vigilance performance. Nevertheless, they suggest that, like excessive heat, cold also impairs the quality of sustained attention when deep body temperature is perturbed (Hancock, 1984, 1986).

Noise

As described by Loeb (1986), noise, or unwanted sound, is the most ubiquitous pollutant in our industrialized society and a major environmental stressor. Accordingly, its effects have been studied extensively in a variety of situations, including those requiring sustained attention (Jones, 1983, 1984). The effects of noise on vigilance performance are intricate and depend on many factors. Two of the more important are the type of noise involved, intermittent or continuous, and task complexity.

Studies with intermittent noise have led to a plethora of conflicting results. In different circumstances, such noise can either enhance or degrade vigilance performance or have no effect at all (Hancock, 1984; Koelega and Brinkman, 1986; Poulton, 1977). Conditions in which noise is loud and continuous, such as might be expected in armored vehicles during combat, have led to more consistent results. Subjects appear to be relatively immune to the adverse effects of continuous noise when required to monitor only a single stimulus source (Blackwell and Belt, 1971; Davies and Hockey, 1966; Jerison, 1959a; Poulton and Edwards, 1974). They are far less immune, however, when attention must be directed to several stimulus sources. For example, Broadbent (1954) and Jerison (1959a) have reported that loud continuous noise degrades the speed and accuracy of signal detections in multidisplay monitoring tasks. The general effects of continuous noise on the quality of vigilant behavior can be summarized as follows: performance is degraded by loud noise (above 90dB SPL) when the information processing or resource demands of the task are high while it remains unaffected by loud noise when the processing demands are low. In addition, performance under low demand conditions can be facilitated by low-level (approximately 64dB SPL) continuous noise that is variegated in character (Hancock and Warm, 1989; Loeb, 1986).

In careful reviews of the literature on noise and vigilance, Jones (1983, 1984) has noted that continuous noise leads to two interesting changes in the manner in which monitors process information. One of these is a tendency for noise to increase their confidence in the adequacy of a detection decision. For example, given a choice of using one of three response categories when interrogating stimulus events for the presence of signals, "Sure Yes," "Unsure," and "Sure No," subjects exposed to noise increased the use of the two extreme categories at the expense of the intermediate one (Broadbent and Gregory, 1965). A similar result has also been reported by Hartley and Shirley (1977). As Jones (1984) has noted, it would appear that the range over which sensory information is considered becomes narrowed in noise, and in terms of signal detection theory, the distance in decision-space separating risky and cautious response criteria is lessened in noise. Hence, in settings in which risky responding is encouraged, such as combat situations wherein detecting the enemy first is vital for success, noise could reduce the likelihood of early target acquisition.

The second noise-related information processing change is in the manner in which monitors interrogate the vigilance display itself. Hockey (1970) has reported that noise induces subjects to follow the tendencies toward attentional narrowing (Easterbrook, 1959), discussed in Chapter 4, and shift their inspection away from peripheral, low-priority events, toward more central high-priority events. Jones (1983) has argued that this effect is essentially strategic in character; resources are invested in some sources of information rather than others. Such a noise-induced tradeoff has potentially important combat implications. It could serve to enhance target acquisition where it is likely that the enemy may be located on the battlefield, but at the same time, render a tank crew more vulnerable to threats from less likely locations.

Vibration

Vibration is a common experience among travelers regardless of whether their vehicles move about in the air, on the land, or in the sea. It is also encountered frequently in the workplace with machinery of all sorts. Accordingly, vibration stress has been a serious human factors concern (Goether, 1971). Surprisingly, however, few studies have focused on the relation between vibration and vigilance performance. The data that are available indicate that, except for situations in which the amplitude and frequency (above 10-15 Hz) of vibration is strong enough to blur vision (see Hancock, 1984; Poulton, 1977), vibration seems to have little impact on the quality of sustained attention. Studies by Schohan et al. (1965) using visual discriminations and Weisz et al. (1965) using both visual and auditory discriminations failed to find any significant effects for vibration on performance efficiency. Indeed, two experiments using vibration at 5Hz, the resonant frequency of the human body to vertical vibration (Poulton, 1977), found that such stimulation enhanced the frequency of signal detections (Shoenberger, 1967; Wilkinson and Gray, 1974). Poulton (1977) has suggested that this effect may be based on an increase in arousal level, but his explanation is not shared by all investigators (Hancock, 1984). All things considered, it would appear that, unless quite severe, vibration is not likely to be a serious environmental threat to the alertness of rotorcraft or armor crews.

Sleep Loss

As described in Chapter 5, a substantial body of data is available to indicate that sleep loss reduces efficiency on a variety of tasks (Anch et al., 1988; Broadbent, 1963; Colquhoun, 1972; Johnson and Naitoh, 1974). As described here, sleep deprivation, in particular, has been found to have a strong impact on the ability of monitors to remain alert. For example, Bergstrom et al. (1973), using a simulated radar task, found that the percentage of target detections dropped consistently from 100 percent to only 70 percent as the amount of time subjects went without sleep increased from 6 to 66 hours. Several other studies have shown that, after one night of total sleep deprivation, the overall speed and accuracy of signal detections declined as did perceptual sensitivity, and that the vigilance decrement can be exacerbated. In air crews, vigilance tasks are found to be the first affected by fatigue. Moreover, the amount of impairment resulting from sleep loss is linked to circadian rhythms. It is greater at night than during the day and reaches its maximum during the early morning hours (Davies and Parasuraman, 1982; Horne et al., 1983).

Williams et al. (1965) have pointed out that, rather than resulting in a system shutdown, the loss of adequate sleep appears to produce brief periods of inefficiency or lapses in what is otherwise normal functioning. These lapses are considered to stem from intervals of microsleep, which become common with fatigue (Hockey, 1986). It is encouraging to know that the effects of total sleep deprivation are not necessarily long-lasting, a point that might be of importance when considering the recovery of armor crews from sleep stress (Anch et al., 1988). In this regard, Rosa et al. (1983) have reported that subjects who suffered performance impairments after 40 or 64 hours of sleep deprivation returned to a baseline level of efficiency after 4 or 8 hours of recovery sleep, respectively. Recently, studies have shown the benefits of brief naps in air crew performance (Rosekind et al., 1991).

Rather than prolonged sleep deprivation, battle scenarios are more likely to include partial deprivation or limitations of normal sleep length. Studies by Hartley (1974), Webb and Agnew (1974), and Wilkinson and his colleagues (Wilkinson, 1968; Wilkinson et al., 1966) have shown that reduced sleep regimens impaired vigilance performance in comparison to control sleep schedules. Along these lines, it is worth noting that acute shifts in the sleep-wakefulness cycle can also affect vigilance performance. Taub and Berger (1973) have reported that signal detectability is impaired in subjects permitted the usual eight hours of rest when their sleep schedules were shifted forward or backward by several hours from their normal bedtimes. A similar result has been reported by Seidel et al. (1984). In addition, Taub and Berger (1969) have described what they have called the "Rip van Winkle effect," in which auditory signal detections were significantly lower after 11 hours of sleep than after the typical 8 hours. As Davies and Parasuraman (1982) point out, it would seem that any alteration in the normal sleep schedule can impair the quality of sustained attention.

Task-Induced Stress in Vigilance

Physiological Indices

Historically, vigilance tasks have been viewed as tedious but benign situations that place little demand on those engaged in them (Dember and Warm, 1979; Parasuraman, 1984). Evidence is accumulating, however, to indicate that vigilance tasks are not benign. Instead, such tasks can be quite demanding and induce considerable stress in subjects. Consequently, armor crew members who must perform tasks requiring vigilance functions during combat may be stressed not only by environmental factors, but also by the tasks they need to perform. This aspect of sustained attention tasks led Hancock and Warm (1989) to suggest that, in order to understand the role of stress in human performance, it is necessary to revise traditional views of stress as an independent environmentally and/or socially determined agent that acts on performance and recognize that tasks themselves can be a significant source of stress.

The stress response of a monitor during a vigilance session can be assessed by measuring the levels of circulating catecholamines (epinephrine and norepinephrine) and corticosteroids released into the bloodstream (Parasuraman, 1984; Wesnes and Warburton, 1983). This method was used by Frankenhaeuser et al. (1971) in comparing subjects' responses with a supposedly overstimulating sensorimotor task, in which they responded to multisensory stimuli with appropriate button-pressing, lever-pulling, and pedal-pushing activities and an understimulating vigilance task, involving the detection of increments in the intensity of visual targets, during a three-hour experimental session. As expected, the complex sensorimotor task produced elevated catecholamine levels indicative of stress. However, both epinephrine and norepinephrine levels were also elevated during the vigilance task, indicating that the latter also induced effort and stress. Similar results for vigilance tasks have been reported by Frankenhaeuser and Patkai (1964) and by Lundberg and Frankenhaeuser (1979).

More recently, Hovanitz et al. (1989) measured the vigilance-induced stress response by means of a frontal electromyogram and found a significant increase in muscle tension over the course of a one-hour session. Moreover, they reported that the task brought on tension headaches in sensitive subjects.

Mood Measures

Still another way to examine the stress induced by sustained attention tasks is through the use of self-reports of mood after participating in a vigil. The initial investigation along this line was conducted by Thackray et al. (1977), who asked monitors to rate their levels of boredom, monotony, irritation, attentiveness, fatigue, and strain at the beginning and at the end of a one-hour vigilance session. The task consisted of a simulated air traffic control radar system that displayed targets flying along specified routes at different speeds. Critical signals for detection consisted of departures from altitude as reflected in alphanumeric readouts on the radar screen. The subjects rated themselves as feeling significantly less attentive and more bored, strained, irritated, and fatigued after the vigil than before its start.

Subsequent studies using the Thackray scales have reported similar mood changes following participation in a watchkeeping session (Hovanitz et al., 1989; Lundberg et al., 1980; Thiemann et al., 1989). In addition, Warm and his coworkers (Dittmar, 1989; Macomber, 1967; Thiemann et al., 1989;

Warm et al., 1991) have reported that subjects feel more sleepy and fatigued after a vigil than at its start, as measured by the Stanford Sleepiness Scale (Hoddes et al., 1973) and a scale of symptoms of fatigue developed by Yoshitake (1978). Indeed, in one study, self-reports of fatigue increased by 120 percent over the course of a 40-minute vigil (Thiemann et al., 1989).

In addition to these investigations, negative mood changes during the course of vigilance performance have also been reported in two additional experiments that had more direct operational bearing. In one of these, Warm et al. (1989) examined the effects of extratask demands and long hours of work on the performance of simultaneous and successive vigilance tasks in a simulated work environment. For 3 consecutive 12-hour days, subjects engaged in 4 1-hour vigilance tasks interspersed with work at a heavy-load or light-load data entry task. They reported becoming more drowsy, strained, and fatigued and they experienced more somatic complaints over the workday and the workweek. These mood changes were maximal with the successive task and the heavy auxiliary workload, suggesting that in order to maintain performance standards in the successive task, subjects expended more processing resources, which led to a greater cost in fatigue and strain.

An interesting report by Johnson and McMenemy (1989) on mood changes among U.S. soldiers during sentry duty is also consistent with the idea that vigilance tasks are inherently stressful and provides striking evidence for the ecological validity of the findings of the other investigations just described. During three hours of simulated sentry duty, soldiers assumed a standing foxhole position and monitored a realistic target scene for pop-up targets—silhouettes of enemy troops. On detecting targets, the soldiers pressed a telegraph key and fired a Weaponeer rifle simulator. Target detection speed deteriorated with time on duty, a result that could have rather disastrous consequences in combat if the enemy's marksmanship is good, and the sentinels' predominant mood shifted during the assignment from one of vigor at the outset to fatigue at the end. Johnson and McMenemy suggest that, in order to optimize sentry duty performance, it should be limited to one hour or less.

Extrapolating to armor crews, sentry duty is often required in the so-called quiet time prior to combat when the crews are preparing defensive positions or waiting to begin offensive action themselves. Clearly, what was once thought to be a relatively nonstressful activity may place a much greater degree of strain on sentinels in the field than previously believed.

Perceived Workload

Additional evidence for the stress of sustained attention tasks comes from measurements of their perceived mental workload. This concept refers to the information processing load or resource demands that are associated with a task (O'Donnell and Eggemeier, 1986). Recently, several investigations of sustained attention used a subjective scale of mental workload known as the NASA Task Load Index, or the TLX. The instrument is a multidimensional scale that provides a global measure of workload and identifies specific components of workload along three demand dimensions (mental, physical, and temporal) imposed on the observer by the task and three dimensions (effort, frustration, and performance) related to the interaction of the observer and the task (Hart and Staveland, 1988). These studies showed that the cost of mental operations in vigilance is indeed high. For example, Gluckman et al. (1988b) reported uniformly high workload responses to both simultaneous and successive sustained attention tasks, and that overall workload levels varied inversely with the psychophysical salience of the signals; the more difficult it was to see the signals, the higher the workload. This result was confirmed by Galinsky et al. (1989), who found in addition that the powerful effect of event rate in vigilance was reflected directly in the perception of mental workload. The fact that workload scores in vigilance can be brought under psychophysical control enhances the validity of these subjective ratings (see Natsoulas, 1967).

Vigilance studies by Deaton and Parasuraman (1988), Decker et al. (1991), and Dittmar (1989) also found overall workload scores at the upper end of the TLX scale. These values are generally higher than those obtained for tasks such as memory search, choice reaction time, mental arithmetic, and grammatical reasoning (Dittmar, 1989). In all of these experiments, the major factors that contributed to overall workload were mental demand and frustration, a result that provides further indication of the stress of sustained attention. Moreover, it appears that stress effects may be so pervasive that they are more difficult to alleviate than performance effects, at least by noninvasive means. More specifically, Warm et al. (1991) found that providing subjects with brief whiffs of air containing the scent of mugget or peppermint can enhance the probability of signal detections in vigilance compared with plain air control conditions. Although overall performance was affected by the olfactory stimulation, neither fragrance made the task seem less demanding in terms of TLX workload ratings or reduced the feelings of stress obtained from self-report mood measures.

OPERATIONAL RELEVANCE

Workload Transition

Current Army doctrine calls for crews to remain with their tanks at the periphery of a battle zone for up to 72 hours prior to combat. During this time, there is relatively little to do. With the order to engage the enemy, however, the crews will suddenly be thrust into a period of high workload and stress. What are the implications for the efficiency of performance at this juncture of a prior period of relative inactivity? The question of workload transition on the battlefield is the central issue of this volume. Unfortunately, while there is a considerable literature on vigilance, very little information is available on the transition problem with regard to the quality of sustained attention. Nevertheless, the information that is available suggests that vigilance efficiency could be threatened considerably by a shift in the workload level.

Assuming that the modern battlefield will feature an intermingling of friendly and enemy forces, it would appear that one consequence of the onset of combat would be an increased event rate with respect to potential targets. A similar situation is found in the nuclear power plant following an abnormality. Scores of lights and warnings may be illuminated, but only a small percentage of these may contain useful diagnostic information.

A study by Krulewitz et al. (1975) addressed this issue in the laboratory. These investigators examined the effects of abrupt shifts in event rate in a low to high as well as in a high to low direction and found that such shifts had strong effects on monitoring efficiency. The frequency of signal detections for subjects shifted from a low to a high event rate was considerably poorer than that for control subjects maintained on the high event rate throughout the vigilance session. Conversely, a shift in the opposite direction resulted in enhanced performance on the part of the shifted subjects. A similar result has been reported by Wiener (1977) in a study in which the event rate was not altered within a session, but instead between sessions. Wiener's finding suggests that the event rate shift effect is most likely a contrast phenomenon in which prior experience determines the perceived magnitude of stimulus events (see Corso, 1967). Consequently, the high resource demands of a fast event rate in combat may be exacerbated by the lower demands of the lower event rate prior to the onset of combat.

Still another aspect of the post-transition phase compared with the prior passive waiting period is that team members will probably be confronted with more dual-task requirements. For example, the air crew may need to fly a crippled airliner while simultaneously engaging in demanding fault diagnosis and problem solving, and the tank commander may find it necessary to watch for both hostile aircraft and ground forces. A recent study by Gluckman et al. (1988a) demonstrated that efficiency is degraded when two vigilance tasks must be handled simultaneously and that this effect is strongest when resource demands are increased by the presence of a successive task in the dual-task ensemble.

Further work by Gluckman on dual-task vigilance performance has indicated that, as in the case of event rate, changes in workload wrought by shifts in dual-task requirements during a vigil can also have a deleterious effect on performance efficiency. This effect, however, is quite different from that which results from alterations in event rate. More specifically, Gluckman (1990) has reported that subjects shifted from single-task to dual-task monitoring (low to high workload) during a vigil did as well on the dual-task assignment as controls who were maintained on that assignment throughout the vigil. By contrast, subjects shifted from dual-task to single-task monitoring (high to low workload) performed more poorly immediately after the shift compared with controls who were maintained on the single task continuously. A result of this sort suggests that the cost in resource expenditure incurred by a high workload during combat may perseverate and have a negative impact on subsequent tasks requiring sustained attention (e.g., sentry duty) that armor personnel may have to perform after combat. When compared with the effects of shifts in event rate described by Krulewitz et al. (1975) and Wiener (1977), Gluckman's (1990) findings also suggest that the effects of workload transitions on vigilance performance are complex—they seem to depend on the precise manner in which such changes are brought about. This interpretation is supported in a recent report by See (1992), which indicated that shifts in workload brought about by changes in signal salience produced still a different result from the Krulewitz et al. (1975) and Wiener (1977) experiments. In See's investigation, subjects shifted from high-salience to low-salience signals performed in a manner equivalent to their continuous low-salience controls, while subjects shifted in the opposite direction performed in a manner similar to their continuous high-salience controls.

Given that the quality of vigilant behavior may be affected adversely by increments in workload, can anything be done to minimize the potential problem of workload transition and to enhance the general vigilance level of tank crews? Some suggestions toward these ends are offered below.

Remediation

Engineering Solutions

In a cogent analysis of human factors principles in the control of vigilance, Craig (1984) suggested a number of general approaches for enhancing the quality of sustained attention in operational settings. Two of these, reductions in signal uncertainty and the moderation of environmental sources of stress, might be followed by focusing on enhanced engineering design.

In Craig's analysis, the phrase *signal uncertainty* has broad meaning. It refers to anything that might aid monitors in detecting small, transient, or otherwise inconspicuous targets. In view of what is known with regard to the importance of signal amplitude and duration in vigilance in the tank environment, devices for aiding target acquisition, such as thermal imaging or computer-assisted detection systems, might be built to amplify the intensity of such critical signals as hot spots and weapon flashes and increase their dwell time of such signals on the crews' target acquisition displays. Computer aids might also be developed to provide crews with information as to the most probable times of appearance and spatial locations of targets and thus reduce the effects of both temporal and spatial uncertainty on vigilance efficiency.

As noted earlier, the sensory modality of a signal plays an important role in the quality of vigilant behavior, and sensory redundant displays aid in detection efficiency. Accordingly, thought might be given to ways of taking advantage of this effect by designing a form of radar-sonar system for tanks that would make use of analogous audio-visual signals, as has been successfully demonstrated for submarine sonar monitors (Lewandowski and Kobus, 1989). Such a system might increase overall efficiency in target acquisition. It might also reduce the powerful effects of event rate, since these effects can be eliminated in the laboratory when subjects are permitted to search for targets by alternating their inspection of analogous auditory and visual displays (Galinsky et al., 1990).

Throughout this chapter emphasis has been placed on the importance of resource utilization as a way of understanding vigilance performance. It is clear that successive tasks drain more processing capacity than simultaneous tasks. Hence, designers should strive whenever possible to provide simultaneous displays for target acquisition functions. This might be achieved by the use of instruments that furnish crews with immediate reference standards against which events can be compared instead of forcing them to rely on short-term memory to separate signals and noise.

In addition to these psychophysically oriented solutions, Craig (1984) has suggested that still another means by which the observer's uncertainty about the signal to be detected might be reduced and the likelihood of target acquisition enhanced is to employ multiple monitors under the assumption that failures to detect a target are likely to be uncorrelated; thus, what is missed by one monitor might be detected by another. In this way, detection probability by the team of monitors may be greater than that of only one monitor.

Team monitoring is an attractive possibility for enhancing target acquisition in armor crews, since Army doctrine calls for overlapping fields of inspection on the battlefield (Armor Field Manual 17-12-1, *Tank Combat Tables*, no date). Unfortunately, the experimental evidence with regard to the effectiveness of team monitoring in vigilance is too equivocal at present to permit a strong endorsement of this practice. While some experiments have demonstrated an improvement in signal detectability for teams of monitors compared with lone monitors (Baker et al., 1962; Konz and Osman, 1977; Mico, 1965; Morgan and Alluisi, 1965; Wiener, 1965), other studies have reported no advantage for monitoring teams (Bergum and Lehr, 1962). In at least one case, performance for multioperator teams was poorer than that of single monitors working alone (Ware et al., 1964). The effects of team monitoring are complicated by the fact that social interactions between monitors plays a role in determining the effectiveness of the procedure. For example, a study by Klinger (1969) showed that the performance of a monitor is enhanced by the presence of a coactor, but only when the coactor served as a potential evaluator by having access to the quality of the monitor's performance.

It is worth noting that the lack of consistency in team monitoring studies was first pointed out by Davies and Tune (1969) several years ago. Little work has been done since that time to clarify the issue. Moreover, except for one study involving signal density (Bergum and Lehr, 1962), none of the available experiments has explored the influence of important psychophysical variables on the effectiveness of team monitoring. Given its potential applicability to target acquisition in armored combat, the team concept warrants further investigation.

Unlike a factory environment or that of the air crew in fixed-wing aircraft, both of whom can be under the control of the intrinsic interests and the wishes of management, battlefield conditions are more capricious, and the battlefield is a more difficult arena in which to modify sources of environmental stress. Noise and vibration are likely to be unavoidable, and complete noise abatement is probably not advisable, since noise in battle can be informative as well as distracting. In contrast, the elimination of temperature extremes of the sort that can degrade vigilance efficiency in tanks or helicopters would appear to be worthwhile. This can be accomplished by building appropriate cooling and heating systems into such vehicles and/or by providing protective clothing that can insulate crew members from climatic extremes. These steps seem to be especially necessary if tank crew members are to remain buttoned up inside their vehicles for several hours, as in chemical warfare scenarios.

Training

A third approach to the control of vigilance recommended by Craig (1984) and also by Parasuraman (1986) is training. Considerable evidence exists to indicate that training with target cueing or with knowledge of results can have a beneficial effect on performance in tasks requiring sustained attention (Decker et al., 1991; Dittmar et al., 1985; Warm, 1977; Warm and Jerison, 1984; Wiener, 1984). With regard to their vigilance functions, crews of any team confronting vigilance problems may profit from instructions designed to optimize response strategies. More specifically, it may help crew members develop more effective procedures for coping with the vigilance challenges that confront them in combat situations to advise them of such effects as the tendency of monitors to: (1) transfer signal probability estimates from one situation to another, (2) ignore low-probability areas under spatial uncertainty, (3) become more conservative in responding over time, (4) ignore peripheral stimuli in noise, and (5) become more certain (perhaps unduly so) of signal and nonsignal decisions in noise. This training of operators to understand the biases and tendencies in their own performance has an analogy in decision making discussed in Chapter 8, wherein such debiasing procedures have proven successful.

The most impressive testimonial for the potential benefits of training comes from Fisk and Schneider's (1981) finding that the decrement function can be eliminated when vigilance tasks become automatic. Fisk and Scerbo (1987) provide several suggestions for how training should be carried out to maximize automatic processing development. Appropriate strategies for this type of training are discussed in Chapter 11. Fisk and Scerbo (1987) have also pointed out that training for automatic processing can make vigilance performance more resistant to the effects of environmental stress and increased mental workload, findings that add to the potential importance of a good training regimen and that fit well with Wilkinson's (1969) claim that familiarity with a task is a primary way to insulate performance against the effects of stress. As for stress itself, evidence is also available that indicates that training can have an important role in helping individuals to develop appropriate coping strategies (Hockey, 1986; see also Chapter 4).

REFERENCES

Adams, J.A.
    1956   Vigilance in the detection of low-intensity visual stimuli. *Journal of Experimental Psychology* 52:204-208.
Adams, J.A., and L.R. Boulter
    1964   Spatial and temporal uncertainty as determinants of vigilance performance. *Journal of Experimental Psychology* 64:127-131.
Adams, J.A., and J.M. Humes
    1963   Monitoring of complex visual displays: Training for vigilance. *Human Factors* 5:147-153.
Adams, J.A., J.M. Humes, and N.A. Sieveking
    1963   Monitoring of complex visual displays. Effects of repeated sessions and heavy visual load on human vigilance. *Human Factors* 5:385-389.
Alluisi, E.A.
    1966   Attention and vigilance as mechanisms of response. Pp. 201-213 in E.A. Bilodeau, ed., *Acquisition of Skill*. New York: Academic Press.
Anch, A.M., C.P. Brownian, M.M. Mitler, and J.K. Walsh
    1988   *Sleep: A Scientific Perspective*. Englewood Cliffs, New Jersey: Prentice-Hall.

Baker, R.A., J.W. Ware, and R.R. Sipowitz
   1962   Signal detection by multiple monitors. *Psychological Record* 12:133-137.
Bell, C.R., K.A. Provins, and R.W. Hiorns
   1964   Visual and auditory vigilance during exposure to hot and humid conditions. *Ergonomics* 7:279-288.
Benor, D., and E. Shvartz
   1971   Effect on body cooling on vigilance in hot environments. *Aerospace Medicine* 42:727-730.
Bergstrom, B., M. Gillsberg, and P. Arnberg
   1973   Effects of sleep loss and stress on radar watching. *Journal of Applied Psychology* 58:158-162.
Bergum, B.O., and D.J. Lehr
   1962   Vigilance performance as a function of paired monitoring. *Journal of Applied Psychology* 46:341-343.
Blackwell, P.J., and J.A. Belt
   1971   Effect of differential levels of ambient noise on vigilance performance. *Perceptual and Motor Skills* 32:734.
Bowers, J.C.
   1983   Stimulus Homogeneity and the Event Rate Function in Sustained Attention. Doctoral dissertation, University of Cincinnati, Cincinnati, Ohio.
Broadbent, D.E.
   1954   Some effects of noise on visual performance. *Quarterly Journal of Experimental Psychology* 6:1-5.
   1963   Differences and interactions between stresses. *Quarterly Journal of Experimental Psychology* 15:205-211.
Broadbent, D.E., and M. Gregory
   1965   Effects of noise and of signal rate upon vigilance analyzed by means of decision theory. *Human Factors* 7:155-162.
Colquhoun, W.P., ed.
   1972   *Aspects of Human Efficiency: Diurnal Rhythm and Loss of Sleep.* London, UK: English Universities Press.
Colquhoun, W.P., and A.D. Baddeley
   1964   Role of pretest expectancy in vigilance decrement. *Journal of Experimental Psychology* 68:156-160.
   1967   Influence of signal probability during pretraining on vigilance decrement. *Journal of Experimental Psychology* 73(1):153-155.
Colquhoun, W.P., and R.F. Goldman
   1972   Vigilance under induced hyperthermia. *Ergonomics* 15:621-632.
Corcoran, D.W.J., J. Mullin, M.T. Rainey, and G. Frith
   1977   The effects of raised signal and noise amplitude during the course of vigilance tasks. Pp. 645-664 in R.R. Mackie, ed., *Vigilance: Theory, Operational Performance and Physiological Correlates.* New York: Plenum.
Corso, J.F.
   1967   *The Experimental Psychology of Sensory Behavior.* New York: Holt, Rinehart and Winston.
Craig, A.
   1984   Human engineering: The control of vigilance. Pp. 247-291 in J.S. Warm, ed., *Sustained Attention in Human Performance.* Chichester, UK: Wiley.
   1985a   Field studies of human inspection: The application of vigilance research. Pp. 133-144 in S. Folkard and T.H. Monk, eds., *Hours of Work: Temporal Factors in Work-Scheduling.* Chichester, UK: Wiley.

1985b   Vigilance: Theories and laboratory studies. Pp. 107-121 in S. Folkard and T.H. Monk, eds., *Hours of Work: Temporal Factors in Work-Scheduling*. Chichester, UK: Wiley.

1991   Vigilance and monitoring for multiple signals. Pp. 153-172 in D. L. Damos, ed., *Multiple Task Performance*. London, UK: Taylor and Francis.

Craig, A., W.P. Colquhoun, and D.W.J. Corcoran
1976   Combining evidence presented simultaneously to the eye and the ear: A comparison of some predictive models. *Perception and Psychophysics* 19:473-484.

Davies, D.R.
1985   Individual and group differences in sustained attention. Pp. 123-132 in S. Folkard and T.M. Monk, eds., *Hours of Work: Temporal Factors in Work-Scheduling*. Chichester, UK: Wiley.

Davies, D.R., and G.R.J. Hockey
1966   The effects of noise and doubling the signal frequency on individual differences in visual vigilance performance. *British Journal of Psychology* 57:381-389.

Davies, D.R., and R. Parasuraman
1982   *The Psychology of Vigilance*. London, UK: Academic Press.

Davies, D.R., and G.S. Tune
1969   *Human Vigilance Performance*. New York: American Elsevier.

Deaton, J.E., and R. Parasuraman
1988   Effects of task demands and age on vigilance and subjective workload. Pp. 1458-1462 in *Proceedings of the Human Factors Society 32nd Annual Meeting*. Santa Monica, California: Human Factors Society.

Decker, A.B., J.S. Warm, W.N. Dember, and P.A. Hancock
1991   Effects of feedback on perceived workload in vigilance performance. Pp. 1491-1494 in *Proceedings of the Human Factors Society 35th Annual Meeting*. Santa Monica, California: Human Factors Society.

Dember, W.N., and J.S. Warm
1979   *Psychology of Perception, Second Edition*. New York: Holt, Rinehart and Winston.

Dember, W.N., J.S. Warm, J.C. Bowers, and T. Lanzetta
1984   Intrinsic motivation and the vigilance decrement. Pp. 21-26 in A. Mital, ed., *Trends in Ergonomics/Human Factors, I*. Amsterdam: Elsevier (North-Holland).

Dittmar, M.L.
1989   Sex Differences and Stress In Vigilance Performance. Doctoral dissertation, University of Cincinnati, Cincinnati, Ohio.

Dittmar, M.L., J.S. Warm, and W.N. Dember
1985   Effects of knowledge of results on performance in successive and simultaneous vigilance tasks: A signal detection analysis. Pp. 195-202 in R.E. Eberts and C.G. Eberts, eds., *Trends in Ergonomics/Human Factors II*. Amsterdam: Elsevier (North-Holland).

Doll, T.J., and T.E. Hanna
1989   Enhanced detection with bimodal sonar displays. *Human Factors* 31:539-550.

Easterbrook, J.A.
1959   The effect of emotion on cue utilization and the organization of behavior. *Psychological Review* 66:183-201.

Fisk, A.D., and M.W. Scerbo
1987   Automatic and control processing approach to interpreting vigilance performance: A review and reevaluation. *Human Factors* 29:653-660.

Fisk, A.D., and W. Schneider
1981   Control and automatic processing during tasks requiring sustained attention: A new approach to vigilance. *Human Factors* 23:737-750.

Frankenhaeuser, M., B. Nordheden, A.L. Myrsten, and B. Post
    1971   Psychophysiological reactions to understimulation and overstimulation. *Acta Psychologica* 35:298-308.
Frankenhaeuser, M., and P. Patkai
    1964   Catecholamine excretion and performance under stress. *Perceptual and Motor Skills* 19:13-14.
Galinsky, T.L., W.N. Dember, and J.S. Warm
    1989   Effects of Event Rate on Subjective Workload in Vigilance Performance. Paper presented at the meeting of the Southern Society for Philosophy and Psychology, Chicago, Illinois.
Galinsky, T.L., J.S. Warm, W.N. Dember, E.M. Weiler, and M.W. Scerbo
    1990   Sensory alternation and vigilance performance: The role of pathway inhibition. *Human Factors* 32:717-728.
Gluckman, J.P.
    1990   Changing Task Demands in Sustained Attention: Effects on Performance and Perceived Workload. Doctoral dissertation, University of Cincinnati, Cincinnati, Ohio.
Gluckman, J.P., W.N. Dember, and J.S. Warm
    1988a   Capacity demand in dual-task monitoring of simultaneous and successive vigilance tasks. Pp. 1463-1465 in *Proceedings of the Human Factors Society 32nd Annual Meeting*. Santa Monica, California: Human Factors Society.
Gluckman, J.P., J.S. Warm, W.N. Dember, J.A. Thiemann, and P.A. Hancock
    1988b   Subjective Workload in Simultaneous and Successive Vigilance Tasks. Paper presented at the meeting of the Psychonomic Society, Chicago, Illinois.
Goether, W.F.
    1971   Vibration and human performance. *Human Factors* 13:203-216.
Gopher, D., and R. Kimchi
    1989   Engineering psychology. *Annual Review of Psychology* 40:431-455.
Green, D.M., and J.A. Swets
    1974   *Signal Detection Theory and Psychophysics*. New York: Krieger.
Griffin, J.A., W.N. Dember, and J.S. Warm
    1986   Effects of depression on expectancy in sustained attention. *Motivation and Emotion* 10:195-205.
Guralnick, M.J.
    1972   Observing responses and decision processes in vigilance. *Journal of Experimental Psychology* 93:239-244.
Hancock, P.A.
    1984   Environmental stressors. Pp. 103-142 in J.S. Warm, ed., *Sustained Attention in Human Performance*. Chichester, UK: Wiley.
    1986   Sustained attention under thermal stress. *Psychological Bulletin* 99:263-281.
Hancock, P.A., and J.S. Warm
    1989   A dynamic model of stress and sustained attention. *Human Factors* 31:519-537.
Hart, S.G., and L.E. Staveland
    1988   Development of NASA-TLX (Task Load Index): Results of empirical and theoretical research. Pp. 139-183 in P.A. Hancock and N. Meshkati, eds., *Human Mental Workload*. Amsterdam: North-Holland.
Hartley, L.R.
    1974   A comparison of continuous and distributed sleep schedules. *Quarterly Journal of Experimental Psychology* 26:8-14.
Hartley, L.R., and E. Shirley
    1977   Sleep loss, noise and decisions. *Ergonomics* 20:481-482.

Hatfield, J.L., and M. Loeb
   1968   Sense mode and coupling in a vigilance task. *Perception and Psychophysics* 4:29-
             36.
Hockey, G.R.J.
   1970   Effect of loud noise on attentional selectivity. *Quarterly Journal of Experimental
             Psychology* 22:28-36.
   1986   Changes in operator efficiency as a function of environmental stress, fatigue, and
             circadian rhythms. Pp. 44.1-44.49 in K.R. Boff, L. Kaufman, and J.P. Thomas,
             eds., *Handbook of Human Perception and Performance: Volume II, Cognitive
             Processes and Performance*. New York: Wiley.
Hoddes, E., V. Zarcone, H. Smythe, R. Phillips, and W.C. Dement
   1973   Quantification of sleepiness: A new approach. *Psychophysiology* 10(4):431-436.
Horne, J.A., N.R. Anderson, and R.T. Wilkinson
   1983   Effects of sleep deprivation on signal detection measures of vigilance: Implica-
             tions for sleep function. *Sleep* 6:347-358.
Hovanitz, C.A., K. Chin, and J.S. Warm
   1989   Complexities in life stress-dysfunction relationships: A case in point-tension headache.
             Journal of Behavioral Medicine 12:55-75.
Jerison, H.J.
   1959a   Effects of noise on human performance. *Journal of Applied Psychology* 43:96-
             101.
   1959b   *Experiments on Vigilance: The Empirical Model for Human Vigilance*. WADC
             Report No. 58-526. Wright-Patterson Air Force Base, Ohio: Aero-Medical Labo-
             ratory, Wright Air-Development Center.
   1963   On the decrement function in human vigilance. Pp. 199-212 in D.N. Buckner and
             J.J. McGrath, eds., *Vigilance: A Symposium*. New York: McGraw-Hill.
Jerison, H.J., and R.M. Pickett
   1964   Vigilance: The importance of the elicited observing rate. *Science* 143:970-971.
Johnson, L.C., and P. Naitoh
   1974   *The Operational Consequences of Sleep Deprivation and Sleep Deficit*. Report
             No. AGARD-OGRAPH-193. Paris, France: Advisory Group for Aerospace Re-
             search and Development.
Johnson, R.F., and D.J. McMenemy
   1989   Target detection, rifle marksmanship and mood during three hours of sentry duty.
             Pp. 1414-1418 in *Proceedings of the Human Factors Society 33rd Annual Meet-
             ing*. Santa Monica, California: Human Factors Society.
Jones, D.M.
   1983   Noise. Pp. 61-95 in R. Hockey, ed., *Stress and Fatigue in Human Performance*.
             Chichester, UK: Wiley.
   1984   Performance effects. Pp. 155-184 in D.M. Jones and A.J. Chapman, eds., *Noise
             and Society*. Chichester, UK: Wiley.
Joshi, A., W.N. Dember, J.S. Warm, and M.W. Scerbo
   1985   Capacity Demands In Sustained Attention. Paper presented at the meeting of the
             Psychonomic Society, Boston, Massachusetts.
Kantowitz, B.H.
   1985   Channels and stages in human information processing: A limited analysis of
             theory and methodology. *Journal of Mathematical Psychology* 29:135-174.
Kerslake, D.M., and E.C. Poulton
   1965   Initial stimulating effect of warmth upon perceptual efficiency. Transient per-
             petual efficiency variation on temperature increase, noting arousal level. *Aero-
             space Medicine* 36:29-32.

Klinger, E.
 1969 Feedback effects and social facilitation of vigilance performance: Mere coaction versus potential evaluation. *Psychonomic Society* 14:161-162.
Koelega, H.S., and J.A. Brinkman
 1986 Noise and vigilance: An evaluative review. *Human Factors* 28:465-482.
Konz, S., and K. Osman
 1977 Team efficiencies on a paced visual inspection task. *Journal of Human Ergology* 6:111-119.
Krulewitz, J.E., and J.S. Warm
 1977 The event rate context in vigilance: Relation to signal probability and expectancy. *Bulletin of the Psychonomic Society* 10(5):429-432.
Krulewitz, J.E., J.S. Warm, and T.H. Wohl
 1975 Effects of shifts in the rate of repetitive stimulation on sustained attention. *Perception and Psychophysics* 18(4):245-249.
Lanzetta, T.M., W.N. Dember, J.S. Warm, and D.B. Berch
 1987 Effects of task type and stimulus heterogeneity on the event rate function in sustained attention. *Human Factors* 29:625-633.
Lewandowski, L.J., and D.A. Kobus
 1989 Bimodal information processing in sonar performance. *Human Performance* 2:73-84.
Loeb, M.
 1986 *Noise and Human Efficiency.* Chichester, UK: Wiley.
Loeb, M., and J.R. Binford
 1963 Some factors influencing the effective auditory intensive difference limen. *Journal of the Acoustical Society of America* 35:884-891.
 1968 Variations in performance on auditory and visual monitoring tasks as a function of signal and stimulus frequencies. *Perception and Psychophysics* 4:361-367.
Loeb, M., T.K. Noonan, D.W. Ash, and D.H. Holding
 1987 Limitations of the cognitive vigilance increment. *Human Factors* 29:661-674.
Lundberg, U., and M. Frankenhaeuser
 1979 *Pituitary-Adrenal and Sympathetic-Adrenal Correlates of Distress and Effort.* Report No. 548. Department of Psychology, University of Stockholm, Sweden.
Lundberg, P.K., J.S. Warm, and W. Seeman
 1980 Sustained Attention and the Type A Individual: Attentive, Aroused and Able. Paper presented at the meeting of the Midwestern Psychological Association, Chicago, Illinois.
Lysaght, R.J., J.S. Warm, W.N. Dember, and M. Loeb
 1984 Effects of noise and information-processing demand on vigilance performance in men and women. Pp. 27-32 in A. Mital, ed., *Trends in Ergonomics/Human Factors I.* Amsterdam: Elsevier (North-Holland).
Mackie, R.R., and J.F. O'Hanlon
 1977 A study of the combined effects of extended driving and heat stress on driver arousal and performance. Pp. 537-558 in R.R. Mackie, ed., *Vigilance: Theory, Operational Performance, and Physiological Correlates.* New York: Plenum.
Mackworth, N.H.
 1948 The breakdown of vigilance during prolonged visual search. *Quarterly Journal of Experimental Psychology* 1:6-21.
 1961 Research on the measurement of human performance. Pp. 174-331 in H.W. Sinaiko, ed., *Selected Papers on Human Factors in the Design and Use of Control Systems.* New York: Dover (Reprinted from Medical Research Council Special Report Series 268, London, UK: HM Stationery Office, 1950).

Macomber, R.M.
 1967   Effects of Noise on Stress and Performance in Sustained Attention Tasks. Unpublished Senior Thesis, University of Cincinnati, Cincinnati, Ohio.
McFarland, B.P., and C.G. Halcomb
 1970   Expectancy and stimulus generalization in vigilance. *Perceptual and Motor Skills* 30:147-151.
McNicol, D.
 1972   *A Primer of Signal Detection Theory.* London, UK: Allen and Unwin.
Metzger, K.R., J.S. Warm, and R.J. Senter
 1974   Effects of background event rate and critical signal amplitude on vigilance performance. *Perceptual and Motor Skills* 38:1175-1181.
Mico, H.C.
 1965   On the most efficient use of two observers in vigilance tasks. Pp. 449-453 in *Proceedings of the Second Annual Congress on Ergonomics.* Dortmund, London, UK: Taylor and Francis.
Milosevic, S.
 1974   Effect of time and space uncertainty on a vigilance task. *Perception and Psychophysics* 15:331-334.
Montague, W.E., C.E. Weber, and J.A. Adams
 1965   The effects of signal and response complexity on eighteen hours of visual monitoring. *Human Factors* 7:163-172.
Moore, S.F., and S.J. Gross
 1973   Influence of critical signal regularity, stimulus event matrix and cognitive style on vigilance performance. *Journal of Experimental Psychology* 99:137-139.
Morgan, B.B., and E.A. Alluisi
 1965   On the inferred independence of paired watchkeepers. *Psychonomic Science* 2:161-162.
Natsoulas, T.
 1967   What are perceptual reports about? *Psychological Bulletin* 67:249-272.
Nicely, P.E., and G.A. Miller
 1957   Some effects of unequal spatial distribution on the detectability of radar targets. *Journal of Experimental Psychology* 53:195-198.
Nuechterlein, K.H., R. Parasuraman, and Q. Jiang
 1983   Visual sustained attention: Image degradation produces rapid sensitivity decrement over time. *Science* 220:327-329.
O'Donnell, R.D., and F.T. Eggemeier
 1986   Workload assessment methodology. Pp. 42.1-42.49 in K.R. Boff, L. Kaufman, and J.P. Thomas, eds., *Handbook of Perception and Human Performance: Volume II, Cognitive Processes and Performance.* New York: Wiley.
Parasuraman, R.
 1979   Memory load and event rate control sensitivity decrements in sustained attention. *Science* 205:924-927.
 1984   The psychobiology of sustained attention. Pp. 61-101 in J.S. Warm, ed., *Sustained Attention in Human Performance.* Chichester, UK: Wiley.
 1985   Sustained attention: A multifactorial approach. Pp. 493-511 in M.I. Posner and O.S. Marlin, eds., *Attention and Performance I.* Hillsdale, New Jersey: Erlbaum.
 1986   Vigilance, monitoring and search. Pp. 43.1-43.39 in K.R. Boff, L. Kaufman and J.P. Thomas, eds., *Handbook of Perception and Human Performance: Volume II, Cognitive Processes and Performance.* New York: Wiley.
 1987   Human computer monitoring. *Human Factors* 29:695-706.

Parasuraman, R., and D.R. Davies
  1976   Decision theory analysis of response latencies in vigilance. *Journal of Experimental Psychology: Human Perception and Performance* 2:578-590.
  1977   A taxonomic analysis of vigilance performance. Pp. 559-574 in R.R. Mackie, ed., *Vigilance: Theory, Operational Performance and Physiological Correlates*. New York: Plenum.
Parasuraman, R., J.S. Warm, and W.N. Dember
  1987   Vigilance: Taxonomy and Utility. Pp. 11-32 in L.S. Mark, J.S. Warm, and R.L. Huston, eds., *Ergonomics and Human Factors: Recent Research*. New York: Springer-Verlag.
Pepler, R.D.
  1953   *The Effect of Climatic Factors on the Performance of Skilled Tasks by Young European Men Living in the Tropics. 4. A Task of Prolonged Visual Vigilance.* Medical Research Council Applied Psychology Unit Report No. 156/53, London, UK.
Poulton, E.C.
  1977   Arousing stresses increase vigilance. Pp. 423-459 in R.R. Mackie, ed., *Vigilance: Theory, Operational Performance and Physiological Correlates*. New York: Plenum.
Poulton, E.C., and R.S. Edwards
  1974   Interactions and range effects in experiments on pairs of stresses: Mild heat and low frequency noise. *Journal of Experimental Psychology* 104:621-628.
Poulton, E.C., R.S. Edwards, and W.P. Colquhoun
  1974   The interaction of the loss of a night's sleep with mild heat: Task variables. *Ergonomics* 17:59-73.
Rosa, R.R., M.H. Bonnet, and J.S. Warm
  1983   Recovery of performance during sleep following sleep deprivation. *Psychophysiology* 20:152-159.
Rosekind, M.R., P.H. Gander, and D.F. Dinges
  1991   Alertness management in flight operations: Strategic napping. Pp. 1-12 in *Aerospace Technology Conference and Exposition*. Long Beach, California.
Scerbo, M.W., J.W. Warm, V.S. Doettling, R. Parasuraman, and A.D. Fisk
  1987a   Event asynchrony and task demands in sustained attention. Pp. 33-39 in L.S. Mark, J.S. Warm, and R.L. Huston, eds., *Ergonomics and Human Factors: Recent Research*. New York: Springer-Verlag.
Scerbo, M.W., J.S. Warm, and A.D. Fisk
  1987b   Event asynchrony and signal regularity in sustained attention. *Current Psychological Research and Reviews* 5:335-343.
Schneider, W., and R.M. Shiffrin
  1977   Control and automatic human information processing: I. Detection, search, and attention. *Psychological Review* 84:1-66S.
Schohan, B., H.E. Rawson, and S.M. Soliday
  1965   Pilot and observer performance in simulated low-altitude high-speed flight. *Human Factors* 7:257-265.
See, J.E.
  1992   Effects of Transitions in Signal Salience on Vigilance Performance. Masters thesis, University of Cincinnati.
Seidel, W.F., T. Roth, T. Roehrs, F. Zorick, and W.C. Dement
  1984   Treatment of a 12-hour shift of sleep schedule with Benzodiazepines. *Science* 224:1262-1264.

Sheridan, T.
    1970   On how often the supervisor should sample. *IEEE Transactions on System Science and Cybernetics* SSC-6:140-145.
Shoenberger, R.W.
    1967   Effects of vibration on complex psychomotor performance. *Aerospace Medicine* 12:1265-1269.
Smith, R.P., J.S. Warm, and E.A. Alluisi
    1966   Effects of temporal uncertainty on watchkeeping performance. *Perception and Psychophysics* 1:293-299.
Swets, J.A.
    1977   Signal detection theory applied to vigilance. Pp. 705-718 in R.R. Mackie, ed., *Vigilance: Theory, Operational Performance and Physiological Correlates.* New York: Plenum.
Taub, H.A., and F.H. Osborne
    1968   Effects of signal and stimulus rates on vigilance performance. *Journal of Applied Psychology* 52:133-138.
Taub, J.M., and R.J. Berger
    1969   Extended sleep and performance: The Rip Van Winkle effect. *Psychonomic Science* 16:204-205.
    1973   Performance and mood following variations in the length and timing of sleep. *Psychophysiology* 10:559-570.
Teichner, W.H.
    1974   The detection of a simple visual signal as a function of time of watch. *Human Factors* 16(4):339-353.
Thackray, R.I., J.P. Bailey, and R.M. Touchstone
    1977   Physiological, subjective and performance correlates of reported boredom and monotony while performing a simulated radar control task. Pp. 203-215 in R.R. Mackie, ed., *Vigilance: Theory, Operational Performance, and Physiological Correlates.* New York: Plenum.
Thiemann, J.A., J.S. Warm, W.N. Dember, and E.B. Smith
    1989   Effects of Caffeine on Vigilance Performance and Task-Induced Stress. Paper presented at the meeting of the Southern Society for Philosophy and Psychology, New Orleans, Louisiana.
U.S. Department of the Army
    No date *FM 17-12-1 Tank Combat Tables.* Fort Knox, Kentucky: U.S. Army Armor School.
Ware, J.S., R.A. Baker, and E. Drucker
    1964   Sustained vigilance II. Signal detection for two-man teams during a 24-hour watch. *Journal of Engineering Psychology* 3:104-110.
Warm, J.S.
    1977   Psychological processes in sustained attention. Pp. 623-644 in R.R. Mackie, ed., *Vigilance: Theory, Operational Performance and Physiological Correlates.* New York: Plenum.
    1984a   An introduction to vigilance. Pp. 1-14 in J.S. Warm, ed., *Sustained Attention in Human Performance.* Chichester, UK: Wiley
Warm, J.S., ed.
    1984b   *Sustained Attention in Human Performance.* Chichester, UK: Wiley.
Warm, J.S., and E.A. Alluisi
    1971   Influence of temporal uncertainty and sensory modality of signals on watchkeeping performance. *Journal of Experimental Psychology* 87:303-308.

Warm, J.S., and D.B. Berch
1985   Sustained attention in the mentally retarded: The vigilance paradigm. Pp. 1-41 in
        N.R. Ellis and N.W. Bray, eds., *International Review of Research in Mental Retardation (Volume 13)*. Orlando, Florida: Academic Press.
Warm, J.S., W.N. Dember, and R. Parasuraman
1991   Effects of olfactory stimulation on performance and stress in a visual sustained
        attention task. *Journal of the Society of Cosmetic Chemists* 42:199-210.
Warm, J.S., B.D. Eppe, and R.P. Ferguson
1974   Effects of knowledge of results and signal regularity on vigilance performance.
        Bulletin of the Psychonomic Society 4:272-274.
Warm, J.S., S.R. Howe, H.D. Fishbein, W.N. Dember, and R.L. Sprague
1984   Cognitive demand and the vigilance decrement. Pp. 15-20 in A. Mital, ed., *Trends
        in Ergonomics/Human Factors 1*. Amsterdam: Elsevier (North-Holland).
Warm, J.S., and H.J. Jerison
1984   The psychophysics of vigilance. Pp. 15-60 in J.S. Warm, ed., *Sustained Attention
        in Human Performance*. Chichester, UK: Wiley.
Warm, J.S., M. Loeb, and E.A. Alluisi
1970   Variations in watchkeeping performance as a function of the rate and duration of
        visual signals. *Perception and Psychophysics* 7:97-99.
Warm, J.S., and R. Parasuraman, eds.
1987   Vigilance: Basic and applied. *Human Factors* 29:623-740.
Warm, J.S., R.R. Rosa, and M.J. Colligan
1989   Effects of auxiliary load on vigilance performance in a simulated work environ-
        ment. Pp. 1419-1421 in *Proceedings of the Human Factors Society 33rd Annual
        Meeting*. Santa Monica, California: Human Factors Society.
Webb, W.B., and H.W. Agnew
1974   The effects of chronic limitation of sleep length. *Psychophysiology* 11:265-274.
Weisz, A.A., C. Goddard, and R.W. Allen
1965   *Human Performance Under Random and Sinusoidal Vibration*. Aerospace Medi-
        cal Research Laboratories Report No. AMRL-TR-65-209. Wright-Patterson Air
        Force Base, Ohio.
Wesnes, K., and D.M. Warburton
1983   Stress and drugs. Pp. 203-243 in R. Hockey, ed., *Stress and Fatigue In Human
        Performance*. Chichester, UK: Wiley.
Wiener, E.L.
1965   The performance of multi-man monitoring teams. *Human Factors* 6:179-184.
1977   Stimulus presentation rate in vigilance. *Human Factors* 19:301-303.
1984   Vigilance and Inspection. Pp. 207-246 in J.S. Warm, ed., *Sustained Attention in
        Human Performance*. Chichester, UK: Wiley.
1985   Beyond the sterile cockpit. *Human Factors* 27:75-90.
1987   Application of vigilance research: Rare, medium or well done? *Human Factors*
        29:725-736.
Wilkinson, R.T.
1968   Sleep deprivation: Performance tests for partial and selective sleep deprivation.
        Pp. 28-43 in L.A. Abt and B.F. Reiss, eds., *Progress in Clinical Psychology,
        Volume 7*. New York: Grune and Stratton.
1969   Some factors influencing the effect of environmental stressors upon performance.
        Psychological Bulletin 72:260-272.
Wilkinson, R.T., R.S. Edwards, and E. Haines
1966   Performance following a night of reduced sleep. *Psychonomic Science* 4:471-472.

Wilkinson, R.T., R.H. Fox, R. Goldsmith, I.F.G. Hampton, and H.E. Lewis
   1964   Psychological and physiological responses to raised body temperature. *Journal of Applied Physiology* 19:287-291.
Wilkinson, R.T., and R. Gray
   1974   Effects of duration of vertical vibration beyond the proposed ISO "fatigue-decreased proficiency time," on the performance of various tasks. *Proceedings of the AGARD Conference on Vibration and Combined Stresses In Advanced Systems.* No. 145. Oslo, Norway: AGARD/NATO.
Williams, H.L., O.F. Kearny, and A. Lubin
   1965   Signal uncertainty and sleep loss. *Journal of Experimental Psychology* 69:401-407.
Williges, R.C.
   1969   Within-session criterion changes compared to an ideal observer criterion in a visual monitoring task. *Journal of Experimental Psychology* 81:61-66.
Wingate, P.
   1972   *The Penguin Medical Encyclopaedia.* Harmondsworth, Middlesex, UK: Penguin Books.
Yoshitake, H.
   1978   Three characteristic patterns of subjective fatigue symptoms. *Ergonomics* 21:231-233.

7

Geographic Orientation

For a tank crew, developing an accurate mental model of the environment in which the battle is likely to take place is especially important during the critical period prior to the onset of a battle. The performance of this task is mediated by a number of general factors: workload, stress, fatigue, and environmental conditions. This chapter focuses on some of the general factors involved in the development of the team commander's model of the world and how those factors affect his geographic orientation and workload. Although each of the factors mentioned above mediates a tank commander's battlefield success, his ability to maintain geographic orientation (i.e., awareness of one's location in the world) may be the most critical. The successful tank commander needs to know where he is (present position), where he is going (objective), and the position of both friendly and enemy forces (knowledge of his battle area) at all times, in order to complete the mission. Without this knowledge, situational awareness (knowledge of the dynamically changing environment) may be lost, and completion of his portion of the battle plan may not be executed successfully. If the firepower of his team is critical to the success of the mission, the battle could be lost.

The following pages provide a general review of the theoretical basis of geographic orientation. Then, drawing the close analogy between navigation in tanks and in helicopters, we describe the specific navigational tasks confronted by operators of these two vehicles. The chapter concludes by placing these tasks in the context of the phases of workload transition.

Although geographic orientation is critical for the tank crew, it is equally important for at least one other transition team, the helicopter, whether an emergency medical services craft suddenly called for a rescue mission, or a combat vehicle called into battle. Even in systems in which the world of concern is small, such as the nuclear power plant, geographic or spatial orientation will become critical if the operator must diagnose the location and topology of a fault within the complex interconnections of the system.

WHAT IS GEOGRAPHIC ORIENTATION?

Geographic orientation is not a term defined by Webster. But, using Webster's definition for geography and orientation, it may be approached as the sum of two terms: (1) geography: the features, especially the surface features of a region, area or place and (2) orientation: position with relation to the point of the compass; familiarization with, or adaptation to, a situation or environment; specifically in psychology, interpretation of the environment as to time, space, objects, and persons. Deaver (1949) defines orientation as encompassing two psychological senses: awareness of one's spatial and temporal position within an environmentally defined frame of reference, with respect to mental rotation.

Thus, we can define geographic orientation as: (1) awareness of one's relationship to physical features (especially the surface features) of a region, (2) one's awareness of relative location within that region (e.g., the center or the edge), and (3) one's temporal awareness of when one should arrive at locations within that region.

For tank commanders or helicopter crews, geographic orientation refers to their knowledge of the environment through which they are moving and to the relationship between where they are, where they should be, and where they are going. Since the visual scene is continuously changing, geographic orientation is a dynamic process. It requires navigators to focus their visual attention on the immediate environment, to maintain directional control and to avoid obstacles, while simultaneously relating information in the visual scene (a forward view) to remembered landmarks or those depicted on hand-held or electronic maps (a downward view). Correlating the outside visual scene with maps that depict the same area is cognitively demanding and requires mental rotation and rescaling at least. The difficulty of this task is further increased when objects that are visible in the forward field of view do not appear on the map, objects are represented by labels or symbols rather than pictures, and significant landmarks are obscured by other terrain features, reduced visibility, or both.

How do operators attain and maintain geographic orientation during operations? Before we can understand this process, we should examine some of the general factors involved. The following sections will review:

(1) The issue of constraints on spatial awareness: What physical features permit and constrain people's orientation in the world around them?

(2) Spatial frames of reference: How do people represent or understand their position in the world?

(3) How do factors such as confirmation bias (e.g., expectancies) and object comparison processes (i.e., comparing map objects or symbols with viewed objects) affect orientation?

(4) Language: How do people communicate relative positions (i.e., use verbal information to aid in self-orientation and that of others)?

(5) Timing: How do people remain aware of where they should be while on the move?

REAL-WORLD CONSTRAINTS ON SPATIAL AWARENESS

The world around us provides a basic structure within which our orientation is defined. It determines both how position and movement can be defined and measured and how we can come to know our position (i.e., how we can achieve orientation). According to Shepard (1984), the most pervasive and enduring constraints in the world in which we have evolved are likely to have become internalized in the nervous system. As a consequence, such internal constraints may be both so abstract, and so much a part of ourselves, that we are ordinarily unaware of them. The following may be considered the fundamental constraints on our experience of geographic orientation.

Space is three-dimensional and locally Euclidean. Rigid motion of an object can be defined by six degrees of freedom: three are translational and three are rotational. The earth's gravitational field determines a locally unique upright that is orthogonal to an approximately flat surface. When, as observers, we are constrained to this surface, we possess: (1) a unique top (the head) and bottom (the feet) defined by our standing orientation, (2) a unique front and back defined by the direction we are looking and our direction of travel, and (3) a basic laterality that defines our right and left sides (Shepard, 1984) but is less salient than the vertical and fore-aft dimensions.

There are more subtle constraints that may be internalized as well. For example, on a flat horizontal surface, a person may move in any direction defined with respect to the north-south, east-west frame of reference. North-south and east-west are not abstract concepts, since they may be internalized with respect to consistent phenomena in the world (e.g., the sun rises in the east and sets in the west; and when one faces east, north is always on the left, and south on the right). This frame of reference may be contrasted to the earth's magnetic field, a natural phenomenon that is not directly visible but that provides a cue to direction when depicted by a compass.

Frames of Reference

Frames of reference are the basic spatial cognitive models by which we define where we and others are in the world. As such, frames of reference are obviously critical elements in any account of human navigation. Three different frames of reference have been proposed as crucial to successful geographic orientation and locomotion. The first, one's egocentric or ego frame, is defined with respect to an observer's body (e.g., above/below, front/back, and left/right).

The second, a container, world, or environmental frame, defines location with respect to physical or imaginary world lines or surfaces. The most familiar container frame, altitude, is defined by the physical dimension of feet above sea level (up/down) and the more imaginary latitude (north/south) and longitude lines (east/west) is defined by degrees, minutes, and seconds. Other container frames can be defined with respect to more concrete boundaries, such as tree lines or rivers. The most important feature of container systems is that their utility diminishes as the observer gets farther and farther away from the relevant lines or features. Thus, earth latitude/longitude coordinates would provide a very poor reference system for locating features on the surface of Mars, and position relative to streets in New York yields poor localization for places in Trenton.

The third type of reference frame is an object-centered frame, in which locations and directions are defined relative to fixed landmarks (e.g., mountaintop, valley, outlook tower). In some ways it shares properties with both the container and the ego frames. It can be defined with respect to axes running parallel to the top/bottom, front/back, left/right, or sides of some object. Thus, it is very similar to the container frame in that it has important world lines or surfaces. However, it is similar to the ego frame as well, inasmuch as the concept of left/right is involved.

Although all three frames and their associated dimensions can be of critical importance for an individual, their perceptual availability differs greatly. For example, the gravitationally defined up/down dimension is accessible in all three frames by vestibular and visual cues (e.g., objects typically have perceptually distinct tops and bottoms). However, vestibular cues are subject to the effects of motion. The front/back direction is also generally quite salient. Even though front/back is not as invariant a dimension as gravity, it is useful. Front/back is available in the egocentric frame (e.g., what can and can not be immediately seen or approached by natural locomotion) and given in the object-centered frames (e.g., the distinct front and back of those objects). The limitation to the usefulness of this dimension is that, in the egocentric frame, front/back changes with the orientation of the observer relative to an object while, in the object-centered frame, it depends on the presence of a natural front and back to the object.

Rather than being an unwanted complication, the presence of more than one reference frame may be a prerequisite for navigation. The key to navigational awareness is a comparison and verification process: Am I (ego frame) where I should be (world frame)? When these two representations map onto each other, geographic orientation is maintained; visible objects correspond to those that are expected to be in a particular location in the world. When they do not, disorientation will result, which is a potentially disastrous condition during any combat mission.

For example, Wickens (1989a, 1989b), in his discussion of the multidimensionality of navigational performance, suggested that spatial awareness (one category of navigation performance) is based on the congruence between the ego and world frames of reference. The navigator attempts to maintain congruence between his position and orientation in a world frame specified by a physical or cognitive map (see Tolman, 1948, for a discussion of cognitive maps) and what he can see in his ego frame (e.g., his forward field of view). The cognitive representation, which is normally derived from earlier map study and verbal reports, may be stored as a spatial representation (cognitive map) or as a route list (a serial list of verbal descriptors, such as "follow the right fork of the river for three miles then turn west"). The congruence model states that two views, or frames, are congruent if two pairs of points can be brought into a one-to-one relationship (see Maxwell, 1975, for the mathematical formalization of the congruence concept). In the present case, this means that a person is oriented if he can match two points visible in the scene with two points on a physical or cognitive map.

Although both frames of reference are compared to maintain spatial orientation, they tend to serve rather different functions. For example, we use the world frame to convey compass heading and cardinal directions (north, east, south, and west), while we use the ego frame to convey relative bearing (right, left, front, and back) and clock direction (e.g., aircraft at a 2:00 bearing) when verbally communicating. Similarly, in the control of locomotion we tend to use the ego frame to characterize the more dynamic, "inner-loop" variables related to vehicle control (pitch, roll, and yaw) and obstacle avoidance; we use the world frame to characterize the control of more slowly changing "outer-loop" variables (position relative to large-scale terrain features).

Reference Frame Comparisons

Shepard and Hurwitz (1984), in a study of mental rotation during route following, found that reaction time increased significantly as the route that was followed departed from an up/down map direction. They suggested that a compensatory mental rotation of the egocentric frame of reference was performed in order to judge the direction of turns as the route deviated to the left or right.

Two forms of spatial rotation are required for navigation: (1) Physically rotating a map, or its mental representation, so as to keep the depicted or imagined direction of travel always pointing directly away from the map reader; a track-up orientation. This horizontal rotation may be accomplished by physically rotating a paper map to a track-up orientation or by mentally rotating a map that was stored in a north-up orientation. (2) Mentally rotating a two-dimensional plan view of the environment that is perpendicular to the line of sight to yield an imagined perspective view. This forward mental rotation is used to compare a mental image with the perspective forward field of view. Evidence for the reality of these mental rotations can also be found in studies by Aretz (1988); Cooper and Shepard (1973); Shepard and Metzler (1971); Eley (1988); Evans and Pesdick (1980); Harwood (1989); Hintzman et al. (1981); Levine (1982); Shepard and Hurwitz (1984); and Sholl (1987). Each type of rotation requires time, and the processes seems to be additive.

These studies have shown that the time needed to visually compare two stimuli increases linearly with the angular misalignment between their orientations. Aretz (1991) found that the time required to mentally rotate a map to bring it into alignment with the external scene increased from 3.7 to 4.2 seconds as the difference in orientation increased from 0 to 180 degrees in a helicopter flight simulation.

If one considers this rotation effect in terms of a static environment, the milliseconds required to perform this task seem insignificant. However, when considered in the context of a real-world dynamic navigational task, where object and scene recognition is a continuous process, the magnitude of this time-consuming process becomes evident and the greater time demands are also more likely to cause errors.

Biases in Geographic Memory

A mentally generated scene used for comparison with a forward field of view may be stored in memory. Typically, it is derived from map study prior to the start of a mission. However, it has been found that figures (such as symbols or icons on a map), especially those with odd shapes, are difficult to orient in mental space. Therefore, heuristics (rules of thumb) may be adopted to facilitate the coding and retrieval of the spatial orientation and location of these figures. Principles of perceptual organization suggest that people use two such heuristics, rotation and alignment, and that both lead to subtle, but important, biases.

When it is difficult to remember the exact positions or rotations of figures, either or both of these principles of perceptual organization (i.e., rotation and alignment) may be invoked for anchoring figures in frames or shapes in space. When the rotation heuristic is applied, the natural axes of a figure and the axes of its frame of reference converge. When the alignment heuristic is applied, two or more nearby figures group together.

As a consequence of invoking the rotation heuristic, people tend to remember figures as being more rotated in memory such that their primary axes are oriented so as to be similar to the principle axes of the reference frame (Braine, 1978). Since vertical and horizontal are natural axes for describing both figure and frame in sensation, perception, and language, these are the most likely candidates for rotation (Rock, 1974). Thus, invoking the rotation heuristic will generally result in figures being remembered as being more vertical or more horizontal than they actually were.

Alignment is related to the phenomenon of perceptual grouping. As a consequence of invoking the alignment heuristic, people tend to remember figures that gravitate toward a simpler structural grouping than they actually possessed. When this heuristic is invoked, arrays of figures are remembered as being more orderly or aligned than they were. What is remembered, then, is a compromise between the actual stimulus pattern and a more regular, easily remembered pattern (Gogel, 1978).

These heuristics may be invoked during the formation or encoding of representations of the visual world, during the storage of these representations, as well as in the later use of these representations. They are approximation techniques that facilitate memory, but at the expense of distortions of locations and orientations. The heuristics may also allow inferences when information is incomplete; for instance, when comparisons are made across regions that have not been stored together. In these cases, best guesses must be made about relative orientation or alignments of stored representations. For example, Tversky (1981) found that these biases affected performance in map reproduction, recall, and recognition memory and that they were adopted in storage, when spatial positions were difficult to encode, as well as in inferences to fill in gaps of knowledge. Tversky presented evidence for systematic distortions in memory for real-world maps, artificial maps, local environments, and visual forms. For all of these diverse stimuli, the distortions have the same characteristics reflecting alignment and grouping heuristics. For example, the position of stars is remembered by aligning them with one another to form meaningful structures (i.e., constellations).

The alignment and rotation heuristics have been demonstrated in the way people remember familiar, naturally occurring stimuli, as well as for new information acquired from artificial stimuli (Palmer, 1980). They have been demonstrated for information acquired from artificial navigation (e.g., path following in a laboratory study) of environments, information acquired from maps for visual forms, as well as geographic entities (Stevens and Coupe, 1978).

Particularly important for navigation is the finding that spatially extended stimuli (e.g., highways and mountains) induce their own axes in the normal course of perception (Braine, 1978; Howard and Templeton, 1966; Rock, 1974). These coordinate axes, which can serve as an induced container frame, may interact with object-centered reference frames. This causes the container axes and the object axes to appear, or be imagined, to be in greater alignment than they actually are. For example, during a recent field study, emergency medical services (EMS) helicopter pilots were asked to draw maps of their service areas. Their maps depicted highways that generally parallel northwest to southeast mountain ranges as straight lines (Battiste et al., 1989). The east and west ranges of hills in the San Francisco Bay area serve as a container for this area, thus spatially extended stimuli (highways, powerlines, etc.) are remembered as being more aligned with these hills, than they actually are. But this does not affect their ability to perform required piloting tasks.

Hierarchical anchoring is another important heuristic that people use to help them remember geographic information. For example, Stevens and Coupe (1978) presented evidence that people remember the position of large geographic units, such as states, remember which cities belong to which states, and then use the location of the state to remember the locations of the cities. However, systematic distortions may result from using this strategy. For example, subjects report that Reno is farther east than San Diego. However, comparing these two cities on a map, one can easily determine that Reno is the more westerly city. This occurs because the state of Nevada is thought to be east of California. Since Reno is a city in Nevada, it is thought to be east of any city in California. Thus, this heuristic makes it difficult to directly compare locations nested within different higher-order units.

While Tversky (1981) presented evidence for systematic distortions in remembered location and orientation, other researchers have demonstrated systematic distortions of distance relations among elements. Thus, two points are judged to be closer when they are within the same object or contour (container frames) than when they are in different objects or contours (container frames) (Coren and Girgus, 1980). For example, a distance within a large city would be judged closer than an equal distance between two cities.

Reference points also affect distance judgments. Distances between objects and a point of reference that is near are overestimated, while distances between objects and a point of reference that is distant are underestimated. That is, spatial discrimination is greater when closer to a point of reference.

Reference points can also induce asymmetry in distance judgments. Ordinarily, places and landmarks (i.e., important points of reference) are judged to be closer when places are compared with landmarks than when landmarks are compared with places (Sadalla et al., 1980). That is, when proceeding toward a landmark from a place, the distance would be judged closer than when proceeding from the landmark to a place. Thus, reference points and figural properties also affect how spatial knowledge is organized in memory and yield systematic errors in distance judgments.

The problem of remembering spatial locations of figures is similar to the problem of remembering the order of a list of verbal items; for both, structure promotes memory but may induce distortions. Whether or not these biases exert significant influence on the absolute recognition procedure employed in a navigational task is unclear. For example, would a tank commander or a locomotive conductor become confused if the viewed curvature of a mountain is greater than the simplified (i.e., straightened) mental representation of the mountain?

Another potential distortion is related to the way people forget particular image features that might be used for object comparisons. An assumption made by some researchers in this area, which is supported by pilot interviews, is that during map study, people imagine a three-dimensional representation of a feature depicted on two-dimensional maps. These three-dimensional images are later remembered for comparison with their view of the "outside" scene (Eley, 1988). Do people, during map study, imagine three-dimensional forms for comparison with their forward field of view? Do they forget these distinctive shapes when comparing their mental representation to the actual figure? How well is seasonally variable ground or vegetation texture imagined when studying a map, and how much of this detail is remembered?

Biederman's (1987) work on the basic components of object recognition may provide a useful framework for understanding landmark memory and forgetting. Also relevant here is the fact that memory of object shapes tends to be biased toward the symmetrical representation, as mentioned earlier.

Language

As studies in the field of linguistics (Fillmore, 1968) and psycholinguistics (Clark, 1973) make clear, the fundamental spatial facts of the world are reflected not only in our perceptual and cognitive structures, but also in the way we talk about the world. For example, there is considerable evidence suggesting that the primacy of the up/down dimension affects not only how we see and think about the world, but also the very words we use to talk about the world.

With regard to language, children learn and successfully use terms pertaining to up, down, front, and back long before they master terms pertaining to left and right or to north, east, south, and west. Also, the terms *up* and *down* are universally used to refer to any directions in the horizontal plane (e.g., he traveled up North, they went down South, "he walked up to the front of the room," "they walked down the street together").

Clark (1973) also noted the significance of referring to the direction of the reference object as *up* (e.g., they climbed up to the top), suggesting that things above the ground plane are more accessible than things that are below. Therefore, the upward direction seems to cognitively dominate the downward direction.

As global navigation grew in importance and with the invention of the magnetic compass, the unique poles of the earth became more appropriate, accessible, and invariant reference points. And since most of the global navigators and map makers came from the northern hemisphere, the association between spatial proximity and the absence of linguistic markings would favor the north pole as the reference point for up. These reasons can somewhat explain why the direction of north has come to mean up in navigation and communication among navigators, and also why north is conventionally oriented at the top of maps.

In a simple universe, with only one natural frame of reference (egocentric frame), one might not have a need to imagine rotations in space. However, our daily world, and the world of pilots and tank crews, coordinating with each other and with fixed bases on the ground, are greatly complicated by the fact that people who must coordinate their activities may occupy many different ego frames of reference over time (as a result of locomotion) and space (there may be more than one moving observer). Thus, as two vehicles move independently about a common terrain, the relations between the principal directions of each frame constantly change. Although the upward vertical direction remains aligned across all of these frames (egocentric, object, and container), what was on the "right" may move to the "left" (if the viewer moves) or what is on the right for one observer may be on the left for another because it is perceived from a different vantage point. Mental rotations of perceived and expected scenes or placing ourselves in the perspective of another may facilitate anticipation, planning, and communication in such a world.

Timing

While orientation in space is an important issue addressed by the concept of frame of reference, the equally important issue of orientation in time is not. Many aspects of the tank commander's duties involve timing: arriving at initial battle position on schedule, crossing way points on time, and coordinating arrival times with other teams. It is the tank commander's responsibility to monitor the passage of time during maneuvers. Although most commanders wear watches, continuous monitoring is not possible because other tasks require their attention. Thus, temporal orientation involves more than whether or not the tank commander has a watch.

How do people maintain temporal orientation? Gibson (1968) argues that there is no such thing as the perception of time, but only the perception of events and surfaces. Events, in particular locomotion, do not occur in space but in the medium of an environment that is rigid and permanent. Gibson argues that abstract space is a "ghost" of the surface world, and that time is a ghost of the events of the world. Following his logic, it is not difficult to understand that humans are not very astute time estimators. However, humans are very good at perceiving events. Pilots, during low-level flight, know when to start looking for features in the terrain that they plan to use as orienting landmarks. Typically, when clocks are not used, pilots' estimates of clock time are based on relative distances and speeds of travel. This method of keeping track of time (e.g., tracking physical events) is very different from keeping track of clock time.

There is considerable support for Gibson's belief that time is a ghost abstracted from event structure. For example, Hart (1978) obtained evidence suggesting that people do not perceive time directly but employ strategies for monitoring its passage. She used subjective time estimates as indices of workload and found that commercial airline pilots' abilities to actively keep track of time varied as a function of the demands of other flight-related duties. When pilots were asked to estimate 10-second intervals, Hart found that the estimates increased from about 10 seconds with no competing activity to 14 seconds in the presence of a difficult concurrent tracking task. She also found that the variability of their estimates increased with higher task demands. Hart asserted that, as task demands increased, there is less attention available for active time estimation. Similar results were obtained during a simulation conducted at Wright Patterson Air Force Base (Gunning, 1978).

During the active mode of time estimation, there are many timekeeping techniques: tapping, counting (both aloud or silently), using remembered events, counting heartbeats, etc. These methods are used to fix an individual's attention on the passage of time and makes the process more concrete. However, these externalized methods are easily disrupted by more compelling activities and are impractical in an operational situation.

In response to the problem of estimating time under very high levels of workload, Hart suggested that people seem to switch from an active production mode to a "retrospective mode" of time estimation. With retrospective estimation, people use the number of events that occur during an interval as a measure of the amount of time in that interval. In her study, Hart found that extreme levels of workload began to yield produced durations that were less than the 10-second interval. This is predicted by her model for high-workload situations in which the number of task events per unit time is high. And she obtained reports consistent with this model during interviews with the pilots; time seemed to pass quickly when they were very busy and slowly when they were not—a feeling we have all experienced. The pilots in Hart's study also were aware that they made consistent errors of estimation under conditions of high workload.

Hutchins (1983), during his cross-cultural studies of the Island Navigators of the South Pacific, found that these navigators also used the passage of events (star points relative to a reference island) to estimate trip duration, time of arrival at way points, and arrival time at the destination island. The results from Hart's laboratory, simulation studies, and Hutchins' field studies would seem to support Gibson's assertion that we do not, or cannot, actively keep track of time directly, but that we track events that provide estimates of time. The implications of the workload-related biases in time estimation for navigation are direct. To the extent that the expectancies for landmarks along a route are based on the passage of time when traveling at a given speed, then time estimation errors can distort the sense of when landmarks may be expected. Depending on how time estimation is distorted, landmarks may be expected too early, yielding a premature sense of lostness, or too late, creating the possibility that a landmark would be overlooked if it was passed before it was expected.

Mental Models of Navigational Tasks

Since there are many ways to solve a complex problem, the solutions most likely to occur to a researcher are those that arise from the traditional assumptions of his or her own culture. Hutchins's (1983) chapter on Micronesian navigation shows how easily such cultural biases can mislead an "unbiased" observer, and how convincing an inaccurate explanation can be to the formulator, even in the face of relatively serious anomalies. What we want to do is not model how a scientist conceptualizes a task, but rather how real problem solvers conceptualize the task. In doing this, we need to identify how the task is actually solved and the internal processes that are employed. It is necessary to determine how the problem solver defines the task, the set of operations used to operate on his or her representation of the task, and how these relate to the set of operations required in the world. Then we may ask the question: How could one operate on that representation to produce the decisions required to accomplish the task? For example, the Island navigators in Hutchins' chapter use a mental image of a reference island moving along a defined track (defined by a mental star map) to determine their exact location along a route between two islands.

The task of terrain navigation as performed by helicopter pilots (during low-level and nap-of-the-the-earth, NOE, flight) and tank commanders more closely approximates that of the Polynesian navigator, the Eskimo, and the Touareg nomads, than that of a typical ship or aircraft navigator. The helicopter pilot and tank commander, like the Micronesian navigators, must determine and update their position in the world by discriminating, inter-preting, and organizing subtle terrain distinctions in an environment that appears to be uniform.

Wickens (1989a, 1989b) proposed a model of navigation to explain the way cognitive models are developed and used for navigation by helicopter pilots in NOE or contour flight conditions. He reported that there is little information in the form of a well-developed model that directly pertains to the task of navigation when surrounded by terrain. Hence, the model he proposed consists of components derived from research in the area of visual perception and spatial cognition, coupled with information gained by con-sultation with operational pilots.

The components of the model are presented in Figure 7.1, which pro-vides an integrated framework for the information that preceded this section and can be used to integrate the tank commander's task for the consider-ation of workload transition. Through the use of this model, which seems to capture both the dynamics and the components of the navigational task, experiments can be designed to address the fundamental characteristics of the navigational task.

In such a model, a key component is the need for the navigator to compare the perceptual view of the world, which is ego-referenced and shown in the lower right of the figure, with more abstract goals and expec-tations of where one should be. The latter are often expressed in a world frame of reference (e.g., "I should be heading northwest"). The mental transformations necessary to compare the two representations (e.g., "Am I where I should be?") are shown at the bottom. These may take time and mental effort and be subject to error. Furthermore, the navigation process may depend on long-term memory and geography, whose distortions were discussed above, as well as working memory, whose demands impose a major source of workload.

GEOGRAPHIC ORIENTATION: TANKS AND HELICOPTERS

Since little research exists on tank navigation, this review borrows heavily from research experience in rotorcraft operation, a system that is in many respects analogous to the tank. An indepth analysis of navigational seg-ments of different types of vehicles (i.e., automobiles, fixed- and rotary-wing aircraft, and tanks) reveals that the navigational demands of the tank and the helicopter have far more in common with each other than with their

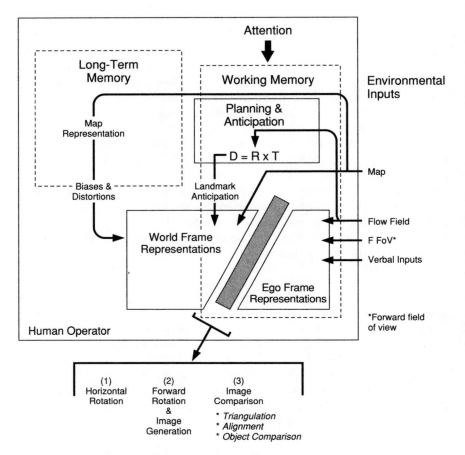

FIGURE 7.1   The Wickens Model of Navigation.

corresponding ground and airborne counterparts (automobiles and fixed-wing aircraft, respectively). For example, both fixed-wing pilots and automobile drivers typically follow paths with tight lateral constraints—highways and roads for the automobile driver and airways or preselected courses for the fixed-wing pilot. The automobile driver and fixed-wing aircraft pilot can usually follow their selected route with little regard for surrounding terrain features, in marked contrast to the tank driver and rotorcraft pilot (during low-level flight), who must use surrounding terrain features to identify the route to be followed. Hence, we now consider the common features of the navigational problems presented by these two systems.

Tank crews and the pilots of military or civilian helicopters flying at very low altitudes are faced with a challenging situation. They operate so close to the ground that local terrain features may obscure their view of significant landmarks, thus reducing their visual range and making it difficult to relate local terrain features in a more global context. Often, tanks and helicopters move freely through terrain, without an explicit, visible or electronic, route to follow. While there are many degrees of freedom in this environment (tank and helicopter crews are not limited to roads or electronic routes as are automobiles and fixed-wing aircraft flying typical cross-country routes), it is more difficult to maintain the desired course, and natural and artificial obstacles pose a very real threat. In this environment, helicopter and tank crews must correlate cues viewed in the external scene with information on paper maps to maintain geographic orientation, avoid obstacles, and maintain their course. Instruments that provide pilots with information about speed and altitude are relatively inaccurate at low altitudes and slow speeds, and electronic aids are intermittent at best, because they require line-of-site with the source to work properly. There are no instruments in tanks to aid in geographic orientation.

Before a mission, helicopter and tank crews study maps of the environment in which they will operate to select a route that offers the most direct path to their destination (given terrain contours, obstacles, etc.), distinctive visual cues (to aid in geographic orientation), and cover (if there is an enemy threat). They select specific features that they will use during the mission to verify their location and identify choice points (e.g., intersections of rivers, hilltops, clearings, groves of trees). They might identify linear features that can provide a visible "route" to follow (e.g., ridge lines, river valleys). However, military crews generally do not select constructed structures for reference (things change) and avoid following roads (the enemy threat is greater there).

Tank and helicopter crews incorporate the available information into a cognitive model or mental map of the environment through which they will travel. The mental representation might be spatial—a mental image of the map (a plan view) or a series of perspective mental images of how significant features in the environment are likely to look when viewed from the cockpit of a helicopter or turret of a tank (a forward view). Alternatively, they may store this information as a route list—a series of verbal commands (e.g., "travel down the valley for two miles then bear right") or descriptions (e.g., "follow the creek that runs beside the cliff") that are remembered and executed during the mission.

During a mission, helicopter or tank crews view features in the external scene and compare them to a paper map or their mental images. They must mentally transform the stylized images on two-dimensional maps into mental images, which represent a perspective view of the object, which is rotated into alignment with the forward field of view, for comparison with the external scene. If they continue to see expected features on time and in the correct order, they know where they are; visible terrain features correspond with their expectations and they can correlate their position with a location on the map. When they pass a distinctive feature (e.g., a water tank depicted on their map) or an intersection of linear features (e.g., two ridge lines intersecting), then they know precisely where they are. However, if a single landmark is symmetrical, they may know generally where they are (e.g., approximately two miles from a water tower), but not their precise position (e.g., approximately two miles west of the water tower) or their direction of travel. In this case, they may look for a second reference point, check the compass, look at the sun, or infer direction from previous cues. When using a ridge line that extends for some distance as a geographic reference, a crew knows only that they are traveling in the correct direction, but not their precise location.

Depending on the familiarity of the terrain, the availability of distinctive features, and the quality of premission planning, maintaining a route may be relatively easy or very difficult. For example, when a crew must rely on subtle variations in terrain to judge location, it may be extremely difficult to relate the visible features in the forward scene to contour lines on the map. This task is particularly difficult if surface contours are masked by vegetation. Furthermore, the appearance of terrain and vegetation varies seasonally and from one region to another, requiring adaptation and inference. There may be considerable ambiguity about whether a particular feature is, in fact, the one a crew expects to see or the specific feature depicted on the map.

As the time between landmarks increases, uncertainty about current position may increase if additional cues are not available for the crew to verify that they are, in fact, where they think they are. At some point, the crew will begin to look for the next expected landmark. If it does not appear by the expected time, the crew may begin to consider the possibility that they are lost. If a feature that is similar to their expectations appears, the crew may identify it as the expected feature. If it is not, it may take some time before they accept the growing evidence that they are not where they are supposed to be. At this point, the crew must take action to reestablish their position. A helicopter pilot might gain altitude or a tank commander drive to the top of a hill to find a distinctive landmark. If this is not possible, the crew may carefully survey the surrounding terrain and try to find a pattern of features on their map that corresponds to what they see. However, it is much more difficult to find a pattern somewhere on a map that corresponds to the forward scene than to verify that a visible feature is where it is supposed to be relative to the vehicle. Alternatively, they may try to retrace their path until they find a familiar landmark. However, the mental preparation performed before the mission will be of little help here, as terrain features and relationships will not correspond in the expected sequence.

Thus, maintaining geographic orientation requires helicopter and tank crews to continuously correlate the visual scene with the map. To do this, they must accurately estimate their speed and distance traveled. Estimates of when to begin looking for a landmark, when a choice point has been missed, or what features should be visible at any point in time are based on subjective estimates of the distance traveled and time elapsed since the last known location.

When operating at night, tank and helicopter crews rely on night vision devices (that intensify light or display infrared imagery) to provide them with information about the external scene. Although they could not perform required missions as well without these devices, their use imposes considerable additional load on the pilots: field of view is limited, acuity is reduced, depth cues are distorted, subtle textures necessary to identify a particular feature may be missing, and objects or terrain features may look very different than expected. Furthermore, greater navigational precision is required at night; obstacles that can be seen and avoided during the day may be invisible at night. Thus, pilots rely on maps to spot potential obstacles. However, this information is useful only if they know exactly where they are. For these reasons, maintaining geographic orientation becomes significantly more difficult, and overall performance capabilities may be reduced. For example, pilots are more likely to fly slower and higher at night, and over sand, where texture supporting accurate distance estimation is absent.

In tanks and helicopters, crew members communicate with each other through an intercom system (high ambient noise levels and physical barriers, in some cases, preclude direct conversations) and with other helicopters, ground personnel, etc., through radios. Navigational and geographic orientation information is usually conveyed verbally, although crew members may use gestures as well (e.g., point to features in the environment or on a map). In helicopter nap-of-the-earth flight, navigation may take as much as 90 percent of the navigator's time, and communications between the pilot and navigator about navigation, 25 percent of both pilots' time. Army aviators use 1:50,000 scale maps that depict terrain contours (e.g., hills and valleys), vegetation (e.g., fields and groves of trees), bodies of water (e.g., rivers, streams, and ponds), and some cultural features (e.g., roads, buildings, bridges, water tanks, and towers). During premission planning, helicopter or tank crews plot their route on the map, identify critical choice points, and select additional features that they will use to verify their position. In flight, the navigator follows the route of flight on the map, giving the pilot verbal cues about what he should see, when he should begin or end a turn, and potential obstacles. In addition, the navigator scans cockpit instruments, verbalizing relevant information to the pilot. The pilot generally keeps his eyes focused outside the cockpit, telling the navigator what he sees in the external scene and verifying that he does (or does not) see specific landmarks described by the navigator. In a tank, the commander is responsible for navigation, passing verbal steering commands to the driver; particularly when the tank is buttoned up because the driver's field of view is too restricted to maintain geographic orientation.

Helicopter or tank crews use or mix a number of different frames of reference when exchanging information among themselves or transmitting to another vehicle: (1) ego-reference/spatial (e.g., a landmark is in front, to the right, or to the left of the pilot; the driver should turn right or left); (2) ego-reference/clock position (e.g., a feature is at the observer's or recipient's 2 o'clock position); or (3) world-reference/compass heading (e.g., the pilot should look for a stream running north-south; an enemy tank is located 5 miles northwest of a friendly tank; another vehicle should turn 20 degrees to maintain a new heading of 280 degrees).

Ego-referenced directions are the easiest to process (Aretz, 1990); they require minimal mental transformation or interpretation. Clock positions are less intuitively obvious than right/left directions, although they provide more precise information. However, clock position may be ambiguous if the sender's and receiver's points of reference (i.e., head position) are significantly different. Furthermore, extracting spatial information given in a verbal form may require additional mental transformations. When giving ego-referenced directions, the originator of the message must mentally project himself into the point of view of the intended recipient, an activity that imposes additional cognitive demands and is subject to error. In both the tank and helicopter environment, the reference frame problem is compounded because the direction of travel of the vehicle may not correspond to the direction the operator is facing.

Spatial information that is world-referenced (i.e., to a numeric or verbal compass position) is more precise than other forms and does not require that the sender or recipient project themselves into another's ego-reference. However, steering commands referenced to compass position presuppose that the recipient knows the current heading. In helicopters, the pilot responsible for flying may have no idea what his current heading is because he is focusing on the external scene, rather than on the instruments. Thus, a flight navigator might couple an ego-referenced command (e.g., turn right) that requires minimal mental transformation with a world-referenced modifier (e.g., turn right; now you're heading due west) to improve the pilot's orientation. In tanks, there is no compass on the instrument panel, and the metal body of the tank interferes with the accuracy of hand-held compasses. Therefore, compass headings are not used for steering commands in tanks.

In addition to the problems associated with the use of different reference systems, tank and helicopter crews often operate in unfamiliar environments in which crew members do not share a common knowledge base about the names and appearance of significant landmarks. Thus, information about these landmarks must be transferred on the basis of their physical appearance (e.g., a small round pond, a dry river bed, a saddle-back hill), rather than by unambiguous names (e.g., Jones' farm, White Mountain, Route 50). Given the potential differences in personal experience, descriptive terms may have very different meanings for different crew members. For example, what looks like a pond to one may look like a lake to another. A 500-foot hill may look like a mountain to a midwesterner, but a person from Colorado would describe it as a small hill, and so on. Furthermore, lack of familiarity with local vegetation may make the description process particularly difficult; it is easier to identify a grove of trees by name than by physical appearance.

The preceding description of navigational demands of tanks and helicopters can also be interpreted within the more theoretical framework of research on geographic orientation. In the following section we employ this framework to introduce laboratory research results that have implications for navigational performance in armored vehicles.

NAVIGATION AND WORKLOAD TRANSITION

When people travel long distances over indistinctive terrain, they often either physically mark the terrain or mentally accentuate whatever distinctive features they can find in the environment (Lynch, 1960). Helicopter pilots and tank commanders during premission planning use both object and container reference systems. On a map, which is usually oriented north-up, distinctive objects (terrain features) are selected to delineate a planned route to the destination and to identify features or objects that will serve as orienting stimuli for different route segments. Additional large-scale features, usually linear (e.g., a mountain, valley, or tree line) are selected to contain the mission area. During the mission, the tank commander or helicopter pilot will use all three frames of reference—ego, object, and container. The ego reference system, the most proximal, is used for local course guidance (e.g., keeping the vehicle moving toward the goal) and obstacle avoidance; hence, it is particularly relevant for communications with the driver. The object reference system, a less proximal system, is used to identify current location and general course guidance (direction of travel) to the next object or waypoint. Finally, the container, a more distal reference system, is used to determine the degree of lostness (e.g., when the container boundary is reached prior to a planned location or waypoint, the tank commander is no longer sure of their precise position).

Helicopter pilots and tank commanders use both object and container reference systems during the planning and execution of their missions. The object reference system is used to plot a planned route through an area. The container reference system is used to determine the mission boundaries. During the mission, the object reference system is used to determine exact position to maintain geographic orientation. The container reference system is used to determine the degree of lostness (e.g., whether they have gone past a location that they had planned to use as a waypoint or location fix and are now no longer sure where they are).

Multiple reference systems can provide a tank commander with flexibility. To the extent that environmental conditions (battlefield conditions) vary, a tank commander must invoke different strategies to accommodate this variability.

The Premission Phase

During the premission phase, the tank commander is assigned an area of responsibility and battle mission objective. He has to develop a mental model of the area where the battle will be joined. This model includes memorizing the area based on maps (north-up) and verbal reports given by the battalion staff intelligence officer. From these reports, the tank commander must develop a plan of attack. This plan consists of a spatial representation of the terrain and the locations of all friendly and known enemy positions. From this spatial representation (usually developed as overlays on a map), the tank commander must select a route to his team's initial battle position and on to the final objective. While selecting the route, waypoints will be selected to break the route into segments. These distinctive features allow the tank crew to periodically update their knowledge of where they are (so they will not go too far in the wrong direction), recognize points where course changes will be made, and compare planned versus actual time taken to move between points (to stay on schedule). This plan is developed in conjunction with or communicated to battalion headquarters and platoon commanders. The workload during this phase of the mission depends on the amount of time available to accomplish these tasks and the quality of information available. The planning phase is information-intensive. In developing a mental model of the mission area, the tank commander might mentally rotate the north-up map into a track-up perspective to visualize the route and to brief the platoon commanders. In communicating the plan to battalion headquarters, it is likely to be expressed in polar coordinates with reference to a north-up map, so the plan can be correlated with that of other teams. However, in communicating the plan to platoon commanders, the information is likely to be expressed from an ego-centric perspective: first platoon will be on my right, second platoon to my left, etc.

During the planning phase of a mission, the tank commander's workload is driven primarily by the difficulties of incorporating vast quantities of information, both verbal and spatial, into a spatial (cognitive or paper) map. Aretz (1990), in his study of spatial cognition and navigation, found that map complexity accounted for most (7 percent) of the explained variance in the task. Thus, as map complexity increases, so does processing time and workload. Also, the need to mentally rotate different map frames to communicate information both up and down the chain of command would affect workload.

The Operational Phase

During the operational phase, the tank commander must move his forces from their current location to their initial fighting position. He must continually correlate his position in the world (forward field of view) with his map route (world view) to maintain geographic orientation. This is accomplished by orienting the map to correspond to the direction of movement (track-up) to align the two frames of reference. During this phase, time estimation is very important for determining when objects or features in the terrain, which are used to confirm geographic orientation, should appear. Also, the tank commander must update his estimated time of arrival (ETA) at the initial fighting position based on his estimate of how far he has gone and how long it is likely to take to cover the area remaining. This may be critical, if the initial engagement time must be coordinated with other teams.

Transition From Rear Staging Position to Initial Fighting Position

The accuracy with which a tank commander must know his team's position during the move to the initial point depends on the proximity of other friendly and enemy positions and the degree to which a precise transition to the initial fighting position is critical to mission success. That is, if the team is trying to stay masked during the transition, then required accuracy could be very high; if surrounded by enemy forces, maintaining a route designed to maintain cover is critically important. During this phase, communications between the tank commander and either platoon or battalion commanders would be very different. For instance, situation reports to battalion headquarters would be given in terms of polar coordinates (world view), while reports from each platoon commander might be given from an ego-centric view (right/left, front/back, or clock positions) of each tank. In the latter case, the tank commander must integrate information from each ego-centered perspective to form a coherent picture of the entire situation into a single frame of reference.

The workload during this phase of the mission is likely to be moderately high. The tank commander must perform multiple tasks, in parallel and serially: (1) continuously determine his own position and the relative position of members of his team, other teams, enemy forces, and his objective; (2) estimate and update the time between waypoints and his ETA at the initial fighting position; (3) communicate his own and other positions up the chain of command; and (4) communicate route and mission changes down the chain of command. The difficulty of these activities is determined by the speed at which the situation unfolds, the degree to which it unfolds according to plan, the availability of salient cues to maintain orientation, and, most critically, the positional accuracy demanded by mission requirements. The amount of time and effort spent in acquiring geographic knowledge of terrain during the premission phase is also relevant, as this information is unlikely to change during the course of the battle and provides the basic context within which other dynamic events occur.

The Preengagement Phase

Upon arrival at the initial battle position, particularly if the mission calls for immediate engagement, the degree to which previous phases have been completed successfully (e.g., the planning phase and the transition to the initial position) influences the workload experienced during the battle phase. If the team has successfully completed the previous phases, the battle plan could be implemented without further changes. Thus, workload during this phase would be driven by the accuracy of estimates of enemy strength and the degree to which the tank commander's plan took them into account. If the team arrived late, or at the wrong location, the workload during this phase could be very high. In addition to coordinating his team's actual position with other teams, the tank commander may also have to coordinate with infantry and artillery units (to develop a revised plan). This might require extensive communications using different map frames of reference. Even if the tank commander executed the first part of the plan correctly, he may have to develop a new battle plan in response to the environment (terrain, time of arrival—day or night, enemy activity, etc.) or to a change in the mission. His communications load during the development of a new plan would be very high: it must be transmitted both up and down the chain of command.

During a battle, maintaining geographic orientation is critical to the identification of friendly forces and enemy targets. If artillery or close air support is needed, the tank commander, through his fire support officer, would determine where and how much artillery or close air support is required, in relation to their current position. Again, this requires a translation between a world view (artillery and close air support) and the egocentric view (tank commander and fire support officer). Since the commander's tank, and those of his team, are in the battle area, accurate estimates of friendly and enemy positions and accurate communication of those positions are critical to survival.

The Post-Mission Phase

Whether the battle is won or lost, situation and logistics reports must be compiled. First, the tank commander must assess his team, their position in relation to the battle plan, their losses in equipment and men, etc. The verbal reports from individual tank and platoon commanders must be correlated with a map of the area. When receiving reports, the tank commander may orient his map either track-up or north-up. Orienting the map to correspond to the frame of reference of each reporter might facilitate interpreting the (ego-centric) communications of team members (e.g., the platoon on the right reports that the enemy forces at their 3 o'clock position have been eliminated, etc.). A north-up perspective (i.e., the world view) would facilitate communication up the chain of command, wherein the battalion commander must evaluate the report of each team in relation to other teams' successes or failures. The workload during this phase would be influenced by the ease with which a commander could integrate information provided in different frames of reference into a coherent picture of the overall situation.

SUMMARY

Geographic orientation plays a major role in the success or failure of most tank operations. Platoon and tank commanders must continually update their position by comparing different map frames of reference (e.g., their forward view of the world to a paper or remembered map) to determine their position in the world. The level of congruence between different reference frames (and the mental rotation required to bring them into alignment) will be a factor in determining the time and difficulty of the geographic orientation task, as well as the likelihood of errors. Terrain characteristics, required accuracy, familiarity, and planning also affect the level of workload associated with geographic orientation and navigation.

To reduce the tank commander's workload, technological innovations such as electronic chart displays (ECD) and premission planners, which can be taken from the mission briefing and downloaded in ECD computers, should be introduced into tanks. (Their utility has been demonstrated in helicopter operations—Cote et al., 1985.) Low-cost electronic chart display systems coupled with global positioning satellite (GPS) receivers are being developed to determine and display the exact position of a vehicle superimposed on a map, a task currently performed by the tank commander using paper maps, at a considerable cost in time and cognitive effort. The cognitive demands of the geographic orientation/navigation task could be reduced by the installation of an electronic chart display system that is designed to maximize the degree of congruence between the map format, the terrain it depicts, and the tank commander's model of the environment. Different display formats will facilitate the performance of different tasks. The following list of features should allow the system to be both compatible with task requirements and the tank commander's internal model:

(1) The system should support both north-up and track-up map formats. The north-up format will facilitate mission planning (multiple missions can be planned and correlated on the same map) and communication between individuals who do not share the same perspective view of the terrain (e.g., headquarters and artillery). Communication between individuals who do not share the same visual perspective must rely on map coordinate data when transferring information.

The track-up format will facilitate wayfinding, locating targets, and communication between individuals who share the same perspective view of the terrain (i.e., the tank commander and the driver). Individuals who have a shared visual perspective can communicate using visual terrain features correlated with map information to support information transfer.

(2) The planned route and the current position of the vehicle should be depicted on the map display. Depicting the planned route and the vehicle's current position on the map eliminates the need to micronavigate between waypoints (thus, the driver's task becomes one of obstacle avoidance and compensatory tracking between waypoints) and facilitates reorientation if the tank becomes lost or makes an unscheduled detour.

(3) Map features selected by the tank commander during mission planning to identify route transition points (waypoints) or to aid in maintaining geographic orientation should be depicted on the ECD system. The degree of congruence between the map and the terrain, and also the cognitive compatibility between map depictions and terrain features, may be improved if iconic symbology selected by the tank crew during mission planning is used.

(4) Through the use of color and shape coding, contour line information can be accentuated and thus becomes more iconic.

(5) Compass information derived from GPS data, scalable range marks, latitude and longitude, bearing to and from selected points on the display, and variable map scales should be available on demand.

Also, electronic maps must depict the sort of features tank commanders and helicopter pilots actually use for geographic orientation, represented in a form that is most compatible with the way the feature will appear in the forward scene. By reducing the workload associated with navigation, all of the features should allow the tank commander more resources to deal with tactical decision making, planning, communications, and team coordination, issues addressed in the next three chapters.

REFERENCES

Aretz, A.J.
    1988   A model of electronic map interpretation. Pp. 1-5 in *Proceedings of the Human Factors Society 33rd Annual Meeting*. Santa Monica, California: Human Factors Society.
    1990   Map display design. Pp. 89-93 in *Proceedings of the Human Factors Society 34th Annual Meeting*. Santa Monica, California: Human Factors Society.
    1991   The design of electronic map displays. *Human Factors* 33(1):85-101.
Battiste, V., R.J. Shively, and S.R. Delzell
    1989   Geographical features used by EMS pilots to maintain geographical orientation. Poster presented at the Human Factors Society 33rd Annual Meeting, Denver, Colorado.
Biederman, I.
    1987   Recognition-by-components: A theory of human image understanding. *Psychological Review* 94:115-147.
Braine, L.G.
    1978   A new slant on orientation perception. *American Psychologist* 33:10-22.
Clark, H.H.
    1973   Space, time, semantics, and the child. In T.E. Moore, ed., *Cognitive Development and the Acquisition of Language*. New York: Academic Press.
Cooper, L.A., and R.N. Shepard
    1973   Chronometric study of the rotation of mental images. Pp. 75-176 in W.G. Chase, ed., *Visual Information Processing*. New York: Academic Press.
Coren, S., and J.S. Girgus
    1980   Principles of perceptual organization and spatial distortion: The gestalt illusion. *Journal of Experimental Psychology: Human Performance and Perception* 6:404-412.
Cote, D.O., G.P. Krueger, and R.R. Simmons
    1985   Helicopter copilot workload during nap-of-the-earth flight. *Aviation Space and Environmental Medicine* 56(2):153-157.
Deaver, J.
    1949   *A Dictionary of Psychology*. Baltimore, Maryland: Penguin Books.
Eley, M.G.
    1988   Determining the shape of land surfaces from topographic maps. *Ergonomics* 31(3):355-376.
Evans, G.W., and K. Pesdick
    1980   Cognitive mapping: Knowledge of real-world distances and location information. *Journal of Experimental Psychology: Human Learning and Memory* 6(1):13-24.
Fillmore, C.J.
    1968   The case for case. Pp. 1-88 in E. Bach and R.T. Harms, eds., *Universals in Linguistic Theory*. New York: Holt, Rinehart, and Winston.
Gibson, J.J.
    1968   *The Senses Considered as Perceptual Systems*. Boston: Houghton Mifflin.
Gogel, W.C.
    1978   The adjacency principle in visual perception. *Scientific American* 238:126-139.

Gunning, D.
    1978   Time estimation as a technique to measure workload. Pp. 41-45 in *Proceedings of the Human Factors Society 22nd Annual Meeting.* Santa Monica: California: Human Factors Society.
Hart, S.G.
    1978   Subjective time estimation as an index of workload. In *Proceedings of the Symposium on Man-System Interface: Advances in Workload Study.* Washington, DC: Air Lines Pilots Association.
Harwood, K.
    1989   Cognitive perspectives on map displays for helicopter flight. *Proceedings of the Human Factors Society 33rd Annual Meeting.* Santa Monica, California: Human Factors.
Hintzman, D.L., C.S. O'Dell, and D.R. Arndt
    1981   Orientation in cognitive maps. *Cognitive Psychology* 13:149-206.
Howard, I.P., and W.B. Templeton
    1966   *Human Spatial Orientation.* New York: Wiley.
Hutchins, E.
    1983   Understanding Micronesian navigation. Pp 191-225 in D. Gentner and A.L. Stevens, eds., *Mental Models.* New Jersey: Lawrence Erlbaum, Associates.
Levine, M.
    1982   YOU-ARE-HERE maps: Psychological considerations. *Environment and Behavior* 14:221-237.
Lynch, K.
    1960   *The Image of the City.* Cambridge, Massachusetts: MIT Press.
Maxwell, E.A.
    1975   *Geometry by Transformations.* Cambridge, England: Cambridge University Press.
Palmer, S.E.
    1980   What makes triangles point: Local and global effect in configurations of ambiguous triangles. *Cognitive Psychology* 12:285-305.
Rock, I.
    1974   *Orientation and Form.* New York: Academic Press.
Sadalla, E.K., W.J. Burroughs, and L.J. Staplin
    1980   Reference points in spatial cognition. *Journal of Experimental Psychology: Human Performance and Perception* 6:516-528.
Shepard, R.N.
    1984   Ecological constraints on internal representation: Resonant kinematics of perceiving, imagining, thinking, and dreaming. *Psychological Review* 91:417-447.
Shepard, R.N., and S. Hurwitz
    1984   Upward direction, mental rotation, and discrimination of left and right turns in maps. *Cognition* 18:161-194.
Shepard, R.N., and J. Metzler
    1971   Mental rotation of three-dimensional objects. *Science* 171:701-703.
Sholl, M.J.
    1987   Cognitive maps as orientating schemata. *Journal of Experimental Psychology: Learning, Memory, and Cognition* 13(4):615-628.
Stevens, A., and P. Coupe
    1978   Distortions in judged spatial relations. *Cognitive Psychology* 10:422-437.
Tolman, E.C.
    1948   Cognitive maps in rats and men. *Psychological Review* 55:189-208.
Tversky, B.
    1981   Distortion in memory for maps. *Cognitive Psychology* 13:407-433.

Wickens, C.D.

    1989a   Attention and skilled performance. Pp. 71-105 in D. Holding, ed., *Human Skills*, 2nd Edition. New York: Wiley and Sons.

    1989b   *Modeling Cognitive Performance in Aviation Environments: Navigation and Strategic Control.* Personal communication.

8

Decision Making

The extent to which teams successfully deal with transitions to crisis situations depends heavily on the extent to which the right actions are chosen: the process of decision making. Because of the great publicity that decision making failures often receive, we typically hear more about faulty decisions than successes in crisis situations. For example, the disaster at Three Mile Island resulted in part because operators in the control room made a decision to shut off an emergency feed water pump, having misdiagnosed the state of the reactor (Rubinstein and Mason, 1979). Less publicized because of their less disastrous outcomes were the more appropriate decisions taken in response to nuclear power emergencies at the Davis-Bessie and Brownsville plants.

The flight crew on board the Air Florida Boeing 737 at Washington's National Airport in 1982 exhibited faulty judgment in their decision to take off in icy conditions without requesting an immediate deicing (O'Hare and Roscoe, 1991; Van Dyne, 1982). The sluggishly handling plane never gained necessary air speed and crashed into the 14th Street Bridge in Washington, DC. In contrast, the problem-solving and decision-making sequence followed by the flight crew of the United flight 232, which suffered a total hydraulics failure over Iowa, was testimony to the good judgment of the team in crisis—bringing a totally crippled and nearly uncontrollable jet to earth (see Chapter 10).

For tank crews, also, the decisions made under combat stress have a major bearing on the success of the mission and the survivability of the crew. Does one chose to engage the enemy or not? Is it worth risking exposure by following the shortest path to an urgent destination? Or should one follow a longer, slower route, maintaining a low-profile, hidden position?

In most teams, decision-making responsibilities fall most heavily on the team leader—the tank commander, the airplane pilot in command, the hospital physician, or the fire chief. These individuals possess the ultimate responsibility for choosing the appropriate course of action, but other members of the team also play a critical role in communicating the information on which the optimal decision can and should be based.

Analysis of the decision-making case studies mentioned above and of numerous others reveals that shortcomings in decision making may result from limitations in a number of the processes necessary to execute a decision, from initial information gathering to final choice. In particular, it is possible to partition the process into two overall phases: the acquisition and maintenance of situation awareness necessary to diagnose or estimate the most likely state of affairs, and the selection of a course of action. While each of these phases can themselves be analyzed further, as indicated in Figure 8.1, it is instructive to consider examples of how faulty decisions can result from a breakdown of each. The operators at Three Mile Island, for example, made the right choice of action given their diagnosis of the state of the plant—which, unfortunately, had been faulty. A correct choice of action was also made by the commanding officer on the U.S.S. Vincennes (Klein, 1989; Slovic, 1987; U.S. Navy, 1988). Given the information provided to him, that the aircraft approaching the ship was probably hostile, his decision to launch a missile was probably the best one. The tragedy resulting when the missile struck a civilian airliner resulted because the identification of that aircraft was in error. In contrast, the Air Florida crash did not result because the crew failed to diagnose the icing conditions, but because their choice of action was inappropriate given those conditions. In the first half of this chapter, we treat these two phases of decision making separately before discussing how both are related specifically to the transition period. The section concludes by recommending some possible remediations to guard against decision failures.

HEURISTICS AND BIASES IN HYPOTHESIS FORMATION

A necessary, but not sufficient, precondition for good decision making is the existence of a correct hypothesis of the most likely state of the world within which the chosen action will be carried out. Wickens and Flach (1988) have presented an information processing model or framework of the hypothesis formation process, shown in Figure 8.1. Within the model, various biases and heuristics (Kahneman et al., 1982) are identified that may create distortions in hypothesis formation and situation awareness. In the

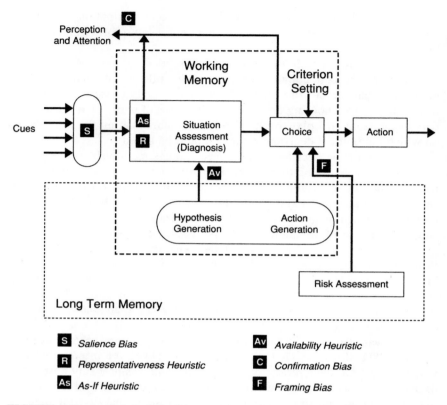

FIGURE 8.1 A model of decision making. Biases and heuristics, denoted by letters surrounded by a square, are discussed in the text. Source: Wickens and Flach (1988). Copyright held by Academic Press. Reprinted by permission.

following, each of these is illustrated as it might be or has been manifest in an applied setting.

When integrating multiple sources of information to formulate a hypothesis, the *salience bias* describes the decision maker's tendency to focus on the most salient (loudest, brightest, most prominent) cue, rather than that which may be most informative and diagnostic, when these are not the same. As one example, in the analysis of the incident aboard the U.S.S. Vincennes when the Iranian airliner was shot down, it was apparent that the salient writing of the word F14 on a message board in the combat information center, following the uncertain hypothesis of the aircraft's identify, contributed to the ultimate misidentification of the aircraft.

Which hypothesis a decision maker chooses to base his or her actions on depends very much on which hypothesis is most *available* in memory, rather than in fact which may be the most likely in the circumstances. This is known as the *availability heuristic* (Tversky and Kahneman, 1974). Thus, the tank commander will find most available the enemy's plan of attack for which he had just been briefed, or which he had encountered in a recent drill, because these would be easily brought to mind. Analysis of the Vincennes incident revealed that the misdiagnosis was the result of interpreting the actions of the radar contact in terms of a predefined script of a hostile attack (U.S. Navy, 1988). That is, an easily recallable sequence of events that would be likely to occur in combat.

Once a tentative hypothesis is formulated, based perhaps on available memories and salient information sources, two closely related forces join to increase the likelihood that available hypotheses will prevail and alternatives will not be considered. The *anchoring heuristic* describes the tendency to stay with a current hypothesis and consider new information that might shift one's beliefs in favor of a different hypothesis less than adequately (Tversky and Kahneman, 1974; Van Dyne, 1982). The *confirmation bias* (Klayman and Ha, 1987; Tolcott et al., 1989) describes the decision makers' tendency to seek new information that supports one's currently held hypothesis and to ignore (or at least downplay) information that may support an alternative hypothesis. Both anchoring and the confirmation bias seem to have been partially responsible for the disaster at the Three Mile Island nuclear power plant, in which operators focused on the inappropriate hypothesis that the water level was high and ignored critical display information suggesting just the opposite (i.e., that the water level was too low, which turned out in fact to be the correct hypothesis). It is easy to envision how the tank commander, with a preconceived hypothesis regarding the nature of enemy intentions, will interpret ambiguous evidence as consistent with these intentions. Tolcott et al. (1989) have found that such a bias is present in the performance of Army intelligence analysts.

EXPERTISE IN DIAGNOSIS

The information flow in Figure 8.1 suggests that human decision makers go through a time-consuming computational process of evaluating and interpreting evidence, relying heavily on the limited capacity of working memory. Yet under time pressure and in potential crisis situations, there is good evidence that expert decision makers—the skilled tank commander, pilot, or nuclear power plant control room operator—may adopt a very different strategy of hypothesis diagnosis in which they simply match the available evidence with the most similar experience already stored in long-term memory (Ebbeson and Koneci, 1981). Klein (1989), for example, has documented that expert fire crew chiefs, when diagnosing the nature of a fire upon first arriving at the scene, go through such a pattern match process, as do expert (but not novice) tank commanders in simulated battle games. The viewed scene is simply compared with a series of mental representations of typical scenes from past experience, to determine which one is an adequate match. In a study of pilot decision making, Wickens et al. (1987) and Barnett (1989) inferred that highly experienced pilots (those with more than 500 flight hours) used a qualitatively different style of pilot judgment than novices, relying less on working memory and more on direct retrieval of the appropriate solutions from long-term memory.

In spite of the apparent advantages of this pattern-matching decision strategy in some contexts, particularly those involving time pressure, the limits of this approach should be clearly noted as well. On one hand, such a technique may be applied effectively only in the domain for which expertise has been developed. Thus, for example, Klein observed that fire chiefs used pattern-matching diagnosis behavior when they diagnosed the nature of a fire, but not when they needed to deal with administrative commands and personnel decisions. On the other hand, although the pattern-matching technique is more rapid, less resource demanding, and qualitatively different, it is not necessarily more accurate than the time-consuming computational technique used by novices. Indeed, Wickens et al. (1987) found little difference in the accuracy of judgments made by high-time versus low-time pilots, only that high-time pilots were more confident in their decisions. As noted in Chapter 4, Koehler and McKinney (1991) found that inflight diagnoses of expert pilots were no better than those of less experienced pilots, and actually suffered more when the problems were nonroutine.

In accounting for these failures, it is reasonable to assume that, because the pattern-matching approach forces a set of environmental cues to match a stored template in memory, it may be relatively more susceptible to the biases in hypothesis formulation discussed above (confirmation, anchoring, and availability). This is because a situation that is generally similar to the mental representation of past experience, but may be different in some key respects, could be classified as identical, with those key differences simply ignored (i.e., anchoring on what is available from past experience). Unfortunately, with the exception of the Wickens et al. (1987) study, few data are available regarding the relative quality of pattern matching versus computational decision making in applied environments. Furthermore, the studies discussed above have defined expertise in terms of years of experience, rather than (necessarily) a high quality of performance. It will be important to continue research that examines decision style and quality as a function of expertise, unconfounded with experience.

CHOICE

Classic decision theory has focused its efforts on ways to integrate the uncertainty and the value associated with prospective outcomes of decision alternatives. That is, a given choice is assumed to have a number of possible outcomes (depending on the uncertain state of the world in which a choice is made) (see Figure 8.2). The option that is favored is assumed to maximize some subjective quantity or preference for the decision maker. It is often assumed that this quantity is the subjective expected utility, which is computed as the utility (subjective value) of each possible outcome for the choice, multiplied by the subjective probability that that outcome will be observed. There are numerous alternative models that have been applied to decision making. For example, it might be assumed that decision makers will minimize losses or will pick the least effortful decision that has some minimum level of expected gain (Slovic, 1987). However, if one option

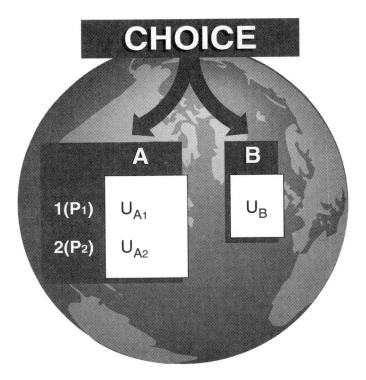

FIGURE 8.2 A hypothetical risky choice. Decision Option A will yield one of two possible outcomes, depending on whether the state of the world is 1 or 2. These states are not known for sure, but are estimated (diagnosed) with probabilities P_1 and P_2, respectively. If state 1 is in effect, outcome A_1, which has utility U_{A1}, will be obtained. State 2 will yield outcome A_2, with utility U_{A2}. In contrast, decision Option B will yield a certain (nonrisky) outcome with utility U_B, no matter which state is true.

promises more attractive outcomes given some circumstances, but the chances of those outcomes are lower than those of less appealing outcomes promised by competing alternatives, how should the conflict be resolved?

A critical concept in such analysis is that of *risk*, typically characterizing an option for which the two or more possible outcomes associated with the choice may differ in their probability of occurrence and do differ in their utility (i.e., cost or benefit). This situation characterizes option A in the figure. For example, a low-probability outcome may be associated with dire consequences and a high-probability outcome may be associated with consequences that are far more benign. In the nuclear power industry, a decision to keep a reactor on line when it has shown a faintly suspicious symptom might be such an example. There is a small probability of a major disaster if the symptom really does herald a failure but a high probability that nothing is wrong.

How bad such a risky option is perceived to be (its expected negative utility) will, of course, depend on how large is the perceived probability of the negative outcome. There are in fact a number of sometimes conflicting influences on perceived probability that may bias the estimate in different directions. For example, very rare events are typically overestimated (explaining why people believe they will win by entering lotteries) (Sheridan and Farrell, 1974; Wickens, 1984). This overestimation is particularly likely to occur when low-probability events are well publicized so that they become available to memory (Slovic, 1987). Humans have a tendency to be overconfident of their own likelihood of success—to underestimate the probability that infrequent, bad things will happen to them (as opposed to someone else) (Bettman et al., 1986). This is one example of the general bias toward overconfidence in human diagnosis and choice.

As shown in the figure, risky options are often paired against "sure thing" options, for which the consequences are reasonably well known: shut the nuclear reactor down and the power plant will surely suffer some disruption, but it also will surely avoid disaster. Research by Kahneman and Tversky (1981, 1984) into the heuristic known as *framing* suggests that, when choosing between a risky and a sure thing option, people respond differently when the outcomes of both options have positive expected utilities, than when both options have outcomes with negative expected utilities. Teams in crisis usually are confronted with a pair of negative outcomes. The tank commander might, for example, choose between a safe retreat, with a sure loss of position but sure preservation of safety, and a risky advance, with a low probability of encountering fatality-inducing battle conditions. In analogous circumstances, when the choice is between negatives, Kahneman and Tversky found that people usually are biased to choose the risky option. When in contrast, the choice is viewed as one between positive outcomes, the choice is more likely to be biased toward the sure thing safe option.

The important feature of this *framing bias* is that the very same decisions may be framed positively—by emphasizing the good characteristics (e.g., probability of winning the battle, preserving crew lives) or negatively (e.g., probability of losing the battle, encountering fatalities), and the difference in framing will influence the choice that is made.

As with our discussion of diagnosis, so also with choice: it appears that expert decision makers do not generally employ a fully analytic strategy. They do not carefully weigh all the alternatives, outcome utilities, and probabilities before arriving at a choice. Rather, evidence suggests that these processes, too, are often circumvented by a decision based on direct memory retrieval. If, in a particular circumstance (evaluated by diagnosis), a choice has proven successful in the past (yielded a favorable outcome), it will be chosen again. Any action that has yielded this outcome can be chosen, not necessarily that with the highest expected utility (Klein, 1989). Such a strategy, in which the first alternative that satisfies all relevant attributes is selected, has been labeled as *satisficing* (Simon, 1955). This characterizes the verbal protocols that fire chiefs give when describing the tactics they choose to fight a fire (Klein, 1989).

Analogous to our treatment of diagnosis, the alternative direct memory retrieval method of decision making shown by experts is not necessarily better than the strategy shown by novices, although it is more rapid and made with less effort. The strategy will lead to the choice of actions that are familiar and easy to recall. Hence, certain biases toward availability may be shown. This appears to be an adaptive strategy in times of stress, when time pressure is intense, as will be the case in most transition situations. We consider now the potential effects of the transition on decision quality.

TRANSITION EFFECTS

The influence of the transition process on decision making may be roughly described from two perspectives: the exchange between pretransition effort and post-transition performance, and the overall influence of stress on transition decision performance.

Pre-Post Exchange

The first section of this chapter has described the extent to which effective decision making is based on accurate situation awareness. One can easily imagine that efficient and accurate judgments in a post-transition period will depend on the fidelity of knowledge gained in the pretransition period. Three kinds of knowledge and preparation would seem to be of use here. The first concerns static knowledge of features that are unlikely to change. For the tank commander, this characterizes knowledge of the geography of the area, the acquisition of which was described in the previous chapter. For the nuclear power crew, this static information is characterized by long-term knowledge of plant operation as well as the more transient knowledge of the repair status of the plant—which lines are open and which are closed. For a disaster relief coordinator, it may involve knowledge of which units and equipment are located where. There is a high payoff in investing resources into acquiring this static knowledge or situation awareness, since it will be unlikely to change and can then be used as a basis for fast and effective decision making after the transition.

Second, there is a class of knowledge and information that can be gathered prior to transition that has uncertainty associated with it. Any decision that will be taken in response to future meteorological conditions, for example, must certainly be of this form. So also will a tank commander's decision based on intelligence about what an enemy might do (Scott and Wickens, 1983). In this instance, it would seem important to prepare for and consider, not only the most likely hypothesis (or state) based on the available cues, but also those conditions of less, but nonzero, likelihood. In short, it is valuable to develop a weighted contingency diagnosis in which crews are prepared for alternate states in proportion to their degree of likelihood. The prepared decision maker should guard against a sharpening of preparedness only for the most likely state. In this way the team will be less likely to misidentify and falsely classify a particular situation, succumbing to the heuristics of anchoring and availability. An important corollary of this strategy is that estimates of uncertainty should be carefully preserved as situation information or intelligence is relayed from person to person or unit to unit. It was in part the failure to relay uncertainty information up the chain of command that led to the disaster in the U.S.S. Vincennes incident (U.S. Navy, 1988).

Third, and most obviously, post-transition decision making can be facilitated by the rehearsal of and preparation for contingency response plans. As noted in Chapter 3, greater pretransition preparation will lead to more efficient post-transition response. But here again, care must be taken to guard against blind following of a preprogrammed procedure, without monitoring its ongoing appropriateness and without entertaining a willingness to modify or abandon the procedure as needed (i.e., to guard against the confirmation bias) (Woods and Roth, 1987).

Stress Effects

The second relevant transition effect on decision making concerns the specific effects of post-transition stress on decision-making performance. Given that many of the stress effects were covered previously in Chapter 4, we present here only a brief review of how the combined effects of noise, danger, and time pressure might be expected to amplify decision-making biases.

Communications

Noise will have a clear and direct degrading effect on communications—the exchange of auditory information necessary for effective decision making. We might also anticipate a specific form of stress bias for the listener to expect and therefore hear the subjectively most likely message. Such was a clear factor responsible for the KLM-PAN AM collision on the runway in the Canary Islands (Bailey, 1989).

Perceptual Tunneling

Stress is known to induce an attentional focusing on the most subjectively important source of information (Broadbent, 1971). Where the subjective importance of an information source does not directly correlate with its true reliability and diagnosticity, major problems could be encountered.

Confirmation Bias

There is at least anecdotal evidence that stress can enhance the confirmation bias, reinforcing still further the belief that the hypothesis or action one has already chosen is correct. This tendency seems to have characterized the operators' behaviors at Three Mile Island (Rubinstein and Mason, 1979) and was diagnosed as a contributing cause of a substantial number of recent accidents in British military aircraft (Chappelow, 1988).

Phonetic Working Memory

It is not difficult to envision how stress, particularly that characterized by noise, can reduce working memory capacity (Hockey, 1986) and therefore the effectiveness of that memory system in storing verbal information necessary for hypothesis testing and evaluation (Mehle, 1982). This is particularly true when the situation is unfamiliar and the operator is less able to rely on pattern-matching techniques.

Spatial Working Memory

Wickens et al. (1988a, 1988b) found that pilot decisions made under the combined stress of noise and time pressure were degraded to the extent that they depended on visualization of the airspace. One might anticipate, therefore, similar effects on decisions that require rapid updating or revision of a mental model of terrain (in the case of the tank commander) or some other visual-spatial environment (i.e., the structure of a ship, building, or plant on fire).

Speed-Accuracy Tradeoff

It has been shown that stress induces a shift to fast, but less accurate, performance on a speed-accuracy tradeoff (Hockey, 1986). Furthermore, given that accurate performance on certain kinds of decisions depends on a time-consuming weighing of various alternatives, it is reasonable to conclude that decision performance following transition will be more error prone, to the extent that it depends on an analytic computational strategy. Alternatively, it can be predicted that the preferred strategy of decision making will be likely to shift to one involving direct memory retrieval, given that the operator has stored the necessary domain-related knowledge base (Klein, 1989).

Remediation

Decision researchers have long been aware of the failures and limitations of human decision making (Slovic et al., 1977). More recently, they have acknowledged the human's very real strengths in this area compared with the capabilities of many artificial intelligence systems (Klein, 1989). To counteract these limitations, four general remediation solutions have been proposed, any of which might be appropriate for the transition environment. Each of these solutions is described below.

Decision Aids

The increasing power and sophistication of computer technology has made more feasible the development of programs that can assist decision making. In each phase, there are two alternative approaches. One involves the development of artificial intelligence/expert system technology in which potential solutions (diagnoses or recommended choices) are computer-generated, to be accepted or rejected by the human operator (Madni, 1988; Rouse et al., 1990). Such techniques would still appear to be somewhat limited unless the optimum decision rules can be clearly and unambiguously articulated, and the decision problem is quite self-contained (i.e., does not involve extracting information from unforeseeable sources). For example, a decision aid in recommending diagnoses of a failed gunnery computer might be appropriate. One that recommends battlefield tactics would be far more tenuous, because of the diversity of factors that should go into such a consideration.

The alternative approach is a decision aid that provides assistance to the human operator but does not recommend diagnoses or actions. Such an aid might, for example, list alternative hypotheses for a diagnosis, to safeguard against the tunneling produced by availability and anchoring. Correspondingly, it might list alternative courses of action (without recommending particular ones). A major potential source of benefit here could be realized in aids that provided an effective and organized display of information cues that could assist in hypothesis evaluation and situation awareness (MacGregor and Slovic, 1986; Scott and Wickens, 1983). Such a display aid could present cues in terms of their information value, in such a way that salience would not distort the overall representation of information. In general, displays that minimize the need for cognitive transformation between what is displayed and what is meant, and that organize information in logical groupings, will aid the decision maker.

Debias Training

An alternative approach to designing aids that will minimize the impact of bias is to train or teach the operator about these biases and heuristics directly. Such debias training has been introduced with the belief that, once a decision maker is aware of the existence of these biases, he or she will be less likely to fall prey to their influence; however, the consensus in the literature is that simple awareness of these biases rarely alleviates them (Fischhoff, 1982).

Some examples of modest success in debiasing have been observed, rendering decision making less susceptible to anchoring (Lopes, 1982) and overconfidence in meteorological forecasting (Murphy et al., 1985). While not yet fully validated as an effective technique, it would seem that providing decision makers with some level of training into the nature of heuristics, and the understanding of probability would be of considerable value in many applied contexts.

Domain Training

An alternative form of training to that used in debiasing is direct training in the domain of the decision itself (rather than in the mechanics of the decision process). Certainly included here would be training in planning and diagnosis or situation assessment. One issue that is not well resolved is the extent to which training to deal with events following crisis should focus on highly specific (but brittle) procedures following. In the context of the nuclear power industry, Woods (1988) has voiced some concern about the dangers of overtraining operators to follow very specific procedures given a particular failure diagnosis. The concern results when the diagnoses on which the procedure is based is itself uncertain (i.e., a diagnosis of the most likely candidate, but not a certain candidate, so that others are plausible). In this case, overtraining on a particular routine or decided course of action to follow given that hypothesis, may lead the operator to follow it blindly, without carefully checking as the decision actions are carried out, to determine whether the routine remains appropriate. As we have seen, this tendency may be exaggerated in times of stress. In this regard, some consideration should be given to training the decision maker to closely monitor the outcomes of the actions following a decision, in order to ensure that the choice was in fact the correct one, and to be prepared to alter those actions as necessary. Such training could make use of the realistic, dynamic simulation facilities offered by SIMNET, a team-oriented tank training facility to be discussed in further detail in Chapter 10. The issue of the specificity with which emergency procedures following should be trained is one for which more research is clearly needed. In at least one domain, programs to train decision makers have demonstrated valid success. Diehl (1991) has reviewed the effectiveness of air crew decision training in a variety of aviation programs and has concluded that such programs substantially reduce the likelihood of erroneous pilot judgments.

Team Cohesion

The final remediation addresses the need to create efficient decision making teams within which the communication of information necessary for optimal diagnosis and choice proceeds in a smooth and unambiguous fashion. Clearly some degree of standardization and redundancy in vocal communications is necessary. But other critical factors involve the spirit, coherence, training, and personality of the team members, and in particular of the team leader. These are issues that are discussed at the end of Chapter 4 and are dealt with again in some depth in Chapter 10; some of them are also addressed in Druckman and Bjork (1991).

SUMMARY

The decision making of teams in transition depends jointly on the decision-making capabilities of the team leader, and on the flow of information via voice communication from other team members and from well configured visual displays. When this information transmission is effective, it provides the basis for good situational awareness or diagnosis of the state of the world that requires a decision. Yet this diagnosis may be hindered or distorted by a number of biases or heuristics, some of which are amplified under times of stress. High degrees of expertise may eliminate some of these problems and produce more rapid decisions.

Diagnosis is often followed by choice, which depends on the accurate assessment of outcomes, their utility, and their risk. Here again, certain biases in risk perception have been identified, and here also the decision process may be facilitated by expertise.

Two categories of transition effects on the decision process may be identified. On one hand, there are certain actions the operator can take before the transition that can improve decision quality (or accuracy) after the transition. On the other hand, the transition itself will induce a level of stress that is likely to systematically degrade certain aspects of the decision process.

The limitations of decision making can be remediated by one of four techniques: computer-based decision aiding, particularly that which emphasizes the display and organization of relevant cues, training of self-awareness of the decision maker's biases, training in the decision domain, and development of team cohesion.

REFERENCES

Bailey, R.W.
1989   *Human Performance Engineering Using Human Factors/Ergonomics to Achieve Computer System Usability* (2nd edition). Englewood Cliffs, New Jersey: Prentice-Hall.

Barnett, B.
1989   Information processing components and knowledge representation: An individual difference approach to modeling pilot judgment. *Proceedings of the Human Factors Society 33rd Annual Meeting.* Santa Monica, California: Human Factors Society.

Bettman, J.R., J.W. Payne, and R. Staelin
1986   Cognitive considerations in designing effective labels for presenting risk information. *Journal of Marketing and Public Policy* 5:1-28.

Broadbent, D.E.
1971   *Decision and Stress.* New York: Academic Press.

Chappelow, J.W.
1988   Causes of aircrew error in the Royal Airforce. In *Human Behavior in High Stress Situations in Aerospace Operations.* NATO AGAARD Conference Proceedings 458.

Diehl, A.
1991   The effectiveness of training programs for preventing aircrew error. In R. Jensen, ed., *Proceedings of the Sixth Symposium on Aviation Psychology.* Columbus, Ohio: Ohio State University.

Druckman, D., and R.A. Bjork, eds.
1991   *In the Mind's Eye: Enhancing Human Performance.* Committee on Techniques for the Advancement of Human Performance. Washington, DC: National Academy Press.

Ebbeson, E.D., and V. Koneci
1981   On external validity in decisionmaking research. In T. Wallsten, ed., *Cognitive Processes in Choice and Decisionmaking.* Hillsdale, New Jersey: Erlbaum.

Fischhoff, B.
1982   Debiasing. In D. Kahneman, P. Slovic, and A. Tverksy, eds., *Judgment under Uncertainty: Heuristics and Biases.* New York: Cambridge University Press.

Hockey, G.R.J.
1986   Changes in operator efficiency as a function of environmental stress, fatigue, and circadian rhythms. In K.R. Boff, L. Kaufman, and J.P. Thomas, eds., *Handbook of Perception and Human Performance, Vol. II.* New York: Wiley.

Kahneman, D., P. Slovic, and A. Tversky, eds.
1982   *Judgment Under Uncertainty: Heuristics and Biases.* New York: Cambridge University Press.

Kahneman, D., and A. Tversky
1981   The framing of decisions and the psychology of choice. *Science* 211(4481):453-458.
1984   Choices, values and frames. *American Psychologist* 39:341-350.

Klayman, J., and Y.W. Ha
1987   Confirmation, disconfirmation and information in hypothesis testing. *Journal of Experimental Psychology: Human Learning and Memory* 94(2):211-228.

Klein, G.A.
1989   Recognition-primed decisions. Pp. 47-92 in W. Rouse, ed., *Advances in Man-Machine Systems Research, Volume 5.* Greenwich, Connecticut: JAI Press.

Koehler, J.J., and E.H. McKinney
1991   Uniqueness of task, experience, and decision making performance: A study of 176 U.S. Air Force mishaps.

Lopes, L.
1982   *Procedural Debiasing.* Technical Report WHIPP 15. Madison, Wisconsin: Human Information Processing Program.

MacGregor, D., and P. Slovic
1986   Graphic representation of judgmental information. *Human-Computer Interaction* 2:179-200.

Madni, A.M.
1988   The role of human factors in expert systems design. *Human Factors* 30:395-414.

Mehle, T.
1982   Hypotheses generation in an automobile malfunction inference task. *Acta Psychologica* 52:87-116.

Murphy, A., W. Hsu, R. Winkler, and D. Wilks
1985   The use of probabilities in subjective quantitative precipitation forecast. *Monthly Weather Review* 113:2075-2089.

O'Hare, D., and S. Roscoe
1991   *Flightdeck Performance, The Human Factor.* Ames: Iowa State University Press.

Rouse, W.B., N.D. Geddes, and J.M. Hammer
1990   Computer aided fighter pilots. *IEEE Spectrum* 27(3):38-40.

Rubinstein, T., and A.F. Mason
1979   The accident that shouldn't have happened: An analysis of Three Mile Island. *IEEE Spectrum* 16:33-57.

Scott, B., and C.D. Wickens
1983   The effects of a spatial information format on decision making performance in a C3 (Command, Control, and Communications) probabilitic information integration task. Pp. 96-99 in *MIT Proceedings of the Sixth MIT/ONR Workshop on C^3 Systems.* Report No. AD-P002887. Urbana, Illinois: Illinois University.

Sheridan, T.B., and W.R. Farrell
1974   *Man-Machine Systems.* Cambridge, Massachusetts: MIT Press.
Simon, H.A.
1955   A behavioral model of rational choice. *Quarterly Journal of Economics* 69:99-118.
Slovic, D.
1987   Facts versus fears: Understanding perceived risk. In F. Farley and C. Null, eds., *Using Psychological Science.* Washington, DC: Federation of Behavioral, Psychological, and Cognitive Sciences.
Slovic, D., B. Fischhoff, and Lichtenstein
1977   Behavioral decision theory. *Annual Review of Psychology* 28:1-39.
Tolcott, M.A., F.F. Marvin, and T.A. Bresdick
1989   *The Confirmation Bias in Military Situation Assessment.* Reston, Virginia: Decision Science Consortium.
Tversky, A., and D. Kahneman
1974   Judgment under uncertainty: Heuristics and biases. *Science* 185:1124-1131.
U.S. Navy
1988   *Investigation Report: Formal Investigation into the Circumstances Surrounding the Downing of Iran Air Flight 655 on 3 July 1988.* Investigation Report. Washington, DC: Department of Defense.
Van Dyne, L.
1982   A false feeling of security. *The Washingtonian* October:112-144.
Wickens, C.D.
1984   Processing resources in attention. Pp. 63-102 in R. Parasuraman and R. Davies, ed., *Varieties of Attention.* San Diego, California: Academic Press.
1992   *Engineering Psychology and Human Performance* New York: Harper Collins.
Wickens, C.D., and J. Flach
1988   Human information processing. Pp. 111-155 in E. Wiener and D. Nagel, eds., *Human Factors in Aviation.* New York: Academic Press.
Wickens, C.D., A.F. Stokes, B. Barnett, and F. Hyman
1988a   *The Effects of Stress on Pilot Judgment in a MIDIS Simulator.* Final Technical Report, Subcontract C87-101376. Savoy, Illinois: Institute of Aviation.
1988b   Stress and pilot judgment: An empirical study using MIDIS, a microcomputer-based simulation. In *Proceedings of the Human Factors Society 32nd Annual Meeting.* Santa Monica, California: Human Factors Society.
Wickens, C.D., A. Stokes, B. Barnett, and T. Davis, Jr.
1987   *Componential Analysis of Pilot Decision Making.* Final Technical Report No. ARL-87-4/SCEEE-87-1. Savoy, Illinois: University of Illinois Aviation Research Laboratory.
Woods, D.D.
1988   Commentary: Cognitive engineering in complex and dynamic worlds. In E. Hollnagel, G. Mancini, and D. Woods, eds., *Cognitive Engineering in Complex, Dynamic Worlds.* London, England: Academic Press.
Woods, D.D., and E.M. Roth
1987   Cognitive systems engineering. In M. Helander, ed., *Handbook of Human-Computer Interaction.* New York: North-Holland.

9

Strategic Task Management

The previous chapter has described the importance of maintaining situation awareness and effective decision making in both the pre- and post-transition period. These elements, however, represent only a part of the cognitive activity required by teams in periods of high workload. A critical activity that we address in this chapter is strategic task management. The operator, faced with a host of tasks competing for attention in periods of high workload, must decide which tasks to perform when, how frequently to switch from one task to another, and when it is appropriate to break off performance of an ongoing task to shift to one of higher priority. Furthermore, to be effective, the shift from one activity to the next should be rapid.

Some aspects of strategic task management are quite similar to those addressed in the previous chapter. For example, the decision made by a tank commander of whether to engage an enemy or retreat is clearly a choice between tasks. But issues of task scheduling and switching are not ones that are typically addressed in the study of decision making. This chapter addresses the issue of task switching and task management at two levels. In the first part, we consider basic laboratory research that has addressed the speed with which humans can initiate, change, and cease tasks. In the second part, we address research in more complex domains that has focused more on when or whether tasks of different priority are performed.

COGNITIVE SWITCHING

Task switching is a pervasive phenomenon in everyday life. Every day we engage in several tasks, switching from one to another with little thought and little apparent effort. We get up, bathe, dress, eat, and go to work. We come home, cook, eat, clean up, recreate, and go to bed. Each activity is focused on specific goals, often requiring that the same things be used in different ways (consider, for example, the different ways we use water in these activities). In each activity, our behavior could be modeled effectively as a special-purpose processor, dedicated to the one act and no other. At different times, we appear to be dressing machines, bathing machines, cooking machines, eating machines, and so on. However, we appear to be more than special-purpose machines, and the clues to our nature become clear at the transitions between activities: we appear to be collections of special-purpose machines, capable of changing from one to another on a moment's notice. The transitions are brief and hardly noticeable in everyday life, yet they are fundamentally important in understanding human behavior.

Strategy Switching

One approach to the study of task switching has been through the study of strategy switching. A person's behavior in performing a task, whether simple or complex, can be described as a strategy. A strategy can be defined as an optional organization of cognitive processes that is designed to achieve some goal in a particular task environment (Logan, 1985a; Logan and Zbrodoff, 1982; Logan et al., 1983). The organization is optional because people can configure their processes in several ways. Often, there are several ways to perform the same task; each one is a different strategy. The cognitive processes are organized because strategic behavior is coherent and planful. Strategic behavior is intentional, organized around the achievement of goals. Some configurations of processes will achieve the goals and others will not. People choose the former. Some configurations of processes will achieve the goals better than others. People try to choose the better approaches. Having adopted a strategy, people will appear as special purpose processors dedicated to the task at hand. But this way of defining strategies highlights the general purpose nature of human activity and provides a way to describe transitions from one strategy to another.

The research of Logan, Zbrodoff, and their colleagues has revealed that people can be relatively rapid at adapting or changing the strategies with which they perform a task. For example, in one task, a variant of the Stroop task (Stroop, 1935), people can either attend to the position of a word (presented above or below a fixation point), or the word's semantic content ("above" or "below"). Depending on the nature of the information presented on a given trial, attending to the one attribute or the other (a difference in attentional strategy) can speed or slow their performance. Logan and Zbrodoff (1982) found that subjects can adopt the required attentional strategy very rapidly (within a half second) if they are motivated to do so, and they will choose one strategy or the other on the basis of the probability that it will best serve their performance (Logan et al., 1984; Zbrodoff and Logan, 1986).

Logan's research on strategy selection of attentional dimensions has parallels in Rabbitt's work (1989) in the selection of speed-accuracy tradeoff strategies. In tasks typifying those in which operators must make a series of rapid choice responses, Rabbitt notes the facility with which subjects seek the strategy that provides the optimal level of performance. For example, if accuracy is important, they will increase in speed until an error is made, and then immediately back off just enough to restore errorless performance on subsequent trials. Similarly, Wickens et al. (1985) have found that, within a dual task paradigm, subjects can shift resources from one task to another within a few seconds, in response to a sudden increase in resource demand (difficulty) imposed by one of the tasks.

The facility with which strategies can be chosen and modified is important and certainly testifies to the flexibility of human cognition. This is an important issue in workload transition periods, for it is evident that a change from pre- to post-transition conditions will normally require a host of different strategies to be adopted, such as a shift to more rapid performance.

It should be noted, however, that most studies of rapid strategy shifting have not been carried out in high-stress conditions, and so, to some extent, the generalizability of this finding of flexibility to the tank crew environment must be treated cautiously. Also, shifting the strategy with which a given task is performed is not the same as shifting between two different tasks—an issue that we now address.

Task Switching

Research on the issue of task switching is made complex because of ambiguity in the issue of "What is a task?" A relatively unexplored research area concerns the hierarchical nature of complex tasks. High-level goals are often accomplished by the attainment of several subordinate low-level goals, and the high-level goals need to be kept in mind while dealing with the low-level goals. This is evident, for example, in navigation tasks in which higher-level goals (e.g., reach a given location) are accomplished by meeting lower-level goals (e.g., come to a given heading).

The research most relevant to this issue is Vallacher and Wegner's (1987) action identification theory. It assumes that action is organized hierarchically and concerns itself with discovering the level at which actions are construed and the circumstances under which people shift the level at which they describe their action. Vallacher and Wegner (1987) argue that the same act can be described at several hierarchical levels. For example, the same act may be described as pressing buttons, dialing a telephone, calling a friend, maintaining social contacts, or searching for meaning in life. Among other things, familiarity with the act encourages high-level descriptions. Vallacher and Wegner show that alcoholics describe imbibing as "getting smashed" whereas nonalcoholics will describe it as "having a drink." People drinking coffee from a 1-pound cup will describe their actions as "picking up a cup," "moving the cup to my lips" and so on, whereas people drinking coffee from normal cups describe their actions as "drinking coffee" or "getting a dose of caffeine."

Vallacher and Wegner argue that levels of action description lower than the one chosen by the actor are performed automatically: the actor need only think of the goal at the level at which he or she describes the action. Lower-level activities will take care of themselves. They argue that people will maintain action descriptions at the highest possible level until something goes wrong. In that case, they switch to a lower-level description to try to discover what went wrong. Thus, we think we are calling a friend until we discover that the number wasn't dialed correctly. Then we pay attention to button pressing, trying to discover whether we executed the sequence incorrectly or the telephone isn't working properly.

Action identification theory is very new and has not been applied to many situations, but it seems very promising, especially in the context of workload transitions. At the very least, it provides a framework in which to understand the complex tasks encountered in workload transition situations. More likely, it will provide a rich source of hypotheses for future research (e.g., what happens to high-level goals when attention is called to low-level goals).

The relatively scarce research that has been done on switching between tasks has considered the concept of task at a relatively low hierarchical level. It reveals that, like strategy switching, task switching can be carried our fairly rapidly.

Jersild (1927) studied the time taken to alternate between similar (adding versus subtracting numbers) and dissimilar alternatives (addition or subtraction versus naming opposites), and found that subjects could alternate between very dissimilar alternatives with virtually no cost (also see Biederman, 1973; Spector and Biederman, 1976). This suggests that strategy engagement time depends on the relation between the strategy to be engaged and the one that went before it. (This theme is discussed at greater length in the section below on disengaging strategies.) More recently, a series of studies on multichannel information processing have revealed that people are able to switch attention from one channel to another, on cue, within a few tenths of a second (Gopher, 1982; Sperling and Dosher, 1986). Interestingly, Gopher has found that individual differences in the speed of switching between two auditory channels provides a valid predictor of differences in performing complex skills, such as those found in bus driving and aviation.

A substantial research program on task switching has been undertaken by Logan and his colleagues, who have examined, independently, the two components of task switching: stopping the first activity and changing to the second activity.

Action can be stopped relatively easily. Highly skilled actions, such as speaking and typewriting, can be stopped very quickly, within a syllable or two or keystroke or two of the stop signal. The same results can be found with experimenter-imposed stop signals and with naturally occurring stop signals such as errors in speaking or typing (for a review, see Logan and Cowan, 1984). Inhibition is difficult only in pathological cases. Schachar and Logan (1990) found that hyperactive children were deficient in their ability to inhibit action, compared with other disturbed children and to normal control children. But even their inhibitory ability can be improved by administration of stimulant medication (methylphenidate) which improves behavioral symptoms of hyperactivity (Tannock et al., 1989).

Action appears to be controllable up to the point of execution. There is no apparent "point of no return" after which action becomes ballistic. This was suggested by behavioral experiments (Logan, 1981; Osman et al., 1990) and confirmed with psychophysiological measures (de Jong et al., 1990). Nevertheless, stopping is strategic. People stop action more quickly when they expect to stop (i.e., when stop signals occur on a greater proportion of trials; Logan, 1981; Logan and Burkell, 1986).

It takes time to stop action, but not much. Actions that are simple and complex, skilled and unskilled, can be stopped in 200-400 milliseconds (for a review, see Logan and Cowan, 1984). The time to stop action increases somewhat as the difficulty of performing that action increases (Logan et al., 1984, 1987).

A variation of the stop-signal paradigm, relevant to the discussion of activity switching, is the change-task paradigm, in which the signal to stop one activity serves as the stimulus to start a different, changed activity. The change-task signal is a type of procedural bridge between the stop task and traditional dual tasks, in which subjects respond overtly to two signals. It provides a simple analog of workload transition situations, in which current (low-workload) activities have to stop suddenly to make way for new, more important (high-workload) activities.

Stopping performance in the change-task paradigm is similar to stopping performance in the stop task. The time to stop action may be a little longer in the change task, but the pattern of results is essentially the same. The most interesting results in the change task involve the overt response to the stop (change) signal analyzed contingent on whether or not the subject successfully inhibited the first activity. If subjects fail to inhibit their responses to the first task and therefore respond overtly to the first task and the stop signal, then overt responses to the change signal are delayed as are dual-task reaction times. However, if subjects successfully inhibit their responses to the first task, there is no competition (Logan, 1985b; Logan and Burkell, 1986; also see Logan, 1982). This suggests that successful inhibition "clears the system," removing residual effects of the inhibited response so that the new response can begin without interference.

The lack of interfering effects from inhibited actions has important implications for workload transitions: it suggests that there should be little carryover across the transition, unless, of course, the operator must pick up and complete the stopped task at a later time—a common occurrence in the real world but rare in laboratory tasks. Provided that people inhibit their pretransition actions, there should be little interference with performance of post-transition tasks. However, the change task has not been explored very broadly, so it is not clear how far the lack of refractory effects will generalize. More research is needed. In particular, it will be important to vary the demands of the post-transition task, as post-transition tasks have been relatively simple in previous research (but see Logan, 1983).

In conclusion, the data suggest that actions can be stopped very easily and rapidly. The difficulty of a stopping action depends somewhat on the complexity of the action being stopped and on the selectivity of the stopping response. Studies of the change task suggest that successful inhibition has few carryover effects for subsequent actions, which is good news for workload transition situations.

Implications for Workload Transition

While the research on task engagement, change, and task stopping has been carried out in fairly basic laboratory paradigms, it is possible to speculate to some extent on generalizations that might be made to more complex high-workload environments.

Engaging Tasks

Engaging tasks take time and resources. Task engagement can be relatively leisurely in low-workload situations, but when workload suddenly increases, time pressure increases substantially and there may not be enough time for engagement. Research suggests that the time for strategy engagement can be reduced in several ways. First, the engagement process can be automatized (see also Chapter 3); the more practice, the faster the engagement process. Again, automaticity is specific, so it will be important to train engagement of each strategy or task separately. In principle, engagement is different from choice, and availability of alternatives does not imply the ability to engage them quickly. Trainees should practice rapid engagement.

Second, the engagement process can be sped up by reducing the degree of choice; the fewer the alternatives, the faster the engagement. The tank commander can reduce the degree of choice for subordinates (i.e., by ordering specific alternatives). That would make engagement easier for the subordinates but it may substantially increase the workload of the commander. A clear chain of command can reduce the degree of choice for commanders and subordinates alike; neither will have to ponder suggestions from unauthorized sources (e.g., "Is that a command or a suggestion?") or decide between conflicting directives (e.g., "Should I obey the sergeant or the lieutenant?").

Third, the engagement process can be sped up by making the conditions for engagement highly discriminable. Fortunately or unfortunately, there may not be much to do here. On one hand, high-workload situations are compelling perceptually (to say the least) and therefore are easily discriminable from low-workload situations. On the other hand, many of the high-workload situations we are considering are either adversarial (onset of combat) or noncooperative (fires or medical emergencies) and therefore cannot be engineered to make conditions more discriminable. One has to take what one gets. However, discrimination can be improved by practice; the performer can be engineered even if the situation cannot.

Disengaging Tasks

Disengaging tasks should not be much of a problem in workload transitions. Tasks can be disengaged very quickly whether the task is simple or complex, whether the performer is novice or skilled. Stopping time depends on the discriminability of the stop signal, but discriminability should be very clear in workload transition situations (e.g., it should be easy to tell when a battle begins). Disengagement may be difficult when some activities must be stopped while others continue (i.e., when stopping is selective), but even then, stopping times are typically less than one second. Studies of the change task suggest that it should be relatively easy to stop one task and begin another, though existing research has not investigated changes from low- to high-workload tasks. In general, more research would be desirable, particularly in workload transition situations, but the data so far are encouraging.

The high stress in workload transition situations may make disengagement difficult. Following the Easterbrook (1959) hypothesis, the high arousal associated with high stress may narrow the range of cue utilization and render the performer insensitive to stop signals. Indeed, case studies of real-world accidents and incidents reveal many examples of such undesirable cognitive tunneling (e.g., Three Mile Island—Rubinstein and Mason, 1979).

TASK PRIORITY MANAGEMENT

The research of Logan and others on task switching described above has laid the foundation for an understanding of the time course and relative ease of activity switching, but it has intentionally focused on research paradigms in which the destination activity of the switch was well defined and the overall time frame of the switching process was short, within a second or so. We now discuss data in which both the identity and the time of the particular tasks to be performed are less constrained, and the time frame of performance is on the order of minutes or longer.

Our interest here is in the nature of human operator task management strategies: the appropriateness of human behavior in selecting what task to do when (Adams et al., 1991). Turning to the operational community, one can find numerous examples of aircraft accidents (in National Transportation Safety Board (NTSB) reports) and incidents (in NASA Aviation Safety Reporting System (ASRS) data) that have resulted from failures of effective task management. Here, for example, one might consider a pilot so preoccupied with geographic orientation that the key task of flight control is neglected and the aircraft is stalled. In this case the optimal task management strategy dictated by the adage "aviate-navigate-communicate" is violated. The account of the Eastern Airlines L1011 crash into the Everglades in 1972, when the flight crew, preoccupied with a landing gear problem, failed to monitor their altitude, is another example (Wiener, 1977). Indeed, significant altitude deviations resulting from task neglect reflect a major concern in the aviation industry because of their growing frequency of occurrence (Granda et al., 1991).

Two general features would seem to be heavily responsible for the success or failure of individuals to appropriately manage tasks in situations such as those described above. First, it is apparent that good *situation awareness* is a key component. Situation awareness describes an understanding not only of geographic orientation, as described in Chapter 7, but also of the state of systems under the operator's control (a breakdown here was partially responsible for the Three Mile Island incident discussed in Chapter 8) and the current responsibilities assumed by equipment automation and by other members of the team. Good situation awareness provides a context or background within which different tasks can be more appropriately selected or dropped. The concept of situation awareness remains somewhat ill-defined, but recent theoretical treatments by Sarter and Woods (1991) and by Adams et al. (1991) have made major advancements in linking the concept both to existing empirical data and to psychological concepts from cognitive psychology.

A second feature critical to effective task management is the concept of task priority, and the implicit or explicit assumption that the optimal task manager will possess a mental priority scale that can provide the basis for appropriately shedding tasks when workload becomes excessive and resuming (or assuming) tasks when workload is relieved. In spite of the importance of this concept, there appears to be few data to indicate the effectiveness of subjective priority in driving task management in operational environments. What evidence is available comes from a set of partially, but not entirely, relevant research domains.

First, we may refer to the National Transportation Safety Board and the Aircraft Safety Reporting System reports on maladaptive task management strategies (Williams et al., 1992). These reports are important because they illustrate the existence of a problem that has major implications for air safety (e.g., the Everglades crash referred to above). Yet, like all accident and incident reports, these accounts provide a tenuous base from which to draw firm conclusions regarding the precise causes of the failure to prioritize tasks. Was it a lack of training? A high level of stress? Poor cockpit design? Poor procedures? Accidents and incidents are usually ambiguous as to their cause.

A second relevant domain is the laboratory research that has been carried out regarding the manipulation of task priorities in dual task performance, following the pioneering work of Gopher and his colleagues (Gopher and Navon, 1980; North and Gopher, 1976; Wickens and Gopher, 1977; see also Goettl, 1991; Sperling and Dosher, 1986; Tsang and Wickens, 1988; Vidulich, 1988). This work generally reveals that, under controlled laboratory circumstances, subjects can fairly accurately modulate the performance level of the tasks in proportion to the implicit or explicit priority given to the task. Furthermore, there appears to be recent evidence that the skill of priority-based performance modulation learned in the laboratory is one that transfers to the operational environment of the aircraft cockpit (Gopher, 1991). Yet even in this domain there are hints of occasional failures. For example, Wickens and Liu (1988) have pointed to a phenomenon of "preemption" in which a lower-priority discrete auditory task may interrupt or preempt the performance of a higher-priority visual one, a preemption that will not take place if the discrete task is visual. Cumming and Croft (1973) note that people may sometimes fail to recognize or anticipate a change in task demands. Clearly, altitude busts in aviation represent failures to appropriately allocate resources to this monitoring task; in the hospital trauma center, one can imagine circumstances in which monitoring of key aspects of a patient's status may be neglected because of high attention demands associated with other aspects of the trauma.

A third domain of data derives from studies that have been carried out from an engineering perspective, based heavily on the formal treatment provided by queuing theory (see Kleinmann, 1991; Moray, 1986; Moray et al., 1991 for good reviews). While much of this work describes the sampling of visual channels (i.e., optimality in a perceptual sense), studies by Tulga and Sheridan (1980), Pattipati et al. (1983), and Moray et al. (1991) considered optimality of task selection using a paradigm in which tasks were represented as boxes moving across a computer screen timeline. Tulga and Sheridan's conclusions regarding the shortcomings in human anticipation when tasks become too numerous are important, as is Moray et al.'s (1991) recent work examining performance when optimal schedules become too complex. However, it is not immediately clear how generalizable data are from paradigms in which tasks are visibly viewable and symbolically represented as boxes in a displayed queue, to those circumstances in which tasks may have various forms of visible or nonvisible evidence for their existence. That is, a waiting task may be an action to be performed that is not triggered by a perceptual event, thus introducing prospective memory (Meacham and Leiman, 1972) as an added (confounding) factor.

Finally, there are a few studies that have examined task management strategies in complex environments with real tasks (Adams et al., 1991). Puffer (1989) studied how students managed the completion of assigned tasks having varying attributes (boredom, difficulty) over the course of a semester. She found that earlier completion of tasks resulted in superior performance, and that more difficult tasks were completed later. However, the time scale of one course semester is far longer than the scale of minutes or a few hours involved in most operational tank engagements. Chou and Funk (1990) and Ruffle-Smith (1979) have examined task scheduling and shedding in high-workload aviation simulation environments, but their research did not extract general principles regarding the form taken by this scheduling.

Two investigations by Wickens and his colleagues examined the degree to which aviators optimally employed task priority as a means of scheduling tasks. That is, were higher-priority tasks consistently performed over those of lower priority when a conflict of demands was present? In both studies, prioritization was examined in simulations in which sudden increases in workload were imposed by unexpected time pressure.

To investigate these issues, Segal and Wickens (1990) required licensed pilots to fly a series of simulated low-level flight segments on a computer-based helicopter simulator. Subjects needed to perform tasks of three well-identified levels of priority: the primary task of flying an accurate altitude and navigating accurately, a secondary task of solving spatial location problems, and a tertiary low-priority task involving discrete keyboard entry to be performed when time allowed.

Collectively, the results of the experiment indicated that pilots performed reasonably optimally in their task management strategies. The primary tasks of both vertical and lateral flight path control were protected from the degrading effects of higher-workload demands. The secondary side task was degraded in its accuracy (but not postponed) during higher-workload periods, while the tertiary housekeeping task was simply not performed (or performed less often) when workload was high. Still, two noteworthy departures from optimal performance were identified. First, when subjects were given the opportunity to reschedule performance of lower-priority tasks to avoid high-workload periods, they did not avail themselves of the opportunity to do so. Instead, they allowed performance on those tasks to suffer during high-workload periods. Secondly, there was some tendency to procrastinate in the performance of the discrete secondary and tertiary tasks; pilots delayed the performance of these tasks rather than performing them early in each flight.

One noteworthy aspect of the experiment was observed in the benefits of preview. Those pilots who were given reliable information regarding the existence of upcoming workload transitions (increases or decreases) performed better on many aspects of the task ensemble than did pilots without such preview, a finding with relevance to the importance of reliable forecast information.

The value of previewed intelligence information in strategic task management should not, however, always be accepted uncritically, particularly if the preview is unreliable. Some studies have shown that preview in task management and scheduling can be detrimental if it is not entirely reliable; or if it is presented in such a way that the visual attention required to integrate and interpret the preview information competes with processing information regarding present system status (Sanderson, 1990; Wickens et al., 1991).

Raby et al. (1989) also performed an aviation-related study of strategic task management in which pilots flew an instrument flight simulation through airport landings at low, medium, and high levels of workload. As in the Segal and Wickens study, continuous flight performance measures were recorded, as well as discrete tasks of various levels of priority, as assessed by an independent group of observers. As in the helicopter simulation study, here too pilots adhered reasonably well to the imposed priority scheme. However, their adherence was imperfect, as they did allow flight performance to suffer as workload increased but did not allow their performance on high-priority discrete tasks to deteriorate. In fact, the amount of time devoted to the latter tasks actually increased as time pressure (and workload) increased. Within the set of discrete tasks, pilots showed reasonable optimality, devoting progressively less time to lower-priority tasks at higher levels of workload. Also, in agreement with the results of the Segal and Wickens (1990) study, it was observed that subjects failed to reschedule those tasks of lower priority. They simply abandoned their performance or did them less accurately.

Although the levels of stress in these two simulations imposed by time pressure and high workload were far less than that imposed in battlefield conditions, the simulations do suggest that appropriate task priorities can be maintained under sudden increases in workload. But they suggest a failure to appropriately reschedule when lower-priority tasks are performed around intervals of lower workload. Such a finding has implications both for the possible utility of task management training and the implementation of computer models of human task scheduling (Shanker, 1991), arguing that these scheduling routines need not be too complex. Equally important are the implications of the preview benefits observed by Segal and Wickens and reinforcing the points made in Chapter 3. The preview can be valuable, if it is reliable and well formatted. Yet it remains evident that full confidence in generalizing these results to operational environments awaits further validation research in complex scenarios.

REFERENCES

Adams, M.J., Y.F. Tanney, and R.W. Pew
  1991   *Strategic Workload and the Cognitive Management of Advanced Multi-Task Systems*. Report No. CSERIAC-91-6. Wright-Patterson Air Force Base, Ohio: Crew Systems Ergonomics Analysis Center.

Biederman, I.
  1973   Mental set and mental arithmetic. *Memory and Cognition* 1:383-386.

Chou, C.D., and K. Funk
  1990   Management of multiple tasks: Cockpit task management errors. Pp. 470-474 in *Proceedings of the 1990 IEEE International Conference on Systems, Man, and Cybernetics*. Los Angeles, California: IEEE.

Cumming, R.W., and P.G. Croft
  1973   Human information processing under varying task demand. *Ergonomics* 16(5):581-586.

de Jong, R., M.G.H. Coles, G.D. Logan, and G. Gratton
  1990   Searching for the point of no return: The control of response processes in speeded choice reaction time performance. *Journal of Experimental Psychology: Human Perception and Performance* 16(1):164-182.

Easterbrook, J.A.
  1959   The effect of emotion on cue utilization and the organization of behavior. *Psychological Review* 66:183-207.

Goettl, B.P.
  1991   Tracking strategies and cognitive demands. *Human Factors* 33(2):169-183.

Gopher, D.
  1982   A selective attention test as a predictor of success in flight training. *Human Factors* 24(2):173-183.
  1991   The skill of attention control: Acquisition and execution of attention strategies. In D. Meyer and S. Kornblum, eds., *Attention and Performance, Volume XIV*. Hillsdale, New Jersey: Erlbaum Associates.

Gopher, D., and D. Navon
  1980   How is performance limited: Testing the notion of central capacity. *Acta Psychologica* 46:161-180.

Granda, T.M., D.H. McClure, and J.W. Fogerty
    1991   The development of an altitude awareness program. Pp. 47-52 in *Proceedings of the Human Factors Society 35th Annual Meeting.* Santa Monica, California: Human Factors Society.
Jersild, A.T.
    1927   Mental set and shift. *Archives of Psychology* 89.
Kleinmann, D.
    1991   Models of attention control. In D. Damos, ed., *Multiple Task Performance.* London: Taylor and Francis.
Logan, G.D.
    1981   Attention, automaticity, and the ability to stop a speeded choice response. In J. Long and A.D. Baddeley, eds., *Attention and Performance, Volume IX.* Hillsdale, New Jersey: Erlbaum.
    1982   On the ability to inhibit complex movements: A stop-signal study of typewriting. *Journal of Experimental Psychology: Human Perception and Performance* 8:778-792.
    1983   On the ability to inhibit simple thoughts and actions: I. Stop-signal studies of decision and memory. *Journal of Experimental Psychology: Learning, Memory and Cognition* 9:585-606.
    1985a   Executive control of thought and action. *Acta Psychologica* 60:193-210.
    1985b   On the ability to inhibit simple thoughts and actions: II. Stop-signals studies of repetition priming. *Journal of Experimental Psychology: Learning, Memory and Cognition* 11:675-691.
Logan, G.D., and J. Burkell
    1986   Dependence and independence in responding to double stimulation: A comparison of stop, change, and dual-task paradigms. *Journal of Experimental Psychology: Human Perception and Performance* 12:549-563.
Logan, G.D., and W.B. Cowan
    1984   On the ability to inhibit thought and action: A theory of an act of control. *Psychological Review* 91:295-327.
Logan, G.D., W.B. Cowan, and K.A. Davis
    1984   On the ability to inhibit responses in simple and choice reaction time tasks: A model and a method. *Journal of Experimental Psychology: Human Perception and Performance* 10:276-291.
Logan, G.D., B.H. Kantowitz, and G.L. Riegler
    1987   On the Ability to Inhibit Selectively: A Model of Response Interdiction. Unpublished manuscript, University of Illinois.
Logan, G.D., and N.J. Zbrodoff
    1982   Constraints on strategy construction in a speeded discrimination task. *Journal of Experimental Psychology: Human Perception and Performance* 8:502-520.
Logan, G.D., N.J. Zbrodoff, and A.R. Fostey
    1983   Costs and benefits of strategy construction in a speeded discrimination task. *Memory and Cognition* 11:485-493.
Logan, G.D., N.J. Zbrodoff, and J. Williamson
    1984   Strategies in the color-word Stroop task. *Bulletin of the Psychonomic Society* 22:135-138.
Meacham, J.A., and B. Leiman
    1972   Remembering to perform future actions. In U. Neisser, ed., *Memory Observed.* San Francisco, California: W.D. Freeman, Inc.
Moray, N.
    1986   Monitoring behavior and supervisory control. Pp. 40.1-40.51 in K. Boff, L. Kaufman,

and J. Thomas, eds., *Handbook of Perception and Human Performance*. New York: John Wiley.

Moray, N., M.I. Dessouky, B.A. Kijowski, R. Adapathya
1991 Strategic behavior, workload, and performance in task scheduling. *Human Factors* 33:607-629.

North, R.A., and D. Gopher
1976 Measures of attention as predictors of flight performance. *Human Factors* 18:1-13.

Osman, A., S. Kornblum, and D.E. Meyer
1990 Does motor programming necessitate response execution? *Journal of Experimental Psychology: Human Perception and Performance* 16(1):183-198.

Pattipati, K.R., D.L. Kleinman, and A.R. Ephrath
1983 A dynamic decision model of human task selection performance. *IEEE Transactions on Systems, Man, and Cybernetics* SMC-13(2):145-166.

Puffer, S.M.
1989 Task-completion schedules: Determinants and consequences for performance. *Human Relations* 42:937-955.

Rabbitt, P.
1989 Sequential reactions. In D. Holding, ed., *Human Skills, Second Edition*. New York: John Wiley and Sons.

Raby, M., C.D. Wickens, and R. Marsh
1989 *Investigation of Factors Comprising a Model of Pilot Decision Making: Part 1. Cognitive Biases in Workload Management Strategy*. Report No. ARL-90-7/SCEEE-90-1. Savoy, Illinois: University of Illinois, Aviation Research Laboratory.

Ruffle-Smith, H.P.
1979 *A Simulator Study of the Interaction of Pilot Workload Errors, Vigilance, and Decisions*. Report No. NASA-TM-78472. Moffett Field, California: NASA Ames Research Center.

Rubinstein, T., and A.F. Mason
1979 The accident that shouldn't have happened: An analysis of Three Mile Island. *IEEE Spectrum* 16:33-57.

Sanderson, P.
1990 Knowledge acquisition and fault diagnosis: Experiments with PLAULT. *IEEE Transactions on Systems, Man, and Cybernetics* SMC-20(1):225-242.

Sarter, N., and D.D. Woods
1991 Situation awareness: A critical, but ill-defined phenomenon. *International Journal of Aviation Psychology* 1:45-57.

Schachar, R.J., and G.D. Logan
1990 Impulsivity and inhibitory control in normal development and childhood psychopathology. *Developmental Psychology* 26(5):710-720.

Segal, L.D., and C.D. Wickens
1990 TASKILLAN II: Pilot strategies for workload management. *Proceedings of the Human Factors Society 34th Annual Meeting*. Santa Monica, California: Human Factors Society.

Shanker, R.C.
1991 Z-Scheduler: Integrating theories of scheduling behavior into a computational model. Pp. 1367-1371 in *Proceedings of the IEEE International Conference on Systems, Man, and Cybernetics*. Los Angeles, California: Institute of Electronics and Electrical Engineers.

Spector, A., and I. Biederman
1976 Mental set and shift revisited. *American Journal of Psychology* 89:669-679.

Sperling, G., and B.A. Dosher
  1986   Strategy and optimization in human information processing. Pp. 2.1-2.65 in K.
            Boff, L. Kaufman, and J. Thomas, eds., *Handbook of Perception and Human
            Performance, Volume I*. New York: John Wiley.
Stroop, J.R.
  1935   *Journal of Experimental Psychology* 18:643.
Tannock, R., R.J. Schachar, R.P. Carr, D. Chajczyk, and G.D. Logan
  1989   Effects of methylphenidate on inhibitory control in hyperactive children. *Journal
            of Abnormal Child Psychology* 17:473-491.
Tsang, P.S., and C.D. Wickens
  1988   The structural constraints and strategic control of resource allocation. *Human
            Performance* 1:45-72.
Tulga, M.K., and T.B. Sheridan
  1980   Dynamic decisions and workload in multitask supervisory control. *IEEE Transac-
            tions on Systems, Man, and Cybernetics.* SMC-10:217-232.
Vallacher, R.R., and D.M. Wegner
  1987   What do people think they're doing? Action identification and human behavior.
            Psychological Review 94(1):3-15.
Vidulich, M.A.
  1988   Speech responses and dual-task performance: Better timesharing or asymmetric
            transfer. *Human Factors* 30:517-529.
Wickens, C.D., and D. Gopher
  1977   Control theory measures of tracking as indices of attention allocation strategies.
            Human Factors 19:249-366.
Wickens, C.D., and Y. Liu
  1988   Codes and modalities in multiple resources: A success and a qualification. *Hu-
            man Factors* 30:599-616.
Wickens, C.D., D. Pizarro, and B. Bell
  1991   Overconfidence, preview and probability in strategic planning. *Proceedings of the
            Human Factors Society 35th Annual Meeting.* Santa Monica, California: Human
            Factors Society.
Wickens, C.D., P. Tsang, and B. Pierce
  1985   The dynamics of resource allocation. In W.B. Rouse, ed., *Advances in Man-
            Machine Systems Research, Volume 2.* Greenwich, Connecticut: JAI Press.
Wiener, E.L.
  1977   Controlled flight into terrain accidents: System-induced errors. *Human Factors*
            19:171.
Williams, H., M.P. Tham, and C.D. Wickens
  1992   *Resource Management in Aviation Incidents: A Review of the ASRS Data Base.*
            Report No. ARL-91-5/NASA-91-3. Savoy, Illinois: University of Illinois, Avia-
            tion Research Laboratory.
Zbrodoff, N.J., and G.D. Logan
  1986   On the autonomy of mental processes: A case study of arithmetic. *Journal of
            Experimental Psychology: General* 115:118-130.

10

Team Leadership and Crew Coordination

Effective leadership and communications among crew members are necessary to ensure optimal team performance during a workload transition. It is necessary for the tank commander to direct the actions of the crew members to form an effective team and to coordinate the actions of his tank with those of other tanks and combat units. The tank environment is a classic example of a small work group embedded in a multigroup setting—a situation demanding effective leadership and crew coordination.

The critical issue is that crew performance must be considered as a team endeavor. While this statement seems to be belaboring the obvious, training in many, if not most, team activities focuses on individual tasks, and evaluation concentrates on individual performance and error. For example, operating teams are composed of surgeons, anesthesiologists, and supporting nurses for each. Medical training, however, concentrates on the specialty, with the implicit assumption that the subgroups will coordinate their activities effectively when they come together to deal with a patient. A growing body of evidence suggests that, when teams face sudden transitions from routine procedures to a medical emergency, coordination can break down and conflicts can occur (Howard et al., in press). Similarly, although flying a modern jet transport, patrol aircraft, or bomber is patently a team endeavor, the formal evaluation and certification of pilots have historically concentrated on individual proficiency. What is characteristically lacking is attention to *processes* by which teams as a unit accomplish their tasks.

Within this context, the key to success in effecting a transition from a standby or vigilance status to an action (combat) posture is in keeping each crew member alert, fully apprised of the operational situation, and prepared for coordinated action. Maintaining a cohesive, efficient team is made more difficult in the tank environment by the fact that communications are degraded by the physical layout and habitability of the vehicle. As noted earlier, face-to-face interaction is generally precluded, with intracrew communications taking place over interphones and interunit communications by radio. Several channels of communications operate simultaneously, creating a need to monitor and screen communications for relevant information. Chemical or nuclear alerts require MOPP gear, which further increases difficulties in communications. Crews transitioning to combat may have spent several days in cramped, poorly ventilated, readiness conditions in or near their tank. It is possible that when the sudden need arises for effective, coordinated communications and action, crew members will be in less than peak physical and psychological readiness.

Clearly, the success or failure of tank crews (and teams in general) in workload transition depends to a large extent on the flow of communication among the team members, how this flow is affected by stress, and how these effects, in turn, are moderated by personality qualities of the team leader and by the organizational structure.

Somewhat relevant here is an extensive literature on group decision making and problem solving (see Davis, 1992, or Hastie, 1986, for a good synthesis). The vast majority of this research has been involved with fairly abstract tasks. Nevertheless, certain conclusions from this work are worth summarizing:

(1) Generally, performance of a group solving a problem or reaching a decision falls somewhere between the average of the individual competencies of group members and the performance of the most competent members. Confidence in decision quality is generally higher than individual competence.

(2) Where performance ranges between these limits depends on a number of other factors: performance appears to be a function of (a) how clearly demonstrable is the correct solution, (b) the length of time the organization remains constituted (improves), (c) the nature of factions that form within the group, (d) the size of the group (improves up to five members), and (e) the persuasiveness and status of more competent (improves) or less competent (degrades) members.

(3) There is little evidence that different structural techniques, such as Delphi or brainstorming, systematically improve decision performance (Hastie, 1986).

(4) There is some evidence that face-to-face settings are beneficial. It also appears that computer-mediated communications allow less dominant

group members to provide more input. Group decisions reached in this computer-mediated manner tend to be more extreme but not necessarily of higher quality (Kiesler and Sproull, 1992).

As noted above, most of the studies have employed fairly abstract tasks (some of the work on jury verdicts is an exception), using naive subjects, in nonstressed conditions, and groups that were constituted specifically for the purposes of the experiment. These characteristics somewhat limit the generalizability of these conclusions to team performance in crisis, the focus of this report. To address the latter domain, we turn instead to one environment—the aircraft cockpit—in which a substantial amount of relevant research has been conducted. Hence, the cockpit environment is the primary focus of this chapter.

AVIATION RESEARCH FINDINGS ON LEADERSHIP AND CREW COORDINATION

On preliminary examination, many issues seem common to tank crews and flight crews. One, of course, is long periods of passive vigilance, which may be supplanted by a high-workload period with high needs for effective, coordinated behavior. A second is a high volume of (often degraded) multichannel communications and the need to comprehend and act on critical information embedded in extraneous transmissions. Also common to many flight as well as tank operations are high levels of fatigue that may impair individual and group function. Finally, the psychological sense of danger and the possibility of fatality following an inflight emergency is certainly common with the tank crew facing battle.

The physical environment of the tank is also clearly less benign and provides less opportunity for face-to-face interaction than does the aircraft. It is also possible that the decision-making and information processing tasks incumbent in tank warfare are less dependent on open communications among crew members, making the issues cited above less serious in this environment. It is possible that the military chain of command and organizational structure may override individual and group idiosyncrasies and result in effective information transfer, even under highly stressful situations (or, conversely, may impede effective interaction).

Despite these caveats, examination of crew performance issues in other military environments, such as shipboard combat information centers, and demanding civilian settings, such as nuclear power plant control rooms and hospital emergency rooms, leads to the tentative conclusion that team effectiveness depends heavily on effective resource management; that is, personnel within the team share information effectively and are appropriately coordinated in their monitoring and task performance responsibilities. In fact, a root cause of the majority of accidents involving aircraft with multiperson crews has proved to be breakdowns in leadership and coordination among crew members resulting in flawed decision making and improper actions (e.g., Cooper et al., 1979).

Analytically we address the role of coordination or resource management in transition teams in this chapter by first describing crew resource management training. We then consider the influences on effective voice communications. Finally, we focus on the broader implications of research on coordinated activities within the team, addressing factors related to organizational climate, leadership, and personality (e.g., Foushee, 1984; Foushee and Helmreich, 1988; Helmreich et al., in press; Helmreich and Foushee, in press). Many of the valid conclusions in these domains come directly from research in aviation; this domain therefore represents the focus of much of this chapter.

CREW RESOURCE MANAGEMENT TRAINING

The aviation community has responded to evidence that failures in *team* coordination have been implicated in a majority of commercial jet transport accidents by initiating formal training in communications and group coordination, known generically as crew resource management (CRM) training. Early courses grew out of traditional management development training, but recent programs have evolved to deal with very specific behaviors and encompass full mission simulation (Line Oriented Flight Training or LOFT) designed to require high complex decision making and group coordination under conditions with a high level of time pressure (Butler, in press; Helmreich and Foushee, in press). This integrated approach to training is augmented by videotaping the simulator session and an intensive debriefing that allows crews to observe their own behavior (Butler, in press).

Validation research in commercial aviation has shown highly significant changes in crew member attitudes and, more critically, positive changes in behavior in operational settings following training (Helmreich and Wilhelm, 1991). Critical elements that determine the success of CRM training include not only courses that address concrete behaviors rather than abstract, psychological constructs, but also strong organizational support for concepts taught and recurrent training accompanied by continuing feedback and reinforcement for the practice of effective teamwork (Chidester, in press; Helmreich and Foushee, in press).

The success of CRM training in aviation has resulted in the adaptation of the approach to other settings in which effective teamwork is essential for mission success. These include operating room teams using simulated patients and videotaped interactions (Howard et al., in press), aircraft maintenance groups (Taggart, 1990), and nuclear power plant control room teams.

The Federal Aviation Administration is also developing plans to adapt CRM training for air traffic controllers.

Given the conceptual similarities, it would appear that the outcomes of tailoring these training approaches to the tank environment would have a high probability of success, not only in improving transitions from monitoring to action, but also in improving overall team effectiveness. This approach would seem to fit naturally into the types of simulations accomplished using SIMNET.

VOICE COMMUNICATIONS

Breakdowns in communications between and within aircrews have been documented as a major source of human error and potential disaster (Hawkins, 1987; Nagel, 1988). The most salient example is the decision made by a KLM 747 pilot at the Tenerife Airport in the Canary Islands to proceed with a takeoff, despite the presence of a second jumbo jet still on the runway (Hawkins, 1987). The resulting collision led to over 500 fatalities. Three features of this accident are worthy of analysis because of their similarity to characteristics of the tank crew environments: (1) the auditory quality of the message was poor—a degradation that may be caused by high ambient noise or by electronic "clipping" of radio messages; (2) the communications were not face-to-face, thereby eliminating many of the nonverbal cues that have been documented to improve communications, particularly with degraded speech (Chapanis et al., 1972; Kryter, 1972); and (3) the environment was stressful (although not involving the stress of combat). The flight crew was on the final leg of a long and fatiguing international flight, weather conditions (and visibility) were rapidly deteriorating, and there was obvious time stress to proceed with the decision action (takeoff) as soon as possible.

These potentially degrading characteristics of communications may be balanced by a list of other factors that can foster good communications. Restricting vocabulary and standardization reduces the possibility of confusing messages, and introducing redundancy, by repeating key messages or key words or echoing auditory with visual displays, ensures that ambiguous or unexpected messages are not interpreted incorrectly. Many short messages can be better understood by providing a redundant verbal context, like "your fuel is low," rather than "fuel low." The likelihood of misinterpretation (and the resulting need for redundancy) is particularly high whenever a message involves conveying information that is unexpected, or negating a statement (e.g., do not proceed) as was the case with the KLM flight. In general, affirmative communications are better understood and more reliably received than negative messages (Wickens, 1992). Using acknowledgments and read-backs can trap errors before they are executed (Helmreich and Foushee, 1988).

Within many multicrew teams, the issue of confusion of the message source is also a very real danger. A large research base in experimental psychology has documented the likelihood of confusion of the source of verbal and nonverbal auditory messages that may be heard simultaneously or in close temporal proximity (Hirst, 1986; Treisman, 1984; see Wickens, 1984, for a summary). Within the tank, this confusion could result between messages intended for any of the four crew members. For the tank commander, this confusion might well be enhanced by the need to monitor both intratank and intertank (i.e., company and battalian level) communications. Research data indicate that confusions of this sort will be lessened (but not necessarily eliminated) if different channels can be made physically distinct—by different voice characteristics, modulation, or apparent spatial location (Treisman, 1964) or by some other clearly discriminable (perhaps visual) cue identifying whom is speaking what.

Flight Deck Communications

Communication patterns among crew members have proven to be the Rosetta stone for understanding the nature of effective and ineffective flight crew performance. Because the flight deck is a constrained environment with well-defined crew roles and well-defined tasks, variations in the quality, quantity, and nature of communications are relatively easy to isolate and quantify. Cockpit voice recorders provide a tangible record of communications in accidents in which crew performance is implicated, and high-fidelity simulators allow experimental manipulation of critical factors and tests of hypotheses regarding determinants of performance.

Foushee and Manos (1981) pioneered a methodology of coding the interpersonal interactions of flight crews from audio tapes of cockpit communications. Their seminal work grew out of an experimental simulation conducted in a Boeing 747 simulator (Ruffle-Smith, 1979). This study consisted of a simulated mission flown by volunteer line crews from an airline's B747 fleet. During the two-segment flight there were several equipment malfunctions requiring the diversion of a scheduled trans-Atlantic crossing under deteriorating weather conditions. Foushee and Manos found that crews with a higher frequency of operational communications and information exchanges committed fewer operational errors and had a more even distribution of workload during critical phases of flight.

Subsequent work has resulted in the development of coding schemata that allow precise delineation of the group processes involved in normal and emergency situations. These have been applied both to experimental simulations and to the cockpit voice recorder tapes and transcripts from aircraft accidents and incidents (Kanki and Foushee, 1989; Kanki et al., 1989). These schemata allow specification of the content of information exchange, sequences of communications among crew members, and shifts in communication patterns during periods of high stress and/or workload. Work in progress by Predmore (1991) further categorizes communications in terms of action decision sequences (ADS), interactions dealing with particular tasks or decisions that face crews in normal and abnormal circumstances. Using data from accidents and from an experimental simulation flown by three-person crews in a NASA B727 simulator, he is exploring the patterns that emerge when crews have to deal with multiple ADSs requiring immediate action. The data from all of these investigations indicate that there is great variability in communications among crews faced with the same stressful flight scenario and that effective crews exchange information and utilize available resources better.

Systematic Observational Studies of Crew Performance

A methodology has also been developed for the collection of reliable data on flight crew performance in both normal line operations and full mission training in flight simulators (LOFT: Line Oriented Flight Training; Butler, in press). In this methodology, expert raters observe crews and make real-time assessments of crew behavior and performance. Data are collected on a rating form, the NASA/UT Line/LOS (Line Operational Simulation) Checklist (Helmreich et al., 1990a, 1990b, 1991) that elicits Likert-scaled ratings of elements of communications practices that have been identified as critical determinants of team performance. Also recorded are comments on special circumstances and unusual reactions. In addition to global ratings of technical proficiency and crew effectiveness, nine human factors components are assessed: (1) conduct and quality of pre-event briefings; (2) effectiveness and openness of communications and processes of decision making; (3) inquiry/assertion/advocacy—the willingness of crew members to question proposed actions and decisions and to propose alternatives; (4) crew self-critique of decisions and actions; (5) leadership/followership; (6) interpersonal relations and group climate; (7) preparation/planning/vigilance; (8) workload distribution and avoidance of distractions; and (9) conflict resolution (when occurring).

Training in the use of the form centers on the concept of specifically defined behaviors (called behavioral markers) that represent effective enactment of the components of each of the nine elements. Data from more than 10,000 actual or simulated flight segments have been collected in several airlines and military units. Of particular concern is isolating the factors that trigger superior and poor overall performance. Comparable data from two airlines show similarities, but also organizational differences, in the determinants of performance. In one organization, the most frequent causes of poor ratings were (1) poor critique, (2) poor inquiry/assertion/advocacy,

(3) ineffective conflict resolution, and (4) poor management of distractions. In a second airline, poor performance was associated with (1) poor inquiry/ assertion/advocacy; (2) poor management of distractions; (3) inadequate briefings; and (4) ineffective conflict resolution. In the first airline, superior performance ratings were triggered by excellence in (1) preparation/ planning/vigilance; (2) establishing a positive group climate; (3) briefings; and (4) conflict resolution. In the second airline, the most frequent causes were (1) group climate; (2) briefings; (3) conflict resolution; and (4) leadership/followership.

Flight operations, particularly long flights involving extended periods of cruise at high altitude, are characterized by periods of low activity and system monitoring followed by transition to high workloads during terminal approach and landing. Inflight mechanical emergencies and changing weather conditions also lead to abrupt workload transitions. The factors cited above, as they determine overall crew performance, also determine readiness for workload transitions and the effectiveness of such transitions.

Leader Behavior

A common element in the observational data on crew performance and in analyses of the causes of accidents is the actions of the designated leader. The captain of an aircraft bears ultimate responsibility for the management of the flight deck, the provision of briefings, planning, management of workload, resolution of conflicts, and the climate of the group. Recognizing that successful performance is a group endeavor requiring the coordinated activities of all members, the leader remains the most important single component. Two patterns of leader behavior have been isolated as causal elements in many accidents and sources of poor performance in experimental simulations (see, e.g., Chidester and Foushee, 1988). One pattern is characterized by autocratic behaviors that inhibit communication from subordinates and result in a hostile group climate, leading subordinates to withhold critical information, even when it is needed to avoid catastrophe. Another reflects a leadership vacuum and failure to coordinate and guide the actions of group members. An important study by Ginnett (1987) examined leader behaviors surrounding initial crew briefings as they relate to crew performance. Ginnett observed airline crews from initial briefings through a three-day scheduled trip. The crews he followed were classified into two groups by independent expert observers. One group had captains who were rated as outstanding in terms of observed leadership and crew coordination. The second had captains who were rated as deficient on these dimensions. Ginnett found that he could predict the overall performance of the crews from behaviors manifested during the initial briefing. Effective captains consistently established a positive group climate and bases for open communications during the briefing. They also expanded the definition of the crew to include cabin personnel and stressed role definitions. Leaders of ineffective crews showed a variety of behaviors but failed to establish the crew as an integrated team.

Leader Personality

Attempts to isolate personality traits associated with effective leadership have resulted in a large literature with many conflicting findings (Hollander, 1985). Part of the difficulty in isolating global factors stems from the fact that requirements for leadership are not common to all groups and are contingent on the group's structure and the nature of task to be accomplished (Fiedler, 1964).

Efforts to use personality traits to select pilots (who ultimately become leaders of their flight crews) have similarly had mixed outcomes (e.g., Dolgin and Gibb, 1988). Problems with the predictive validity of personality measures in aviation may stem from the nature of the performance criterion employed. The overwhelming majority of the research on pilot selection utilized either performance in initial training or success or failure in completing training as the criterion measure. Research by Helmreich et al. (1986b) found personality to be a poor predictor of job performance immediately after completion of training but to have significant relationships with objective performance measures after six and eight months on the job. This phenomenon has been labeled "the honeymoon effect," and it is interpreted as reflecting the fact that initial motivation to obtain a desired position may initially overcome the influence of personality on performance. With the passage of time and familiarity with the work role, however, the underlying relationships between personality and performance emerge. This implies that, if the criterion is the operational performance of experienced pilots, personality may be a valid predictor of leader and crew effectiveness. Recent research supports this view. A set of traits reflecting positive and negative manifestation of two broad, orthogonal dimensions has been used in research with flight crews (Spence and Helmreich, 1978; Helmreich and Spence, 1978). The first dimension consists of traits associated with achievement motivation and instrumental goals (with the negative component reflecting an autocratic, dictatorial orientation). The second consists of traits defining expressivity and interpersonal sensitivity (with the negative components reflecting either subservience and passivity or verbal aggression).

To reduce the personality battery to a smaller set of categorical factors and to reflect the distribution of component variables in the research population, cluster analytic techniques were employed to isolate frequently occurring constellations of traits (Chidester et al., 1991). In a validation of these personality constellations and their relationships with flight crew performance, Chidester and Foushee (1988) conducted a two-day experimental simulation in a Boeing 727 simulator using line airmen assigned to this aircraft. Three experimental groups were formed based on the personality cluster assignment of the captain. The first consisted of crews led by a captain with high levels of positive, instrumental traits and high levels of positive, expressive traits (a group labeled as having the "right stuff"). The second group had captains from a cluster characterized by high scores on negative instrumental traits (e.g., domineering, autocratic) and low levels of positive expressivity (labeled as having the "wrong stuff"). The third group of captains were low on both positive instrumental and positive expressive dimensions (labeled by default as having "no stuff").

Each crew flew a two-day simulation involving five flight segments with two having high workloads, adverse weather, and mechanical problems. Significant differences in performance (based on expert ratings and objective measures of errors) were found as a function of the leader's personality. Crews led by "right stuff" captains performed best across all flight segments; those led by "no stuff" leaders performed worst under all conditions. Crews led by "wrong stuff" captains performed badly on initial segments but showed much improvement in performance by the second-day segment involving high workload and mechanical abnormalities. A theoretical explanation for the latter finding is that crew members became able, over time, to cope with the domineering leader who had strong achievement motivation although he was lacking in interpersonal skills. No interpersonal strategies appear to have allowed crews to overcome the problems caused by captains lacking in both achievement motivation and interpersonal skills.

These personality dimensions have also been shown to relate significantly to the acceptance of training in crew coordination concepts as measured by changes in attitudes regarding appropriate leadership and interpersonal communications (Chidester et al., 1991; Helmreich and Wilhelm, 1989). Those high on both instrumental and expressive dimensions ("right stuff") show the strongest positive, attitude change. Those in the other two clusters showed much less change, and there was evidence that training actually had a regression effect for those low on both dimensions ("no stuff"). A theoretical explanation for the latter finding is that those lacking in attributes whose importance is stressed in leadership and crew coordination training are threatened and respond defensively by changing their attitudes away from the direction advocated.

It is obvious that the personalities of junior crew members also play a role in determining the overall effectiveness of work groups. The multiplicity of combinations possible even in very small groups has had limited empirical investigations and the research base remains sparse.

Automation, Leadership, and Crew Coordination

The introduction of more automated flight management systems has created major changes in flight operations. This has resulted in a reduction in crew complement from three to two, even in widebody aircraft involved in long transoceanic flight. Empirical data are just beginning to accumulate regarding the impact of automation on leadership and crew interaction (Wiener, 1988, in press). One finding is clear: automation, especially with a reduced crew complement, results in a redistribution of workload and may lead to higher levels of workload, especially when reprogramming of flight management computers is required during critical phases of flight such as airport approaches (see also Chapter 3). On a theoretical level, automation of the flight deck may shift the balance of authority away from the captain. In many instances, the copilot may be assigned primary responsibility for programming the flight management system. This can have the unintended effect of shifting information control and, hence, de facto control of the flight to the more junior crew member.

Another outcome of automation is a tendency, implicated as causal factor in several accidents involving automated flight systems, to allow the computer to retain control even in situations in which reversion to manual flight is indicated by evidence of computer malfunction or excessive reprogramming requirements. In some ways this phenomenon, which has been labeled "automation complacency," is another form of erosion of leadership.

Systematic studies of crew behavior in automated aircraft are just beginning. A recent NASA study contrasted the performance of crews flying the same scenario during an experimental simulation flown either in a conventional DC-9 or an automated MD-88 (Wiener et al., 1991). The results provide some justification for concern over the impact of high levels of automation. Although there were generally few differences in performance of the highly automated (MD-88) and less automated (DC-9) crews in their effectiveness in dealing with simulated inflight crisis situations, those differences that were observed tended to favor the DC-9 crews. It is clear that prior to finalizing the design of automated systems either for aircraft or for tanks, simulations that examine the dynamics of crew interaction and performance should be conducted and the results of such investigations should guide hardware development and crew training practices.

Organizational Cultures and Subcultures

Another factor that has been implicated in crew coordination is the culture of the organizations or subunit within organizations in which crews operate (Hackman, 1987). Embedded in the larger study of crew performance have been surveys designed to measure crew members' attitudes regarding optimal crew management (Cockpit Management Attitudes Questionnaire (CMAQ): Helmreich, 1984; Gregorich et al., 1990). Data have now been collected from more than 20,000 crew members in military and civilian organizations in the United States and Europe. The data indicate that, even in a highly regulated environment, organizations and units within them (for example, particular aircraft fleets or bases) show highly significant differences in attitudes indicating the presence of unique norms regarding appropriate behavior that may or may not have formal sanctions. These attitudes have operational significance and have been validated as predictors of crew performance in line operations (Helmreich et al., 1986a). In addition, systematic observational research confirms significant differences in crew performance between aircraft fleets within particular organizations (Helmreich and Wilhelm, 1989; Helmreich and Foushee, in press; Clothier, 1991).

Ethnographic research into organizational cultures and their development and manifestations in crew behavior is under way under a cooperative agreement between J. Richard Hackman (of Harvard University) and NASA. One ultimate outcome of this research should be a better understanding of how to change such norms in order to optimize crew performance. The issues involved are clearly relevant to the tank corps of the Army as evidenced by a review of culture and military performance by Tamir and Kunda (1987).

ENGINEERING MODELS OF COORDINATION

One promising avenue of research, addressing organizational factors in a nonaviation team performance environment, has been the program of research on distributed decision making carried out by Kleinman and his colleagues at the University of Connecticut (Kleinman et al., 1992; Miao et al., in press). Their approach departs from much of the research on group processes by adopting an engineering-oriented quantitative modeling perspective. Examining teams of operators who may be in different physical locations (i.e., not in face-to-face contact) and must solve a common problem with different amounts of information available, they have formed a number of tentative conclusions with direct relevance to the current issues.

For example, they find that human operators within a team tend to overvalue their own information and tasks relative to others (Kleinman et al., 1992); they observe the particular value of a coordinating leader in times of stress induced by information overload (Miao et al., in press); they document substantial differences in team performance induced by differing perceptions of team goals that may be held by members at different vertical levels of the hierarchy; and they note the particularly debilitating effects of uncertainty on team performance.

These effects are complex, and the conclusions, being recent, await further replication. The approach, however, represents a much-needed direction of research, modeling performance limits of mission-oriented teams. Such research, with its controlled, laboratory-based approach, can be used to provide convergence with the more observational techniques employed by Helmreich and his colleagues in the air crew domain.

CREW PERFORMANCE RESEARCH

The preceding discussion reveals that a series of related actions to assess the need for formal training in leadership and crew coordination are recommended. Additional areas for action include assessment of the social psychological impact of automation and reduced crew complement and investigation of the role of personality factors as determinants of crew performance. First, an evaluation of the extent and nature of leadership and crew coordination problems in tank crews is needed. A number of methodological approaches can be used to obtain a valid representation of leadership and crew coordination issues in current battle tanks. These include:

(a) An examination of archival operational records from a social psychological perspective to determine the extent of leadership, communications, and crew coordination problems. Especially important is the isolation of instances of extremely effective and ineffective crew performance, similar to that which has been undertaken with aircrews (see Ruffle-Smith, 1979).

(b) A survey of crew members to determine normative attitudes regarding leadership, crew coordination, and personal capabilities under stressful conditions.

(c) An assessment of communications patterns and their operational implications for tank operations using the research paradigms employed in aviation. A useful research strategy would be to obtain recordings of crew communications (intra- and interunit) from a sample of tanks in both field operations and simulations. Using adaptations of coding schemata employed in flight crew research, it should be possible to analyze communications to evaluate leadership behaviors, gaps in communication, failures in information transfer, and situation analysis and awareness and decision processes and to relate these to indices of unit performance. Comparative analyses of communications protocols from differing organizations (e.g., European-based versus continental United States-based units) should provide some information on the possible existence of different organizational cultures. In particular, protocols should be analyzed to determine the existence of performance, communications, and crew coordination problems during workload transition situations.

(d) Experimental simulations investigating leadership and crew coordination. An investigation of the effects of tank automation and complement reduction on crew communications and performance is required. In addition to more traditional human factors analyses of crew task performance in more automated units, it is vital to determine how crew interactions change as a function of complement reduction. It is becoming increasingly clear that this area was not sufficiently investigated with the introduction of sophisticated automation on the flight deck. The most viable approach would be to conduct full mission simulations (including interunit communications) focusing on the crew interactions, vigilance, decision making, and task performance, using as subjects crew members with experience levels representative of the tank force. The simulations should be of sufficient duration to allow assessment of behavior during workload transition periods. Refinement of coding schemata for analysis of intracrew and interunit communications should allow evaluation of the impact of hardware and staffing changes on group processes and performance.

It is important to note that the fourth crew member in current operational tanks may fill a number of critical roles affecting operational effectiveness outside combat (e.g., watch standing, maintenance, etc.). In assessing the operational significance of complement changes, it is critical to examine all the operational implications of such changes. In particular, the additional crew member could be more beneficial in workload transition situations.

Second, an evaluation of the utility of formal training in leadership and crew coordination should be conducted. Should the existence of significant problems in crew coordination and communications be confirmed through this research paradigm, the next logical step would be the adaptation of existing training approaches in crew coordination to the tank environment and experimental investigation of whether such training influences communications processes and, most critically, crew performance criteria. (It should be noted that the Army is implementing this type of training for rotorcraft crews at the present time.) The training should focus on the particular behavioral skills required for effective team functioning and should provide clear exemplars of positive and negative leadership and interactions.

Tests of the efficacy of such training should include opportunities for crew members receiving formal instruction, to practice the concepts learned, and to receive feedback on their behavior. A conceptual analog to LOFT in aviation is needed with operational scenarios designed to require effective communications and coordination for mission accomplishment. While current simulation training may serve some of these functions, experiences drawn from the incorporation of LOFT into flight training indicate that, to be effective, the simulation scenarios must be designed to exercise the particular skills stressed in the formal training programs. Those charged with administering the simulation training should be given special training in evaluating and debriefing crew coordination and leadership. Utilizing video or audio tapes of crew interaction for both research and crew feedback can greatly enhance the impact of the experience.

Finally, the role of personality as a determinant of tank commander and crew member performance should be investigated. Recent evidence from civil and military aviation suggests the importance of personality, especially that of the leader, as a determinant of crew performance. It is recommended that the operational significance of personality be investigated, first at the level of the tank commander. Assessment of personality constellations of a sample of tank commanders using validated measures in a no-jeopardy situation should be followed by exploration of the relationships between these factors and leadership behaviors and crew interaction patterns. This evaluation could be conducted both in field operations and experimental simulations. Should it be determined that personality accounts for a significant component of performance variance, the utility of several alternative strategies can be evaluated. One strategy involves designing procedures to *select in* for optimal characteristics. This strategy works well when there is a substantial pool of qualified candidates. The alternative strategy, more feasible when there is a limited pool of candidates, is to *screen out* those with personality constellations associated with poor leadership and ineffective crew performance.

Logical follow-on research would investigate the importance of the personalities of junior crew members as determinants of the crew's performance. This leads into investigation of the importance of the mix of personalities comprising effective and less effective crews. As noted, investigations in this area are much more exploratory as the research base is limited.

REFERENCES

Butler, R.E.
  In press   Line Oriented Flight Training: Full mission simulation as Crew Resource Management training. In E.L. Wiener, B.G. Kanki, and R.L. Helmreich, eds., *Cockpit Resource Management*. San Diego, California: Academic Press.
Chapanis, A., R.B. Ochsman, R.N. Parrish, and G.D. Weeks
  1972   Studies in interactive communications I. *Human Factors* 14:487-509.
Chidester, T.R.
  In press   Critical issues for CRM training and research. In E.L. Wiener, B.G. Kanki, and R.L. Helmreich, eds., *Cockpit Resource Management*. San Diego, California: Academic Press.
Chidester, T.R., and H.C. Foushee
  1988   Leader personality and crew effectiveness: Factors influencing performance in

full-mission air transport simulation. In *Proceedings of the 66th Meeting of the Aerospace Medical Panel on Human Stress Situations in Aerospace Operations*. The Hague, Netherlands: Advisory Group for Aerospace Research and Development.

Chidester, T.R., R.L. Helmreich, S.E. Gregorich, and C. Geis
1991   Pilot personality and crew coordination: Implications for training and selection. *International Journal of Aviation Psychology* 1:23-42.

Clothier, C.
1991   Behavioral interactions across various aircraft types: Results of systematic observations of line operations and simulations. In R.S. Jensen, ed., *Proceedings of the Sixth International Symposium on Aviation Psychology*. Columbus, Ohio: Ohio State University.

Cooper, G.E., M.D. White, and J.K. Lauber
1979   *Resource Management on the Flight Deck*. NASA Conference Publication No. 2120. Moffett Field, California: NASA-Ames Research Center.

Davis, J.H., ed.
1992   Special issue on group decision making and problem solving. *Organizational Behavior and Human Decision Processes* 52.

Dolgin, D.L., and G.D. Gibb
1988   *A Review of Personality Measurement in Aircrew Selection*. NAMRL Monograph no. 36. Pensacola, Florida: Naval Aerospace Medical Research Laboratory.

Fiedler, F.E.
1964   A contingency model of leadership effectiveness. In L. Berkowitz, ed., *Advances in Experimental Social Psychology, Volume 1*. New York: Academic Press.

Foushee, H.C., and R.L. Helmreich
1988   Group interactions and nightcrew performance. Pp. 189-227 in E.L Wiener and D. Nagel, eds., *Human Factors in Modem Aviation*. New York: Academic Press.

Foushee, H.C., and K.L. Manos
1981   Information transfer within the cockpit: Problems in intracockpit communications. In C.E. Billings and E.S. Cheaney, eds., *Information Transfer Problem in the Aviation System*. NASA Technical Paper No. 1875. Moffett Field, California: NASA-Ames Research Center.

Ginnett, R.O.
1987   First Encounters of the Close Kind: The First Meetings of Airline Flight Crews. Ph.D. dissertation, Yale University.

Gregorich, S., R.L. Helmreich, and J.A. Wilhelm
1990   The structure of cockpit management attitudes. *Journal of Applied Psychology* 75(6):682-690.

Hackman, J.R.
1987   Group level issues in the design and training of cockpit crews. In H.W. Orlady and H.C. Foushee, eds., *Cockpit Resource Management Training: Proceedings of the NASA/MAC Workshop*. Report No. CP-2455. Moffett Field, California: NASA-Ames Research Center.

Hastie, R.
1986   Review essay: Experimental evidence on group accuracy. Pp. 129-164 in B. Grofman and G. Owen, eds., *Information Pooling and Group Decision Making*. Greenwich, Connecticut: JAI Press.

Hawkins, F.H.
1987   *Human Factors in Flight*. Brookfield, Vermont: Gower Press.

Helmreich, R.L.
1984   Cockpit management attitudes. *Human Factors* 26:583-589.

Helmreich, R.L, T.R. Chidester, H.C. Foushee, S.E. Gregorich, and J.A. Wilhelm
    In press   How effective is cockpit resource management training? Issues in evaluating the
               impact of programs to enhance crew coordination. In T.R. Chidester, ed., *Emerg-
               ing Issues for the Second Decade of Line Oriented Flight Training: Proceedings
               of a Workshop Held at the Pan American International Flight Academy.*
Helmreich, R.L., and H.C. Foushee
    1988   Flightdeck communications. In E. Wiener and D. Nagel, eds., *Human Factors in
               Aviation.* Orlando, Florida: Academic Press.
    In press   Why Crew Resource Management: The history and status of human factors train-
               ing programs in aviation. In E.L. Wiener, B.G. Kanki, and R.L. Helmreich, eds.,
               Cockpit Resource Management. New York: Academic Press.
Helmreich, R.L., H.C. Foushee, R. Benson, and R. Russini
    1986a   Cockpit management attitudes: Exploring the attitude-performance linkage. *Avia-
               tion, Space and Environmental Medicine* 57:1198-1200.
Helmreich, R.L., L.L. Sawin, and A.L. Carsrud
    1986b   The honeymoon effect in job performance: Delayed predictive power of achieve-
               ment motivation. *Journal of Applied Psychology* 71:1085-1088.
Helmreich, R.L., and J.T. Spence
    1978   The work and family orientation questionnaire: An objective instrument to assess
               components of achievement motivation and attitudes toward family and career.
               JSAS Catalog of Selected Documents in Psychology (MS 1677, Vol. 8). Austin,
               Texas: University of Texas.
Helmreich, R.L., and J.A. Wilhelm
    1989   When training boomerangs: Negative outcomes from Cockpit Resource Manage-
               ment programs. *Proceedings of the Fifth Aviation Psychology Symposium.* Co-
               lumbus, Ohio: Ohio State University.
    1991   Outcomes of crew resource management training. *International Journal of Avia-
               tion Psychology* 1:287-300.
Helmreich, R.L., J.A. Wilhelm, S.E. Gregorich, and T.R. Chidester
    1990a   Preliminary results from the evaluation of Cockpit Resource Management Train-
               ing: Performance ratings of flightcrews. *Aviation, Space, and Environmental Medicine*
               61:576-579.
Helmreich, R.L., J.A. Wilhelm, J.E. Kello, and W.R. Taggart
    1990b   *Reinforcing and Evaluating Crew Resource Management: Chock Airman/LOFT
               Instructor Reference Manual.* Technical Manual 90-1. Austin, Texas: NASA/
               University of Texas.
Helmreich, R.L., J.A. Wilhelm, J.E. Kello, W.R. Taggart, and R.E. Butler
    1991   *Reinforcing and Evaluating Crew Resource Management: Evaluator/LOS Instruc-
               tor Reference Manual.* Technical Manual No. 90-2. Austin, Texas: NASA/Uni-
               versity of Texas.
Hirst, W.
    1986   Aspects of divided and selected attention. In J. LeDoux and W. Hirst, eds., *Mind
               and Brain.* New York: Cambridge University Press.
Hollander, E.
    1985   Leadership and power. In G. Lindzey and E. Aronson, eds., *Handbook of Social
               Psychology, Volume 2.* New York: Random House.
Howard, S.K., D.M. Gaba, K.J. Fish, G. Yang, and F.H. Samquist
    In press   Anesthesia crisis resource management training: Teaching anesthesiologists to
               handle critical events. *Aviation, Space, and Environmental Medicine.*
Kanki, B.G., and H.C. Foushee
    1989   Communication as a group process mediator of aircrew performance. *Aviation,
               Space, and Environmental Medicine* 60:402-410.

Kanki, B.G., S. Lozito, and H.C. Foushee
  1989   Communications indexes of crew coordination. *Aviation, Space, and Environmental Medicine* 60:56-60.
Kiesler, S., and L. Sproull
  1992   Group decision making and communications technology. *Organizational Behavior and Human Decision Processes* 52:96-123.
Kleinman, D.L., P.B. Luh, K.R. Pattipati, and D. Serfaty
  1992   Mathematical models of team distributed decision making. In R.W. Swezey and E. Salas, eds., *Teams, Their Training and Performance*. New York: Ablex.
Kryter, K.D.
  1972   Speech communications. In H.P. Van Cott and R.G. Kinkade, eds., *Human Engineering Guide to Systems Design*. Washington, DC: U.S. Government Printing Office.
Miao, X., P.B. Luh, and D.L. Kleinman
  In press A normative-descriptive approach to hierarchical team resource allocation. *IEEE Transactions on Systems, Man, and Cybernetics* 22(3).
Nagel, D.
  1988   Human error in aviation operations. In E. Wiener and D. Nagel, eds., *Human Factors in Aviation*. Orlando, Florida: Academic Press.
Predmore, S.
  1991   Communications and multi-task processing on the flightdeck. In B. Kanki, ed., *Approaches to Studying Group Productivity and Group Processes Using High Fidelity Flight Simulators*. Technical Memorandum. Moffett Field, California: NASA-Ames Research Center.
Ruffle-Smith, H.P.
  1979   *A Simulator Study of the Interaction of Pilot Workload with Errors, Vigilance, and Decisions*. NASA Technical Memorandum No. 78482; A-7354. Moffett Field, California: NASA-Ames Research Center.
Spence, J.T., and R.L. Helmreich
  1978   Masculinity and femininity as personality dimensions. *Society for the Advancement of Social Psychology Newsletter* 4:2-3.
Taggart, W.R.
  1990   Introducing CRM into maintenance training. *Proceedings of the Third International Symposium on Human Factors in Aircraft Maintenance and Inspection*. Washington, DC: Federal Aviation Administration.
Tamir, B., and G. Kunda
  1987   Culture and military performance. Background paper for D. Druckman and J.A. Swets, eds., *Enhancing Human Performance: Issues, Theories, and Techniques*. Washington, DC: National Academy Press.
Treisman, M.
  1984   A theory of criterion setting: An alternative to the attention band and response ratio hypotheses in magnitude estimation and cross-modality matching. *Journal of Experimental Psychology* 113(3):443-463.
  1964   Verbal cues, language, and meaning in selective attention. *American Journal of Psychology* 77:206-219.
Wickens, C.D.
  1984   Processing resources in attention. Pp. 63-102 in R. Parasuraman and D.R. Davies, ed., *Varieties of Attention*. San Diego, California: Academic Press.
  1992   *Engineering Psychology and Human Performance*. New York: Harper Collins.
Wiener, E.L.
  1988   Cockpit automation. Pp. 189-227 in E.L. Wiener and D. Nagel, eds., *Human Factors in Aviation*. New York: Academic Press.

In press Human factors of the high technology cockpit. In *Proceedings of the ICAO Human Factors Seminar, 1990.* Leningrad, USSR.

Wiener, E.L., T.R. Chidester, B.G. Kanki, E.A. Palmer, R.E. Curry, and S.E. Gregovich
1991   *The Impact of Cockpit Automation on Crew Coordination and Communication: I. Overview, Loft Evaluations, Error Severity, and Questionnaire Data.* Contractor Report no. 177587. Moffett Field, California: NASA.

11

Training for Emergency Responses

Performing well in the transition from routine to emergency situations depends on the complex interaction of a host of environmental, organizational, and individual variables. Team effectiveness in an emergency is influenced by numerous factors such as leadership, personality, unit cohesion (Griffith, 1987), physical fitness (Martens and Landers, 1970), and sleep schedule—topics that have been addressed in previous chapters. The main focus of this chapter is on training approaches that can be used to offset decrements in performance that might occur in the transition.

As discussed in the previous chapters, numerous ways to sustain effective performance have been detailed in the literature:

(1) Leadership—soldiers who lack trust in their leadership are more susceptible to battle shock (e.g., Kopstein et al., 1985).

(2) Unit cohesion—variables such as crew stability and common experience are linked to resistance to combat stress (Griffith, 1987). Unit cohesion is developed as a result of working and training as a crew over prolonged periods of time.

(3) Personality—several experiments involving the use of different motor tasks have demonstrated that individuals with moderate levels of trait anxiety perform better than individuals with low or high levels of trait anxiety (Martens and Landers, 1970).

(4) Physical conditioning—fitness may attenuate decrements in cognitive work capacity. Pleban et al. (1985) found that physical fitness had a

beneficial effect in an encoding/decoding task requiring prolonged mental effort, particularly as sleep loss and other stresses began to mount.

(5) Stress management techniques—soldiers who are equipped to manage stress are likely to be more successful than those not so equipped. FM 26-2, *Management of Stress in Army Operations* (U.S. Department of the Army, 1983), was written to assist soldiers in managing stress.

(6) Systems design—technological advances offer the opportunity to enhance the capability of systems, but without the careful consideration of the match of system requirements and cognitive abilities, the promise of technology may not be achieved. The U.S. Army's MANPRINT program (Booher, 1990) has demonstrated that integration of manpower, personnel, training, human factors engineering, system safety, and health hazard considerations in the system design process can enhance soldier performance. Without considering soldier-system interactions, a variety of unforeseen problems can result from the application of technology such as automation (Moray and Huey, 1988).

(7) Job-person match—recent research has demonstrated the potential importance of developing classification-efficient multidimensional assignment measures for increasing operational performance of soldiers (Johnson and Zeidner, 1991). The importance of general cognitive ability to job performance has been well documented (Hunter and Schmidt, 1982). This most recent research on differential assignment theory suggests that important gains in performance can be achieved through differential classification of individuals and assignment of crews. Furthermore, system designers need more refined information about intraindividual abilities to more adequately match equipment and individual capabilities (Zeidner and Johnson, 1991).

(8) Human resource management—commanders and soldiers who search for innovative solutions to labor-intensive tasks, who weigh the costs and benefits of taking prudent risks, and who instill the need for work/rest/sleep discipline should survive longer under demanding conditions than those who do not.

(9) Training—well-learned responses appear less subject to interference from extraneous environmental influences and the effects of sleep loss than less well-learned responses. Also, soldiers who are well trained are more confident in their abilities (e.g., Adams, 1971) and better able to share task responsibilities than those who are less well trained.

The first part of the chapter describes a number of training challenges. The second part provides a training framework and addresses specific findings related to the question of how training can increase the probability of adequate performance. The chapter concludes with a discussion of realistic training approaches and potentially important areas for future research.

TRAINING CHALLENGES

The generic requirements for competent task performance in an emergency situation were outlined in Chapter 1. The specific performance requirements of monitoring, navigation, situation awareness, decision making, strategic planning, communications, procedure following, and perceptual-motor interaction span the continuum from performance of complex, problem-solving tasks to routine, procedural tasks. For example, the crew of any complex system should be capable of performing certain tasks automatically, while the crew leader must possess the adaptability to apply multidimensional thinking and decision making when appropriate. Because the knowledge requirements are so diverse and evolve as people move up in responsibility, the training demands for these different kinds of activities are also very different. This assertion is supported by a recent article by Glaser (1990), who reviewed research findings from studies of three major aspects of competent performance related to the challenges presented above: (a) proceduralized knowledge and skill, (b) self-regulatory skills and performance control strategies to foster comprehension, and (c) structured knowledge and mental models for problem solving. He speculates that procedural skills that are "knowledge lean" may be learned in one way, whereas cognitive skills may be learned in different, more complex ways.

TRAINING AND SKILL RETENTION

The goal of training for emergency responses is to ensure that the method of training induces rapid, accurate performance. It is reasonable to assume that one of the best criteria to guarantee such performance is that the skills called on are retained well. In this regard, a host of variables are known to influence the retention of skills (Adams, 1987; Schendel et al., 1978; Wells and Hagman, 1989). Some of the key variables include: type of task, amount of practice, type of practice, testing, and level of original learning. These variables are discussed in the following paragraphs.

Type of Task

Not all tasks are forgotten at the same rate. For example, procedural tasks are forgotten in days, weeks, or months, whereas continuous control tasks typically are remembered for months or years. Rose et al. (1985) and Shields et al. (1979) found that task characteristics that are readily available from existing documentation are accurate predictors of retention performance. This information can be used to determine the amount and kind of refresher training required to maintain skilled performance.

Based on reviews of the literature and extensive field tests, Rose et al.

TABLE 11.1 Task Characteristics Related to Retention

Job/Memory Aided	Quality of Job/Memory Aids
Length	Definite Step Sequence
Built-in Logic to Steps	Mental Requirements
Number of Facts	Complexity of Facts
Movement Demands	Time Demands

(1985) identified and evaluated a large set of variables that could be used in a model to predict retention loss for specific tasks. The final set of task characteristics is shown in Table 11.1.

Operational definitions of these task characteristics were developed and compiled to form a model. In tests of over 300 individual soldier tasks, these characteristics have been found to reliably predict proficiency levels for individual tasks. In similar research, Rossmeissl and Charles (1988) developed a model to predict the cognitive requirements of human task performance. They identified 12 factors that were particularly important in determining job or task difficulty. These factors, listed in Table 11.2, were found to be significant predictors of task difficulty in tests using Army subjects.

The approaches described above can be used to predict training requirements, and also as a design aid to assist in allocation of functions or tasks between humans and machines. In short, they can be used to "design out" the most difficult training tasks.

Amount of Practice

A skill will not be acquired until it is practiced (Hinrichs, 1976). Observations drawn from a review of the literature on exceptional performance indicate that such performance depends most heavily on enormous motivation and continued practice over a period of years (Schendel, 1987). How-

TABLE 11.2 Cognitive Requirements Model Evaluation Factors

Working Memory	Task Repetition
Quantity of Data	Decision Making
Multiple Processing	Data Interpretation
Time	Problem Solving
Psychomotor	Environment
Long-Term Memory	

ever, as Schneider (1985) points out, "practice makes perfect" may be an overgeneralization.

Schneider (1985) developed guidelines for training high-performance skills based on the proposition that performance results from the interaction of two qualitatively different forms of processing: controlled and automatic. Controlled processing is slow and requires attention from the performer to deal with novel tasks or task rules that are inconsistent over time. Automatic processing is fast and requires little or no attention on the part of the performer. For perceptual tasks, Schneider (1985) found that under conditions of prolonged practice, the processing of information moves from controlled processing to automatic processing, when the task has consistent components. The rules and findings were developed out of basic research on developing visual skills, in which Schneider found that skill development relates to the heterogeneity of components. A consistent task component is one in which the performer makes the same response to a stimulus every time (i.e., the performer pushes the same button every time a red light comes on). A varied component is one in which the performer may respond one way to a signal under certain conditions, and another way under a different set of conditions. Performers show large improvements with practice on consistent task components, but not on varied task components. Subsequently, Schneider's dichotomy of controlled processing (and inconsistent mapping) and automatic processing (consistent mapping) has been extended to accommodate cognitive rule-based skills as well (Kramer et al., 1990).

In an extensive review of the effects of repetition and practice, Wells and Hagman (1989) conclude that repetition, necessary or even desirable, is the key factor in learning, retention, and transfer of skills, but the required amount of repetition depends on the training requirements. They found that, if the goal is to enhance performance of a specific task, then the more repetitions, the better. If the goal is to enhance problem solving and transfer to new tasks, then fewer specific repetitions are recommended along with an increase in variety.

Type of Practice

By systematically altering practice to encourage information processing activities, one can generate enhanced performance capabilities (Schmidt and Bjork, 1989). Experimental evidence shows that conditions that make performance during the acquisition phase most effective are often least effective for learning, as measured by retention and transfer tests (Wickens, 1992). In contrast, conditions that force more elaborate processing during acquisition and that may slow the rate at which performance improves during acquisition often lead to more and better learning and better retention.

An example is guided training, in which the learner is consistently led through the correct sequence of responses. While error-free performance will result during training, the fact that the learner will not have been allowed to choose the responses on his own will depress later transfer. Some guidance will be useful, but too much can be counterproductive. Additional research is needed to understand the processes underlying these empirical findings.

Testing

Testing has been shown to improve the long-term retention of skills better than study alone. For example, in one experiment on the long-term retention of verbal materials, researchers found that an immediate test trial performed after 10 study trials reduced error frequency nearly 50 percent as compared within 10 study trials without the test trial (Allen et al., 1969). Another important reason for testing is that it motivates learners to study by demonstrating to the individuals their skill levels. People are not very good at estimating and reporting their own skill levels. Most studies find low correlations between how well people say they are going to perform and how well they actually perform. In addition, most people overestimate their skills. In one study conducted for the Army, over 75 percent of the soldiers tested predicted higher scores in a rifle marksmanship test than they actually obtained (Schendel et al., 1984).

Level of Original Learning

All of the variables discussed above have been linked to performance after retention. However, the single most important determinant of retention is level of original learning. As an example, Fleishman and Parker (1962), using a three-dimensional flight control task, found high positive correlations (.80 to .98) between learners' initial learning levels and later retention. More important, the strength of these correlations was high and unchanging over retention intervals ranging from one month to two years.

Given that the single most important determinant of skill retention is level of original learning, the key is to ensure a high degree of original learning. Knowledge of results or feedback (externally provided information about the correctness of a response), is commonly regarded as the single most important variable for learning (Winstein and Schmidt, 1990). It is a critical source of information and motivation during learning.

To assure high levels of original learning, overtraining (or mastery training) may be more effective than proficiency training (that is, training one to successful performance). This was demonstrated by Schendel and Hagman (1982), who trained reserve soldiers to perform an assembly/disassembly task. Mastery training was found to be superior to proficiency training across an eight-week retention interval.

In addition to increasing the probability of competent performance after the retention interval, other advantages are associated with higher levels of original learning. These are the ability to perform tasks with minimal mental effort (automatic processing) at lower levels of perceived workload and with less interference from the effects of stress. These advantages are discussed below.

TRAINING AND WORKLOAD

Gopher and Donchin (1986) point out that practice has an important impact on the perception of workload. As parts of task performance become automatic, there is a reduction of resource costs in a system driven by automatic compared with controlled processes. Therefore, the level of practice that an individual has at the time of performance may dramatically reduce perceived workload or increase it instantly when novelty is encountered.

Lysaght et al. (1989), in their review of workload methodologies, point out that training and specific skill acquisition extend an individual's capability to handle workload. However, they go on to point out that certain contributors to high workload, such as the necessity to perceive faster, are not amenable to training. Many of these factors are related to and limited by an individual's cognitive abilities. This is an area of research that requires greater study.

To some extent, training reduces workload at the same time that it improves performance. However, in order to achieve the expected improvement of performance during training, workload reductions may occur at a slower rate than performance improvements. Each time a transition from one position or vehicle to another occurs, workload may be quite high until new skills are mastered, and unfamiliar tasks, procedures, and responsibilities become familiar. Even for crew members who are highly experienced in their current position, transition to a new environment (e.g., being transferred from the United States to a foreign country or from peacetime to wartime conditions) will create a temporary increase in workload and may affect performance.

TRAINING APPROACHES

In the study of complex human performance, Glaser (1990) found that (1) learning takes place by active application of knowledge in the context of working on specific problems, (2) the key to learning complex cognitive tasks was the explication and modeling of the appropriate problem-solving structure and procedures or strategies entailed in competent performance, (3) strengthening of existing knowledge was enhanced by practice that minimized error, and (4) failure or conflict triggered new learning, except for the automatic process of knowledge compilation. Although Glaser (1990) found these commonalities, he found a dichotomy in instructional approaches. In one, the mastery approach, the instructor controls and builds the specific learning sequence. In the other, the learner is in control of the problem-solving approach and shapes his or her experience in an environment that assists and supports his or her performance. This dichotomy may be due to differences in subject matter (cognitive and problem-solving skills versus proceduralized knowledge) as well as a difference in research traditions and values.

Since the learning of complex tasks and performances occurs over weeks and months and goes through many stages, both the mastery and problem-solving approaches to training of complex tasks is required. In a previous section, evidence was presented that the level of original learning is a key determinant of later performance. Assuming this is the case, training approaches must be developed that optimize retention of the array of tasks that must be performed in an emergency situation. For the tank crew, the challenge is how to structure training to ensure that: (1) the crew performs as a coordinated, interactive team; (2) the commander makes the correct decisions given the specific conditions; (3) the crew communicates internally as a team and externally as a member of a larger unit; (4) each member is prepared to fill roles of missing members in the case of undermanning or combat casualties; and (5) each member performs his individual and team roles and tasks in the context of the battlefield environment (external stresses). The primary decision maker, or commander, must have the opportunity to practice emergency problem-solving and decision-making as well as routine proceduralized tasks. Practice under realistic, challenging conditions will allow better use of mental resources for the nonroutine elements of the emergency situation.

The following paragraphs describe three training approaches that appear to have particular relevance for the training of tank crew members, as well as other teams or crews that may be required to respond to emergency situations. While considerable research has addressed the potential dangers in seeking excessive realism in simulator environments (Hawkins, 1987; Jones et al., 1985), the three approaches discussed below are noteworthy because their developers have sought to incorporate those specific elements of realism that encourage positive transfer to operational environments. The three approaches, Simulation Networking (SIMNET), embedded training, and crew or cockpit resource management (CRM) training, provide realistic training and testing to promote the long-term retention of skills. CRM training is discussed in the previous chapter. We discuss below the advantages and disadvantages of the other two training approaches and suggest recommendations for research.

Training Complex Tasks Through
Simulation Networking (SIMNET)

Realistic training improves a soldier's ability to withstand combat stress (Frank, 1982). The realistic sights and sounds of the battlefield help to develop the soldier's knowledge of himself, his enemy, and his weapons. In the earlier examination of the performance processes involved in tank crew performance, it was noted that the tank commander position involves the greatest training and performance demands. Decision-making and problem-solving skills, in addition to procedural knowledge, appear to be the predominant skill requirements for successful performance. This analysis implies that the highest payoff for training in the tank crew environment would involve enhancing the cognitive skills of the commander. In other words, training should enhance the commander's skill to recognize and respond appropriately to new or uncommon problems or create more effective ways to solve old problems. SIMNET provides this opportunity (Ropelewski, 1989). It represents the leading edge in realistic, large-scale, low-cost combat training exercises.

SIMNET was developed by the Defense Advanced Research Projects Agency (DARPA) and the U.S. Army. Training is achieved through a network of disbursed combat simulators. Fully manned and separated, tank platoons and companies can fight battalion-size battles. The battles can involve the full range of command and control and supporting elements, including helicopters and fixed-wing air support. SIMNET allows trainees to practice the range of communication and decision-making tasks and roles in a realistic environment. Its most significant advantage is that it provides the opportunity for interactive training of large numbers of commanders of air and ground units operating from different sites.

SIMNET is a giant whole-task trainer for fighting multiple units. In the SIMNET system there are no reset buttons to allow crews to pause or start over again if something goes wrong. The commanders must plan, communicate, and execute decisions in real time. SIMNET allows individual crew members, as well as battalion commanders, to practice tasks and roles as individuals and units.

The low cost and flexibility of SIMNET compared with most simulators makes it reasonable for use on a routine basis. The system can be used to simulate joint and combined warfare or small unit engagements. It is used on a daily basis at Fort Knox, and was used in Germany to train for the Canadian Army Trophy tank-gunnery competition (Ropelewski, 1989).

The advantages of SIMNET as a realistic trainer are clear. It also provides the opportunity to study learning in a natural setting as suggested by Glaser (1990). The technology permits the conduct of carefully designed experiments to study issues such as: (1) the appropriate type and sequencing of feedback to trainees; (2) the acquisition of decision-making skills; (3) the interaction of individual differences and the acquisition of decision-making skills; (4) the principles underlying the design of training programs to maximize performance in emergency situations; and (5) the interaction of training, workload, and stress variables on performance in a combat-like environment. A major technical challenge for SIMNET is to conduct experiments and provide appropriate feedback without degrading the dynamic, realistic simulation.

In the initial development of SIMNET, the emphasis was placed on the technology of producing a realistic, low-cost simulator. From a training perspective, the value of SIMNET as a trainer would be greatly enhanced if the trainee could receive process feedback as well as battle outcomes. This information would provide the learners with an assessment of the direct outcome of their decisions, as well as an assessment of the processes and procedures used to obtain the outcome. The importance of process information has been confirmed in an extensive body of research that shows that the way in which executives think and make decisions greatly influences their success (Streufert and Swezey, 1986). SIMNET provides the opportunity to give commanders information about the quality of their problem-solving approaches and thereby enhance the probability of adequate performance in emergency situations.

Embedded Training for Practicing Procedural Tasks in the Operational Setting

Embedded training presents an excellent opportunity for the practice and retention of tasks and skills that should be performed automatically in the course of battle. Embedded training is a training capability built into or added onto operational systems. Advances in the sophistication of the tank systems, such as the use of electronic display screens, high-speed integrated circuits and solid-state computers, make it possible to embed training subsystems in the operational equipment. This would allow the tank systems themselves to provide refresher training. New tanks have the potential to integrate embedded training applications into gunnery, tactics, driving, and maintenance training (Hardy, 1988).

Currently, the Main Battle Tank does not have embedded training capabilities. Tank crewmen can practice the tasks associated with preparation for gunnery, but there is no feedback. Embedded training for the Block III

Tank is required to support four principal areas: (1) tank gunnery, (2) tactics, (3) maintenance (i.e., fault isolation/diagnostics), and (4) tank driving. Embedded training must: (1) train individual job tasks through force-level collective tasks (crew through battalion) as required; (2) be capable of providing a series of training exercises for all levels previously mentioned that can be used to train to doctrinally acceptable standards; (3) be able to store and retrieve data; (4) provide realistic computer-generated imagery simulation training exercises that are programmable for individual, crew, platoon, team, and task force level tactical and gunnery training; (5) have the capability to network two or more vehicles into the same computer-generated imagery data base to support specific training exercises; and (6) have the capability for precision laser force-on-force training aboard the vehicle.

An advantage of embedded training is that it can provide high-quality, standardized training tailored to an individual's needs. The embedded training system can assess the proficiency level of the soldier, provide feedback, and keep records of the learner's progress. Another advantage of embedded training in the operational environment is that it can be designed to operate without an instructor. It provides the opportunity to practice the highly perishable skills identified by Rose et al. (1985). Embedded training is better suited to provide refresher training than to provide training for new skills (Oberlin, 1988).

Embedded training as it is currently configured does not provide the opportunity for the commander to practice the complex decision-making tasks required in combat. An important disadvantage is that embedding full-task training exercises may require too much textual instruction because learners' tolerance for reading lengthy screen messages is low. The whole-task training necessary for the commander is better accomplished in a SIMNET-like environment. Nevertheless, given the long periods of underload that often characterize the pretransition phase of teams in transition, it is reasonable to conclude that embedded training could, if properly structured, achieve these important goals: (1) maintain a level of arousal sufficient to guard against vigilance decrements (Chapter 6); (2) maintain or induce situation awareness of the status of the vehicle and the environment (Chapter 7); and (3) achieve the primary goal of delivering knowledge.

Training to Improve Communications and Coordination

The SIMNET system should be adaptable to the investigation of social psychological issues surrounding crew communications and crew resource management, as discussed in the previous chapter.

Aware of the potential benefits of reducing and controlling crew errors resulting from poor leadership and crew coordination, many airlines and units of the military have developed programs to provide training in these areas—programs that have come to be known generically as Crew Resource Management (CRM) training. Primary CRM training programs (often described as the initial awareness phase of training) typically are conducted in a seminar format and include modules on leadership, interpersonal communications, decision making and problem solving, conflict resolution, and stress effects and stress management. Emphasis is placed on the need for open communications despite status and role differences. Military training programs also focus on the need to overcome barriers imposed by military rank structure and officer-enlisted, status differentials without eroding leader authority.

Early programs in aviation were largely derivative from traditional management training and organizational development courses. Later programs tend to focus more directly on issues related directly to flight deck problems and are tailored to highlight issues raised by analysis of operational incidents and surveys to determine baseline attitudes regarding leadership and flightdeck management. The emphasis is on experiential rather than didactic instructional techniques. Many courses employ role-playing of conflict resolution situations, briefings, and post-mission critiques, often employing videotape to record interactions and provide feedback.

A number of strategies are employed to ensure that CRM training has a lasting impact. One is to demonstrate complete organizational commitment to the concepts taught by providing positive role models, incorporating CRM concepts in formal doctrine and operating manuals, and by requiring adherence to the concepts (making failure to practice these concepts and to show effective leadership grounds for termination from flight status). A second is to provide formal recurrent training in CRM concepts and techniques rather than giving only a single training experience. Third, and perhaps most important, is to provide recurring opportunities to practice the concepts and receive reinforcement and feedback. This is accomplished through full mission simulations (LOFT) that have scenarios designed to elicit problem-solving behavior and decision making in abnormal flight situations that have no simple, book solution and no clear optimal course of action. The training impact is also enhanced by making the training without "jeopardy." Crews are free to practice different behaviors without placing their licenses to fly at risk. Perhaps the most successful innovation has been videotaping the sessions and using the tape for post-mission debriefing of crew behaviors. The fourth strategy is to provide regular feedback and reinforcement of CRM concepts during regular performance evaluations. This is accomplished by giving designated evaluators (check airmen) special training in the evaluation and debriefing of leadership and crew coordination practices. Crews are then observed and critiqued following regular evaluations (line checks).

Preliminary data from a NASA-sponsored, longitudinal study of flight crew performance before and after CRM training demonstrates that such training can have a significant positive impact on crew performance, if well implemented (Helmreich, 1991; Helmreich and Foushee, in press; Helmreich and Wilhelm, in press). Multiple measures of training impact are employed and all show consistent, positive change. Dependent variables include: (1) systematic observations of crew performance in line operations and full mission simulations; (2) changes in attitudes regarding crew-related issues; (3) case studies of crew communications from the cockpit voice recorder tapes of relevant aircraft incidents and accidents; and (4) self-reports by crew members of the efficacy of training.

The data indicate that training both improves the performance of less effective crews and further enhances that of competent crews. Although the project is still in the data collection phase, the following findings have been obtained and replicated: (1) Observational data collected on the previously described NASA/UT Line/LOS Checklist show significant improvements in overall performance and crew effectiveness as well as in specific behavioral categories. (2) Highly significant, positive changes in attitudes regarding leader roles, interpersonal communications, and awareness of stressor effects are found. (3) Although the number of accidents involving flightcrews trained in CRM concepts is small, the cockpit voice recorder transcripts of these catastrophes form a slowly increasing data base from which information on crew behavior can be analyzed in a case-by-case fashion (Predmore, 1991). During the past year, two major accidents occurred involving crews with formal CRM and LOFT training. One involved the loss of a cargo door and two engines, the second loss of all hydraulic systems associated flight controls. Both crews faced novel, life-threatening situations for which no standard procedures existed; both crews were faced with extreme stress for an extended period of time. Examination of the communications patterns shows the high workload imposed by the situation and the practice of inquiry, advocacy, critique and careful decision making, even under great stress. One of the captains attributed his crew's survival to CRM training. While not conclusive evidence, these data combined with other evidence represent encouraging evidence. (4) Self-reports of participants overwhelmingly support the utility of CRM training. Specific items on a post training evaluation form ask for ratings of (a) the potential of the training for safety; (b) personal usefulness of the training; and (c) extent to which the training has (or will) change personal behavior on the flight deck. Survey results regarding the value of LOFT are equally positive. Crews find the experience to be an extremely valuable setting in which to put together what they have learned regarding effective crew performance. Participant endorsement of such programs is a necessary but not sufficient indicator. If crews did not perceive the training as useful, it is unlikely that the practices advocated would be internalized.

One negative finding is that a small subset of crew members reject the training both in self-reports of reactions and, attitudinally, in terms of less acceptance of positive crew coordination practices. As previously noted, one determinant of negative training outcomes is crew member personality (Helmreich and Wilhelm, 1989). It appears that personality characteristics may form one of the limiting factors on the efficacy of CRM training. As yet, little progress has been made in determining if additional training or peer pressure can elicit behavior change among those who reject the training. In particular, it is not known whether training strategies and interventions can effect change in personality related behaviors.

The above data suggest that enhancements in crew coordination provided by CRM training may prove to be effective countermeasures against the stress of workload transitions. As previously noted, effective crews employ behavioral strategies that would appear to utilize the combined resources of the group which can serve to compensate for stress-induced individual attentional and cognitive deficits (see Chapter 8). However, full scientific validation of the impact of crew coordination training has involved assessment of crew performance during normal operations and simulated flights with abnormal conditions. Adequate systematic data on the performance of crews during highly stressful, real inflight emergencies are not yet available, beyond the two case studies described above. Although unlikely, the possibility exists that improvements noted after CRM training might disappear in a stress-induced reversion to earlier patterns of behavior.

SUMMARY

In summary, extensive training on those procedures and actions that may need to be taken in an emergency situation may mitigate the negative effects of stress and workload. Training to automate performance of certain tasks may be accomplished through embedded training devices in the tank or on the equipment. Training to enhance the probability of adequate decision processes and crew coordination and leadership issues could be accomplished through a SIMNET environment. Consideration of the appropriate training methodology is based on an analysis of the specific requirements in the emergency situation.

In the long run, the optimal role of training must be established by a careful evaluation of the cost-effectiveness of training versus design in improving system performance (Rouse, 1985). The nature of these tradeoffs (and that involving a third factor—abilities) is beyond the scope of this report but is addressed specifically by the Army's MANPRINT program. The reader is referred to the detailed treatment by Booher (1990) for discussion of these issues.

REFERENCES

Adams, J.A.
1971   A closed-loop theory of motor learning. *Journal of Motor Behavior* 3:111-149.
1987   Historical review and appraisal of research on the learning, retention and transfer of human motor skills. *Psychological Bulletin* 101(1):41-74.

Allen, G.A., W.A. Mahler, and W.K. Estes
1969   Effects of recall tests on long-term retention of paired associates. *Journal of Verbal Learning and Verbal Behavior* 8:463-470.

Booher, H.R., ed.
1990   *MANPRINT: An Approach to Systems Integration.* New York: Van Nostrand Reinhold.

Fleishman, E.A., and S.F. Parker
1962   Factors in the retention and relearning of perceptual-motor skill. *Journal of Experimental Psychology* 64:215-276.

Frank, G.R.
1982   Continuous operations. *Armor* 167-171.

Glaser, R.
1990   The reemergence of learning theory within instructional research. *American Psychologist* 45(1):29-39.

Gopher, D., and E. Donchin
1986   Workload: An examination of the concept. Chapter 41 in K.R. Boff, L. Kaufman, and J.P. Thomas, eds., *Handbook of Perception and Human Performance.* New York: John Wiley and Sons.

Griffith, J.
1987   Toward a conception of military unit cohesion: A summary of results from the cohesion studies of the Army's new manning system. Paper presented at the meeting of the U.S. Army Medical Department Professional Postgraduate Short Course - Research Psychology. Washington, DC: Walter Reed Army Institute of Research.

Hardy, H.C.
1988   Armor training 1997: An application of embedded training. *Armor* 34-36.

Hawkins, F.H.
1987   *Human Factors in Flight.* Aldershot, England: Gower Technical Press.

Hinrichs, J.R.
1976   Personnel training. Pp. 829-860 in M.D. Dunnette, ed., *Handbook of Industrial and Organizational Psychology.* Chicago: Rand McNally.

Hunter, J.E., and F.L. Schmidt
1982   Fitting people to jobs: The impact of personnel selection on national productivity. In E.A. Fleishman and M.D. Dunnette, eds., *Human Performance and Productivity, Volume I: Human Capability Assessment.* Hillsdale, New Jersey: Erlbaum.

Johnson, C.D., and J. Zeidner
1991   *The Economic Benefits of Predicting Job Performance, Volume II: Classification Efficiency.* New York: Praeger.

Jones, E.R., R.T. Hennessy, and S. Deutsch
1985   *Human Factors Aspects of Simulation.* Washington, DC: National Academy Press.

Kopstein, F., A. Siegel, H. Ozkaptan, F.N. Dyer, J. Conn, W. Sliffer, and J. Caviness
1985   *Soldier Performance in Continuous Operations: Administrative Manual for a Briefing and Seminar for Platoon and Guard Personnel.* Alexandria, Virginia: U.S. Army Research Institute for the Behavioral and Social Sciences.

Kramer, A.F., D.L. Stranger, and J. Buckley
    1990   Development and transfer of automatic processing. *Journal of Experimental Psychology* 16:505-522.
Lysaght, R.J., S.G. Hill, A.O. Dick, B.D. Plamondon, P.M. Linton, W.W. Wierwille, A.L. Zaklad, A.C. Bittner, and R.J. Wherry
    1989   *Operator Workload: Comprehensive Review and Evaluation of Operator Workload Methodologies.* Technical Report No. 851. Alexandria, Virginia: U.S. Army Research Institute for the Behavioral and Social Sciences.
Martens, R., and D.M. Landers
    1970   Motor performance under stress: A test of the inverted-U hypothesis. *Journal of Personality and Social Psychology* 16(1):29-37.
Moray, N., and B.M. Huey, eds.
    1988   *Human Factors Research and Nuclear Safety.* Committee on Human Factors. Washington, DC: National Academy Press.
Oberlin, M.
    1988   Some considerations in implementing embedded training. *Human Factors Society Bulletin* 31(4):1-4.
Pleban, R.J., D.A. Thomas, and H.L. Thompson
    1985   *Physical Fitness as a Moderator of Cognitive Work Capacity and Fatigue Onset Under Sustained Combat-like Operations.* Technical Report No. 687. Alexandria, Virginia: U.S. Army Research Institute for the Behavioral and Social Sciences.
Ropelewski, R.R.
    1989   SIMNET training concept hones battlefield skills. *Armed Forces Journal International* 132-136.
Rose, A.M., P.H. Radtke, H.H. Shettel, and J.D. Hagman
    1985   *User's Manual for Predicting Military Task Retention.* Research Product No. 85-26. Alexandria, Virginia: U.S. Army Research Institute for the Behavioral and Social Sciences.
Rossmeissl, P.G., and J. Charles
    1988   Applications of the cognitive requirements model. Pp. 45-50 in A.C.F. Gilbert, ed., *Proceedings of the 30th Annual Conference of the Military Testing Association.* Alexandria, Virginia: U.S. Army Research Institute for the Behavioral and Social Sciences.
Rouse, W.B.
    1985   Optimal allocation of system development resources to reduce and/or tolerate human error. *IEEE Transactions on Systems, Man, and Cybernetics* SMC-15:620-630.
Schendel, J.D.
    1987   *Exceptional Performance.* Technical Report. Alexandria, Virginia: U.S. Army Research Institute for the Behavioral and Social Sciences.
Schendel, J.D., and J.D. Hagman
    1982   On sustaining procedural skills over a prolonged retention interval. *Journal of Applied Psychology* 67(5):605-610.
Schendel, J.D., J.C. Morey, M.J. Granier, and S. Hall
    1984   Use of self assessments in estimating levels of skill retention. *Proceedings of Psychology in the Department of Defense, Ninth Symposium.* Colorado Springs, Colorado: U.S. Air Force Academy.
Schendel, J.D., J.L. Shields, and M.S. Katz
    1978   *Retention of Motor Skills.* Technical Report No. 313. Alexandria, Virginia: U.S. Army Research Institute for the Behavioral and Social Sciences.

Schmidt, R.A., and R.A. Bjork
   1989   *New Conceptualizations of Practice: Common Principles in Three Research Paradigms Suggest Important New Concepts for Practice.* ARI Basic Research Report. Alexandria, Virginia: U.S. Army Research Institute for the Behavioral and Social Sciences.

Schneider, W.
   1985   Training high-performance skills: Fallacies and guidelines. *Human Factors* 27(3):285-300.

Shields, J.L., S.L. Goldberg, and J.D. Dressel
   1979   *Retention of Basic Soldiering Skills.* Research Report No. 1225. Alexandria, Virginia: U.S. Army Research Institute for the Behavioral and Social Sciences.

Streufert, S., and R.W. Swezey
   1986   *Complexity, Managers, and Organizations.* New York: Academic Press.

U.S. Department of the Army
   1983   *Management of Stress in Army Operations.* Field Manual No. FM26-2. Washington, DC: U.S. Department of the Army.

Wells, R., and J.D. Hagman
   1989   *Training Procedures for Enhancing Reserve Component Learning, Retention, and Transfer.* Draft Technical Report. Alexandria, Virginia: U.S. Army Research Institute for the Behavioral and Social Sciences.

Wickens, C.D.
   1992   *Engineering Psychology and Human Performance.* New York: Harper Collins.

Winstein, C.A., and R.A. Schmidt
   1990   Reduced frequency of knowledge of results enhances motor skill learning. *Journal of Experimental Psychology: Learning, Memory, and Cognition* 16:677-691.

Zeidner, J., and C.D. Johnson
   1991   Classification efficiency and systems design. *Journal of the Washington Academy of Sciences* 81(2):110-128.

12

Recommendations for Research

What happens when a team or group is suddenly required to react effectively to a situation after a period of inactivity? Does it perform well or poorly? The many anecdotal reports and case histories of incidents in which there are abrupt shifts from low to high workload suggest that performance is, at times, seriously or dangerously degraded. But, aside from some studies of single variables such as training, sleep patterns, and stress, the research knowledge base on performance after a sudden change in workload is sparse. The ways in which the interaction of different environmental, operational, and individual variables may affect performance or how their combined impact on performance can be reduced by administrative, design, or other changes is not known well understood.

The Panel on Workload Transition was charged to examine the existing knowledge base and to identify and evaluate techniques that might be used to reduce performance decrements during abrupt workload transitions. The panel was asked to pay special attention to what happens to the performance of Army tank crews during sudden increases in workload but also to consider its effect on teams in other situations such as nuclear power plants, commercial airliners, emergency medical services, railroad locomotives, shipboard, and disaster relief efforts.

In carrying out its charge the panel examined what is known about workload and workload transitions and their performance effects, identified existing research results that could be applied now and research that needed to be done to fill gaps in knowledge and inform operational policy. A large number of recommendations appear throughout the report. Those considered by the panel to be most important appear below.

WORKLOAD

Task structure is known to have a significant impact on the workload imposed during the performance of the task. Much is known about the effects of variations in rate of presentation of visual stimuli for discrete tasks or display bandwidth for control tasks; however, the effects of such factors as speed-accuracy tradeoffs, task schedules, and task duration on operator performance under different levels of workload are not well defined, and additional research must be performed. How effective are team members in scheduling tasks appropriately under high levels of workload during a post-transition period?

During most post-transition periods there are many task demands, often with critical time constraints. When performing familiar tasks for which variations in task demands are predictable, completing some tasks ahead of schedule and developing contingency plans for others during periods of low workload can reduce workload and improve performance during later higher-workload periods. Research suggests that people are able to develop more efficient strategies if given the opportunity. But more research is needed on team workload management strategies and their effectiveness. For example, the effect of teammate cooperation—when one underloaded team member takes on some of the tasks usually assigned to another team member who is currently overloaded—on performance is unknown.

Regardless of the specific source(s) of workload at any point in time, adequate training and preparation, adopting strategies and tactics most appropriate for the situation, effective leadership, and smooth crew coordination can counteract some of the detrimental effects of imposed task demands.

The influence of stress, fatigue, training, crew coordination, and environmental stressors may have a significant effect on operator workload in operational situations, but their relationships with operator workload is not yet known, and most theories of workload ignore them. More research is required to attempt to identify the joint effects of these factors. These same factors will also affect operator performance, and they are discussed in the following sections. Quantitative scales need to be developed to rate the attributes that can be placed on these different workload drivers for the development of predictive models of workload.

Continued research and development is needed to validate global operator models of human performance in complex systems. Particular efforts must be focused on modeling components of the team-communication aspects in conjunction with the individual. To what extent does workload increase with two members because of added communications, or does it decrease because of a division of labor?

Before considering automation of function, careful consideration must be given to the well-documented costs of automation. Many times, automation of subsystems does not result in reduced overall workload, but rather replaces one form of workload with another (Hart and Sheridan, 1984). Operators must continue to perform a series of activities, which may appear unrelated, and their direct involvement with and knowledge of the system are reduced, making it more difficult to detect errors or assume control of the system if the automation fails. Another serious question that remains unanswered is who should maintain authority over whether the human or the automated system retains control of the system.

STRESS

Although there have been many recent tragic accidents in which stress may have been a contributing factor, research on the effects of stress in complex systems is sparse. The panel recommends that the Army capitalize on information that has been obtained in environments in which realistic stressors already exist. An example would be an analysis of errors in performance by crews working in situations that are life-threatening to the crew itself (e.g., fire bomb disposal) versus other types of life-threatening situations (e.g., medical staff in an emergency room). A research program is needed in which stressors are not experimentally induced.

Two categories of techniques may be adopted to minimize the degrading effects of stress on human performance: (1) design solutions, which address the task and interface with equipment and (2) personal solutions, which address the operator (through selection strategies or training), the characteristics of the team, or both. Design principles that may minimize the degrading effects of stress include: using familiar elements and eliminating nonessential ones, displaying information that is directly necessary for action, highlighting, and integrating displays. In addition, emergency procedures that must be referred to on-line must be brief and succinct under circumstances in which working memory and attention span are attenuated. Furthermore, procedural instructions should avoid arbitrary symbolic coding and be phrased as actions to be taken, not as prohibited actions or descriptions of the state of the system. Finally, the number of steps to be taken in following emergency procedures should be held to a minimum.

Personal solutions include the adoption of strategies by the operator to minimize the degrading effects of stress. Among the most effective of these are preplanning, anticipating, and rehearsing actions to be taken under stress. Research shows that if individuals can predict, understand, have knowledge of, and have a sense of control over a stressor, they are more likely to develop successful coping strategies. It is also known, however, that simply providing information is one way to reduce uncertainty and increase a person's sense of control over a situation.

The panel endorses the findings and recommendations made by the Committee on Techniques for the Enhancement of Human Performance (Druckman and Swets, 1988) that cognitive approaches to stress management will probably prove the most useful in the military setting. According to Druckman and Swets (1988:125), "The implication of this approach [of providing realistic information in advance] for the military is that individuals should be given maximum knowledge and understanding of potentially harmful situations and as much control over them as possible. This conclusion seems just the opposite of the accepted military philosophy of giving the individual the least amount of information necessary for a given task or situation. In a combat situation it would seem that each soldier should be given as much information as possible about his situation and that of the enemy to help him manage stress levels and maintain arousal at a useful motivational level."

Good team qualities, such as trust, participation in relevant decision making, excellent communications, and a commitment to cooperation are conducive to effective team-building processes. Team building efforts, as well as environmental buffers (e.g., changes in the tank environment), can be employed to minimize communication problems and the stress-related problems associated with decision making and problem solving. To date, communication in tanks has been largely ignored. However, it appears that communication is a key component in successful team performance. Therefore, research is needed to examine the effect of stress on communications.

As noted above, the environment plays an important moderating role in problems arising from communications, stress, decision making, and problem solving, to name a few. Although it is impossible to remove environmental stress from the battlefield, tank crews can be somewhat isolated from its worst effects. It is probably not advisable to completely isolate crew members from battlefield noise, since noise in battle can contain information. In fact, the headphones currently used by tank crews probably do a good job of cutting out much of the unwanted battlefield noise. Unfortunately, these headphones are heavy and constricting. Along with the helmets worn by crew members, they contribute to discomfort and fatigue, both of which degrade vigilance efficiency. Therefore, we recommend that lighter, more comfortable headgear, including sound-isolating headphones, be either purchased commercially or developed.

The design of the suspension of tanks isolates the crew from much higher frequency vibration. However, crew members are still subject to shock from impacts and to accelerations in all directions from the overall movement of the vehicle. None of the existing crew workstations contain any degree of shock isolation, such as could be easily obtained by mounting the crew seats on shock absorbers. None of the current crew seats contain any form of personal restraint, such as seat belts or, more appropriately, 5-point harnesses. The panel recommends that all crew positions be shock isolated and that personal restraints be provided.

We believe that the elimination of temperature extremes inside the vehicle is a worthwhile action that can be taken with existing technology. This could be accomplished by building appropriate cooling and heating systems into armored vehicles and by providing protective clothing that can insulate crew members from climatic extremes. These steps seem to be especially necessary if crew members are to remain "buttoned up" inside their vehicles for several hours or days, as in chemical warfare scenarios.

In the area of displays and controls, there seem to be several small but meaningful changes that could make the job of monitoring and controlling vehicle and mission functions easier for crew members. While we did not perform a detailed analysis of crew workstation displays and controls, certainly the driver's and gunner's workstations could benefit from such an analysis and rearrangement. Likewise, the general area of radio communication, including the placement and design of the radio equipment should be studied with an eye to simplification and usability.

Finally, the relationships among stress (including environmental stressors such as heat, cold, vibration, noise, and danger), fatigue, training, and crew coordination are unknown. Additional research is needed to identify these relationships, particularly in the tank environment, and to determine their unique and joint effects on operator and team performance.

SLEEP PATTERNS AND FATIGUE

The most important recommendation the panel can make in this area is that, before an engagement, tank crews must have a duty schedule, and the cycle time is very important. Sleep is most effective and restorative if it can be brought into phase with the 24-hour circadian rhythm. For example, four hours on duty, eight hours off, four on, eight off is an ineffective duty schedule. Sleep schedules or length of sleep periods should be modulated according to the length of time before onset of the event. In the case of the tank crew, this event would be the beginning of battle.

In addition, sleep periods should be mandated and enforced by the command structure. This is particularly important for operators who perform low-level vigilance monitoring tasks or complex cognitive tasks (i.e., tank commanders). Some research has found that a single two-hour nap, strategically placed, can significantly reduce the periodic decrements of alertness and performance that occurred during 54 hours of sleep deprivation (Dinges et al., 1987).

Research has found that preemptive naps should be scheduled in a staggered manner across time and crew members and that naps must be a minimum of 10 minutes in duration in order to effectively restore the decrements due to sleep loss. However, without additional research, the minimum nap time necessary to prevent or mitigate the degrading effects of sleep loss on performance is unknown.

Countermeasures for sleep loss—stimulants, increased physical activity, naps, monetary incentives, diet, and intensive social contact—can mitigate the deterioration of performance on the first night; however, none of these remedies are effective in overcoming impairments that occur on the second or third nights of continuous operations.

The last important issue that must be addressed in this area pertains to sleep habitability in the operating environment. If the environment does not have some minimum level of comfort and darkness, the amount of peaceful sleep or rest the crew members get may not be sufficient to counteract the negative effects of sleep loss.

TARGET DETECTION AND VIGILANCE

Signal enhancement is a driver of vigilance performance in any task. In view of what is known with regard to the importance of signal amplitude and duration in vigilance, devices for aiding target acquisition such as thermal imaging or computer-assisted detection systems might be built in a manner that amplifies the intensity of such critical signals as hot spots and weapon flashes and also increases the dwell time of such signals on the crews' target acquisition displays.

The sensory modality of the signal plays an important role in the quality of vigilant behavior, and sensory redundant displays aid in detection efficiency. Thus, an alternative technique to pure visual monitoring would be to transfer the signal into an auditory modality. For example, it might be beneficial to attempt to take advantage of this by designing a form of radar/sonar systems for tanks that would make use of analogous audio/visual signals. Such a system might increase overall efficiency in target acquisition and reduce the powerful degrading effects of a high nontarget event rate, since these effects can be eliminated in the laboratory when subjects are permitted to search for targets by alternating their inspection between analogous auditory and visual displays.

Computer assistance systems may be developed that would provide crew members with information as to the most probable times of appearance and spatial locations of targets and thus reduce the effects of both temporal and spatial uncertainty on vigilance efficiency. Given the particularly deleterious effects of sleep loss on low-arousal monitoring environments, we recommend that special consideration be given to adequate sleep for those charged with monitoring and vigilance.

Tasks that are performed in succession require more processing capacity than tasks that are performed simultaneously. Hence, designers should strive to provide simultaneous-type displays for target acquisition functions when possible. This might be achieved by the use of instruments that furnish crew members with immediate reference standards against which events can be compared instead of forcing them to rely upon short term memory to separate signals and noise.

In order to minimize the deleterious effects of vigilance on performance, the panel recommends that the crews be instructed on the biases and nonoptimal strategies of their vigilance functions in order to optimize their response strategies. In addition, training with target cueing or with knowledge of results can have a beneficial effect on performance in tasks requiring sustained attention. Team monitoring is also a possibility for enhancing target acquisition in armor crews since Army doctrine calls for overlapping fields of inspection on the battlefield. While a few experiments have reported an improvement in signal detectability for teams of monitors compared with single monitors, other experiments have reported no team advantage. The effects of team monitoring are complicated by the fact that social interactions between monitors play a role in determining the effectiveness of the procedure. Furthermore, only one study (Bergum and Lehr, 1962) has examined the influence of psychophysical variables on team monitoring effectiveness. Given its potential applicability to target acquisition in armored combat, the team concept warrants further investigation.

GEOGRAPHIC ORIENTATION

The panel recommends that efforts be made to provide armored crew personnel with accurate, possibly electronic, navigational information, capitalizing, whenever possible, on technology (e.g., digitized terrain data bases, the Global Positioning System, and inertial navigational systems). In the design of these navigational maps, consideration should be given to the appropriate frame of reference, to the depiction of updated position information, and to the realistic depiction of terrain features.

Navigational systems should also support both north-up and track-up map formats. North-up formats will facilitate mission planning and communications between individuals who do not share the same perspective (i.e., crews in different tanks). Track-up formats will facilitate wayfinding, locating targets, and communications between individuals who share the same perspective view of the terrain (i.e., members in the same tank crew). Finally, both planned route and current position should be displayed on the map.

COMMUNICATIONS AND DECISION MAKING

Communications in tanks has been largely ignored as an issue, but in other systems (i.e., aviation) it has been identified as a major human factors problem. The panel recommends that the way in which information is presented to the tank commander should be redesigned. At present, the tank commander must piece together information from auditory and visual channels. This adds to the confusion and may result in missed information, resulting in poor decision making and performance. Design efforts must address the potential confusion of the source of communications under high workload resulting from the tank commander monitoring two parallel radio channels and confusing the source of communications within the tank.

Recent studies of expert versus nonexpert decision making in firefighting (Klein, 1989) indicate that the decision making of experts is more rapid and less demanding of their cognitive resources. Research is needed to determine if decisions using this strategy are more accurate than those employing more effortful strategies.

Continued research is needed regarding the effectiveness of *debiasing*— training personnel to understand the effects of biases and heuristics on their decisions—in improving the overall quality of decision performance. Decision makers in complex systems should be explicitly taught about confirmation bias, which describes the decision makers' tendency to seek new information that supports one's currently held hypothesis and to ignore or minimize the importance of information that may support an alternative hypothesis. If a tank commander has a preconceived hypothesis regarding the nature of enemy intentions, he may interpret ambiguous evidence as consistent with these intentions. This bias has been found in the performance of Army intelligence analysts (Tolcott et al., 1989). Care must also be taken by the team leader to guard against following preprogrammed procedures, without monitoring the continued appropriateness of the decision and the commander must be willing to modify or abandon procedures as required.

STRATEGIC TASK MANAGEMENT

The panel has concluded that the research base on how well and effectively people manage or switch activities following a workload transition is quite sparse. While basic laboratory research suggests some facility in this switching, there is a strong need for research that identifies the speed, strengths, and limitations of activity switching in high workload/high stress environments. It is particularly important to examine the extent and prevalence of cognitive tunnel vision (the failure to switch) in emergency situations, such as the Three Mile Island incident. Such research could capitalize well on advanced simulator capabilities, such as SIMNET, in which realisticly stressful conditions can be created, and activities can be recorded digitally.

Evidence that activity switching benefits from both training and clearly distinguishable cues of what tasks are required certainly leads to recommendations regarding the importance of practice in emergency response (see Chapter 11) and of clear, unambiguous communications within the team regarding task assignments, as discussed in Chapter 10.

The benefits of preview for task management, while not based on extensive data, are nevertheless consistent with arguments presented in Chapter 4 regarding the benefits of providing team members with knowledge of likely future stressful conditions. Research is recommended in this domain to examine the effects of partially reliable preview. Finally, the data suggest that, under high levels of workload, tasks are not always rescheduled according to an optimal prioritization scheme. Research should focus on the extent to which this task rescheduling can be trained.

TEAM LEADERSHIP AND CREW COORDINATION

Based on evidence available to date, the panel recommends that complex teams should maintain their integrity over some period of time. Tank crews generally do but civil aviation crews do not, at present. High-level decision makers must consider the personalities of people within groups in addition to technical competence. Crew composition has been found to have a significant effect on performance. There are three possible solutions: crew resource management training, selecting out the "no stuff" operators who have been found to inhibit the development of effective communications, and crew composition/creation. Consideration should be given to implementing crew resource management training in all multiperson teams after it has been demonstrated that such training would be of benefit for that environment. Research is needed to examine the factors that enhance crew compatibility and productivity, as well as the individual characteristics that predict how an individual and team will function productively.

A series of related actions to assess the need for formal training in leadership and crew coordination are recommended. Additional areas for action include assessment of the social-psychological impact of automation and reduced crew complement and an investigation of the role of personality factors as determinants of crew performance.

The importance of the mix of personalities that comprise effective and less effective crews must be examined. Research to date suggests that effective teams have high loyalty, morale, commitment, and effective task performance. Good team qualities include effective leadership, membership mix, commitment/cohesion, cooperation, achievement motivation, effective work methods, clarity of roles and procedures, acceptance and giving of suggestions and criticism, individual initiative, and adaptability. Attempting to achieve this in the tank crews would result in more effective team performance.

To date, no investigation has been carried out on the extent and nature of leadership and crew coordination problems in tank crews. A number of methodological approaches can be employed to obtain a valid representation of leadership and crew coordination issues in current battle tanks; these have been addressed in Chapter 10. Considerable data have been accumulated in aviation on the validation and behavioral impact of crew coordination training. Priority should be placed on conducting research to determine if such training is applicable to tank crews. Further research is also needed to determine the effect of complement reduction on crew interactions (both communications and performance) prior to a change in crew structure. The most viable approach would be to conduct full mission simulations with accurate video and audio recordings.

TRAINING

The panel wishes to stress that training is not a panacea. To enhance performance of a specific task, the more repetition that occurs, the better. And to enhance problem solving and transfer to new tasks, fewer specific repetitions are recommended along with an increase in the variety of tasks that are practiced. The panel recommends that tank crews be trained to the point of automatic processing for proceduralized tasks. To perform in an expert fashion under stress, tank commanders and crews must have a thorough understanding of the system. The lower-level procedural skills required to respond appropriately should be automated, thus freeing attention for the unique aspects of the problem at hand, and this can make vigilance performance more resistant to the effects of environmental stress and increased mental workload. SIMNET allows individual crew members through battalion commanders to practice tasks and roles in as realistic, complex environment as necessary to develop the appropriate skills. The panel strongly encourages the maximum utilization of SIMNET. The technology of embedded training allows individuals to practice procedural tasks in the operational environment, which is also beneficial.

Emergency procedures ought to be more trained so that attentional tunneling does not occur. Thus, emergency problem-solving and decision making, as well as routine proceduralized tasks, must be practiced. Initial training for emergency situations should be given under nonemergency conditions because learning is better in nonstressed environments. But, once learned to some degree of efficiency, those procedures should be practiced under some degree of emergency stress/high workload so that operators will better learn how to respond under those conditions.

On the basis of the research findings, we recommend that emergency procedures be trained to the point of automaticity. The complexity of the system and the nature of human response under stress must be known by the trainer. For simple systems, emergency procedures should be overtrained; however, for complex systems, fault diagnosis should be taught, in which operators monitor the consequences of each step in a procedure for accurate diagnosis.

Considerable benefit can be gained from applying the training programs in crew resource management, successfully validated in an aviation context, to other team environments. The training principles discussed in the preceding chapters provide some practical information on how to design programs to enhance soldier performance. However, as noted by Hinrichs (1976), these principles have not been adequately validated to warrant wholesale application without additional research. They do provide hypotheses amenable to testing. Basic and applied research are most needed in the following areas: (1) the impact of stress on task performance following varying degrees and types of training and (2) the validation of training approaches against performance in a combat-like environment. This research will provide the basis for a comprehensive approach for providing training that will result in a higher probability of competent performance under emergency situations such as tank combat.

REFERENCES

Bergum, B.O., and D.J. Lehr
    1962   Vigilance performance as a function of paired monitoring. *Journal of Applied Psychology* 46:341-343.
Dinges, D.F., K.T. Orne, W.G. Whitehouse, and E.C. Orne
    1987   Temporal placement of a nap for alertness: Contributions of circadian phase and prior wakefulness. *Sleep* 10:313-329.
Druckman, D., and J.A. Swets, eds.
    1988   *Enhancing Human Performance*. Washington, DC: National Academy Press.
Hart, S.G., and T.B. Sheridan
    1984   Pilot workload, performance, and aircraft control automation. Pp. 18.1-18.12 in *Proceedings of the AGARD-Symposium on Human Factors Considerations in High Performance Aircraft Conference Proceedings No. 371*. Neuilly sur Seine, France: NATO Advisory Group for Aerospace Research and Development.
Hinrichs, J.R.
    1976   Personnel training. Pp. 829-860 in M.D. Dunnette, ed., *Handbook of Industrial and Organizational Psychology*. Chicago: Rand McNally.
Klein, G.A.
    1989   Recognition-primed decisions. Pp. 47-92 in W. Rouse, ed., *Advances in Man-Machine Systems Research, Volume 5*. Greenwich, Connecticut: JAI Press.
Tolcott, M.A., F.F. Marvin, and T.A. Bresdick
    1989   *The Confirmation Bias in Military Situation Assessment*. Reston, Virginia: Decision Science Consortium.

Index

Spatial
  awareness, 173-183, 191, 193
  orientation, 24, 172 (*see also*
    Geographic orientation)
  working memory, 102-103, 106, 207-
    208
Speed-accuracy tradeoff, 9, 58-59, 104,
    208, 216, 266
Stimulus
  complexity, 145-146
  uncertainty, 143-144
Stimulus-response compatibility, 67
Strategic
  behavior, 215
  goals, 16
  planning, 24, 250
  shifts, 104
Strategies
  adoption, 10, 19, 61, 64, 66, 85, 109
  cognitive, 70
  coping, 63, 85, 108-111, 267-268
  definition, 215
  development of, 8, 11
  long-term, 17
  performance criteria and, 58-60
  reactive, 62
  resource allocation, 59
  scheduling, 59, 62
  sequential, 62
  switching, 61, 215-216
  task management, 7, 26, 55, 214-228,
    272-273
  team-building, 112
  team workload management, 62, 266
  time-sharing, 61, 62
Stress
  communications and, 230
  coping mechanisms, 108-111, 267-
    268
  decision making and, 104-106, 205,
    206-208, 268
  environmental, 148-155
  human performance and, 9, 10, 24,
    31, 97, 107, 114, 267
  incentives and, 11, 126, 130
  management, 110, 111-114, 249, 259,
    268

  mediating effects, 11, 107-108, 160,
    171
  memory and, 78
  noise, *see* Noise
  physical, 11
  psychological, 55, 95-96
  task-induced, 5, 152-155
  teams and, 114
  training and, 160, 260, 274
  work environment and, 30, 41, 47,
    96-97, 267-268
Stressors
  consequences of, 94-96
  direct, 95-96
  environmental, 4, 9, 33, 44, 57, 85,
    94, 148-155, 266, 268
  indirect, 95
  psychological, 4, 24, 94, 95
  time, 61
Sustained attention, *see* Attentional
  tunneling; Vigilance
System
  complexity, 84
  design, 8, 249
  failures, 29, 66
  safety, 1, 5, 7, 13, 16, 33, 36, 39

T

Tank
  crew, 5, 6, 8-9, 14, 15, 16, 17, 16-24,
    26, 29, 31, 35, 37, 41, 42, 56-58,
    63, 72, 95, 100, 112, 113, 128-131,
    141, 155-156, 157, 159, 171-179,
    180, 181, 183, 184-191, 193, 194,
    198-199, 201, 204, 206, 207-208,
    216, 220, 230, 241, 243, 255-256,
    265, 268-269, 272, 274
  design, 8, 15
  environment, 3, 20, 28, 36, 44, 96-
    97, 148, 229, 231, 233, 234, 242,
    268-269
  workstations, 20-24, 268-269
Target
  acquisition, 5, 11, 20, 22, 24, 58, 59,
    61, 66, 80, 81, 141, 150-151, 158,
    270, 271